RALLYCOURSE

THE WORLD'S LEADING RALLY ANNUAL

Hazleton Publishing

CITROËN WORLD RALLY CHAMPION 2003

Automobiles Citroën - DCCO - Design : NUANCES - 11/2003 - Photo : DPPI

Xsara WRC

CITROËN

www.citroen.com

Contents *Rallycourse* 2003-2004

DIRECTOR
Rob Yarham

EDITOR
David Williams

ART EDITOR
Julian Bigg

COPY EDITOR
Huw Davies

BUSINESS DEVELOPMENT
MANAGER
Peter Mercer

SALES PROMOTION
Laura Fell

RESULTS AND STATISTICS
Paul Haines

CHIEF PHOTOGRAPHER
Reinhard Klein

RALLYCOURSE
PUBLISHED by
Hazleton Publishing Ltd
5th Floor
2 Puddle Dock
London EC4V 3DS
Telephone: 020 7332 2000
Fax: 020 7332 2003

DESIGN by
Fresh Produce

COLOUR REPRODUCTION by
Radstock Repro
Midsomer Norton

PRINTED IN BRITAIN by
Butler & Tanner Ltd, Frome

ISBN: 1-903135-27-3

DISTRIBUTORS
United Kingdom
Haynes Publishing
Sparkford, Nr Yeovil
Somerset BA22 7JJ
Telephone: 01963 440635
Fax: 01963 440001

North America
Motorbooks International
PO Box 1,
729 Prospect Ave.,
Osceola, Wisconsin 54020,
USA
Telephone: (1) 715 294 3345
Fax: (1) 715 294 4448

Rest of the World
Menoshire Ltd
Unit 13 Wadsworth Road,
Perivale,
Middlesex UB6 7LQ
Telephone: 020 8566 7344
Fax: 020 8991 2439

ACKNOWLEDGEMENTS

PHOTOGRAPHS APPEARING IN
RALLYCOURSE 2003-2004 HAVE BEEN
CONTRIBUTED BY: the incomparable
McKleins – Reinhard Klein, Bob McCaffrey,
Colin McMaster and Tony Welam – Colin
Taylor Productions, Gavin Lodge, Martin
Sharp, Willy Weyens and Brian Young.

THE EDITOR OF RALLYCOURSE WISHES
TO SALUTE THE DILIGENCE, TOLERANCE
AND ZEAL OF THE FOLLOWING IN THE
PRODUCTION OF THE 2002-2003 EDITION:
Julian Bigg, Hugh Bishop, Adam Cathersides,
Hannah Curry, Huw Davies, Lisa Franklin,
Mike Greasley, Andrew Haill, Paul Haines,
Ross Hyde, Reinhard Klein, David Limage,
Michel Lizin, Gavin Lodge, Bob McCaffrey,
Colin McMaster, Neil Perkins, Peter Procter,
Martin Sharp, David Thomson, Tony Welam,
Willy Weyens, Jerry Williams, Rob Yarham
and Brian Young.

www.rallycourse.com

World Rally Crown for new Prince of Wales.

Subaru powers Petter Solberg to beat the world.

With a commanding performance in the World Drivers' Championship, Viking Petter Solberg and Welsh co-driver Phil Mills gain World Rally glory at the Wales Rally GB in the awesome Subaru Impreza. Winning the 2003 FIA World Rally Championship for drivers/co-drivers, Subaru's sixth World title and seventh victory in the Rally of Great Britain in the last decade. So whether you're negotiating a tricky track in the forest or a tight wet bend on the Queen's highway, the Impreza is still king. Visit your loyal Subaru dealer for details.

Impreza GX Sport from £14,950* WRX from £19,995* STi £24,995

* Prices exclude mica/metallic paint at £250. Impreza range fuel consumption in mpg (L/100km); Urban 18.2 (15.5) to 23.0 (12.3), Extra Urban 33.2 (8.5) to 43.5 (6.5), Combined 25.4 (11.1) to 32.8 (8.6). CO₂ emissions 206 to 265 (g/km).

FOREWORD
by Petter Solberg
Rallycourse 2003

I cannot quite believe that I am World Champion! This is what I have wanted ever since I first drove a rally car, but sometimes this year, I thought it was only a dream. It has been such hard work, with so much pressure and so many rallies close together at the end, and we have had to fight for every point. It is just amazing!

Everybody wants to congratulate the driver, but it is a team effort, you know. I want to thank my co-driver Phil Mills and everybody at Prodrive and Subaru, because they have worked so hard this year. Thanks to them, this year has been better than I thought possible!

NEW STARS FOR OLD

Editor's Introduction

It is an enticing prospect: Petter Solberg, the newly crowned World Champion, confronting Sébastien Loeb, Markko Märtin and Marcus Grönholm. Will the new generation take over? Will the 307 restore Peugeot hegemony? Will Carlos Sainz's knack of mastering unfamiliar terrain enable him to set a new record for World Championship rally victories? Will François Duval become the youngest driver to win a World Championship rally? In any event, the new, often-derided points-scoring system means that the 2004 World Rally Championship is almost certain to be close.

The Junior World Championship is likely to be just as intriguing. There will be a host of new cars and new names, and in a sign that it is being recognised as the fastest route to the top, Timo Jouhki's most recent find, Jari-Matti Latvala, will take on Suzuki's cosmopolitan quartet.

Perhaps all this smacks of the childish optimism of a fairy tale, but it seems necessary to offset the palpable decline of rallying in Britain. The sport is stuttering here. Most of the recent news, from Richard Burns's blackout at the beginning of November, to the decline in Colin McRae's fortunes, to the Hyundai-triggered collapse of Motor Sport Developments, to Channel 4's failure to increase the audience for rallying, has been bad. The promised television-led breakthrough into the national consciousness hasn't happened. It was rather summed up by *The Independent*, feasting on Neath magistrates' barrage of fines and bans for speeding on the 2002 Rally GB, when it published a photograph of Freddy Loix captioned as Burns.

From any number of other countries, the perspective is somewhat different. Solberg has a fan club that follows him to most parts of the globe, Loeb's matches the Norwegians for size and raucousness when it does appear and whereas most people in rallying might have struggled to find Estonia on a map a few years ago, Märtin's legion of supporters have made the Baltic republic's flag instantly recognisable. The fans provide the colour, but in a commercial age, the reassuring evidence for the future is provided by the mushrooming television figures in France and Germany; on the Rally of Great Britain, the scrum of French journalists made talking to Loeb an achievement in itself.

There is nothing as sure as change and it's instructive to witness the charismatic power of a young, successful sportsman. Peugeot has consciously sought to make the car the star, on the not unreasonable basis that it sells 206s, not Grönholms, but while a successful car is the first ingredient, 2003 piercingly illustrated that a driver's standing in his home country – allied to the manufacturers' or importers' desire to make use of it – can make a world of difference. Consider the contrasting fortunes of McRae and Sainz at Citroën. To pursue the argument further, it's a wonder that the manufacturers aren't hunting more urgently for the next Röhrl or Biasion.

We may not be witnessing the end of civilisation as we know it, yet it isn't necessarily parochial to be pessimistic. At the time of writing, 17 days before the deadline to register for the 2004 World Championship, Ford is still wavering and it's impossible to know which team Märtin and Duval will drive for, or even if they will drive at all. It is certain that there will be fewer manufacturers registered than in 2003 and that consequently there will be fewer works cars to televise. The income of the TV rights-holding company, International SportsWorld Communicators, is likely to drop as a result. The optimists maintain that four manufacturers is a realistic average, given economic factors and any car maker's natural reluctance to fund a losing team on a long-term basis, but the sport is on uncertain ground. There are legitimate concerns over ISC's future, given the scale of the investment David Richards has been required to make, the investment climate, the FIA's reluctance to agree a longer-term contract and the declining number of World Rally Car manufacturers.

The latest upheaval is no doubt part of the cycle, partly economic, partly sporting, in which support for the World Championship would plot as a rollercoaster curve on a graph. Historically, it is still at a respectable level. The concern is that any further shocks could pitch it into headlong decline and that recent uncertainty has been exacerbated to a fair degree by the FIA. The arguments for and against change are considered in more detail elsewhere in the book, but the running skirmish between the rulemakers and the participants is in itself an indictment of the former. Are the FIA's procedures and structures really so defective that any radical change rapidly turns into a crisis? It has a right not to be bullied by the manufacturers, but the latest turn of events recalls the whimsical autocracy of Jean-Marie Balestre, the scrapping of the supposedly over-mighty BPICA and Max Mosley's confrontation with Toyota in 1995. Older enthusiasts must quite hanker for the benign neglect of the CSI.

Jerry Williams echoes some of these concerns in an intriguing interview with Solberg's co-driver, Phil Mills, while Martin Sharp provides his customary piercing insight into the most recent technical developments, exemplified by the Focus RS 03. It redoubles one's admiration for M-Sport, although one wonders why a host of new rules make scarcely any attempt to reduce the cost of World Rally Cars.

The Paris-Dakar Rally was a novelty when *Rallycourse* was first published. It's now an established highlight of the motorsport year and Neil Perkins analyses its unique and growing appeal to drivers and manufacturers. Hannah Curry provides a clear-sighted analysis into the British Championship, while Andrew Haill and David Thomson investigate the British National and Asia-Pacific arenas with corresponding thoroughness. We also profile Märtin and Jouhki, and analyse the emergence of the Viking superstar himself, Solberg.

Rallycourse has a well-established tradition of being the supreme visual record of the past season. In keeping with that tradition, the McKleins have once more served up a photographic feast.

David Williams
London, November 2003.

A GRIP THAT NEVER SLACKENS

ADVERTISEMENT FEATURE
Michelin 200th World Championship rally victories

For Markko Märtin and "Beef" Park, it was a historic moment. Their victory on the 2003 Neste Rally Finland was the first on this event for an Estonian driver. To Märtin, who had watched the event as a boy, it was proof that he could succeed on a rally that sorts the men from the boys. But as the Anglo-Estonian crew stood on the bonnet of their Ford Focus WRC RS and acknowledged the applause, they were also celebrating a landmark for Michelin. 30 years after Jean-Claude Andruet and "Biche" had won the very first World Championship rally, the 1973 Monte Carlo, in their Alpine-Renault A110, Märtin and Park had achieved Michelin's 200th victory in the World Rally Championship. It was a landmark commemorating decades of tireless endeavour.

The contrast could not have been more pronounced. Märtin's Focus is four-wheel drive, produces in excess of 300 bhp, weighs 1,230 kilos and uses 18-inch diameter wheels on asphalt. Andruet's flyweight Alpine was two-wheel drive, gave 180 bhp, weighed little more than half as much as a Focus and ran on 13-inch rims. The Rally Finland is one of the fastest in the world, drivers such as Märtin routinely averaging 120 km/h on the rollercoaster forest roads around Jyväskylä. On the 1973 Monte, Andruet faced blizzards in the Ardèche, milder temperatures and sunshine on the hairpin-infested roads closer to Monte Carlo, and made use of a range of tyres, from "racers" to narrow, studded snow tyres.

The contrast is the essence of the challenge and the appeal. No other form of motorsport involves competing in such a breadth of conditions, sometimes within the same event. It's a tribute to Michelin's all-round excellence that it has succeeded on such a wide range of rallies: since the World Championship was established, it has won 20 times in Corsica, on pure asphalt, 19 times on the Swedish, on ice and snow, and 18 times apiece on the Monte – which might be said to blend Corsica with Sweden – and on Finland's loose-surface forest tracks. The engineers in Clermont-Ferrand can justly claim to be as versatile as the drivers themselves.

There is scarcely a rally driver of note who hasn't worked and won with Michelin. It has partnered 16 car manufacturers and over 40 drivers to victory on World Championship rallies. Since 1973, it has taken 34 world rally titles, including the 2003 World

Championship for Manufacturers with Citroën.

Its involvement in rallying dates back well before the World Championship. Michelin-equipped drivers swept the board on the 1954 Monte Carlo Rally, for example, but its formal involvement dates from 1963, when appropriately enough, it met a request for support from Citroën.

The goal remains the same, but the challenge has changed constantly. When Alpine-Renault dominated the 1973 World Championship, winning six of the 13 rounds, rallies generally included 40-45 special stages and the average stage length was 30-50 kilometres. There were no service restrictions to speak of and tyres were therefore tailored to specific stages. Michelin would devise a tyre not just for a given surface, but a given temperature.

If rallying had an age of excess, it was surely the Group B era in the mid-1980s. The cars – roadgoing prototypes that combined the emerging technologies of four-wheel drive and turbocharging with racing car construction – fired the imagination of engineers, drivers and spectators alike. Michelin had to adapt to power outputs of more than 500 bhp and in 1986, it took no fewer than 11,000 tyres to the Monte Carlo Rally.

Since then, the rallies have become shorter, typically including 15-20 stages, with an average stage length of 20-25 kilometres, but tough restrictions have been imposed on the tyre manufacturers. Service limitations were introduced in the 1990s and restricted the opportunity to change tyres. They are no longer made for specific stages, but for a much broader range of conditions. A dry-weather Tarmac tyre is much more likely to be used on damp roads, for example, and it is not unusual for a tyre choice to be made two hours before it will be used in anger. It's a far cry from servicing almost in sight of the stage start.

The demands become still more exacting in 2004, when the opportunities to change tyres are likely to be restricted still further. Versatility and reliability will be at a premium.

On Tarmac in particular, width restrictions have imposed new demands on tyre manufacturers. In the 1970s, wheel diameters rarely exceeded 15 inches, but they were as much as 11 or 12 inches wide. Progressive tightening of the rules has enforced a maximum tyre width of nine inches – which means the wheel is little more than seven inches wide – while a maximum

tyre diameter of 650mm means that wheels are no more than 18 inches in diameter. It's an exacting technical challenge for the tyre makers. Wheel diameters would certainly have reached 20 inches if the regulations permitted. A Ferrari or Lamborghini road car with the equivalent power has tyres about twice the size.

Michelin has responded to evolving circumstances with constant innovations. It was the first tyre manufacturer to introduce slicks to rallying, unveiling the SB9 on the 1974 Tour of Corsica. When they were banned in 1995, it displayed similar ingenuity in creating the N-pattern, a tyre that could withstand dry roads and cope with the damp. In 1998, it took asphalt rallying a step further by producing the FP, or Fort Potentiel generation. It looked the same, but its impact was revolutionary. At Michelin's urging, teams had to stiffen bodyshells by 15-20% to make the most of the tyres' extra grip. Michelin has rarely been beaten on Tarmac since.

Michelin also pioneered the use of pressure-regulating valves that effectively dealt with the problem of rising temperatures leading to rising pressures. They were eventually banned by the FIA.

The same ingenuity is applied to all surfaces. The Nora was originally developed for Citroën to use on the 1965 Monte, but it became the staple tyre for any loose-surface rally and it thrived into the 1980s. Jean-Pierre Nicolas, now Peugeot's Sporting Director, but a linchpin of Peugeot's driving squad in the 1970s, remembers testing for the 1978 Safari, tracking clouds around Nairobi in the hope of finding a storm that would allow Michelin to assess its latest mud tyres. The result was the sole all-French Safari victory, in which the "tractor-pattern" Michelins were one of the vital components in a memorable triumph for his Peugeot 504 Coupé.

Nicolas has fond memories of his Monte Carlo victory the same year, when he drove a private Porsche, but had full service from Michelin, with a van and a full range of tyres at the start of every stage, but the innovation that stands out in most drivers' minds is ATS, or appui temporaire souple – the run-flat inserts originally developed for motorcycles for the Paris-Dakar Rally, when the system was referred to as bib-mousse. It has changed driving styles, allowing drivers to cut corners with something near impunity, obliging teams to strengthen cars to exploit their

tyres' enhanced capabilities.

As Didier Auriol, the 1994 World Champion with Toyota and Michelin explained, "It was every driver's dream! You could push to the limit and what was more, you could do so without taking risks. It was a big step forward. Even if you got a puncture, you could keep going. It permitted a driving style that's harder on the car and its components."

To the fan, tyres are easy to overlook. Drivers and engineers never do so. They know that the right choice of tyre can win a rally, that a new tyre can be worth a season's engine development.

"Tyres put all your engineering efforts on to the ground. If that is not so good, then you can do whatever you want, but you're not going to be winning. You're not moving forward, you're not braking, you're not steering, so it's pretty crucial," as Märtin put it.

ATS naturally stands out, but driver after driver cites Michelin's rigorous attention to detail. Across the generations, they admire its consistency and its expertise.

Warming to his theme, Märtin commented: "I find Michelin a very easy company to work with. They are very professional, they always have good information and good products. They don't have many failures. They are very good in sorting out problems. If they are weak on some kind of surface or

conditions, they can respond to it and fix it, so I think that's pretty impressive."

He had listed not just Michelin's attributes, but its objectives.

Sometimes, as it did when it introduced the FP Tarmac tyre, Michelin might advise one of its partners to modify its car, but it believes it is just as important to make tyres that suit the car, as the Rally Department Manager Aimé Chatard explained.

"We make tyres for all our manufacturers. If your car is heavy and hard on tyres, we will make a tyre for you. If it is light and has good suspension, we can make a special tyre to suit, but we treat all our partners the same. The tyre will then be offered to other manufacturers to try. Our strategy is the same: rallying is research."

9

The new Focus was an instant sensation, confirming
Markko Märtin's brilliance and sprinkling a little stardust
on its creator, Christian Loriaux.

REVIEW OF THE YEAR
By David Williams

I t's an unwritten rule in sport that every champion will be brought down in the end by younger, hungrier rivals, that today's lords of the jungle become tomorrow's mincemeat. Yet it is hard to credit that it took the discovery of Richard Burns's brain tumour to give Colin McRae even a prospect of a World Championship drive in 2004.

Beyond question, 2003 was a watershed. Unusually though, the end of an era wasn't brought about by fresh technical regulations. Whatever new phase rallying is entering, it can't be summarised as Group 4, Group B, Group A or by any other FIA-designated handle, because World Rally Cars live on. Whether 2003 was the zenith of the WR Car epoch remains to be seen, but it certainly elbowed aside the dominant drivers of the past decade, McRae and Tommi Mäkinen, and heralded a battery of new, non-technical regulations.

It was McRae's fall that encapsulated change. That's not a judgement made from a jingoistic British perspective: although Mäkinen has won fewer World Championship rallies, he has outscored McRae in championship terms four to one and there's a respectable case for regarding him as the better driver. The difference is that Mäkinen departed willingly. He's mulled over retirement for some years and the two-year stint at Subaru was always likely to be a swansong. He didn't seem demob happy, exactly, but Tommi placidly accepted his new role as Petter Solberg's sidekick and plainly finds the idea of not living out of a suitcase irresistible.

In contrast, McRae has been overtaken by events. He went to Citroën rather than cut his coat to Ford's cloth and signed a one-year deal, because it gave him maximum room for manoeuvre if he didn't take to life in a French team. The idea that doing so might leave him without a drive in 2004 never crossed the mind. There were those willing to predict that he wouldn't lay a glove on his young French team-mate, Sébastien Loeb, on Tarmac, but none who supposed that he might struggle to master the Xsara in any circumstances. Nevertheless, for the first time in his life, McRae was confronted with a car he couldn't tame. His results contrasted poorly not just with Loeb's, but with Carlos Sainz's. If a team is an engine, the Spanish veteran is its turbocharger. His desire to understand and refine a car borders on the obsessive and he is not only a tireless worker, but unlike McRae, has a strong command of French. He fitted in a good deal more quickly and while he scored only one victory – a classic success on a new rally, in Turkey – he was a fine second in Corsica and would have won in Argentina but for a misunderstanding with his co-driver, Marc Martí. At 41, Sainz took on a new lease of life. Only a painful case of kidney stones on the eve of the Sanremo Rally hinted at middle age.

Citroën has been predictably coy as to why it chose in the end to retain Sainz after lengthy negotiations with a driver six years younger, but the effect of impending unemployment was stunning and dismaying to behold. There were signs that McRae was coming to terms with the Xsara until he was sacked. Thereafter, with no prospect of a works drive in 2004, his form crumbled. The aggression that had made him such a formidable opponent melted away. The number 17 Xsara turned up at service point after service point without a scratch on it. Its driver had nothing to report. Away from the car, he would admit that he was more aware of the dangers than he had been in his 20s and that in his new circumstances, he didn't have the incentive to take risks. The fire and brimstone had given way to milk and water.

'I'm out of the championship battle and I'm up against guys fighting for the world title. It's like dropping out of the slipstream,' he explained wanly.

Fans across the globe were incensed that their hero had been discarded in his prime. Their response was not shared by the men who hire and fire, the team managers. McRae's erstwhile boss at Citroën, Guy Fréquelin, might have claimed that choosing Sainz

BETWEEN
THE TIDES

CYPRUS

authoritatively on the best way to drive a rally car –
there isn't a single correct way – but advancing
technology has at the very least encouraged a different
approach. As McRae himself observed, the Xsara is
some way removed from the Impreza 555 in which he
became World Champion almost a decade ago.

Who knows what McRae might have achieved if
Ford had bowed to the wishes of Motorsport News
readers, ditched Duval and reinstated Britain's first
World Rally Champion? After all, Duval likes to throw
a car around. But there were signs too that
commitment and not just speeds have crept a little
higher. McRae couldn't think of any advantages to
being an older rally driver and while experience still
counts to a large degree, the sport may be reaching
the point at which rally drivers aren't automatically at
their best over 30. Loeb will be 30 not long after this
book is published, in fact; it's good to see that there is
still a place for drivers who don't even take up the
sport until they're 23, but 30 must seem a long way

*Big oil is back, in a small way: BP joined forces with Ford
in mid-season and Shell threw its weight behind Skoda,
albeit perhaps with the Fabia in mind rather than
venerable Octavia (below).*

rather than McRae was the hardest decision of his life,
but the truth was that there was no great clamour for
the Playstation royalties millionaire. The man who had
embodied Colin McRae Rally has been supplanted by
the Playstation generation, by the likes of Solberg,
Markko Märtin and François Duval. The writing was
on the wall when Subaru re-signed Solberg as early as
May and Citroën made sure that Loeb was under lock
and key soon afterwards. By the time McRae was told
that he was a free agent in August, there were only
crumbs left on the table.

McRae is a special case, for a number of reasons.
There is nothing wrong with his eyesight or his
reactions and one suspects that he hasn't lost the
appetite for driving at life-threatening speeds on
narrow roads bordered by trees either. What he has
lost is the desire to do so for its own sake, without a
worthwhile shot at the World Championship, without
a full works car and a full works salary. One suspects
too that Citroën would have extracted much better
value from its investment and need not have agonised

between Sainz and McRae if it had gone to greater
lengths to find an engineer who could build up a good
rapport with the Scot.

Nevertheless, McRae does belong to a different
generation and not simply because he doesn't care for
playing computer games. One of the reasons that he
didn't thrive in the Xsara was that it reflected 21st-
century thinking, in that it was developed for a
different driving style. Märtin began rallying in a Lada
Samara, Loeb in a 106 and Duval in a Saxo; the only
member of the Playstation brigade who took to the
stages in a rear-wheel-drive car was Solberg, who
chose a Volvo 240. In the main, the rising stars didn't
learn their craft opposite-locking in rear-wheel-drive
cars with live axles. They tend to have less expansive
driving styles, more akin to a racing driver's and very
much in tune with modern tyres, suspension
developments and transmission technology: twiddling
the active differential knobs on the dashboard can
make a Xsara oversteer like a Mark 2 Escort, but it
won't make it quicker. It's impossible to pronounce

off to Duval, who was born in November 1980, or to
Ford's semi-official number three, Mikko Hirvonen,
and a lifetime away to Jari-Matti Latvala, the 18-year-
old whom the Finnish driver manager, Timo Jouhki,
and M-Sport's Director, Malcolm Wilson, have given a
works-prepared Focus.

At 35, McRae said that he had become conscious
of how much he had got away with; the sense of
immortality diminishes with maturity. However, safety
also concerned younger drivers. Neither Solberg nor
Märtin is given to dwelling on the risks, but they were
disgusted that the FIA decided to ban gravel notes and
it was Märtin, not the drivers' usual shop steward,
Sainz, who led the drafting of a letter of protest to the
FIA President, Max Mosley.

It was a telling illustration of how the sport has
changed: when Shekhar Mehta was a works driver in
the 1970s and '80s, gravel notes didn't exist. On the
Monte Carlo Rally, professional drivers had ice note
crews, as they had had since BMC had developed the
idea in the 1960s. The Monte's shifting combination of

Tarmac and snow was considered uniquely perilous and more than justified hiring experienced crews to make last-minute amendments to pace notes. Well before Mehta became President of the World Rally Championship Commission, the technique had spread to other rallies – outside the World Championship to boot – and acquired its new name. One can appreciate Mehta's view that gravel notes are a luxury, not a need and there is no gainsaying that he survived any number of attempts at the RAC, the Acropolis and Portugal without them. He would argue that gravel note cars and crews are an expense that the sport can no longer indulge in a post-September 11 world, in

which car manufacturers' profits and willingness to spend on rallying are declining in unison. On the other hand, rallies are shorter now and cars are stronger. The tempo has consequently increased and while drivers will adapt to circumstances – they're meant to be versatile, after all – there have been quite enough bone-breaking accidents in recent years to suggest that their fears are well founded.

The changing of a generation is never a neat exercise like the changing of the guard. Sainz is still very much in harness, Marcus Grönholm is a few months older than McRae, but has a Peugeot contract until 2006, and as Richard Burns points out, he first

contested a full World Championship season in 1998, just two years before Solberg. Burns is only 32, incidentally and has secure employment with Subaru for the medium term, while Peugeot was happy to sign Freddy Loix, who is a little older. Two of the four drivers fighting for the World Championship on the final round might be termed part of the old guard. The qualifications don't alter the fact that a new generation is assuming a dominant role. Between Grönholm's victory in Argentina and Gilles Panizzi's in Catalonia, five months passed in which all seven rallies fell to drivers who were under 30 and had each won his first World Championship round within the previous year.

They had acquired the experience to complement natural ability and the will to win. It would be unwise to assume that the likes of Burns are henceforth consigned to number-two status and that their championship-winning days are behind them, but two years at Peugeot have done his reputation real damage. He is no longer seen as a 'strike' driver who can carry the attack to the opposition.

There is an element of fashion guiding manufacturers' thinking, but there is also a trend and it's a paradox that Ford, which didn't feature in the most closely fought World Championship yet, has made the running. To a large degree, Wilson had no

choice but to be bold. Having blithely launched driver fees through the £3,000,000 barrier, Ford's mounting losses meant that it could no longer afford megastar money. Given a choice between McRae and a heavily revised Focus, Wilson recognised that Christian Loriaux's car was his team's sole chance of remaining competitive in the medium term and perhaps of surviving at all in the longer term. Ford is said to have toyed with the idea of re-hiring McRae. Yet while there would have been substantial publicity benefits, the company has been in a conspicuously parsimonious mood and it is not alone. McRae saw no reason why he should drive for a pittance and was

under no obligation to do so, but neither Ford, nor Subaru, nor the World Championship's handful of sponsors and associated commercial partners were in the mood to splash out the £5,000,000 needed to keep him in action. If he doubted that the sport had moved into leaner times, he had only to consider Sainz's drastically reduced fee and consequent replacement of Luis Moya with Martí.

From the manufacturers' viewpoint, it wasn't simply a question of money. They also want young men who habitually overlook the risks and haven't grown too accustomed to having their demands met.

In many respects, M-Sport's post-McRae season

15

Is that an EVO you're driving...

...or are you just pleased to see me?

The new Mitsubishi Lancer Evolution VIII delivers an awesome 276bhp, goes from 0 - 60 mph in just 4.42 seconds (source: Autocar Magazine) and is capable of reaching speeds of up to 157mph. It has a new 6 speed manual transmission, improved aerodynamics and outstanding warranty. The Evolution VIII boasts enhanced acceleration and stability through the new Super Active Yaw Control system. And, if this is not enough, for an additional £2,000 there is the FQ300 upgrade, boosting power to 301bhp for total exhilaration. Evolution VIII. A true rally car for the road from just £26,999 OTR.

Available now from official Mitsubishi Ralliart dealers

The official number to call: 0845 330 2002

www.mitsubishi-cars.co.uk

**MITSUBISHI
MOTORS**

The Fabia (above right) displayed glimpses of promise, without justifying the decision to rush it into action months ahead of the original schedule. Snow is part of the sport's appeal, snow tyres one of its abiding mysteries.

was a triumph. The 2003 Focus was an acclaimed demonstration of the combined talents of Wilson's ex-Prodrive Technical Director, Loriaux, and his team. It was a pacesetting car that wrested the technological initiative away from the French manufacturers, while Märtin amply rewarded Wilson's judgement and the doubters who suggested that Ford might complete 2003 without a win were silenced. Ingenuity and determination went a long way towards compensating for straitened circumstances. There are those who believe the World Championship would be a very one-sided contest indeed if M-Sport had PSA's resources.

But the Focus had rather too much in common with the hare and rather too little in common with the tortoise. Lancia possessed a knack of launching cars that not only set the pace, but went the distance. In fact, Ford had a respectable finishing record in 2003, but a knowledgeable bookmaker wouldn't have given odds on Märtin hitting trouble by the end of the season, for Loriaux's Focus was all too vulnerable to niggling problems, usually with the hydraulics or the electronics.

The World Championship was won by those old-fashioned virtues, reliability and weight of numbers. It was always likely to be a two-horse race, for only Peugeot and Citroën could afford to pay the three drivers that winning the World Championship for Manufacturers demanded. Ultimately, there was almost nothing to choose between them, the wins and the points divided almost equally. As their new stars gained confidence, Ford and Subaru were able to challenge for victory with growing frequency, despite their cars' periodic fits of temperament, but neither had started the season with their eyes on the manufacturers' title, as they were no more able to hire a third established driver than Hyundai.

Peugeot Sport management were predictably irritated by suggestions that the 206 was getting long in the tooth, Panizzi's victory in Spain after a salvo of fastest stage times in the dry as well as the wet rather proving the point, but it wasn't a vintage season by Vélizy's standards. As the team's Director, Corrado Provera, acknowledged, the opposition had inevitably closed in; it would have been remarkable if it had not, given that Ford had re-engineered its car from stem to stern, that Citroën had acquired Sainz, along with a useful financial injection to extract more from the Xsara and that Peugeot had made no major technical advances in more than a year. That said, it wasn't primarily Grönholm's curiously erratic form that cost the team dearly, but crumbling reliability. In the early months of the season, the 2002 World Champion remained an irresistible force, winning three of the first five rallies, while Burns was a safe bet for a finish in the top three. On that basis, even as the opposition strengthened, Peugeot ought to have had a secure lead in the manufacturers' series at any rate by the middle of the season. Instead, it lost ground to Citroën thanks to a succession of mechanical mishaps, from Grönholm's wrongly plumbed petrol tank on the Acropolis, to the wheel bearing failures that hamstrung Grönholm and Burns in Finland, to the gearbox and turbo problems that cost the latter points in Greece and Argentina. Ford's fragility was understandable; Peugeot's was harder to explain or to forgive. The most likely explanation is that reliability waned as the opposition waxed and Peugeot's drivers were therefore obliged to push their machinery beyond its limits.

Peugeot's handling of Burns was also open to question. Relations were civil – Burns would usually give Provera a box of cigars when jetting in from his tax haven in Andorra – and it's impossible to tell whether the 206 could have been re-engineered to his liking, but it seemed a pity that Peugeot's regimental approach to running a rally team meant that the possibility was never explored with much vigour. Lancia and Toyota managed to cater for driver preference without blunting their competitive edge and Burns's inability to feel at one with the car left the team a cylinder short. While Peugeot had not simply coped, but thrived in comparable circumstances with François Delecour and Didier Auriol, its adversaries have grown a good deal stronger in the years since

WALES EMERGES
AS A CENTRE OF EXCELLENCE
FOR MOTORSPORT AND PERFORMANCE ENGINEERING

Wales Rally GB Motorsport Initiative

A new motorsport initiative, which will bring together all the key public and private sector partners in Wales, was announced by Andrew Davies, Minister for Economic Development and Transportation, Welsh Assembly Government at Wales Rally GB 2003.

Facilitated through the Welsh Development Agency and Welsh Assembly Government, this new scheme will allow specialist teams in Wales to develop business, infrastructure, education and tourism opportunities.

This announcement also received a major boost with the news that Ford is to base its prestigious Auto Academy in Wales, 2004 and funding has been granted to provide a new £10 million cutting edge 'Auto Technium', a research and development incubator facility for companies wishing to embrace design, development and testing to world class standards.

Andrew Davies Minister for Economic Development and Transportation, Welsh Assembly Government.

FORD
Auto Academy
coming to
WALES

MOTORSPORT STRATEGY

WALES RALLY GB
MOTORSPORT INITIATIVE

WDA
AWDURDOD DATBLYGU CYMRU
WELSH DEVELOPMENT AGENCY

Noddir gan
Lywodraeth
Cynulliad Cymru
Sponsored by
Welsh Assembly
Government

Email: paul.r.jones@wda.co.uk

THINK BUSINESS WALES   THINK EDUCATION WALES   THINK TOURISM WALES   THINK MOTORSPORT WALES

THINK WALES RALLY GB

and Burns ought to have been a more formidable presence than either of his predecessors.

The 206's patchy finishing record compared unfavourably with the Xsara's utter dependability. The Citroën's ruggedness was evident when both works cars finished the 2002 Safari at the first attempt and by 2003, serious mechanical maladies were news. McRae's car caught fire in Argentina, while Loeb's blew its engine in Greece. Sainz lost 40 seconds and three places thanks to an electrical fault in Catalonia, just as McRae was foiled by a faulty electronic throttle on the Acropolis, but these were very isolated failings. The cars were evidently lifed very precisely indeed, making the three-mile trip from the Tour of Corsica's service area to scrutineering on a transporter for example, but Citroën scored points more consistently than Peugeot and made huge strides in making the car as competitive on dirt as it has always been on asphalt. The new drivers confirmed that it was nervous at speed on bumps and significant progress by Argentina was owed largely to new top mounts and revised suspension settings, tuning dampers and bumpstops to match the ingenious hydraulic anti-roll bars. Loeb's searing pace in Australia owed something to a lengthy test after the Rally Finland.

Although his team's results vastly exceeded Fréquelin's cautious predictions, if it had a weakness, it was caution. It unaccountably failed to order Loeb onto the attack when Harri Rovanperä's 206 was ailing in Cyprus – how Loeb would have yearned for the two extra points as he prepared for the showdown on the Rally of Great Britain – and its tyre choice on asphalt was occasionally unimaginative too.

The FIA wants to put a stop to Peugeot-Citroën battles, or anything similar and strange as it seems in the light of 2003 policy making, it wants to create a situation in which drivers such as McRae are not cast adrift at 35. Nonetheless, thanks largely to the governing body's actions, there has rarely been a season of such marked contrasts. One might have expected those within the sport to revel in a year of breathtaking competition, of new names coming to the fore and championship battles going to the wire; a little complacency might have been forgiveable. Instead, the second half of the season was characterised by a profound sense of despondency. Talk of expansion – more teams, more drivers, more television – was replaced by uncertainty and conflict,

pitting most of the manufacturers and drivers against the FIA and Citroën against the rest. It was a watershed not just for McRae and Mäkinen, but for the FIA and the television rights-holding company, International SportsWorld Communicators. June's World Council decision to expand the series to 16 rallies in 2004, in the teeth of noisy opposition from ISC and every manufacturer bar Citroën, was a signal that the FIA ran the sport and not ISC's owner and Prodrive Chairman, David Richards, nor the participants, the car manufacturers. Just possibly, Richards will get his extended rights deal, but there no longer seems much likelihood of a rallying equivalent of the Formula 1 Concorde Agreement, nor of there being television income to parcel out between the main players. The FIA has no plans to turn Peugeot and Subaru into the equivalents of Ferrari and McLaren.

The sense of dismay was understandably mingled with outrage. The press learnt that Richards and most of the manufacturers were being ejected from the World Rally Championship Commission in October before the participants. The manufacturers stressed that they had no objection in principle to the World Championship being enlarged, but they were adamant

Petter Solberg's star quality is not in doubt. He has few rivals when it comes to driving a car, none when it comes to working a crowd.

that 2004 was not the year to do it – not when profits were dwindling and budgets were being slashed.

It is fair to say that they didn't argue their case well. Rallying is adminstered no more democratically than any other sport, but the manufacturers were at least given the courtesy of being invited to devise cost-cutting regulations to ease the pain of extra rallies. Instead, they were unable even to agree to hang together; the one proposal they put forward, that 20-minute service allocations should be cut to 15, was subsequently criticised by Fréquelin. As a result, they neither secured a compromise on 15 rallies (the FIA might have been prepared to bring Mexico in and make Japan wait for a year) nor had much influence on new regulations that may therefore cause turmoil. ISC was the one organisation to provide a detailed breakdown of its costs and it's easy to see why the FIA lost patience with the car makers when every query was met with the response that the item in question didn't cost much. It was difficult to credit at times that the indignant manufacturers were often the same people who had warned that the 1,000,000 rally car was nigh. The competitive urge seemed to interfere with a sense of self-preservation.

McRae and Sainz had been in a parlous position from June onwards, when championship expansion was accompanied by a new driver nomination rule, stipulating that three-car works teams had to include

at least one driver who hadn't finished in the top three of a World Championship rally in the previous three years. From then on, Citroën was compelled to jettison one of its older hands. Changing the rules again in September, making two-car teams mandatory, therefore made no odds to the 'junior' PSA team, but it infuriated Peugeot, which had assembled a three-car line-up consisting of Grönholm, Loix and Harri Rovanperä based on the June rule.

There was no reasonable defence to offer for altering the regulations twice in three months. In other respects, the FIA has a case of sorts. By stipulating two-car teams, it will end Peugeot-Citroën duels, but it will offer Subaru a chance of winning the manufacturers' crown and who knows, may give Skoda or Suzuki a realistic chance of success; under the present rules, Skoda continues merely to make up the numbers, although rushing the Fabia into action so early might have been calculated to make it look second-rate. Reducing costs and adding rallies – assuming the two aren't entirely contradictory – may make the difference between manufacturers staying out or coming in; it may mean that there are enough teams in future to fight over McRae's signature even if he isn't in the first flush of youth. Introducing new rallies does more than answer criticisms that the championship hasn't justified its 'world' tag. It also recognises that the fastest-growing car markets are not in the sport's European heartland. The governing body could argue that it was preparing for stormy weather ahead.

There was no denying that in the meantime it had whipped up a storm of its own. It has consistently failed to justify adding rallies in 2004 rather than 2005

or 2006, it has managed to jettison the sport's biggest worldwide name and aggravate a mood of uncertainty. Hyundai might have departed anyway for its own reasons, but the prolonged speculation over Ford's and Skoda's future participation stemmed from the June World Council meeting.

The worst may lie ahead. Some of the sport's most level-headed figures believe that the new regulations for practising and servicing will be unworkable. Doing away with recce cars might cut transport costs, turning airfreight into a practical alternative to seafreight, but most teams expect to send some equipment by sea and given the 2004 calendar, they could need more equipment, not less. Moreover, cramming the competitive action into the afternoon threatens to reverse much of the progress made in adapting rallying to media deadlines, to say nothing of the chaos that may result from practising each morning at the same time as spectators are flooding into stages. The possibility of there being no footage to screen one day is a real one. It is easy to understand and sympathise with competitors who saw nothing wrong with the present system. Less servicing has an appeal, restoring an element of endurance and perhaps reducing speeds, but combined with fewer cars, it risks creating processional rallies in which the leader coasts to victory over the walking wounded. In television terms, it may be raw poison.

The FIA also managed the unlikely feat of making people feel sorry for Richards. He's the sort of personality who tends to inspire respect rather than affection, but even his detractors would recognise that he has made more effort than anyone else to sell rallying to television and has run up the losses to

IN SUCCESSFUL BUSINESSES,

every member of the team is vital.
Whatever they do, wherever they are.

WE NETWORK THEM.

prove it. The FIA's new policy, with fewer works cars and fewer visits to a centralised service area, flies in the face of Richards's blueprint and threatens to undermine much of what he has achieved. Richards is perceived as having overstepped the mark in his dealings with organisers and his policy irritated many of the sport's diehard fans, but it was at least coherent and in the light of the most recent audience figures, it cannot be argued that he isn't fulfilling his brief. The FIA doesn't appear to have an altogether clear picture of what it wants the World Championship to become and given its treatment of the present promoter, it's difficult to see why anyone else would wish to sink millions into the sport if he throws in the towel.

Its attitude towards the manufacturers raises echoes of 1995. Back then, the FIA seemed not to understand that Toyota would take its humiliation over the Catalan turbo restrictor scandal seriously. It wouldn't simply change its name from Toyota Team Europe to Toyota Rally Team and swagger back into the fray like some brass-necked Formula 1 outfit. There is a real danger that the FIA drives away manufacturers now; none of them – even a maker as devoted to four-wheel drive as Subaru – are compelled to be involved.

Rallying has an intrinsic appeal. It's the one form of motorsport that involves something resembling a road car and something resembling an ordinary road. Provided it remains adaptable, it should survive, but there are grounds for fearing that 2003 may have been the end of a golden age. The flurry of new rules have been an exercise in ripping off the tablecloth on the assumption that the china will never break.

THE SWEATSHOP APPROACH TO RUNNING A RALLY TEAM

If a car manufacturer were seeking an object lesson in how not to run a rally programme, it need look no further than Hyundai. Failing to improve on fourth place over a four-year campaign was perhaps unfortunate and certainly no disgrace, considering the lack of a motorsport tradition in Korea. However, the collapse of its World Championship involvement in a welter of recriminations and legal action beggared belief.

No doubt the full circumstances will become apparent over the next year or two, as the case between Hyundai Motor Corporation and Motor Sport Developments picks its way through the German courts. It would be unwise to rush to judgement in the meantime. Some maintain that MSD was the victim not of Korean callousness exactly, but of a different mindset, in which suppliers are regarded as expendable without any disrespect necessarily meant or implied. From the other side, it appears that Hyundai felt it wasn't kept in the picture by its own rally team.

Some suggested that if Hyundai needed to see the books so badly, MSD might have conceded the point before accounts were due to be filed and the breakdown became public. Others insisted that the Milton Keynes concern had the same budget as M-Sport, despite the pronounced contrast in results; it should be pointed out that unlike M-Sport, MSD was also responsible for engine development and public relations, and that it was based in a more expensive part of the country. When MSD was so strapped for cash that it couldn't maintain a test programme or even bring a motorhome, it was difficult to avoid the impression that Hyundai had lost interest, which in itself was evidence that it didn't fully appreciate what motorsport could offer. There was no denying that the Accent was doing as badly in the showroom as it was on stage, but with a little more investment, it might at least have done something positive for the company image, even if the model's was past rescuing.

Whatever the rights and wrongs of the dispute, Hyundai should surely have been able to avoid becoming the only manufacturer to miss a scheduled rally since registration was introduced to the World Championship in 1995. If the relationship with MSD had to end, it need not have been so messy and so brutal. Teams come and go in motorsport, but it isn't often that their demise is accompanied by the use of words such as 'honour' and 'dignity'. It was inexcusable that MSD staff learnt that they had lost the contract, and hence their jobs, from the internet.

As MSD sources suggest, Hyundai probably won't have much difficulty in finding staff for its new, Russelsheim-based team, assuming the project goes ahead; there are always people who think they can do a better job. But Hyundai should remember that international motorsport is a powerful means of giving a faceless organisation an image, even a personality, and whatever its concerns and grievances, its recent conduct fosters precisely the kind of backward, alien impression it is seeking to dispel.

REVIEW OF THE YEAR
The Accent WRC was never an outstanding rally car, but respectability was within its grasp until the money dried up.

IN EVERY KIND OF BUSINESS,
there are times when you only get one shot
at something. You can't afford to be let down.

WE MAKE SURE YOU WON'T BE.

Trust matters. Whether it's at the FIA World Rally Championship or in the corporate boardroom, you need to know your equipment is going to work. It's something you shouldn't even have to think about. You can believe in Inmarsat technology. Our high-speed, high-quality communications are all about reliability. With our sophisticated satellite network, connectivity is constant. So when something absolutely needs to get through, it does. At the FIA WRC, our high-speed data communications and fast, mobile internet connectivity instantly and reliably relay crucial data to teams and drivers, ensuring everyone can concentrate on the road ahead. When you need one less thing to worry about, trust Inmarsat to deliver.

For more information about Inmarsat solutions, visit www.inmarsat.com/data

inmarsat
Total Communications Network™

EXCLUSIVE GLOBAL PARTNER OF THE FIA WORLD RALLY CHAMPIONSHIP

an **inmarsat ventures** company

Petter Solberg has the priceless knack of making you feel important. It's as though signing an autograph or giving an interview requires the same commitment and gives the same pleasure as setting a fastest stage time. It comes naturally, for Solberg has no shortage of warmth, but it's an instance of a relentless, obsessive quest for perfection. An intelligent, thoughtful man, he recoils from the idea that his job begins and ends with driving a car.

Midway through the season, he said earnestly that 'fans are important'. It was an arresting statement: fans are fun, fans are gratifying, but important? His emergence as Norway's most popular sportsman is remarkable, considering that in his childhood, rallying was banned and the sport has nothing like the traditional following it has in other Nordic countries. Nevertheless, it's difficult to believe that international companies such as Subaru and British American Tobacco care very much whether a Norwegian rally driver is moderately or wildly popular in his homeland; it isn't going to shift many cars or cigarettes. Besides, European sportsmen are allowed all too often to be tortured souls, too wrapped up in the business of winning to be expected to spare much time for their fans.

Yet to Solberg, it matters a great deal. Turning on the charm can't fail to please an employer and while it won't make many odds in Norway, it certainly helps on promotional tours to Japan or the United States. As Carlos Sainz has proved, a high public profile is a powerful tool. In a sport funded very largely by car manufacturers, the ability to attract and to please sponsors can make a crucial difference. After winning the Rally of Great Britain, Solberg sounded mildly apologetic for not having devoted more time to his fans.

Nevertheless, it would be wrong to suggest that he is purely calculating. There is no denying the sense of obligation to his supporters, nor that there is a side of him, rather like Ari Vatanen or the late Henri Toivonen, that revels in the adulation – 'Hollywood' Solberg indeed – and another part that takes an instinctive delight in sharing success. An effervescent, telegenic, engaging personality, Solberg is the extrovert's extrovert.

The desire to please doesn't generally extend to rivals. If Solberg was a cricketer, he would be worth selecting for his sledging ability alone. He is quick to point out that Markko Märtin has contested more World Championship rallies than he has, adroitly ignoring the fact that Märtin has tackled somewhat fewer in a works car, and is just as ready to suggest that Sébastien Loeb – whom he notes in passing, started rallying a year sooner than he did – built up experience in Super 1600 cars; it sits a touch awkwardly with his claim that learning how to make pace notes is one of the key skills. Loeb learnt how to make them, certainly, but notes made in a 130 or 200 bhp Saxo probably won't serve much purpose in a 300 bhp Xsara – to say nothing of the fact that Solberg was driving cars near the family home in Spyderberg from the age of six and competing from his early teens. He proclaims just as cheerfully that Peugeots, Citroëns and above all Fords have more power than his Subaru. In Australia, he said that he thoroughly enjoyed the duel with Loeb, but that he hadn't wanted to take the lead too soon, as he needed the pressure to perform. It paints a picture of a man toying with his opponents. It's not that they're bad drivers – perish the thought – but it feeds the notion that they are inferior.

In contrast, Solberg thoroughly enjoyed having Tommi Mäkinen as a team-mate, paying fulsome tribute to the Finn's advice and generosity. Younger drivers would do well not to be won over by this

touching portrayal of pupil and master: talented, ambitious drivers whose careers aren't on Mäkinen's trajectory may not get such a cuddly reception.

For the foreseeable future, any other driver will surely struggle at Subaru. Following in the footsteps of Röhrl and Biasion, Sainz and Mäkinen, Solberg has worked industriously to mould the team around him.

'It's worth to put in everything and then you get everything back,' he says. He is quick to praise his mechanics, conspicuously so after the overnight resurrection of his Impreza before his outstanding Tour of Corsica victory, and he is more than ready to lead by example. The long-term contract with Subaru fuels team spirit; so does buying the beers after a victory. He has learnt not to dwell in public on mechanical problems and other setbacks, although the comments about Prodrive's engines are certainly intended to increase the pressure on the engine department. He still feels the surge of frustration, but he realises that harping on about it neither wins friends nor ultimately makes him feel better.

Like Sainz, he is a tireless tester, endlessly fascinated by shock absorber and differential settings, quite capable of ringing his engineer, Pierre-Yves Genon, between rallies to suggest a tweak for the next event.

Can he imagine a perfect car?

'There will never be a perfect car, never,' he replied

PROFILE
Petter Solberg
By David Williams

Solberg seized and celebrated the championship with characteristic panache. The enthusiasm is infectious, even Tommi Mäkinen (below left) entering into the spirit of the occasion.

quickly. 'I can't say you can't get good cars, but if you stop, you think, "Bloody hell, I've got a good car now," then you will start to lose. I always have to develop and do small things all the time.'

The lack of complacency is admirable, but Solberg loves cars and engineering far too much to want there to be such a thing as a perfect car. Worrying away at perfection is part of the fun.

However, the difference between Solberg the budding star and Solberg the World Rally Champion has far less to do with presenting an image and much more to do with self-discipline, a determination to learn and extraordinary resilience. A degree of exasperation had begun to steal over the team when an early accident on the Monte Carlo Rally was followed by another in Turkey. While his opponents piled up the points, the Norwegian doggedly insisted that he had been unlucky. Opportunities to score well

on rallies that suited the car were slipping away.

But Solberg drew the appropriate conclusions. At 28, he grasped that a man of his talent didn't need to win from the front. He developed and adhered to a new tactic of driving with a sliver of caution at first and gathering speed gradually. A finely judged victory in Cyprus was followed by an electrifying second place in Finland, when faulty Peugeot wheel bearings brought Richard Burns within striking distance at the last moment; one suspects that beating the man scheduled to become his 2004 team-mate was as much a source of delight as the two extra points.

The points were crucial in the end. In seeking to explain why Solberg won and Loeb lost, one could point to Loeb running out of petrol in Turkey or tot up any number of other mishaps that befell the two. The telling difference came in October. Solberg was in a trough of despair after Sanremo, aghast not so much

FROM SPYDERBERG TO SUPERSTARDOM

that he had retired early, but that the latest Pirellis and active suspension appeared to have brought Subaru no closer to being competitive on Tarmac. All the brilliance displayed in Finland and Australia threatened to count for nothing. Stealing Corsica against the odds, with a car that had been all but written off against a telegraph pole, was an achievement that deserves to pass into rallying legend. His quip that he would sponsor the telegraph pole belied a supreme demonstration of willpower.

Scoring well in Catalonia and withstanding the pressure of being the favourite in Britain contrasted with Loeb's uneven performance after seizing the initiative in Sanremo. There are qualifications to be entered on the Frenchman's behalf, such as the mix-up with Michelin over the available tyres in Catalonia and team orders in Wales, yet it would be impossible to argue that the wrong man won. Solberg had trumped the experts who had proclaimed Loeb as the favourite.

Solberg wouldn't entertain the idea that Loeb deserved the crown. He didn't dominate the season – no one did – but he had seized his opportunity. Above all, he might point to Australia and revel in the claim that he has never lost a battle yet. There are experienced observers within Prodrive who regard him as the fastest driver ever to have worked for the team. The first world title – it's difficult to believe that there won't be more – surely isn't the culmination of a career. Solberg is enjoying success far too much for that. It will only fuel his desire for more.

2003 RALLY CAR SPECIFICATIONS

PEUGEOT 206 WRC

Team Manager	Jean-Pierre Nicolas
Chief Engineer	Michel Nandan
Sponsors	Marlboro/Total/Clarion

ENGINE		CHASSIS	
Cylinders	4 in-line	Steering	Rack and pinion (power assisted)
Mounts	Transverse/front	Front suspension	MacPherson strut, Peugeot damping
Capacity	1997 cc		
Bore & stroke	85 x 88 mm	Rear suspension	MacPherson strut, Peugeot damping
Compression ratio	–		
Valves/camshafts	16-valve/DOHC	Wheel sizes	7 x 15/8 x 18 in Speedline
Fuel system	Magneti Marelli Step 9	Tyres	Michelin
Turbocharger	Garrett TR30	Front brakes	295-355 mm discs, 4-/8-pot calipers
Max. power	300 bhp @ 5250 rpm		
Max. torque	550 Nm @ 3500 rpm	Rear brakes	294-355 mm discs, 4-/6-pot calipers
Oil contract	Total		
TRANSMISSION		**DIMENSIONS**	
Gearbox	5-speed, Xtrac sequential	Overall length	4005 mm
Drive type	4WD	Overall width	1770 mm
Clutch/differentials	Triple-plate carbon/hydraulic active differentials	Wheelbase	2468 mm
		Weight	1230 kg
		Front track	1647 mm
		Rear track	1621 mm
		Body	3-door steel

SUBARU IMPREZA WRC2003

Team Manager	David Lapworth
Chief Engineer	Steve Farrell
Sponsors	555, Pirelli

ENGINE		CHASSIS	
Cylinders	Flat-4	Steering	Rack and pinion
Mounts	Front, in-line	Front suspension	Struts with TCA, Bilstein/Prodrive or Sachs damping
Capacity	1994 cc		
Bore & stroke	92.0 x 75 mm	Rear suspension	Struts with lateral and triangle links
Compression ratio	8:1		
Valves/camshafts	16/4	Wheel sizes	7 x 15 in. (dirt) 8 x 18 in. (asphalt)
Fuel system	Subaru sequential injection		
Turbocharger	IHI	Tyres	Pirelli
Max. power	300 bhp @ 5,500 rpm	Front brakes	Alcon 330–366 x 32 mm ventilated discs
Max. torque	48 kg/m @ 4000 rpm		
Oil contract	–	Rear brakes	Alcon 305 x 28 mm ventilated discs
TRANSMISSION		**DIMENSIONS**	
Gearbox	Prodrive 6-speed	Overall length	4405 mm
Drive type	4WD	Overall width	1770 mm
Clutch/differentials	AP carbon, Prodrive mechanical diffs with hydraulic control	Wheelbase	2535 mm
		Weight	1230 kg
		Front track	1510 mm
		Rear track	1510 mm
		Body	4-door steel

FORD FOCUS WRC

Team Manager	Malcolm Wilson
Chief Engineer	Christian Loriaux
Sponsors	BP

Engine		Chassis	
Cylinders	4 in-line	Steering	Rack and pinion (assisted), 2.0 turns lock to lock
Mounts	Transverse/front		
Capacity	1995 cc	Front suspension	MacPherson struts, Reiger damping
Bore & stroke	84.8 x 88.3 mm	Rear suspension	MacPherson struts, Reiger damping
Compression ratio	–	Wheel sizes	5–8 x 15–18 in.
Valves/camshafts	16/DOHC	Tyres	Michelin
Fuel system	Ford/Pectel electronic injection and ignition	Front brakes	Brembo 300/380 mm ventilated discs with 4/8-pot caliper
Turbocharger	Garrett	Rear brakes	300/315 mm ventilated discs, 4-pot caliper
Max. power	300 bhp @ 6500 rpm		
Max. torque	550 Nm @ 4000 rpm		
Oil contract	BP	Dimensions	
		Overall length	4152 mm
Transmission		Overall width	1770 mm
Gearbox	Xtrac 240 6-speed sequential	Wheelbase	2635 mm
		Weight	1235 kg
Drive type	4WD	Front track	1470 mm
Clutch/differentials	Hydraulic/electronic Xtrac differentials, hydraulic/electronic control	Rear track	1487 mm
		Body	Unitary 3-door steel

CITROEN XSARA WRC

Team Manager	Guy Fréquelin
Chief Engineer	Jean-Claude Vaucard
Sponsors	Total/Michelin

ENGINE

Cylinders	4 in-line
Mounts	Transverse/front
Capacity	1998 cc
Bore & stroke	86 x 86 mm
Compression ratio	–
Valves/camshafts	16-valve/DOHC
Fuel system	Magneti Marelli MR3
Turbocharger	Garrett
Max. power	300 bhp @ 5500 rpm
Max. torque	520Nm @ 4000 rpm
Oil contract	Total

TRANSMISSION

Gearbox	Xtrac 6-speed, sequential
Drive type	2WD (front)
Clutch/differentials	Triple-plate carbon, hydraulic active differentials

CHASSIS

Steering	Rack and pinion (power assisted)
Front suspension	MacPherson strut, Extrem Tech damping
Rear suspension	MacPherson strut, Extrem Tech damping
Wheel sizes	8 x 18in.
Tyres	Michelin
Front brakes	376 x 28 mm Alcon discs, 6-/8-piston calipers
Rear brakes	278 x 20 mm discs

DIMENSIONS

Overall length	4167 mm
Overall width	1770 mm
Wheelbase	2555 mm
Weight	1230 kg
Front track	1568 mm
Rear track	1568 mm
Body	3-door steel

MITSUBISHI LANCER WRC2

Team Manager	Sven Quandt
Chief Engineer	Mario Fornaris
Sponsors	Mitsubishi Oil, Michelin

ENGINE

Cylinders	4 in-line
Mounts	Transverse/front
Capacity	1996 cc
Bore & stroke	85.5 x 86.9 mm
Compression ratio	8.5:1
Valves/camshafts	16/DOHC
Fuel system	Electronic injection
Turbocharger	Mitsubishi twin-scroll
Max. power	300 bhp @ 5500rpm
Max. torque	55 kg/m @ 3500 rpm
Oil contract	Mitsubishi Oil

TRANSMISSION

Gearbox	Xtrac sequential 6-speed
Drive type	4WD
Clutch/differentials	Carbon triple-plate clutch, electro-magnetic differential options

CHASSIS

Steering	Rack and pinion (assisted)
Front suspension	MacPherson strut
Rear suspension	MacPherson strut with wishbone, Ohlins damping
Wheel sizes	5/6/7/8 x 15 in. 8 x 18 in.
Tyres	Michelin
Front brakes	AP 4/8-pot caliper, 310/370mm ventilated discs
Rear brakes	4-pot caliper, 300/320mm ventilated discs

DIMENSIONS

Overall length	4360mm
Overall width	1700mm
Wheelbase	2600 mm
Weight	1280 kg
Front track	1550mm
Rear track	1550 mm
Body	4-door steel

HYUNDAI ACCENT WRC3

Team Manager	David Whitehead
Chief Engineer	Graham Moore
Sponsors	Michelin

ENGINE

Cylinders	4 in-line
Mounts	Transverse/front
Capacity	1998 cc
Bore & stroke	85 x 88 mm
Compression ratio	9.2:1
Valves/camshafts	16/DOHC
Fuel system	Hyundai/Pectel electronic injection
Turbocharger	Garrett
Max. power	300 bhp
Max. torque	520Nm
Oil contract	-

TRANSMISSION

Gearbox	Xtrac 6-speed sequential
Drive type	4WD
Clutch/differentials	AP ceramic triple-plate/ active differentials.

CHASSIS

Steering	Rack and pinion (power assisted)
Front suspension	MacPherson struts, Proflex or MSD damping
Rear suspension	MacPherson struts, Proflex or MSD damping
Wheel sizes	7 x 15/8 x 18 in.
Tyres	Michelin
Front brakes	AP 304/370 mm (4-/6-pot calipers)
Rear brakes	AP 304/370 mm (4-pot calipers)

DIMENSIONS

Overall length	4200 mm
Overall width	1770 mm
Wheelbase	2440 mm
Weight	1260 kg
Front track	1550 mm
Rear track	1550 mm
Body	3-door unitary steel

SKODA OCTAVIA WRC

Team Manager	Pavel Janeba
Chief Engineer	Dietmar Mettrich
Sponsors	Shell

ENGINE

Cylinders	4 in-line
Mounts	Transverse/front
Capacity	1999 cc
Bore & stroke	82.5 x 93.5 mm
Compression ratio	–
Valves/camshafts	20/DOHC
Fuel system	ALS electronic injection
Turbocharger	Garrett
Max. power	300 bhp @ 6250 rpm
Max. torque	501 Nm @ 3250 rpm
Oil contract	Shell

TRANSMISSION

Gearbox	6-speed Prodrive sequential
Drive type	4WD
Clutch/differentials	Triple-plate/active differentials

CHASSIS

Steering	Rack and pinion (power assisted)
Front suspension	MacPherson strut, Ohlins damping
Rear suspension	MacPherson strut, Ohlins damping
Wheel sizes	7 x 15 in./8 x 18 in.
Tyres	Michelin
Front brakes	Alcon ventilated discs, 6-piston calipers
Rear brakes	Alcon ventilated discs

DIMENSIONS

Overall length	4511 mm
Overall width	1770 mm
Wheelbase	2441 mm
Weight	1250 kg
Front track	1430 mm
Rear track	1394 mm
Body	5-door steel

SKODA FABIA WRC

Team Manager   Pavel Janeba
Chief Engineer   Dietmar Mettrich
Sponsors   Shell

ENGINE		CHASSIS	
Cylinders	4, in-line	Steering	Rack and pinion
Mounts	Front, transverse	Front suspension	MacPherson struts, Reiger damping
Capacity	1995 cc		
Bore & stroke	82.5 x 93.5 mm	Rear suspension	MacPherson struts, Reiger dampers
Compression ratio	8.7:1		
Valves/camshafts	20/DOHC	Wheel sizes	6 x 15 in. (dirt) 7 x 18 in. (asphalt)
Fuel system	Injection		
Max. power	300 bhp @ 5,500 rpm	Tyres	Michelin
Max. torque	600 Nm @ 3,500 rpm	Front brakes	304 x 28/376 x 32 mm discs, 4-/6-pot calipers
Oil contract	Shell		
		Rear brakes	304 x 28/355 x 28 mm discs, 4-pot calipers
TRANSMISSION			
Gearbox	Xtrac/Unic 6-speed sequential	**DIMENSIONS**	
Drive type		Overall length	4002 mm
Clutch/differentials	4WD, active limited slip differentials	Overall width	1770 mm
		Wheelbase	2462 mm
		Weight	1250 kg
		Front track	1565 mm
		Rear track	1485 mm
		Body	5-door steel

RENAULT CLIO SUPER 1600

Team Manager   -
Chief Engineer   Gilles Lallement
Sponsors   -

ENGINE		CHASSIS	
Cylinders	4, in-line	Steering	Rack and pinion
Mounts	Front, transverse	Front suspension	MacPherson struts , Ohlins/ Renault damping
Capacity	1598 cc		
Bore & stroke	79.5 x 80.5 mm	Rear suspension	Trailing arms, coil springs and Ohlins/Renault dampers
Compression ratio	-		
Valves/camshafts	16/DOHC	Wheel sizes	6 x 15 in. (dirt) 7 x 17 in. (asphalt)
Fuel system	Magneti Marelli MF4 injection		
Max. power	220 bhp @8,800 rpm	Tyres	Michelin
Max. torque	20 kg/m @ 7000 rpm	Front brakes	AP 343 mm ventilated discs , 4-piston calipers
Oil contract	—		
		Rear brakes	AP 263mm discs, 2-piston calipers
TRANSMISSION			
Gearbox	Sadev 6-speed sequential	**DIMENSIONS**	
Drive type	FWD	Overall length	3809 mm
Clutch/differentials	Twin-plate/Sadev clutch-type limited slip differential	Overall width	1783 mm
		Wheelbase	2472 mm
		Weight	1000 kg
		Front track	1600 mm
		Rear track	1600 mm
		Body	3-door steel

FIAT PUNTO RALLY

Team Manager   —
Chief Engineer   Sergio Limone
Sponsors   —

ENGINE		CHASSIS	
Cylinders	4, in-line	Steering	Rack and pinion
Mounts	Front, transverse	Front suspension	MacPherson struts, Bilstein damping
Capacity	1579 cc		
Bore & stroke	82.5 x 74.7 mm	Rear suspension	MacPherson struts, Bilstein damping
Compression ratio	12.5:1		
Valves/camshafts	16/DOHC	Wheel sizes	6 x 15 in. (dirt)
Fuel system	Magneti Marelli MF4 injection		7 x 17 in. (asphalt)
Max. power	215 bhp @ 9,000 rpm	Tyres	Michelin
Max. torque	20 kg/m @ 6,500 rpm	Front brakes	300/355 mm ventilated discs, 4-piston calipers
Oil contract	—		
		Rear brakes	Brembo 240 mm discs, 2-piston calipers
TRANSMISSION			
Gearbox	Hewland 6-speed sequential	**DIMENSIONS**	
Drive type	FWD	Overall length	3800 mm
Clutch/differentials	Single-disc, cerametallic/Plate-type limited slip differential	Overall width	1782 mm
		Wheelbase	2460 mm
		Weight	1000 kg
		Front track	-
		Rear track	-
		Body	3-door steel

VOLKSWAGEN POLO S1600

Team Manager   —
Chief Engineer   Gilles Vandecaveye
Sponsors   —

ENGINE		CHASSIS	
Cylinders	4, in-line	Steering	Rack and pinion
Mounts	Front, transverse	Front suspension	MacPherson struts, Ohlins damping, anti-roll bar
Capacity	1598 cc		
Bore & stroke	86.9 x 76.5 mm	Rear suspension	Trailing arms, coil springs, Ohlins dampers, anti-roll bar
Compression ratio	—		
Valves/camshafts	16/DOHC	Wheel sizes	6 x 15 in. (dirt) 7 x 17 in. (asphalt)
Fuel system	Bosch 3.1 injection		
Max. power	215 bhp @ 8,750 rpm	Tyres	Michelin
Max. torque	180 Nm @ 6,250 rpm	Front brakes	300/355mm ventilated discs, 4-pot calipers
Oil contract	—		
		Rear brakes	280mm ventilated discs, 2-piston calipers
TRANSMISSION			
Gearbox	6-speed sequential	**DIMENSIONS**	
Drive type	FWD	Overall length	3891 mm
Clutch/differentials	Sintered metal clutch/clutch-type limited slip differential	Overall width	1799 mm
		Wheelbase	2482 mm
		Weight	1000 kg
		Front track	1600 mm
		Rear track	1600 mm
		Body	3-door steel

PEUGEOT 206XS

Team Manager —
Chief Engineer —
Sponsors —

ENGINE

Cylinders	4, in-line
Mounts	Front, transverse
Capacity	1587 cc
Bore & stroke	78.2 x 82 mm
Compression ratio	–
Valves/camshafts	16/DOHC
Fuel system	Magneti Marelli injection
Max. power	200 bhp
Max. torque	185 Nm
Oil contract	–

TRANSMISSION

Gearbox	Sadev 6-speed sequential
Drive type	FWD
Clutch/differentials	Cerametallic single-plate/ZF limited slip differential

CHASSIS

Steering	Rack and pinion
Front suspension	MacPherson struts, Peugeot damping
Rear suspension	Trailing arms, torsion bars, Peugeot dampers
Wheel sizes	6 x 15 in. (dirt) 7 x 17 in. (asphalt)
Tyres	Michelin
Front brakes	295/345mm ventilated discs, 4-pot calipers
Rear brakes	278mm discs, 2-pot calipers

DIMENSIONS

Overall length	3826 mm
Overall width	1765 mm
Wheelbase	2455 mm
Weight	1000 kg
Front track	–
Rear track	–
Body	3-door steel

FORD PUMA 1600

Team Manager —
Chief Engineer Philip Dunabin
Sponsors —

ENGINE

Cylinders	4, in-line
Mounts	Front, transverse
Capacity	1597 cc
Bore & stroke	80 x 79.45 mm
Compression ratio	–
Valves/camshafts	16/DOHC
Fuel system	Pectel electronic injection
Max. power	210 bhp @ 8,750 rpm
Max. torque	–
Oil contract	–

TRANSMISSION

Gearbox	Hewland 6-speed sequential
Drive type	FWD
Clutch/differentials	Cerametallic/Clutch-type limited slip differential

CHASSIS

Steering	Rack and pinion
Front suspension	MacPherson struts, Dynamics damping
Rear suspension	Transverse beam, trailing arms, Dynamics dampers
Wheel sizes	6 x 15 in. (dirt) 7 x 17 in. (asphalt)
Tyres	Michelin
Front brakes	Alcon 300/355 mm ventilated discs, 4-piston calipers
Rear brakes	Alcon 260mm discs, 2-piston calipers

DIMENSIONS

Overall length	3984 mm
Overall width	1802 mm
Wheelbase	2446 mm
Weight	1000 kg
Front track	1580 mm
Rear track	1565 mm
Body	3-door steel

SUZUKI IGNIS 1600

Team Manager —
Chief Engineer Paul Barnard
Sponsors —

ENGINE

Cylinders	4, in-line
Mounts	Front, transverse
Capacity	1597 cc
Bore & stroke	81.0 x 77.5 mm
Compression ratio	13:1
Valves/camshafts	16/DOHC
Fuel system	Suzuki injection
Max. power	205 bhp @ 8,500 rpm
Max. torque	18.4 kg/m @ 7,250 rpm
Oil contract	–

TRANSMISSION

Gearbox	Suzuki 6-speed sequential
Drive type	FWD
Clutch/differentials	Single-plate/Multi-plate limited slip differential

CHASSIS

Steering	Rack and pinion
Front suspension	MacPherson struts, Reiger/Kayaba damping
Rear suspension	3-link beam axle, Reiger/Kayaba damping
Wheel sizes	6 x 15 in. (dirt) 7 x 17 in. (asphalt)
Tyres	Michelin
Front brakes	Brembo 300/355mm ventilated discs, 4-piston calipers
Rear brakes	Brembo 278mm discs, 2-piston calipers

DIMENSIONS

Overall length	3550 mm
Overall width	1740 mm
Wheelbase	2360 mm
Weight	1000 kg
Front track	1530 mm
Rear track	1489 mm
Body	3-door steel

OPEL CORSA 1600

Team Manager -
Chief Engineer Charlie Nichol
Sponsors —

ENGINE

Cylinders	4, in-line
Mounts	Front, transverse
Capacity	1598 cc
Bore & stroke	mm
Compression ratio	–
Valves/camshafts	16/DOHC
Fuel system	Motec injection
Max. power	215 bhp @ 8,750 rpm
Max. torque	199 Nm @ 6,250 rpm
Oil contract	–

TRANSMISSION

Gearbox	Xtrac 6-speed sequential
Drive type	FWD
Clutch/differentials	Single-plate/Clutch-type limited slip differential

CHASSIS

Steering	Rack and pinion
Front suspension	MacPherson struts, anti-roll bar
Rear suspension	Trailing arms, coil springs
Wheel sizes	6 x 15 in. (dirt) 7 x 17 in. (asphalt)
Tyres	Michelin
Front brakes	300/355 x 28 mm ventilated discs, 4-piston calipers
Rear brakes	280 x 9.6 mm discs, 2-piston calipers

DIMENSIONS

Overall length	3817 mm
Overall width	1770 mm
Wheelbase	2491 mm
Weight	1000 kg
Front track	1556 mm
Rear track	1556 mm
Body	3-door steel

VUELA, MARKKO, VUELA!

INTERVIEW Markko Märtin By David Williams

'Markko is a quiet guy, but I think he's a bit of a nutter,' observed M-Sport's Technical Director Christian Loriaux. He was reflecting on one of the most memorable images of the 2003 season, of Märtin's Focus silhouetted against a blue Argentine sky, the road far beneath, out of the picture. The vicious, first-leg yump put paid to the local hero and short-odds Group N favourite, Marcos Ligato, as well as Ramon Ferreyros. Predictably, Märtin's World Rally Car was more robust than the South Americans' less highly modified Mitsubishis, but he had had the brow cautioned in his pace notes. On the spur of the moment, he decided to take it flat out. The photograph made the front page of the regional paper.

With almost any other professional rally driver, Loriaux's verdict might have been a reproach, even a cause for alarm: popular wisdom assumes that they're all nutters, especially the younger ones. But Märtin appears so meek, so reserved, so diffident, that it's hard to credit that he is a professional rally driver at all. Far from criticising, Loriaux had been as delighted as anyone that his 2003 re-design and the boyish-looking, 28-year-old Estonian had combined to such spectacular effect. Even after the engine blew, the photograph remained a symbol of Ford's resurgence.

In certain respects, Märtin fits the pattern. He has always loved cars and cannot remember how old he was when he began driving, only that he was young enough to be sitting on his father's lap as he steered the family Lada. Living just outside the university town of Tartu, he took every chance to drive in fields or on frozen lakes. There was never the

least doubt that he would try his hand at rallying at the first opportunity and two months after his 18th birthday, he was competing in a self-prepared Lada Samara.

Few outstanding drivers have serious doubts over their abilities. Didier Auriol is typical of the breed. He watched his first rally and instantly concluded that he could do better. In contrast, Märtin had embarked on the painstaking modification of the Samara in the hope that he might be good enough not to be disgraced. When it turned out that he was good enough, he decided to see if he could hold his own in a competitive Group N car. When he mastered that too, he gladly accepted a drive in Group A. He has reached the top of the sport he loves like a high jumper raising the bar, never quite sure where his limits lie. For a decade, he has made a habit of exceeding his own expectations.

Yet he saw winning the 2003 Acropolis, his first World Championship success, as a vindication rather than a transformation.

'It was just a relief. I lost Acropolis [in 2002] and many times I have lost some podium places, because of some strange problems, so it was a relief to finally get it and show I think more to everybody else that we are capable of winning, because people who are not so closely involved, they don't see that actually there is a reason why we get this or that,' he said.

'I think for an Estonian it's already a bit unbelievable to be in a top factory team for a championship. Five or six years ago, people said that was impossible for an Estonian driver to be in that position, so already that I think was more than myself or other people

imagined was possible and then to win a rally was probably a smaller step. If you are good enough to get that position, it was expected that you should be able to do that as well.'

Regardless of his driving ability, his background entirely justified modest expectations. If it hadn't been for the fall of the Iron Curtain when he was 13, it is practically inconceivable that he would have ended up leading Ford's rally team. In Soviet times, if he was lucky, he might have found himself in a works Lada. Just possibly, a few dedicated spectators in a British or Finnish forest might have nodded to one another that he looked quick; a magazine somewhere would have squeezed in a diverting paragraph, musing that this Communist class winner might be a genuine contender in decent machinery. As Märtin points out, many top 'Russian' drivers during the Cold War were in fact Estonians, but despite the two countries' geographical similarity, politics had ensured that Estonians achieved none of the international success of their northern neighbours, the Finns. There were no fellow countrymen to offer advice or provide a yardstick and he was brought up in a society that neither encouraged nor entertained high expectations.

Estonian independence in 1991 presented the opportunity to travel, but it didn't flood the country with capitalist riches. As a child, he remembers 200 cars contesting local rallies. When he began competing, recession had bitten so hard that he was seeded 14th, yet last. Estonia has a population of under 1,500,000 and no great natural resources.

Shyness hasn't prevented Märtin

from fighting tooth and nail to flout precedent and surmount every obstacle. His second rally car couldn't have provided more of a contrast to the Lada. It was a Group N Escort Cosworth that he bought from Ken Skidmore in Lancashire and it proved not just that he was determined, but unafraid to trust his own judgement.

'I like to do things differently from the others, because everybody bought the cars from Finland and the Finnish guys when they got those cars, they got them from UK, so I thought, "Let's skip the Finns and go direct to Britain." In '96, I was 20. I had Motoring News and thought, "That looks quite good," so I flew to London, took a train to Leeds or Manchester or wherever it was, and it ended up in a container and came to Estonia. I can't really remember why, but I just decided to do it that way.

'It was my first time [in Britain]. I must say it was brave, because it tied up all the money as well! I was lucky it wasn't complete crap, that car.'

Subsequently, when he fell out with Toomas Kitsing, he decided to find a British co-driver.

'I thought if I am going to get the co-driver, I should have a lightweight British co-driver! I don't know where that idea came from as well, but it is a bit related to there are no co-drivers with World Championship experience in Estonia, so that was almost the only choice, to go abroad,' he said.

Märtin has developed an arresting turn of phrase in English and – it goes practically without saying – a dry, self-deprecating sense of humour. They're an indication of a growing self-belief.

His father's haulage company had

paid for the Escort, but it wouldn't have taken the son to the next stage. The Escort wasn't a true match for a Lancer, in fact, and Märtin was debating what to do after selling the Ford when he was offered a drive in the Estonian Oil Company's Group A Celica. That led to his first taste of World Championship competition in Finland, in 1997 (the gearbox broke) and several further forays on to the world stage the following year, which produced ninth place on the RAC.

The following season, Märtin persuaded EOS to fund an Escort World Rally Car and with it, he made the breakthrough. He was eighth on the Swedish, beating Ford's new starlet, Petter Solberg. Granted that the Norwegian was under strict orders to finish, but he did have a works car. Märtin had caught the eye of that shrewd talent scout, Ove Andersson, and he was soon back in a Toyota, with works backing for the first time in his life. Character-istically, Andersson didn't satisfy a young man's hunger for money. Instead, Märtin was given discreet assistance to keep the Corolla running. Money was tight enough for him to be genuinely anxious if he knocked a spotlight off – not exactly a concern for either Solberg or Sébastien Loeb at comparable stages of their careers – but he became a regular top-ten finisher and an occasional points scorer.

In 2000, following Toyota's switch to Formula One, the support was stepped up. For the first time, Märtin had a pre-rally test. TTE engineers were impressed that he listened and learned. Further development released a little more power and as he was prepared to try the

softer suspension settings long rejected by Auriol and Carlos Sainz, the Corolla ended up quicker than it had ever been in its factory prime, albeit no longer a match for the very latest machinery.

If it hadn't been for Toyota's withdrawal, he might have started 2000 as a works driver, but the dream became a reality soon enough. In Australia that year, he joined Subaru. It hardly mattered that his Impreza caught fire and wrecked its propshaft as early as the second stage. He had a contract for 2001. On the Rally GB when he was back in the Corolla, his mechanics swapped overalls with some of their Subaru counterparts, hid in the van and leapt out to surprise him at final service; they were thrilled for him.

With Prodrive, it pays to have a good lawyer. Although Märtin, along with the world at large, was given to

The 2003 Focus might have been made for Markko Märtin, the combination taking its first victory on the Acropolis (below). But his confident handling of the 2002 car (far left, on the Swedish) convinced Ford of his potential.

understand that he was joint number two with Solberg, that wasn't what it said in the small print. He was guaranteed only nine of the 14 rounds of the World Championship and as extra sponsorship failed to materialise, his experience of non-European rallies was confined to the recces. While Solberg prepared for the start, Märtin all too often packed for the flight home.

'I am happy that they gave me a chance to be in a factory car. It was great to see a team like Subaru and work for a team like Subaru, but I am disappointed that they didn't do what they promised me and I feel that cost me almost a year of my development. I should have had a full season 2001 and I came to 2002 still with no experience from long-haul rallies. I should have had that full season already under my belt and 2002 would have been a lot easier.

'I am not talking about me and Petter. That's not the point: it was more like me and Toshi [Arai], because I was staying away from them when Toshi was doing them and I don't think they should have had to choose between me and Toshi,' he said.

He makes his point clearly, but without rancour. Asked what he learnt from his year at Banbury, he answered, 'Put everything on paper.'

He can be trenchant when he wishes. Although he went well, he took a predictable dislike to a rally as rough as the Safari. When it was put to him that it was a priceless link to motorsport's 19th-century origins, he responded that cars had also improved since then.

Results were solid rather than startling. Märtin is a cautious, incremental driver. He grew up not being able to afford to crash cars. He has an intense loathing for damaging them on rough roads – another unusual characteristic for a rally driver – that Ford came to regard as a handicap and he was sent testing in Spain not long before the 2002 Acropolis with orders to try to break the Focus. At Prodrive, Solberg was compared to McRae, Märtin to Burns. His most eyecatching performance was on the World Championship round he knew best, Finland, when he ran as high as third until he damaged the exhaust and suspension on a yump. He finished fifth. It was no surprise that he was released at the end of the season, but nor was it that he promptly replaced François Delecour at Solberg's old team, Ford. The Norwegian might have seemed the brighter star, but Märtin's intrinsic worth had been recognised.

Not unnaturally, there are plenty of drivers who will discuss their setbacks and failings in only the most cursory terms. Self-criticism is something they we were pretty slow there, learning the car and everything. I expected to go well in Sweden and there I had a chance. That was a bit of a blow, I think.

'I don't want shit like that again in Sweden, because it sort of really slowed down my progress all this year, because a couple of rallies after that I really didn't want to make a mistake. I wanted just to try and finish and make sure I didn't do anything stupid any more,' he recalled some months later.

He got closer still to victory on the 2002 Rally GB, only to be caught cold by Solberg on the first long stage on Sunday morning.

'I think RAC – or Rally GB – really Marcus [Grönholm] gave us the chance to fight for victory, so we both sort of really didn't deserve it. GB was a good fight and I think I learnt a good lesson there: the long stage I was too slow, not pushing enough and that cost me

MARKKO MÄRTIN INTERVIEW
Märtin (top right) and 'Beef' Park have learnt and thrived together, from their days in Corollas, when every penny counted, to World Championship pacesetters on almost any terrain in a Focus.

do in private. In contrast, Märtin dwells on failure. Almost any other driver would have stressed the highlights of 2002: leading the Acropolis by a country mile until getting a puncture, beating his team-mate, Colin McRae, at Sanremo, or coming within a whisker of victory on the Rally of Great Britain. Pumped hard enough, Märtin will concede that he was happy to lead in Greece and surprised that he was almost a minute in front when the tread peeled off one of his Pirellis, but he talks at greater length about the embarrassing, agonising crash in the shakedown that prevented him from contesting the Swedish and led to a carpeting from his boss, Malcolm Wilson.

'I was angry myself. I really thought I had a good chance there to get a decent result and kick-start my season. I was taking really no risk in Monte Carlo and probably my first rally win.'

It's as though discussing failure helps him to analyse and confront it. He admits that he likes to spend a few stages assessing the pace – and that he isn't a morning person. Others suggested at the time that his fitness and consistency needed to improve. However, he hadn't expected to win rallies in 2002 and began 2003 still shrinking from any predictions. Nevertheless, he had become lead driver. It was thanks chiefly to a budget cut that obliged Ford to dispense with Sainz and McRae, but Wilson grinned wolfishly when it was put to him that Ford might well go through the season without a win. Märtin said that he would have preferred another season as the understudy: better to learn than to get out of his depth.

But by then he had suffered the

introvert's worst nightmare: he had become a national hero, making the transition from back page to front page. It isn't that Estonia lacks successful sportsmen, but they have tended to be weight-lifters or long-distance runners and cautiously, Märtin suggests that they lack the perceived glamour and certainly the wealth of a rally driver. He describes fame as 'quite bad,' for although he isn't mobbed in public, he can't go out for a quiet drink, while buying something in a shop is liable to lead to a request for an autograph.

It culminated in his victory on the Rally Finland, when Estonians not only seemed close to outnumbering Finns in Jyväskylä, but the Prime Minister, Juhan Parts, flew in for the occasion.

Märtin isn't interested in politics and wondered why Parts had bothered.

"I think it was better for the sport, for people in Estonia. It meant a lot more to me to know that some of the people in our team were happy about it, who had been working hard for it,' he said.

But can't he see that it isn't a question of whether Parts can tell a rally car from a taxi? It's

a measure of his success that Parts feels the need to be associated with it.

'It's getting too big now. I can't control it any more. That's a bit bad,' he concluded, a little unhappily.

If fame has in some respects surprised and dismayed Märtin, he no longer needs to be goaded into admitting that he is good. The moment he drove the 2003 Focus, he sensed he had a car in which he could attain the goal of winning in Finland, the rally he had first watched as a spellbound 15-year-old. It was much more satisfying than winning the Acropolis.

'That was the rally I always wanted to do well and I had a discussion with Michael [Park] before the beginning of this season, and he said, "You're never going to do well in Finland, because you expect to do so well yourself and you have so much pressure on yourself, and people come to watch and everybody else expecting you to do well". He was just saying like expectations are pulling

down my results almost. It's very special. I always thought that is the rally to win. It's the ultimate driver's event. Maybe if you have a fantastic car and you are not the absolute best, you can win it, but shit drivers can't win it, that's for sure!'

Victory carried its dangers too. It had been a dream for so long that Märtin had to persuade himself that it wasn't an end in itself, that he had other obstacles to confront and goals to meet. He accepts that he even now needs to become a little more consistent.

Nevertheless, he has adapted with impressive speed to team leadership. The treadmill pressure doesn't give him much time at home, little time to play basketball or ride a mountain bike, but he maintains that he is fundamentally lazy and needs a challenge. Although Finland has secured his place in rallying history, it wasn't the turning point. There was no blinding realisation, but earlier in 2003, Märtin finally accepted that the sky is the limit.

THE GENTLE ART OF WINNING

It's an indication of Märtin's ability that other people's co-drivers were convinced of his potential long before he was. When he was lured back into a Toyota, few people were happier than another semi-works Toyota man, Michael 'Beef' Park. At the time, the diminutive Herefordshire man — the mocking nickname has stuck since schooldays — was navigating Abdullah Bakhashab, but Park was ambitious.

'We sort of sussed out — me and Robert Reid — that this Markko Märtin was the next boy coming along that was going to be very good and it was really quite funny, we were hatching a plan then before I'd even met him as to how I was going to get to co-drive for him! Then he turned up in the same team as us, which made it a damn sight easier.

'He was very much like everybody thinks of him. He was very, very quiet and almost shy. He kept himself to himself. I got to know him quite a bit during that year and it turned out that he didn't actually like his co-driver that he had. You could tell they didn't get on as early as that rally in Greece. It was changing tyres and this guy was sat in the car, with Markko changing tyres on his own and I thought, "Summat odd going on there," so I sort of hatched a plan to get to know him better!' Park recalled.

Other co-drivers were also interested — Denis Giraudet and Per Carlsson, for instance — but Märtin wanted English pace notes and a native English speaker. It was a risk for both sides.

'For Markko, it was a massive risk, because one, he didn't know if he would get his sponsors the following year. Kitsing was the guy who first brought EOS on board, so Markko had to approach them and see with all the turmoil if it could carry on. Obviously, he didn't know also if he'd get on with the English language and for me, I turned down quite good money with Abdullah Bakhashab to do it and basically said to Markko I would do the first year for nothing to get given the chance. We both did it for a pittance.'

Park has contributed fully to Märtin's success: it took a year of gentle persuasion to convince him to put any detail into his pace notes. Few have a greater insight into a personality than the co-driver.

'He's got to the stage where he knows he should be setting top-three stage times on nearly every stage he does and if he doesn't, he's letting himself down. He doesn't strike you as somebody who ever really takes a car by the scruff of the neck, but we definitely had stages in Finland this year, when we had the problem with the car on day two, he drove completely wild. He lost the plot if you like. He decided he was just going to go flat out and got to the end and said, "Oh, sorry about that, I just had to get it out of my system." He was just completely wild, jumping like a maniac and sideways everywhere, and braking late. He got to the end of the stage and the time wasn't particularly good, which he knew, because he can't drive like that. He's almost like a racing driver on gravel. I really think he thinks so much about his driving, he isn't all about aggression.

'He does know his rules very, very well. He's very inquisitive. He's always asking questions. He's never one to think that co-driving is my job and driving is his job. It's quite good, because I know I can't try to pull the wool over his eyes, because he knows better!'

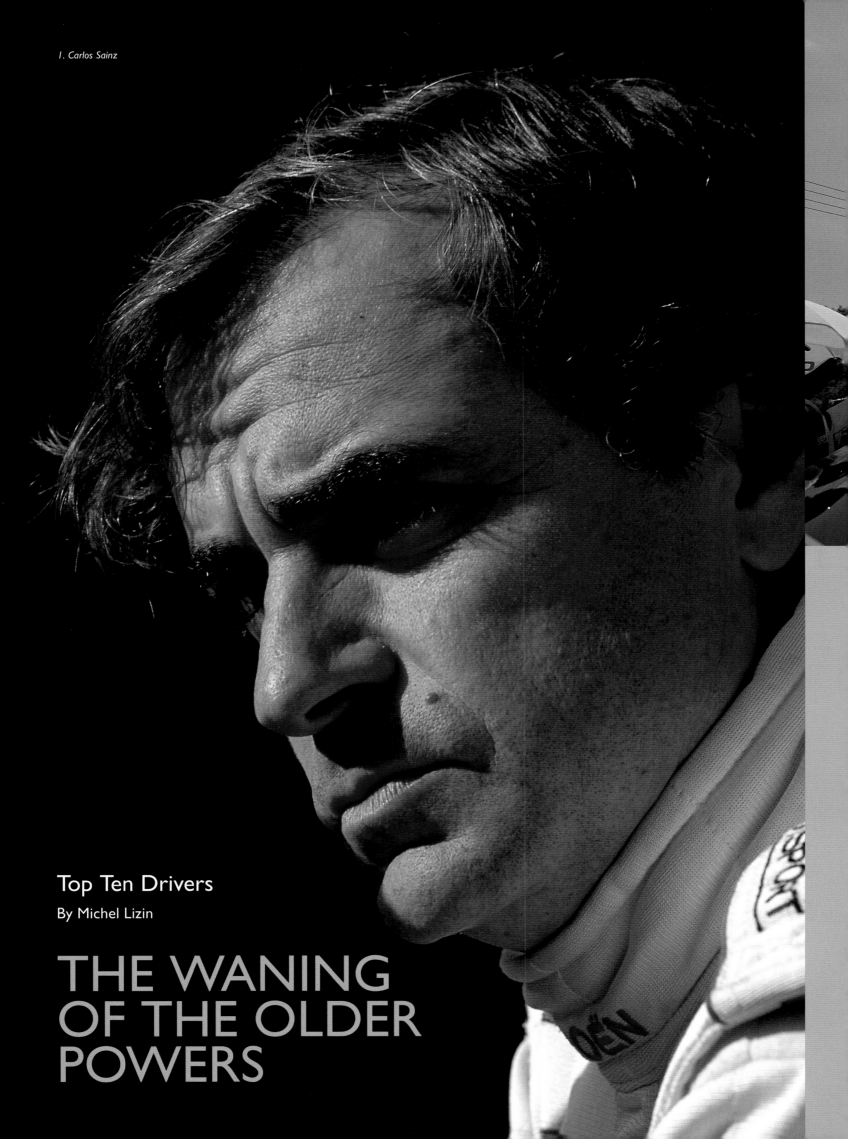

Top Ten Drivers

By Michel Lizin

THE WANING OF THE OLDER POWERS

What has become of the Mäkinens, the McRaes, the Auriols and the Burnses? Since June 2003 rally victories have been monopolised by three men of the new generation: Petter Solberg, Sébastien Loeb and Markko Märtin.

'These guys have taken rally driving to a higher level than ever,' McRae said recently. Praise indeed, coming from the man long felt to be the greatest talent in absolute terms on asphalt and on dirt.

Thanks to his resounding successes early in the season, as well as for his driving style, Marcus Grönholm counts as part of this 'new wave'. He is a little older, granted, having already won two world titles, but he has taken time to get up to full speed, and he started tapping into his full potential only from 2000.

Yet even though the old hands have suffered from the rise of this new breed, the driver who has best carried the fight to them is the oldest hand of all: Carlos Sainz; he is not the oldest in age – Auriol is four years older – but he is the most experienced. With his future in the balance at the end of 2002, Sainz drew from adversity a desire, a fierceness and a toughness which command respect. After 15 years at the highest level of his sport, the Spaniard succeeded in astounding everyone.

1. CARLOS SAINZ

He is no longer the fastest of all, but his season has been quite simply exceptional. The most senior of all the drivers refused to be forced into retirement, made financial sacrifices to stay in the game and found incredible energy to draw on in hostile circumstances. His 2003 campaign has been of an exemplary consistency and, amazingly, seems to demonstrate a gradual increase in ability. He adapted with alacrity to the Xsara WRC, taking an active role in its development, and playing no small part in honing its all-round competitiveness. To the great surprise of observers, and Sainz himself, consistently being one of the front-runners propelled him to the head of the race for the title at the crucial point.

Just as in Hollywood an actor receives an award for 'lifetime achievement', Sainz wins the honour of heading the 2003 Top Ten not only for the quality of his performances, but also in appreciation of all he has brought, and still brings, to rallying.

2. PETTER SOLBERG

His irrepressible celebrations of each victory are a wonderful advertisement for rallying. The Norwegian oozes *joie de vivre*, yet now shows great maturity. His 2003 season is a perfect example. He opened with a rather silly excursion on the Monte, and encountered a few difficulties in finding his feet in Sweden. Things went much better thereafter, with results sometimes dependent on the quality of Pirelli's tyres. Among his great feats of the year, the intense battle which pitted him for three days against Loeb in Australia, and the way, in Corsica, that he made light of difficult weather conditions demonstrated his great mental strength as much as his speed. Petter also admits to having a soft spot for his second place in Finland, snatched on the very last stage.

Solberg is the very embodiment of the modern driver: as analytical and painstaking as he is quick, obsessed with anything that may in any way bring him even one-tenth of a second of extra speed.

3. SEBASTIEN LOEB

3. Sébastien Loeb

Was there ever a driver who had a more dazzling rise to the top, who progressed so swiftly to such a level of competitiveness and reliability on all surfaces? 'Seb' isn't the youngest around. He'll be 30 soon, but he was nearly 23 when he started his first rally, and in 2003 he has contested his first ever full World Championship season.

Certainly, until now, Loeb has starred 'only' on Tarmac, but his habit of battling it out for victory until the very end, demonstrated on his second start in Australia, hints that his first victory on dirt won't be long in coming. The speed of his development has in no way changed him: he is still just as natural and accommodating as ever. From this equilibrium he gains a serenity that lets him believe that nothing is impossible, and that there is no reason why he can't compete with the very best in the forests of Finland or Great Britain, or anywhere else.

4. MARKKO MÄRTIN

Along with the two drivers who precede him in this list, Markko is part of the new generation starting to dominate world rallying. He loses nothing to the others in terms of speed, but in the first half of the year his performances suffered from the development problems of the innovative Focus WRC 03. The Estonian had no need to worry, since ultimately he was greatly aided by a car which, as he was fond of saying, fitted him like a glove.

At the wheel, Märtin has developed a very distinctive driving style, keeping slides to a minimum and making full use of the car's agility. This is not to say that he is never spectacular. In Finland he put in what was possibly the drive of his life by pushing the limits of the possible further than even the local specialists had ever managed. As much at ease on Tarmac as on dirt, he is capable of winning in all conditions.

4. Markko Märtin

5. Marcus Grönholm

5. MARCUS GRÖNHOLM

Marcus is proof, after all, that extra-terrestrials don't exist. Since 2000, when he exploded on to the scene behind the wheel of his Peugeot, the Finn has been considered unbeatable, clearly having arrived from another planet. In 2003 he turned out to be human after all. He is still among the best drivers in the world, but no more than that – as if that wasn't good enough.

Three runaway wins showed that he has lost none of his skill, but mistakes in Monte Carlo, Australia, Sanremo and Britain pointed to a degree of fallibility in coping with the maladies afflicting his car. The 206 WRC's most recent World Championship campaign has not been nearly as unblemished as the one before. Mechanical niggles of all kinds blighted the performances of its drivers. Grönholm made the mistake of trying single-handedly to atone for the failings of his team. The intent was laudable, but it was a little too ambitious.

6. Richard Burns

6. RICHARD BURNS

It has been very difficult to get the measure of Richard Burns in the past year, either in terms of his driving or in terms of his relationship with his car. Beyond question, the Briton quickly put into action his plan of driving for points, but this move has all the appearance of being a rationalisation of an inability to win since being in the 206 WRC, unless it was more to do with an inability to overcome his stablemate Grönholm.

Burns was a lot closer to winning in 2002 in his first season with Peugeot than he was in 2003. His admirable consistency and his tactic of scoring points right across the board allowed him to be in the battle for the title right to the end, only to be deprived of his chance by a blackout at the wheel of his road car. Is the crown worth, as he asserts, the change of image?

7. Colin McRae

7. COLIN MCRAE

This isn't the first time that Colin has had a strange season. Early on, he was up with his team-mates yet without managing to wrap up a victory. Thereafter, on several occasions, bad luck dogged him, while never afflicting his colleagues. The turning point of his campaign came perhaps in Argentina, when his car was totally destroyed by fire. After this, the Scot's performances were solid without ever hinting that he could win. McRae made no bones about it: he had never felt at home behind the wheel of the Xsara, never quite being able to display his characteristic fluid driving style.

The FIA's summer decisions took him by surprise and took the wind out of his sails. Maybe without his even realising it, doubt crept into his mind, and the spectre of unemployment – in the World Championship – did not help him bring his season to a satisfactory ending.

8. François Duval

8. FRANÇOIS DUVAL

Duval is another one who had an odd season. It began bizarrely in Monte Carlo and continued catastrophically in Sweden before the clouds cleared away with a magnificent first World Championship podium in Turkey. Thereafter François chopped and changed between good and bad until he put his finger on the problem that was undermining his performance: the lack of precision, or, more exactly, the lack of consistency in his pace notes. The bad was very bad in Finland and Australia.

This was what prompted the Belgian to react by going back to the drawing board. The rebuilding of his confidence and the reconstruction of his driving started at Sanremo and immediately bore fruit. In Corsica, on incredibly difficult and treacherous terrain, Duval led for much of the rally. Over the three days he steered clear of all snarl-ups to achieve his second podium place. His talent is undeniable; the fulfilment of his potential is back on track.

9. FREDDY LOIX

The hard times appear to have had no effect on Freddy. For five years now he has been denied the chance to express himself behind the wheel of a car that is either competitive or suited to his style. Yet he never fails to give of his best from the moment he is behind a wheel and under starter's orders.

In a team in which the rot set in over the months, the Belgian never let any bitterness show. Unlike Armin Schwarz, who progressively let his shoulders droop, understandably, he gave his all for as long as a car was provided. His determination was rewarded with one point for Hyundai, hard-earned in Australia, then a few more with Peugeot as Burns's GB stand-in. Taken on – indeed, thrown a lifeline – by Peugeot, Loix will at last have the chance to fulfil some of the expectations that were placed in him in 1997 and 1998 at Toyota. The ball is in his court now.

9. Freddy Loix

10. GILLES PANIZZI

Twice, the rain let Panizzi display his talents. At Sanremo, a sudden downpour and a daring choice of tyres allowed him to leap from fifth to second. Changeable climatic conditions worked in his favour in Catalonia too, leading as they did to a victory. This was great consolation at the end of a season that had otherwise been particularly trying.

In Monte Carlo, Panizzi cracked mentally as much as physically. Like Burns, he had been put off his stride by the Tarmac behaviour of the 206 WRC. It had become if not unpredictable, perhaps a little edgy. In Germany, in Sanremo and to an extent in Corsica, his driving lost some of its confident efficiency, before he magnificently made amends in the final miles of Catalonia. On dirt, Gilles has had too few chances to show how he has improved, but he finished a fine fifth in Turkey. It is up to him now to prove at Mitsubishi that he has become the finished article he has always wanted to be.

10. Gilles Panizzi

"POSSUM" BOURNE

The expression 'larger than life' might have been coined with 'Possum' Bourne in mind. His enthusiasm for rallying was barely contained and the grin habitually stretched from ear to ear. He loved telling it straight. Within a few minutes of meeting him, at a press day before the 1986 Olympus Rally, he offered me a ride around the stage. I had never been in a Subaru of any kind, nor in a US forest, so the offer was too good to miss. Within a few more minutes, we dived briefly into a large bush. Car and occupants emerged none the worse for wear and Bourne, characteristically, was apologetic and amused; few professional drivers could describe an accident or a near-miss with such relish.

It was very much part of his self-deprecating manner. Rallying hardly dominates the sports pages in New Zealand and he cheerfully admitted that the nickname, which he earned after crashing his mother's car swerving to avoid a possum, was the making of him. No one called him Peter.

Bourne's talents went a good deal further than telling a good yarn for the press. Perhaps he was too destructive to get the best out of a 1980s Subaru on the Safari and there was an impetuous streak to his driving, but his seven consecutive Australian titles and three Asia-Pacific crowns proved that he was much more than a domestic phenomenon. His best World Championship result – third on home ground in 1987 – didn't do him justice.

Certainly there was steel behind the smile. In the early days of its involvement in rallying, Bourne personified Subaru. He was the first man to compete in the cars outside Japan, the first to win rallies in them and might easily have been the first to be shown the exit when Prodrive became the works team in 1990. However, he was nothing if not persistent. He was co-opted into the official team in the Far East and gained his first two Asia-Pacific Championships in factory cars. He remained a staunch customer for top-line machinery until WR Cars soared beyond domestic budgets, and he nagged his way into the money for his successful 2000 Asia-Pacific bid and 2003's Production World Championship campaign. He had after all continued driving after the Rally Australia accident that cost his co-driver, Rodger Freeth, his life in 1993.

Bourne was incapable of being a mere driver. He turned 'Possum' Bourne Motorsport into a thriving business, did much to inspire the career of his Australian number two, Cody Crocker, and gladly joined committees. Bourne was a participant and naturally campaigned for what he saw as better Group N rules when he switched from WR Cars.

His own death came quite unexpectedly last April. He was involved in a collision with another competitor while practising for the Race to the Sky hill climb on South Island, as he returned gently to the bottom of the course. He was 47. It's commonplace to describe someone as irreplaceable. In his case, that was unquestionably true.

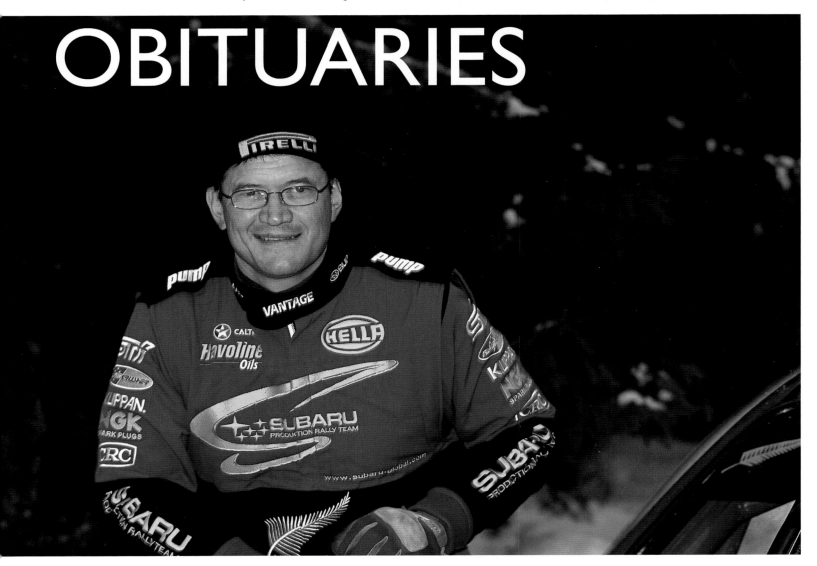

OBITUARIES

HOWARD MARSDEN

When Howard Marsden succumbed to cancer in August, there was a universal thread to the tributes and the obituaries: Howard was a gentleman. The mind's eye pictures a courteous, softly spoken man. He possessed a knack of making whoever he was talking to seem important and it was in no sense for show. A range of people remember his kindness, whether it took the form of advice or practical support in their careers. He had some of the soothing charm of a respected village doctor.

Marsden wasn't just reassuring, but boundlessly competent. A long and distinguished career in motorsport spanned different companies, disciplines and continents. He first became involved with Alan Mann Racing in 1963, working on Ford's first serious foray into European motorsport. He subsequently had a hand in everything from the cars used in the film Chitty Chitty Bang Bang, to racing with Lola, Frank Williams and Steve McQueen.

When he moved to Australia in the 1970s, he inspired one of the most successful periods in Ford's racing history, then joined Nissan and directed the team that secured four consecutive Australian Rally Championships with the likes of George Fury and Ross Dunkerton. Nissan subsequently put him in charge of an assortment of racing programmes, from Le Mans to saloon racing and the ill-fated World Rally Championship bid with the Sunny GTi-R; it might have fared better if he had had more control of the project.

Marsden spent the final years of his life back in Australia, firstly with Tickford, then with Ford itself. He had a deep understanding of the demands of competition and a flair for getting the best out of people. At 61, he was in no sense a figure from the past. He will be much missed.

MARK LOVELL

It came as a shock to most of the mourners at his funeral to learn that Mark Lovell had decided beforehand that the Oregon Trails would be his last rally. Thanks partly to his success with Prodrive and Subaru, the SCCA Pro-Rally Championship – the US national series – had become increasingly professional. Lovell had returned to rallying purely for pleasure and at 43, the added pressure was turning it into a chore. He had a young family. Rather than wait until the end of the season, he had decided to stop in July.

Lovell was one of the most gifted British rally drivers in a generation, a sportsman of vast natural talent, and he had never been in the habit of crashing cars. The disclosure added poignancy to the knowledge that he and Roger Freeman had died after hitting a tree on the first corner of the first stage.

It was one of Lovell's most attractive characteristics that he had always made rallying seem fun. He never betrayed much sign of being under pressure and he combined a dislike for toeing the official line with an unflagging reluctance to take himself too seriously. It seemed odd that the outside world often regarded him as smug and aloof.

Lovell's ability was swiftly recognised and nurtured. Early successes in an RS2000 led to the Escort Turbo Championship, to membership of the British Junior Rally Team and to a works drive in the Turbo's recalcitrant production offspring, the Escort RS Turbo. The fact that his father was the Weston-super-Mare Ford dealer did no harm, but Lovell deserved his opportunities. There was no trail of tangled metal to excuse: his driving brought to mind a batsman who always has time to play his shots. He had judgement as well as speed. There was never any question of his career being damaged by the RS Turbo's numerous failings. He won the 1985 Shell/Autosport Championship in a Nissan 240RS – beating Willie Rutherford and the four-wheel-drive Sierra built by RED, the team Lovell drove for in the Open series – then took the Open Championship the following year in the RS200, against heavy-calibre opposition from Audi, Austin Rover and Peugeot. He was still only 26.

Driving Mike Little's Sierra Cosworth, he lost the title in 1987 to Jim McRae and RED's Sierra, but took a wonderful victory on the Ulster after a breathtaking duel with Bertie Fisher. On that occasion, Lovell was up well before dawn to make sure that he was ready for the challenge of Fermanagh and Tyrone. Yet the relationship with Ford soon began to curdle. The idea took hold that he was a 'Tarmac expert,' he was sidelined into the Dutch and Tarmac Championships, and Ford management offered the wounding observation that he had been born with a silver spoon in his mouth. It was an arresting charge for a manufacturer simultaneously promoting Carlos Sainz. Lovell's approach was engaging, but liable to exasperate his employers. His career never recovered after he was ordered to hand the 1989 Manx to his team-mate, Russell Brookes.

Lovell made a fleeting return in a Group A Celica before gracefully withdrawing from the fray. A successful car shipping business he developed latterly with Freeman led to an involvement in the World Championship's logistics – as much of a challenge in its way as taming an RS200.

By then, he had been persuaded to dip a toe in the water once more by making gravel notes for Toshihiro Arai and when Prodrive wanted a safe pair of hands for Subaru's first involvement in US rallying, Lovell duly collected the 2001 SCCA crown. A few weeks before his death, he won his class at Pike's Peak.

He was certainly capable of applying himself, but lacked single-mindedness. It would be glib to pronounce that he didn't fulfill his potential, to speculate that he might have achieved something akin to Colin McRae's or Richard Burns's success had he been handled differently, but this would overlook the fact that rallying is a sport, not a duty. Lovell never lost sight of that.

ROGER FREEMAN

If one's image of a lawyer is of a donnish man with owlish spectacles and a predilection for Latin, then it was hard to credit that Roger Freeman was a solicitor. Pint in hand, regaling his audience with an anecdote in a foghorn Warrington accent, Freeman was one of the lads. But for a journalist cornered for a persuasive and vigorous defence of his driver, Mark Lovell, the fluent command of detail gave an insight into how Freeman won cases.

Freeman was combative in the nicest possible way and his loyalty to his drivers was unflinching. When Lovell was stopped for speeding on a road section shortly after rolling his RS200 on the 1986 Scottish, Freeman, mindful of the substantial points tally on his driving licence, took advantage of the traffic cop's confusion and handed over his own.

For Lovell and Freeman alike, their best years in rallying were together. They enjoyed one another's company – it was difficult not to enjoy their company, in fact – but Freeman appeared to extract a little more speed from Lovell than anyone else. He didn't hesitate to tell Lovell when he thought he wasn't driving well and cheerfully used anger as a spur. However, there was nothing reckless about it and it was a painful irony that they died together in the autumn of their professional careers, in what should have been a relatively stress-free arena. Certainly, Subaru USA's Impreza was a far cry from the Mike Little-prepared RS200 in which they won the 1986 British Open title.

There was no motorsport tradition in the family and Roger came across the sport by chance. He began by servicing for Keith Billows, then turned to navigating for Richard Stamp in a Dolomite Sprint and developed a passion for maps – Warrington isn't far from classic Welsh road rally country – and came to national prominence in the early 1980s with one of those talents who never quite captured a works drive, Terry Pankhurst. He impressed John Taylor, the driving force behind the British Junior Team and most of Ford's attempts to find another Roger Clark at the time, and it was chiefly for that reason that he ended a fruitful partnership with Phil Collins to join Lovell midway through 1986, when Ford decided that it no longer wanted Peter Davies in the car.

Rallying held an irresistible lure, but it was never Freeman's all-consuming passion. He was a keen rugby player, in League in his youth, in Union, which he thought rather easy by comparison, in his 40s. Married with two children, he was a family man above all and he gave up navigating Lovell when he felt it demanded too much time away from home. On his return in the 1990s, when Prodrive wanted his no-nonsense capabilities to guide Subaru's Japanese find, Toshihiro Arai, it was never on a full-time basis. He was a loveable rogue – he saw both sides of a set of bars – but always capable of inspiring affection and admiration.

ROCCO THEUNISSEN

Rocco Theunissen's death was a terrible shock. He was just 30 and in the prime of life when he died suddenly of meningitis while resting at his family's holiday home in Malta on April 19.

Theunissen treated rallying as a hobby, but he was the kind of amateur who could give the professionals a run for their money. During the week, he was Commercial Director of the family business, Milo Coats. At the weekend, the Dutchman became a formidable adversary in a Corolla World Rally Car, twice winning the Dutch Open Championship and following that with two wins in the Belgian Division 1 series, in 2000 and 2002.

He took up rallying at the age of 22, driving a Sunny, but quickly progressed to an Impreza, winning Dutch Group N titles in successive years before taking the plunge and buying a Group A Impreza in 1998, beginning a fruitful association with the Belgian team, Future World.

His last rally was the 2003 Boucles de Spa, on which he came fourth, complaining of severe headaches. He will be remembered as an amiable personality, a quiet man for whom rallying was purely fun.

Rocco Theunissen

PETER HARPER

In different circumstances, Peter Harper might have been as revered and recognised as Paddy Hopkirk. There was little to choose between them when they were team-mates at Rootes, but whereas Hopkirk achieved lasting fame with BMC driving Minis, Harper, the Rootes dealer in Stevenage, stayed put. Rallying was a more carefree, less lucrative activity then, having any sort of works car was a bonus and the business came first.

There was nothing amateurish about Harper's approach to the sport though. He had taken it up in the 1950s and he was the first driver to be paid expenses by Rootes (the princely sum of £10 per day) never mind a salary. The company finally agreed that drivers needed paying when he pointed out that a succession of Montes, Alpines and Tulips entailed a good deal of time away from work.

A former Spitfire pilot, he was also an accomplished racing driver, winning the Index of Thermal Efficiency at Le Mans 1961 with Peter Procter in a Sunbeam Alpine and competing with some success everywhere from Goodwood to Silverstone and Sebring.

If it hadn't been for an agonising homologation mix-up, in which the paperwork specified bigger valves than fitted to the car, he would have vanquished the Austin-Healeys and taken a richly deserved victory on the 1965 Alpine in a works Tiger, but he wasn't simply a Tarmac driver. He won the 1958 RAC in a Rapier in dreadful conditions and he was regularly the top British finisher on the Monte, usually in Rootes machinery that was never likely to win outright.

By the 1960s, the Rapier was getting long in the tooth, the Tiger took an age to develop and the Imp never became the promised worldbeater. Harper occasionally raced Mustangs and Cortinas for Alan Mann, before taking up rallycross in Imps.

A neat yet aggressive driver, he was a gentleman, keen to win, but always willing to encourage younger team-mates. He died last summer after a short illness, at 82.

Twenty-five years ago a young Frenchman named Thierry Sabine decided to conquer the Sahara with a group of fellow French motorsport enthusiasts. Over the next few years, the following swelled, as an annual event was established to seek out some of the remotest trails and tracks on the planet.

The rally became a notable addition to the motorsport calendar. Both two- and four-wheel manufacturers began to take a keen interest and its reputation grew, as each route across North Africa and the Saharan wastelands became more of a challenge to the discerning enthusiast.

Yamaha, BMW and Cagiva controlled proceedings in the motorcycle category then, and have been superseded by the dominant Austrian KTM outfit. Porsche's and Lada's four-wheel triumphs gave way to years of domination by Citroën's and Peugeot's Group

B derivatives. Mitsubishi and Schlesser-Renault have achieved success in recent years, with Nissan, Volkswagen and BMW all developing machinery for stronger assaults in 2004. Prodrive, meanwhile, is already working on costings and business appraisals for a possible entry into the contest.

Well before the end of the 20th century, the rally had become an off-road equivalent of the Le Mans 24 Hours, but it also earned itself an infamous reputation. Numerous fatalities and serious accidents have marred the first 25 years of the Dakar and Sabine himself lost his life in a helicopter crash in his beloved Ténéré Desert in 1986.

But in Britain, it has failed to capture the public's imagination. Raise the Dakar with the man in the street and you might trigger memories of Mark Thatcher going missing for three days between Mopti and Gao in

Mali back in 1982, or references to 'that race across Africa where people get killed'. Few prominent British rally drivers have even taken part and one of the handful of successful British competitors in recent years was the BMW factory rider, John Deacon. The Cornishman had begun to put the Dakar on the map in the UK when he was killed while competing in Syria during the 2001 Masters Rally.

British co-drivers such as Fred Gallagher, Bobby Willis and Matthew Stevenson remain firm supporters of the rally and are actively involved each year, although Gallagher has switched to team management with the Nissan Rally Raid Team.

The Dakar thrives, despite mounting geo-political problems in the region, column inches of bad press the world over and its readiness to turn its back on the FIA and FIM as and when the organisers see fit –

THE SUPREME CHALLENGE

INSIGHT The Dakar Rally   By Neil Perkins

All photographs Willy Weyens

another characteristic that invites comparison with Le Mans, in fact.

Sabine's name lives on through the Thierry Sabine Organisation (TSO) and the Dakar has established itself firmly in rallying folklore, especially in France, Italy and Spain. It now has a fair claim to being the greatest motorsport event in the world.

Logistically and in terms of the sheer scale of its organisation, it has no rivals. Figures released by TSO show an increase from 297 to 343 competitors since 2001, 186 reaching the finish in 2003. The 2004 event will start in Clermont-Ferrand for the first time and will pass through seven countries. It is expected to attract an even bigger entry.

The 2003 Dakar was aired on television for 19 hours and attracted around 5,000,000 viewers per day in France alone. Footage was shown in 188 countries, on 72 channels and broadcast for an estimated 340 hours. The official Dakar website was visited 33,000,000 times by an estimated 1,000,000 web surfers.

But the Dakar is also adopting some of the World Championship's innovative ideas. Plans are afoot to fit tracking systems in the lead vehicles, and the images and data will be broadcast live both on the internet and in the satellite press offices. In-car cameras are to be installed and the use of automatic tyre deflation systems on 4x4 vehicles may be prohibited.

The Frenchman, Stéphane Peterhansel, is the most successful competitor in the history of the Dakar, having taken six victories on motorcycles. On four wheels, he led from the moment the rally entered Tunisia in 2003 and lost a potential victory to his Mitsubishi team-mate, Hiroshi Masuoka, on the penultimate stage in Egypt, eventually finishing third behind the veteran Frenchman, Jean-Pierre Fontenay. Masuoka's victory was Mitsubishi's eighth and the team's third successive triumph.

'I first took part in the Dakar when I was 22 years old,' Peterhansel recalled. 'I won for Yamaha for the first time when I was 26. The Dakar has a special appeal that I cannot describe. When we leave Europe and arrive in Africa each year that magic returns. Now I have made the switch to four wheels and am trying to become the second driver to win in both disciplines.'

The only competitor to have achieved this feat so far is TSO's Director General, Hubert Auriol.

Mitsubishi's grip on the 2003 Dakar never slackened, victory going eventually to Hiroshi Masuoka (below left), while Miki Biasion got the measure of the Sahara. Variety is part of the appeal, the event welcoming everything from Jan De Rooy's monstrous Daf truck (below) to VW's diesel-powered Tareks, looking for all the world like mid-'60s Porsche prototypes.

'January would not be the same without the Dakar. For sure, its roots are French. That is because it was the brainchild of the French. We do not want to lose that tradition, but the organisers appreciate that the event now has more global appeal. That makes winning next year all the more important for me to make up for the disappointment of this year,' Peterhansel added.

Many regard the Dakar as a retirement home for veteran racing and rally drivers: Ari Vatanen, Ukyo Katayama, Eric Bernard, Jacky Ickx, Grégoire de Mevius and Henri Pescarolo have been keen competitors recently. But Vatanen and Italy's double World Champion, Miki Biasion, disagree.

'To go to Africa is to see the real world and to be at peace with yourself,' said Vatanen, the Dakar winner in 1987, 1989, 1990 and 1991, and the winner of a record 46 Dakar special stages.

'Dakar has a special place in my life. It was a fantastic opportunity for me to return this year and meet all my old friends again. This race and the people you meet along the way put life into perspective. The race is becoming more competitive all the time. The old Dakar Rallies were endurance races. That is still the case to an extent, but cars are more developed today and drivers are taking more risks and pushing that much harder.'

'It is true that the Dakar has a reputation for taking retired World Championship drivers,' Biasion admitted. 'But that is not exactly true. Mitsubishi now have a 20-year-old French driver called Nicolas Misslin and he has been showing potential this season. Cross-country rallying requires a different mental approach, enormous concentration and physical fitness. There are several young drivers out there and Mitsubishi now has a Young Driver Programme for the future.'

Biasion – who won his first Dakar stage in 2003, between Abu Rish and Sharm El-Sheikh in Egypt – has been co-driven by Tiziano Siviero for 25 years and took all but three of his international rally successes with his loyal partner. Siviero now combines navigating with event organisation and is responsible for running the Por Las Pampas round of the FIA World Cup in Argentina.

'I was fortunate to be involved in world rallying through the greatest times in the 1980s and early 1990s,' Siviero observed. 'Events such as the Safari, Acropolis and RAC were fantastic rallies. They were adventures. Cars such as the Group B Lancias were extremely powerful and exciting for spectators. But times change and rules change. The World Championship is not even a shadow of its former self and that is a big shame.

'I talk to people in Italy and they much prefer to watch cross-country rallying on television these days. These type of events are the only traditional rallies that remain. The footage is spectacular and it is easier to understand a car going from point A to point B than it is to explain a series of loops each day. I am sure that there will be a new world championship soon for six- or seven-day long-distance rallies. Other manufacturers such as Toyota and Ford are already showing an interest in joining the likes of Volkswagen, Nissan and Mitsubishi. This series has a great future.'

The Florida-based Briton, Vic Elford (an early, pacesetting Dakar competitor in a Subaru) has the distinction of being one of only a handful of drivers to make a successful transition from rallying to international circuit racing. The 2002 FIA World Cross-Country Champion, Jean-Louis Schlesser, is another to have succeeded in both disciplines.

The Moroccan-born Schlesser moved in the opposite direction to Elford, switching to the desert

after taking a pair of Group C sports car world titles with Mercedes. He has influenced the regulations to such an extent that he has been able to remain competitive in a two-wheel-drive buggy, powered over the years by Seat and Renault motors and latterly by a Ford V6.

Schlesser is a talented engineer in his own right and won the Dakar in 1999 and 2000 . The former Williams Formula 1 test driver wouldn't contemplate a return to single-seater racing.

'For me, the desert is home. A rally like the Dakar

is like no other. It is you and your car against the elements and the perils of Africa,' he said.

A former co-driver in both the French and World Rally Championships, Dominique Serieys took over the day-to-day management of Mitsubishi Motor Sports following Ulrich Brehmer's death from cancer. Serieys and his team at Mâcon, near Lyon, have developed an Evolution of the Mitsubishi Pajero into the car to beat. He won the Dakar with his fellow Frenchman Bruno Saby in 1993.

'Every year we sit down with the Mitsubishi board and discuss budgets for the following year,' Serieys explained. 'But one event stands on the top of the list in terms of priority and that is the Dakar. This year we entered a few rounds of the FIA World Cup, but the emphasis was and still is on developing a car to win the Dakar. While Mitsubishi develops a new World Rally Car for next year's WRC, the media's attention has been on our cross-country programme.

'Every year my family knows that they will lose me for two months for the Dakar. It is a fact of life. The event is a massive commitment for a professional team and a huge logistical operation for the organisers. We will pass through seven countries in 2004. We arrange a lot of our own catering, but I can't imagine the logistical task of having to arrange for the feeding of over 2,000 people in Africa for 17 days.

'I was lucky to survive a serious accident in Libya in 2000, but that has not deterred me from returning every year. There are times when you hit the wall and think enough is enough, but the magic of Africa and the Dakar Rally always makes you come back.'

Only a handful of individuals have taken part in all 26 Dakar Rallies in various capacities. One is Auriol and another is the French agency photographer, Eric Vagliou.

'I couldn't imagine a New Year's Eve without being involved in the Dakar,' Vagliou promised. 'It is a magic race. I also work in Formula One and the World Rally Championship, but I have been lucky enough to have captured all the Dakar Rallies and have some fantastic memories – like the time we were forced to spend the entire day and night stranded in the car in the Ténéré by the most violent sandstorm you could imagine. There was absolutely zero visibility. It was quite frightening. That is what makes the Dakar so special – it is totally unpredictable.'

I first worked on the event as a Motoring News staff reporter in 1988, travelling with Peugeot's team manager, Jean Todt, in a small management plane. The scale of the TSO operation was impressive even then, but the event has reached a new level in recent

seasons as cross-country rallying becomes an increasingly important weapon in car manufacturers' marketing arsenals. I have worked on the last five Dakar Rallies as a press officer for various organisations, including TSO in 2002.

The Amaury Sports Organisation – TSO's holding company – is an arrogant creature. It can afford to be. It runs the Tour de France cycle race, Dakar and the Le Touquet beach race, and has been linked strongly to acquiring the rights to Le Mans in recent months. Staff are proudly French.

Each evening on the Dakar there is a competitor briefing in the bivouac. The TSO chief officials, Auriol and Patrick Zaniroli, preach to the assembled throng in articulate French, as a British translator attempts to keep up, his message frantically relayed to the ever-growing English-speaking rally community via numerous dusty headsets.

Miss out on the following day's vital GPS points or intricate details about route amendments and a competitor could be in trouble. If you don't have a good command of French, then you have to make alternative arrangements. That's never easy for the large Polish, Scandinavian, German, Hungarian and American communities on the Dakar.

A little more consideration for the non-French speaking community would earn the Dakar organisers far more respect from foreign competitors and the international press. It's quite extraordinary how many Dakar first-timers can be heard muttering under their breath about TSO's harsh and unfriendly attitude towards them.

The Dakar's massive medical and catering operations are handled with almost Foreign Legion-like precision by individual teams. There is a separate PC Air to handle the complex aviation timetable – never easy on an event which relies on daily flights to remote military airbases and sand strips in the middle of desolate countryside for four or five Antonov AN-74 cargo planes, a Safair Hercules and up to eight smaller passenger planes per day.

Then there's the impressive bivouac clean-up operation, run by a team of Paris airport staff who use the Dakar as an annual adventure in Africa. Litter, discarded equipment and waste oil products are all removed, leaving the bivouac area – home for up to

2,000 people each night – near its original condition. The same cannot be said perhaps for the myriads of Africans who bear witness to 21st-century technology descending upon their corner of the world for a very short space of time before the return to poverty and normality.

That the Dakar grows in stature and prestige, regardless of its imperfections and its idiosyncracies, is a testament to a high level of planning, slick organisation, its global reputation and the importance now placed on the contest by motor manufacturers. Perhaps the organisers should put a little more emphasis on looking after their international guests in a more hospitable manner, but the Dakar could be entering an even more significant phase of positive development.

The transformation of the World Rally Championship and its assumed rise in stature have alienated it from many people. A chasm has now appeared between world and domestic rally championships, as the step up to the world's premier rally series becomes ever more difficult. There is no suitable feeder system into the World Championship for up-and-coming drivers – the 1600 Cup and Group N Production Cup aside – and John Smith can no longer compete against his heroes in a showroom Subaru or a budget Opel Corsa.

ISC has set its targets and outlined its goals for the progression of the World Championship, but there have been stumbling blocks along the way and television revenues and marketing have not been an overwhelming success. Financially, perhaps, the world series is overstretching itself to reach its targets. The Dakar Rally and the FIA World Cup for Cross-Country Rallies could be about to benefit from the World Championship's weaknesses.

But even if Colin McRae and Tommi Mäkinen join the fray, there's still room for John Smith. He could enter his near-standard T1 Pajero in the Dakar Rally and sit cross-legged in the bivouac with the top drivers, perhaps discussing the day's competition, without requiring a special pass to allow him into a private catering area or a VIP zone. Nor does a journalist need to book an appointment via a management team to talk with a top driver. Perhaps the Dakar has kept the good old days of the World Championship very much alive.

THE DAKAR RALLY INSIGHT
The manufacturers are displaying renewed interest in cross-country rallying and above all in Dakar. BMW and Chevrolet (left) made tentative forays, while Nissan inevitably gained a much higher profile for its fleet of pick-ups, not least by hiring Dakar's unquestioned superstar, Ari Vatanen (above).

MILLS AND VROOM!

INTERVIEW Phil Mills   By Jerry Williams, Chief Sub-Editor, *The Daily Mail*

He once memorably insisted he would quit competition for team management by the time he was 40. Remind Phil Mills of that now he's hit the big Four Zero and he snorts a short, embarrassed laugh. No one likes to be ambushed by their past predictions, but not everybody finds a world title suddenly within their grasp at that age. For Mills, his electrifying partnership with Petter Solberg has provided just that.

As we talk, he leans forward almost aggressively across the table. Yes, he knows he said all that about management.

'But believe me, I still get exactly the same buzz in the car and I've got unfinished business in competition. I wanted to be British Champion and I wanted to be Welsh Champion before. I've done all that. Being World Champion is a hard nut to crack, but that's what I most want. I think the two of us are capable of doing that job.'

Even as the 2003 crown came within reach, the master plan, he insisted, remained an all-out bid in 2004. It was an urgent little speech and it came as a

jolt because if you watch big Phil at work, words that spring to mind are: solid, dependable, phlegmatic, measured. Typically, the Subaru will pull in shimmering with heat, maybe a bit torn up at the edges. Solberg jumps out for lengthy, detailed talks with his engineers, sometimes walking jerkily round the car, propelled by nervous energy. Then he turns to a throng of journos and snappers, explaining in colourful language how he wrested triumph from disaster or, dejectedly, how it all went wrong.

Mills, meanwhile, sits oblivious in his bucket seat, intent on documents, schedules, maps. There's none of the flightiness of a Luis Moya here, no Nicky Grist-style vying with his driver for interviewers. Phil doesn't do upfront. His guiding principles are thoughtfulness, watchfulness, getting it right – the rock that Petter rests on.

Of course, he will talk, and pleasantly. However, it's clearly not his top choice and you can easily slip into thinking: great bloke, good chap to have next to you in the trenches and a top co-driver but no communicator.

In different circumstances, you find real depths and passion. Rallying flows rich in his veins and it comes from growing up in the tiny Powys village of Trefeglwys. The Mills family home sat on a lane constantly used for road rallies, including the legendary Eagle and Pace-maker. Ten minutes away loomed Hafren forest, scene of the RAC Rally, the Welsh and, as Mills says, 'God knows how many Welsh club events'.

From an early age, he and his dad were out in the lane at dead of night to watch a road rally selective or over to Hafren to feast on forest racing. It fostered an abiding love of the sport and now, 30 years later, that arms him to speak out powerfully against what he sees as needless destruction of its basics.

We talk in the garden of his house in a tiny, exclusive development deep in the Welsh countryside, near Newtown. His partner Helen and little daughter Sioned pop in and out. A red kite drifts lazily past. The sky is a pastel blue Michelangelo would have killed for in the Sistine Chapel.

But despite the idyllic surroundings Mills is plainly vexed. It is the Monday after that black weekend when

Ask any competitor, "What did you like most about New Zealand?" and they'd all say, "Wow, Whaanga Coast, that was phenomenal."

'Likewise, Hafren and Dyfi were the sort of stages that made Rally GB what it is and I think we've got to question what the hell are we doing? We're taking away the ingredients that made the cake special in the first place.

'So why not have central service in Builth Wells on the Friday, which means we can take in the Hafrens and Dyfis? Then go to South Wales for the weekend. And look at the mechanics, they now have three slots of 20 minutes' mayhem during the day and 45 minutes in the evening. The rest of the time they're just sitting around. So the

shifts to the sport's future.

'Now new rules have been proposed for the World Championship that I really don't like, including no gravel crews and using some sort of 1000 Pistes [recce] system. I think they will leave us at a point where it's actually dangerous. You can only cut down events so far and we're right on the limit.

'Some of those involved in making these decisions probably don't realise what speeds we do now and how very vital gravel crews are. It can be a matter of the one slippery corner where because of the gravel crew's input you come down an extra gear. And that's the difference between crashing and staying in the rally. Also what we're forgetting is that we are the World

an up-to-date view. It's time for some fresh, younger blood I'm afraid, rather than people who haven't sat in a rally car for 25 years.'

Suddenly, he sits back with a half smile. It all reminds me of the star sixth-former dissing a senior teacher's lessons before stopping short and wondering at his own nerve!

Then: 'Yes, well, I recognise that's all a strong statement and there are people who won't like to hear it.' But, he adds, it would be false of him not to speak his fears and feelings.

Some of the championship's power-suits would do well to heed Mills. He has no hidden agenda and he represents the yeoman backbone of the sport. This is a man who once crammed 88 events

Phil Mills (with Solberg in Subaru's motorhome) has played a key role in honing the Norwegian's colossal ability. Their victory in Australia was one of their most accomplished.

Mark Lovell and Roger Freeman were killed in America. The desperate news comes against a background of emerging hints about the FIA's plans for World Championship rallying.

'I think what happened to Mark and Roger is a big wake-up call for us. He was such a smooth, non-crashing driver. If it can happen to them, then we're all at risk,' Mills says.

Everyone, he states, is angry over future rules that could detract from safety just as a ghastly accident points to the need to bolster it. And then it pours out of him, the trigger a simple question about his likes and dislikes in the championship as it stands. He speaks in a typically soft, mid-Wales lilt. This is a monologue from the heart.

'I think all the changes that have happened in the WRC over the last few years have altered it hugely. Now it's at a level where it's cut to the limit. As for centralised servicing, well it's a great thing, but only up to a point. I think we should have the Friday somewhere else and then Saturday and Sunday in a central park. Because we're now in one place all three days we've lost stages such as Hafren and Dyfi on Rally GB and Whaanga Coast in New Zealand.

sport has gone for them. It's a bore. And it can't be much fun hanging around for three days as a journalist either. So yes, I reckon we've gone over the mark with the changes, good though some of them were.'

He thinks part of the problem has been television wagging the dog too often.

'Take the Acropolis ceremonial start. It cost a huge amount in time and money to get us all down there from Lamia, but not one TV station I saw used it. Then, we stand outside the casino in Monte Carlo for a big group picture. That's an awful lot of effort and expense and not one TV station used it. So why are we doing these expensive things? You've got to question it. I agree you can't encourage TV enough, but if they're not using properly what is provided then somebody's got to start asking questions. So for God's sake, don't talk about cutting back on the recce to save money, look at things like that instead. I don't believe it is essential for TV to have the service park in one place for all three days. In the Iraq war I saw broad-casts from the top of a moving tank.'

Suddenly, there is a pause in the torrent of words. But it is only to give him time to change up a gear as he

Championship, at the top of the sport and we're getting to the stage that doing Killarney or Donegal would be ten times more interesting than Catalonia and it shouldn't be like that. Again, I think we've got to ask what the hell we're doing.

'Eventually, for instance, spectators will tire of having to walk five or six kilometres to see the cars. And look what we had in Monte Carlo where we had three stages run in one day and it was total chaos. So now we're talking about cutting the recce to two days, which means fewer stages per day and more people crowded into smaller areas. Can't people see what they are doing to the sport? Then there's the fact that there is no consultation with the crews at all, ever. That's my biggest, biggest dislike of the way things are. We have never been asked one single time for our input. I can't believe it.

'I really don't know why this should be. Is it the pig-headed attitude of the people who administer things? I suppose in the end you must say yes it is. The sport has always been run in a dictatorial way. Why for instance don't the reigning world champion driver and co-driver sit on the commission? They would have

into under two years; who has won world-level rallies and also built and driven his own Lada at the opposite end of the sport. This is a man who has been Welsh and British Champion Co-driver, and in 20 years has amassed a deal of experience in team administration.

As we talk on his sporting life seems to divide into three golden periods. The early times in Wales were all make do and mend your own car – couldn't be otherwise for a lad learning the motor trade and at college. But they were days of great camaraderie, with thriving mid-Wales motor clubs the centre of social life.

'We had to build our own cars and the cheapest thing we could find was a Lada. The Challenge was brilliant for us, because the rules stopped you doing anything expensive, so I went to a scrapyard, bought a car for £15 and an engine for £20, put a roll cage in and we all prepared it. After college or work we'd work on our cars till two a.m. I was earning about £40 a week and £35 went on the car. We were road rallying every weekend and stage rallying in this old Lada.'

In the Lada, it may surprise you to learn, he was Mills the Driver, pedalling his way to second overall in the Challenge two years running in 1988 and '89. Today, he looks back on such exploits with a shy fondness, but adamantly insists he has no desire to repeat them.

'Well, yes, I had a lot of fun, but I did soon realise driving was not for me, just something to get out of my system.'

He's happiest in the office seat, where he could indulge his lifelong fascination with maps – 'Really, I'm a cartographic anorak' – and via literally hundreds of road rallies, he moved into a bigger pond with Brian Bell and the BTRDA Championship.

'Do you know, I did 99 events with Brian and we joke every now and then that we ought to do that elusive 100th one. I'm sure it will happen some time.'

But Mills was by then managing a local Honda dealership and things were getting sticky with his bosses over time spent competing. Then his habit of being in the right place at the right time rescued him and shot him into golden phase two.

'I had the offer to partner Sebastian Lindholm in the British Championship in a VW and also to do the Thailand Championship with Mark Higgins as a private entry.'

fact, all the necessities at World Championship level. Cue Mills, who just happened to be working in the office at the time!

'Well, Petter then came over for the M-Sport Christmas party, we met in a pub in Cockermouth and got well lagered up talking rallying all night. What really clinched it for me was his enthusiasm to beat everybody in the world. He was just bursting with it.'

The new pairing hit it off well and the recollection brings a big grin to Mills's face: 'Oh, it started with this unbelievable string of results. Like people were saying, "Who are this crew just turning up and leading the Acropolis Rally?" It just can't be!'

The honeymoon lasted a year and a half until a chink in Ford's contract armour led Prodrive to park its tanks on Wilson's lawn and snatch away his superstar in the making. The deal saved them both financially, says Mills.

'We were having to raise some money to pay a few bills at Ford for the next year, which was fair enough, given the programme, but it was going to be very difficult. We were both in debt, Petter massively so from his national rallying days back in Norway. He was already struggling to pay that off. So the

Prodrive deal wiped all that out instantly.'

But the ensuing furore took a heavy toll of driver, co-driver – and Wilson himself.

Mills promises: 'Without question it was the hardest month of my life and Petter's too. I wouldn't say nervous breakdown, but the stress was simply huge. It was a hideous time. We had this great deal, but also all the weight of the moral obligation to Malcolm, who had given Petter and me everything.

'Malcolm obviously took it very, very hard and it all got terribly personal. But then on Rally GB when we won he was the first to congratulate us. That really broke the ice, because he meant it. We talk now and there's no real problem there any more.'

'But the transition time was very, very difficult. We had six crashes in a row with Subaru, because it was all still preying on our minds. Some in the team were starting to ask questions, but we couldn't be 100% honest, because of the legal side of it. OK, so nobody wants that sort of thing, but perhaps in some ways we can look back and say it was a good thing to happen early on, because Petter came out of it all ten times a harder man, as I did too. It's history now, gone and I don't ever want it back again.'

In the last half hour his normally open face has clouded over, shut against the world. Even the memory of that period seems to physically oppress him. But then we get back to how he and Petter have moulded themselves into a smooth, rally-winning machine and his eyes brighten again. When we next talk at length, fresh from their brilliant, tightrope Rally Australia win over Sébastien Loeb, he will be even more full of it.

'Everything's coming together. What a fantastic weekend,' he'll say. 'You know, we didn't feel nervous at all, because every time Seb took some off us, we'd take it back and we were just giggling in the car about it all.'

But now, in his garden, he's at pains to point out that the road to success was long and difficult.

'For instance, our pace note system is only now fully ready so we can attack properly and that's after hours of discussions over many months. And the mental approach is ready too. Most important, we know now how and when to attack.'

Another thing they had to work at was ridding Solberg of the habit ingrained from rallycross days of trying to be fastest round every bend.

It was the moment for a big-balls choice. The dealership job was comfortable and well paid, with a company car. There was no money in the two rides. Nevertheless, Mills took the icy plunge and – right time, right place again – he also got work at Malcolm Wilson Motorsport as a freelance co-ordinator. Within a fortnight that blossomed into a full-time job.

Now he looks back and says: 'Those nine years or so with Malcolm were some of my best. Competing in UK and Thailand, co-ordinating the Irish Tarmac championship, running cars for the Jolly Club in Italy, doing the odd World Championship round and looking after the Middle East drivers. Then there'd be the hire cars for people like Jarmo Kytölehto and Harri Rovanperä. Every day it was rallying, a fabulous time. What I learned at M-Sport will always stand me in good stead.'

And, of course, it led him straight into his third, enduring golden period. He'd already shown he could hack it at world level after another lucky break saw him contest Corsica in 1996 with Armin Schwarz. Now the catalyst was Wilson's quest for a youngster to mould into championship-class material – 'a truly brilliant thing for him to do'.

Eventually, after a worldwide search, Solberg shone out as the special talent. But neither he nor his then co-driver had a clue about pace notes, recces – in

A LIFE LESS ORDINARY

You can see Mills is hugely grateful for the way in which the World Championship has expanded his life. The enthusiasm is as refreshing as chilled Chablis and strawberries on a scorching day. Ask, for instance, if he thinks the World Championship is verging on Formula One's self-absorbed demi-monde and he rushes into an eloquent denial.

'No, no, no. In F1 they just go airport, hotel, paddock, airport and we still see countries. Stages usually end in a village and on the recce you stop and have a coffee or something and get chatting to the locals. If you went to those countries as a tourist there's no way you'd venture into some of those little villages.

'Take the communities tucked away in the mountains of Corsica or Italy: absolutely fabulous. On Sanremo last year we stopped for a cup of tea in a tiny village and there was a hunting party going out after wild boar. Well, because I do a lot of shooting we got talking as best we could and they were showing me all their guns and equipment and you could never, ever do that as a tourist.

'Many of the countries I've been to I'd like to revisit with the family one day. I've stayed in some gorgeous places, especially like the old monasteries in Portugal. This may sound mad but I'd like to spend time cycling in Corsica and I'd like to explore Africa more and go into Argentina more.'

He finds the South American country fascinating – 'not Third World but not 21st century either, somewhere in between'.

He also takes an engaging delight in the way rallying has opened doors to people outside his usual orbit, such as co-driving the present King of Jordan.

'One year I won the Jordan Rally with Mohammed Bin Sulayem – Ronan Morgan couldn't do it as his sister was getting married. Then the next year, Mo gave away his Escort Cosworth to the then Prince Abdullah, who also needed a co-driver and Mohammed recommended me.

'Now there's no way that Phil Mills, mechanic from mid-Wales, would ever have come into contact with the next King of Jordan. But I sat next to him in a rally car for ten days, took many personal phone calls from him, went to the palace for tea

and so on. It was a great experience.'

He relishes that the sport has brought him many lasting friendships. Petter may now be his biggest mate, but there are also people such as Robert Reid, Michael 'Beef' Park, Mark Higgins, Stephen Finlay and Nicky Grist.

'"Beef," for instance, does clay and target shooting like me so we've spent a lot of time together doing that. I talk to Robert a lot about the sport. Mark lives just over the hill there. Then back in the early '90s I used to compete with people like Stephen and we're all still friends.

'I maintain contact from back to the BTRDA and beyond, not just with Brian Bell. David Bell, Wynne Jenkins from road rally days, Peter Thompson – Dave Campbell from the Welsh road rally championship lives in Perth now, so I meet him every year for a beer – and there's Mike Kidd, of course. So many people.'

As he says with real insight, the shared danger of competition is a powerful glue.

'When you sit in a car together and win and lose and survive crashes you form an unusual bond. I remember with Mark for instance, we had the most horrendous accident in Kielder in the Nissan. Mark broke his back. I had to pull him out of the car and then pushed him around in a wheelchair for ten days. We've never mentioned it since. But there's always this unspoken bond that brings us together.'

When he talks about events, his clear favourite was the Safari ('bonkers hard work, but a huge challenge and a proper adventure') but his Number One rally as a co-driver is New Zealand: 'It has those long, flowing stages with no massive drops or big jumps to worry about, an event where you can just sit back and concentrate on doing a perfect co-driving job.'

Ask him to nominate the worst event in the championship and he hesitates. I think he's just too nice to want to slag off hard-working organisers.

Eventually he says: 'Well, I think the least enjoyable would have to be Catalonia. It's all in the north now and there's no grip on the roads there. You're sliding all the time, which isn't very pleasant, because you know you could hit something. Then there's the format. It's a national rally. It's not a World Championship rally.'

But the judgement is quickly followed by a caveat.

'Saying that, it's probably the best organised event you go to. The people are fantastic and any questions are answered before you even ask them!'

'Now, Petter knows we don't have to be quickest round every single bloody corner. We understand now that you can make a mistake or have a problem and get the time back over ten stages, not one. So, yes it's just sort of happened we've got where we are, but with a lot of thought and it's taken time.

Through all the vicissitudes, he says they have developed a strong personal friendship that cements their competition relationship. As he puts it, 'I think with some of the other crews, they sort of get on, because they have to: you do your job and I'll do mine. But I like to think we're on a better level than that. Yes, Petter is an emotional character and actually, I think that's lovely. It shows he's more than just a driving robot.

'Yes, we do have fairly serious discussions about even minor things although I don't think we'd ever fall out. I know now when to lift him and he knows the same with me.'

However, he reflects that it's healthy they live 1,500 miles apart. Everything might be just too intense otherwise.

'At the start we'd be on the phone to each other ten times a day. But now it's nice to have a little distance as well. You've got to have that bit of space.'

PHIL MILLS **INTERVIEW**
The meticulous Mills established his credentials as a works co-driver with Mark Higgins at Nissan (below), but years of patient endeavour have truly paid off with Solberg.

The conversation runs on. Phil tells me his favourite rallying era is Group 4: 'It was Waldegård and Pond and Mikkola; the Escort, the Sunbeam Lotus, Chevette HSR, Manta 400 and TRV8 that left such an impression on me as a youngster.'

A man of parts is Mr. Mills and one of surprises, too. In fact, he has one more up his sleeve.

'Come on, let me show you something,' he says and takes me to see the pride and joy he's squirrelled away. I recognise the mint condition blue Sunbeam Lotus instantly.

Mills looks surprised. 'Oh, you know about these, then?'

'Phil,' I say, 'I ran two in the 1980s. They were incredible motors.'

He agrees: 'So far ahead of their time back then, fantastic machines.'

This one spent ten years as a showroom talking point and is 15,000 miles perfect.

'I've been after it for years,' says Mills. 'Don't drive it often but it's great for a blast in the lanes. The only things I can't find so I can show it are some CN36 tyres. But they're looking around in corners of the factory for me.'

Actually, my advice is forget the CN36s and fit some modern rubber. You need all the help going with these things. I crashed both of mine, spinning one into a North Circular barrier and one into a mountain near Llangollen. Let that be a lesson to you Millsy, soulmate and true believer!

Photograph Gavin Lodge

BREATHLESS IN
DOUGLAS

INSIGHT Manx Rally

By David Williams

All photographs Gavin Lodge

It took a small band of Dutch marshals to remind me why I had bothered going there in the first place. There's nothing like an early retirement from a rally to induce a sense of futility and I was gloomily contemplating the cost of taking part in the Manx, inwardly thanking God that I'd negotiated a way of getting off the island that night when we fell into conversation with the visitors marshalling a chicane on Injebreck.

They had flown in for the occasion, but on previous visits they had been quite prepared to take a ferry from the Netherlands to Newcastle, then drive across northern England to Heysham and take the boat to Douglas. As one of them explained, 'It is a rally with a name'.

The Manx most certainly has a name. Indeed, it is unique. Its reputation and atmosphere make it distinct from other Tarmac rallies in the British Isles, never mind anywhere else. The atmosphere is owed partly to being held in a tourist destination of a kind, partly because motor sport is such an integral feature of

Manx life. Some fondly recall impromptu races in Minis hired from Mylchreest's, the island's famously tolerant Rover dealership, others the tobacco-funded glitz when Rothmans sponsored the rally and stunt flying displays were part of the circus. In the years since, European Championship status has sometimes brought a Continental feel. As it has often been the concluding round of the British Championship, it has hosted its share of tense championship showdowns and well-lubricated celebrations.

Mylchreest's aside, it is not an especially friendly place. Advertisements in the ferry terminal for cheap deals to get off the island during the TT are a reminder that not everyone thrills to the sound of an engine at high revs; most of the hotels on Douglas Promenade bring to mind a 1950s boarding house and their owners rarely trouble to disguise the fact that they're running the place for their benefit, not yours. It takes a measure of dedication to make the trip, considering the prices the Steam Packet Company charges to get on to the island rather than off it.

The ferries and the hotels are in a way part of the challenge, but only in the sense that they're additional hurdles to jump before getting a crack at the stages. Whether the Manx is the fastest Tarmac rally in the world is a matter of debate, but there is no denying that it was the first international rally in Britain to need

Certain drives enter into legend and Tony Pond's crushing victory on the 1982 Manx was one of them (left). Even Walter Röhrl's Porsche couldn't hold a candle to the Chevette. Martin Rowe (centre, winning in a Mégane) and Mark Higgins, victorious in an Astra, have proved that Manxmen can be contenders, not merely hosts.

The fact that it was had a good deal to do with the commitment derived from the weeks Pond had spent, year after year, learning the terrain.

On that basis, one of the greatest Manx drives was surely Patrick Snijers' win six years later. Driving for a British team, Prodrive, meant that his BMW was well adapted to bumpy moorland asphalt after a test near Glen Rushen mines, but the Belgian had never set eyes on the place before and his speed contrasted strikingly with the edgy performance of his European Championship rival, Fabrizio Tabaton.

Ari Vatanen's 1976 victory in an Escort that teetered through most corners on two wheels was in a similar category, but it isn't often that talent gets the better of experience. Jari-Matti Latvala added still further to his reputation by holding second in 2003, but the Manx got Ford's newest star in the end. After just two practice laps, he had managed to cram every bad corner into his pace notes, but not a single bump; his gravel note crew – an unimagined refinement when Vatanen won a quarter of a century previously – provided a valuable if not infallible safety net.

Tabaton was perhaps the most prominent but by no means the sole visitor not to have realised the time and effort that British and Irish drivers put into mastering the Manx. Malcolm Wilson recalls spending a night driving up and down the road variously known as Injebreck or the Baldwins; another leading British name admits that after days of relentless practice, he bolted slicks on the recce car and did a complete lap of the route one night.

The 1966 winner, Dennis Easthope, used to drive from memory and briefly led all the visitors in his Porsche in 1976. Listen to a three-times winner such as Mark Higgins and it's tempting to suppose that all top Manx drivers can just about dispense with pace notes. Martin Rowe – another triple victor – promises that it isn't so and he was surprised how much he had forgotten when he took the wheel of a Group B 037 as part of the 40th anniversary celebrations during the

rally last summer. He agrees that the Manx makes demands similar to the Rally Finland.

'I remember the first time we did the National rally in '93, it was an open recce,' Rowe said. 'The part from Brandywell Cottage over the jumps and down to Sartfield Hairpin, I drove up and down it on my own. There are six right-hand corners and that section there I just memorised. One of my mates was watching and he said, "Bloody hell, you were the only person who didn't lift or change down." That was purely because I'd learnt those six corners and the inch-perfect lines through there.

'So I figured, if you're going to make a bit of time up, you're going to have to do it on the quick stuff and the dangerous stuff, so I learnt that section and then I learnt the section down through the Baldwins, and that, even in the Lancia this year, was just amazing. You get to the bottom and the hairpin and you sort of take a big breath: you haven't breathed for five minutes! The buzz you get is great – you come down through there and the wing mirrors are against the side of the car, they're flattened against the door sort of thing. So yeah, there are parts of Finland where the locals know it and some of them have in their notes, "This is it," and the co-drivers don't even read the notes, because they know they can't keep up. In a way, the Baldwins are that quick.'

As Rowe said, every rally is someone's local event. If the event is big enough and the local hero is good enough, his feats will make headlines. But since it began 40 years ago as a road rally, the Manx has become far more than a highlight of the British calendar. You don't meet Dutch marshals in Catalonia.

chicanes to ensure that it complied with limits on average speeds and it is certainly one of the fastest Tarmac events. Colin McRae loves it and has suggested wistfully that the stages are World Championship standard; a compact route with short road sections is also part of the appeal.

High speeds, innumerable bumps and a relatively small number of roads have combined to create its reputation. Indeed, even motorcycle racers have voiced the opinion that competing on such narrow roads is lunacy. Manx lanes are exhilarating and satisfying, but pure ability is rarely a substitute for prior knowledge. There is also the awareness that it can be an unforgiving place and that the weather is an additional hazard. On a July evening when the Home Counties were basking in sunshine, a good proportion of the first leg in 2003 was swathed in fog. Nevertheless, it was hard to believe just how quick many of the roads are.

It's a feature that has regularly surprised and dismayed visitors. The feats of the late Tony Pond, once a resident of the island and the first driver to win the rally four times, are rightly part of Manx legend. It's the 1982 victory that stands out, for he trumped no less a driver than Walter Röhrl in a breathtaking display at night. Pond's Chevette should never have been a match for Röhrl's 911.

THE SVENGALI OF HELSINKI

PROFILE Timo Jouhki   By David Williams

Photograph Gavin Lodge

There are team managers who, given the opportunity, would gladly have thrown Timo Jouhki into a pit of vipers. Some have refused to deal with him at all, others maintain that he is a gentleman whose word is his bond. It is entirely natural that he is disliked and even feared, for at the best of times, driver managers occupy an ambivalent position. From a manufacturer's perspective, they can be useful intermediaries in talking round a stubborn superstar, but they tend to be viewed as obstacles in the process of getting drivers to jump through more hoops for less money.

Jouhki has generated more hostility than most of his breed. Marcus Grönholm suspects that Jouhki's associates used to brief against him in Finland – a rare instance of Finnish solidarity breaking down – but it's not the way Jouhki defends his drivers, but the way he builds them up in the first place that marks him apart. He is a shrewd and powerful man, which doesn't necessarily add to his popularity; but whereas managers in rallying are generally seen as doing their best for their charges, Jouhki is sometimes perceived as selling their services in exchange for their souls. Fairly or otherwise, he is portrayed as rallying's Mephistopheles.

It began when he approached Tommi Mäkinen more than a decade ago. At the time, Juha Kankkunen was the sole Finnish driver winning at World Championship level and to national dismay, both Carlos Sainz and Didier Auriol had conquered the 1000 Lakes. The horrific prospect loomed of Finnish drivers following the Swedes into decline. Jouhki sensed a need and an opportunity. He had long been involved in rallying: his sister was Pentti Airikkala's first wife, Hannu Mikkola was a family friend and Jouhki had competed with some success himself, twice finishing in the top ten on the 1000 Lakes, driving Kadetts. He recognised that Mäkinen had the ability, but neither the means nor the persuasiveness to cement a works drive.

Jouhki not only possessed the negotiating skills, but the money. The family is reckoned to have been Finland's richest before the rise of Nokia and he

Part racehorse owner, part trainer, Timo Jouhki (far left) has created an unparalleled stable. It started with Tommi Mäkinen (left), but Jari-Matti Latvala (above) promises a new dimension.

had experience in the field, having ploughed some money into Kankkunen before he became a works driver. The deal done with Mäkinen was that Jouhki would manage him and buy him drives. If Tommi struck it rich, Jouhki's firm, Pro-Racing, would take a substantial percentage – reputedly up to half of his earnings – in return for having taken the risk in the first place.

It was a huge gamble. In July 1994, Mäkinen was on the point of throwing in the towel. A few weeks later, he won the 1000 Lakes. Both his career and the deal flourished. Mäkinen is the only driver to have become World Rally Champion four years running and Jouhki's bet brought such abundant returns that he repeated the process with Harri Rovanperä and Toni Gardemeister. Rovanperä spent several years as a works driver with Seat and when that foundered, Jouhki gave the Jyväskylä driver the means to revive his flagging reputation by renting a Grifone-tuned Corolla for him for the 2000 Rally Finland: Rovanperä was third, having held second for much of the rally, and signed for Peugeot soon afterwards. Similarly, good results in a Grifone 206 helped secure Gardemeister's place with Skoda. It's the sort of agreement that sounds as though it might not withstand fame and fortune. Jouhki insists that none of his 'stable' has ever queried the terms. Mäkinen – not a man given to extravagant displays of emotion – says simply that he would not have become World Champion without him.

In the past, Jouhki has remained firmly in the background, like most of his kind. There are no rallying equivalents of Willi Weber or the late Mark McCormack. But while Jouhki is not the sort of man to be found in front of a TV camera, the spotlight was unavoidably thrown on him in 2003 not because of his best-known and most successful driver, Mäkinen, but thanks to his latest recruit, Jari-Matti Latvala. The new signing has an irresistible, Guinness-Book-

TIMO JOUHKI **PROFILE**
When a youthful Mäkinen (top right) manhandled a Group A Sunny, even Jouhki scarcely imagined that his drivers might feature in most works teams, from Harri Rovanperä at Peugeot (above) to Toni Gardemeister at Skoda.

of-Records appeal as the youngest works rally driver yet. Latvala was barely 18 when he contested the Acropolis and the Focus drive was arranged with Malcolm Wilson before Latvala was old enough to hold a Finnish driving licence. Finally, Jouhki was prepared to discuss his system in some detail.

In this case, Jouhki is seeking not so much to boost a driver's career as to create a driver in the first place. Signing Latvala is an unprecedented gamble, for the deal was done before he had even contested a rally. Like many gifted drivers, Latvala first took the wheel when barely old enough to walk. Partly because Jouhki knew his father, who was a successful clubman, he soon learned of the son's potential, although he has a network of scouts across Finland in any case. Rallysprints admit drivers from the age of 16 in Finland and when Latvala began to win his class every time he took the wheel of his Corolla GT, Jouhki made his approach.

Most driver managers have lawyers and accountants. Jouhki's facilities go considerably further. Latvala was tested on two different roads, one narrow, one wide and fast – 'a 1000 Lakes' road,

as Jouhki put it – with the veteran co-driver, Timo Hantunen, then given a psychological test, then sent to Britain for analysis and coaching with Airikkala, who predicted that he was a future World Champion. Once Jouhki was satisfied with the assessments, Latvala began competing in Britain, chiefly because the Motor Sports Association licenses 17-year-olds to rally. When a Group N Clio was deemed inadequate, he was switched to a Lancer.

For 2003, Jouhki agreed terms to put his newest prodigy in an M-Sport Focus World Rally Car in Britain and a Group N Subaru in Italy, the latter to provide the Tarmac experience that Finns don't get at home. Rather to Jouhki's surprise, Wilson suggested that Latvala should attempt four World Championship rounds as well as the British series. Latvala contested around 25 rallies in 2003, fitting school and exams in between, sometimes doing his homework on aeroplanes. The press lapped it up.

'I have never had so inexperienced rally guy. In some ways it is a risk, but you have to be confident. We are aiming high. He is very mature for his age,' Jouhki

explained. 'When analysing this whole thing, we are the only people with complete organisation. We have media people, gravel note people, everything.'

Indeed he does. M-Sport was a little surprised to discover that Latvala turned up for his first rally in a Focus with a Jouhki-appointed engineering adviser, Esko Reiners.

'This is just my way of doing things. I feel it's much more exciting. You can see more your input, you can see the nurturing working all through and so on. Of course, it involves a whole lot more risks. It's not a simple process of management as some people are doing it from ready-made, entering into teams young guys that already have been professionals. It's totally other way of thinking really,' Jouhki elaborated.

'If we compare with what we had to make as an input in Juha [Kankkunen] and now with either Mikko Hirvonen or Jari-Matti, we are in totally another ballgame. Of course, the fees of the drivers have gone up also considerably, but so have the costs. Probably the sums you can get later on now are much, much, much higher, but then again, if you compare them to the cost, relative yield

is probably not that much more. But yes, the risks are higher. And as I probably mentioned, when I started with Juha I had no intention of doing it as professional or anything like that. It was much much more a hobby and an enthusiasm on the sport. I didn't start it with the intention of becoming a manager.'

Given the cost of hiring an M-Sport Focus, the bet becomes an investment only if top rally drivers continue to be multi-millionaires. Jouhki remains sanguine. He isn't surprised that rally drivers' salaries have risen so greatly. He reckons they are in proportion to the increased earnings of ice hockey or basketball players and reflect the greater media interest in rallying. Plenty of drivers – Richard Burns and Colin McRae included – will be earning substantially less in 2004, but if Latvala is capable of winning World Championship rallies within five years, as Jouhki believes, his earning power should be spread over a longer period than any other driver's.

In Finland at least, Jouhki has his imitators. It's a society in which a wealthy businessman is more likely to fancy the idea of having his own rally

driver than his own football or rugby team, as he might in Britain. None of them operates with anything like Jouhki's systematic efficiency. Indeed, Pro-Racing is unique. Other organisations, including M-Sport and Prodrive, have tested drivers, while Ford used a psychological test as part of its Rallysearch competition in 1987. The difference is that driver is at the beck and call of a single car manufacturer, either committed for years, regardless of the car's competitiveness, or vulnerable to being discarded whenever the marketing weathercock swivels.

Yet Pro-Racing also provides a striking instance of private enterprise getting the better of an official body, as Finland has quite the best-organised and financed junior rally team in the world. It's difficult to know whether institutional weakness, Jouhki's judgement and willingness to spend, or chance are the deciding factors, but at present, there is no immediate sign of the Finnish Junior Team producing another Mäkinen or Kankkunen. Yet rallying isn't Jouhki's full-time occupation. At 52, he is chairman of the family firm, now a Swiss-based investment concern, and that takes up half of his time.

Even good junior teams produce their share of able drivers who don't make the grade at World Championship level. Jouhki admits that he has had his

share of failures too, but they aren't well known. His track record has made him more powerful still; Wilson was prepared to put some of his own money into Hirvonen and Latvala in large part because they come with Jouhki's blessing. The Pro-Racing stamp makes it much easier to regard them as an investment than a risk.

Pro-Racing's development mirrors the evolution of professional sport. The idea that rally drivers might earn enough money to be treated not simply as an investment, but the basis of a self-financing company would have been unthinkable 30 years ago. Jouhki's success is remarkable principally because it has been achieved in something most countries regard as a minor sport, yet one that devours money on an epic scale.

Nonetheless, rallying has entered a phase that will test Jouhki's nerve and might empty the pockets of a less shrewd operator. The convulsions that hit the sport in the latter months of 2003 threaten to stretch manufacturers' budgets to the limit and may whittle their numbers. The willingness or even the ability to experiment with new drivers will be correspondingly reduced for the foreseeable future. Works drives and works support threaten to dry up and it is already certain that there will be fewer factory seats available in 2004.

This may be a concern for a Jussi

Välimäki or a Martin Stenshorne, but it's not an immediate problem for Hirvonen and Latvala. In that respect, the current turn of events will tilt the odds further in Jouhki's favour, as manufacturers acknowledge. M-Sport needs customers and turnover. Jouhki is in this for the long haul and therefore neither needs nor expects an immediate return.

Besides, he is prepared to adapt to changing circumstances. Few Europeans are as clannish as the Finns, but Jouhki maintains that he is quite prepared to consider developing non-Finnish drivers. It's an arresting thought. By and large, Finns stick together and they speak an impenetrable language. There would naturally be fears of getting second-best treatment, but if approached, it would be an offer that any ambitious driver would find hard to refuse, regardless of nationality.

Any talented young driver can now expect to attract people offering advice in exchange for a share of the future proceeds, yet it's difficult to imagine Jouhki acquiring many imitators. A stock market-based scheme developed by Slipstream in Britain to push Neil Wearden amongst other drivers is defunct. Its rapid rise and fall tended to confirm the view that stockbrokers are bookies in pinstripes. It's perhaps worth remembering too that Pro-Racing isn't Jouhki's only business.

It's difficult to predict the returns too. Prodrive's long-serving Subaru rally team director, David Lapworth, regards the megabuck deals done at the turn of the century as a 'blip'. Although he doesn't go into detail, it's a fair description of the overheated blend of economic growth, an optimistic projection of television-fuelled exposure and the marketing policies of Ford and Peugeot. Salaries are dropping, in glaring contrast to the cost of the cars. It's a market with peaks and troughs like any other, but Lapworth believes that that was a peculiarly dizzy peak.

Sporting eminence doesn't last for ever – look at Welsh rugby – and it isn't enough that rallying retains its appeal in Finland, for Jouhki relies just as much on its popularity in countries that produce cars. But that's a very widely spread risk indeed.

RE-INVENTING THE WHEEL

TECHNICAL REVIEW

By Martin Sharp

There were new rally cars, new systems and quicker stage times, but the outstanding technical development of 2003 was a triumphal exercise in blending new wine in an old bottle. The Ford began the year as the oldest World Rally Car design, but in the shape of the Focus RS WRC 03, it ended it as the freshest. It was a transformation that rivals immediately identified as the new benchmark.

Additionally, a number of important new solutions were introduced, notably the Citroën Xsara's grip-optimising, passive anti-roll bar system and Prodrive/Subaru's 'active' pitch and roll control arrangement, which was fitted to Petter Solberg's Impreza WRC for the Sanremo Rally.

Skoda launched the genuinely new car, but Ford created the stir. The eyecatching 2003 Focus was rarely out of the limelight from the moment it appeared on the Rally of New Zealand in April. The fruit of Christian Loriaux's work since he joined M-Sport/Ford from Prodrive/Subaru in January 2002, it set new standards, in particular as a most impressive example of the application of the laws of physics to current technology and regulations.

The Belgian engineer began compiling the specification and initial sketches as soon as he joined M-Sport. As the engineer responsible for the radical-for-the-time Imprezas that took Richard Burns to the World Championship in 2001, he saw no room for compromise.

'The championship now is so tight that you need to go with the optimum everywhere. You can't afford to go and say, "OK we've got this car, it's very good on the slow rallies and we're going to win on the slow rallies, and then on fast rallies it doesn't matter, we'll win the championship with that". You can't. It's so competitive, you have to have a car that can potentially win all 14 [rallies], or that you think that can win all 14.'

His original re-engineering of the Impreza dates back to 1999, and employed the admirable strategy of getting as much of the car's weight as low and as central as possible. Four years of technological progress have provided still more scope, which the 206 and the Xsara have exploited to good effect. Today, many more performance-related areas of the car require optimisation, which often demands increasingly sophisticated solutions. Aerodynamic efficiency is now firmly one of these areas.

The styling of the 2003 Focus is radically different from its predecessor and Loriaux was surprised to encounter little Ford corporate styling influence or restriction on the shapes of the all-new 2003 body panels. Its near-DTM look is essentially functional and aerodynamic efficiency is a key element.

Aerodynamics have comparatively little influence on handling on slower events such as the Tour of Corsica and the Cyprus Rally, although they do have an important influence on cooling on very hot rallies,

such as Cyprus. However, on fast stages such as Finland's, the effects are much more pronounced. Aerodynamically generated forces usually begin to have a useful effect at around 60 mph. But aerodynamic forces are relative to the square of the vehicle speed, which means, for example, at 50 mph there's just one-quarter of the aero force available at 100 mph, not one-half.

So in Finland, where rally cars regularly corner – and jump – at speeds in excess of 100 mph, downforce counts, significantly influencing grip and the amount of time the wheels are on the ground. There can, of course, be a balancing effect too, whereby the high-speed handling characteristics of a nose-heavy WR Car can be honed by its aerodynamic appendages.

A spindly rear spoiler and other body parts of equally low aerodynamic efficiency meant the 2002 Focus lost out on fast rallies. In recent times, Peugeot was the first to raise the aerodynamics game with the 206, most obviously with its latest rear wing, which first appeared in Greece in 2002. The Impreza then appeared with its 'toast rack' rear wing on the 2003 Monte and Citroën arrived in Turkey with a similarly be-finned aerofoil.

However, installing suitably efficient aerodynamic equipment on the Focus – in particular at its rear – necessitated some lateral thinking. FIA regulations demand that extra front or rear body parts do not exceed the extremities of the standard car in plan view. There is little scope for a rear wing of the scale required today on the European Focus, the model on which previous Focus WRCs were based. However, the Ford is a world car: it sells in the United States, where stringent Federal crash test regulations demand bigger front and rear bumpers. By basing the homologation of the RS WRC 03 on the longer US car, M-Sport released the space required to accommodate a rear aerofoil of a useful size, together with a front bumper arrangement that could be modified to provide positive aerodynamic and cooling advantages.

Testing of 206 rear wings on Focuses confirmed the scale of the advantages to be gained and the resulting homologated Ford device also incorporates vertical fins to improve the car's stability in yaw, reducing an overly sideways stance at speed. Not dissimilar in shape to the Peugeot device, the latest Ford rear wing has 'bow-legged' side supports to maintain the visibility of the high-mounted rear light clusters.

Loriaux had a shrewd idea of what he wanted aerodynamically and eight hours in MIRA's wind tunnel in the spring of 2002 established that the basic design provided it. Four days of secret testing on an airfield finalised the specification and four hours back in the wind tunnel in late March this year confirmed that the team was close to its target. It incorporated stringent goals, as anybody who has witnessed the car on a special stage at speed will testify.

The tapering, inverted NACA-duct-shaped roof

scoop is also of note. This is open at its tapered rear end and at speed, air is compressed as it travels into the duct, then 'spits' out of the other side, expanding as it does so, thereby increasing in velocity before hitting an important part of the rear wing and enhancing its effectiveness.

Beneath the re-styling, the car's bodyshell is entirely re-engineered, as is its roll cage. This assembly, and a revised hydraulic system, are the only changes to have increased in weight. Ford relied entirely on 3D CAD software, considerably speeding design and build. All the roll cage pick-up points into the chassis have been revised to improve the load paths through the structure, which is now 20% stiffer.

Loriaux's 100% survey of the Focus has resulted in a myriad of detail packaging changes, all aimed at improving the weight distribution. Anything that could be lightened is lighter; anything that could be mounted lower in the car is lower. Pendant pedals have given way to organ-type, sprouting from a footwell-mounted pedal box with the master cylinders also on the floor. There's now just one lever on the floor; this operates the handbrake, unless the automated gearchange mechanism fails. If that happens the driver simply pops a clevis pin and that lever then becomes the mechanical gearchange. The thinking is logical: resorting to the back-up gearchange usually means the hydraulic system has failed, so the handbrake wouldn't be much use anyway.

The main danger to the occupants of a WR Car comes from side impacts, so the Focus's side 'crucifix'

roll cage bars have been re-designed, while the extensively revised cage also sits slightly further outboard. Additionally, courtesy of a transmission tunnel narrowed by 30-40mm, the driver and co-driver sit closer together. Bringing a couple of 75-kilo human beings closer to the car's centre of gravity has weight balance advantages, in keeping with the main philosophy; bolting the co-driver's seat directly to the floorpan also helps.

The thinner tunnel is possible thanks to another Loriaux innovation, a lightweight, super-thin titanium propshaft, which sits neatly in the tunnel with the exhaust system. It is the first time a three-piece propshaft with two supporting bearings has been seen on a WR Car, other than as a prototype. The auxiliary mechanical gear lever/three-piece prop were proven in competition on Mark Higgins's 2002 Focus on the Rally GB.

The longitudinally arranged Xtrac gearbox and centre diff assembly remains. New gearbox internals brought some weight saving initially, further reductions following the 'tidying-up' of pipe runs and pump locations, and the introduction of a revised transfer box housing at Sanremo.

The main weight gain in the new hydraulic system is from running accumulators, unlike the previous 100-bar system. The new system operates between pressures of 100 and 150 bar, with its main accumulator located low in the rear of the car, by the rear bumper. The car appeared first with a Moog valve actuating just

The 2003 Focus retained most of the 2002 car's virtues, but was competitive in a much wider range of conditions. Subaru's boldness (above) wasn't rewarded as richly, its 'active' dampers running into teething problems.

the semi-automatic clutch and improved filtration was required to ensure clean fluid during rallies. At Sanremo, three more Moog valves were introduced to actuate the active differentials.

Loriaux's suspension design for a car that is to all intents and purposes new is of particular interest. The conventional MacPherson front struts have slightly increased travel , while the Reiger dampers have been lightened. There are also small changes in suspension geometry. Its rear suspension, however, is very different from the MacPherson – or Chapman – strut arrangement of its predecessor. The latter was very heavy and devised early in the design process during 1998 — indeed earlier than some FIA clarifications on WR Car rear suspension design.

Weight reduction and optimised kinematics were the primary reasons to opt for the entirely new system. The front and rear inner wheelarches are re-shaped to enable the car to ride lower, yet with extended wheel travel all round and improved cooling at the front.

Ford officially describes the 2003 Focus's rear suspension as 'trailing arm struts'. Loriaux describes it as having trailing links and lateral links, which it has, shrewdly arranged. The lower mountings of the dampers are also judiciously positioned, where they meet the uprights. These coil-over, remote-reservoir Reiger shock absorbers are particularly lengthy and the whole deal facilitates favourable geometry, within the enlarged wheelarch. It is perhaps worth noting that, on initial submission of the arrangement, official opinion was that the system could never work. Mayonnaise and ketchup might aid the digestion of those words, perhaps?

Since Cosworth Racing took over the development of the iron-block Duratec 'R' engine in May 2000 it has managed to shave 25% of the weight from what was a comparatively heavy unit. When the car was launched in 2003, the total engine performance increase over the three years was eight per cent, but the initial development of 'a new and clever way' was introduced at Sanremo.

Essentially, software strategy developments have improved the interaction of Cosworth's engine management system and the car's chassis systems, with the overall effect of improved driveability and higher performance. Mechanical changes to the engine were made earlier in the year, in order that these new strategies could be introduced. The Cosworth engineer, Alex Hitzinger, explained: 'We have just really started with this strategy. It gives us already a good advantage and there is still more potential there.'

Cosworth belongs to the Ford Motor Company, as does Pi Research, and Pi was brought in to develop the

Focus's electronics in 2002. The resulting package for 2003 is quite possibly the most sophisticated in the World Championship.

The essence of the 2003 Pi electronics system is a power distribution system, using software strategies to control electrical loads. A less power-hungry, 200-amp/hour, alternator can be used, permitting more engine output. Far less wiring and an absence of circuit breakers or relays halves the weight of conventional WRC electronics.

Switching is achieved using Field Effect Transducers, or 'Mofsets'. These offer a new way of controlling high power and are used to control small devices that pass large amounts of current. They can be switched on and off via the CAN – Control Area Network – or one of many processors in the car, enabling detailed on-board computer decisions to be made about operating strategy. Being an entirely solid-state system, packaging is better, and the electronics are sited lower and further to the rear of the car than previously.

Current-carrying mechanical switches are exceptionally rare. Driver-operated controls not directly concerned with driving the car are located in a lightweight, membrane-switch panel positioned between the crew on the floor. This is of a type often used in fighter aircraft and saves about one kilo. The panel is linked to the CAN communications network, as is its latest ultra-lightweight plastic and carbon fibre dashboard, which saves 750 grammes.

Since Pi's involvement, the weight of the electrical components has been reduced by 25%. Its preliminary system shaved ten kilos from the 2002 car, and the latest system saves eight more.

Nine Pi engineers are assigned to the programme: four software engineers at its Cambridge base and five electronics experts at M-Sport in Cumbria. Pi's M-Sport-based Operations Manager Andy Warr (son of the ex-Lotus Formula 1 Team Manager, Peter) travels to events, where typically two Pi engineers are on hand.

The engine ECU and chassis controller are flagship Pectel T10S four-processor units, each using identical twin Motorola 32-bit 25MHz processors and two 40MHz DSPs – Digital Signal Processors. These are well proven, and although more advanced equipment could have been used, it wouldn't have brought much extra performance.

The power controller is the latest component in the car's electronics system, and is networked to the engine and chassis controllers. Some 18 months' development were required before the team was prepared to run it in competition. This system accounts for every electrical action, from constant and

complex actuations depending on specific differential maps, chassis sensor inputs and engine operational requirements, to more mundane tasks such as turning on the heated windscreen. Even the mundane functions change from event to event.

'For instance, Finland requires you to run with side lights and rear lights on the road, and now instead of having to do a whole bunch of rewiring on the car we just tell the box that we want the lights to come on under certain conditions, so the driver doesn't have to think about switching the lights on,' Warr explained.

The heart of the latest Focus lies in its chassis controller. The main decisions are made here, based on information from 40 analogue sensors on rally cars (64 on test cars) plus 15 digital inputs for wheel and shaft speeds. Four CAN buses talk to the other electronic components and there are two RS232 links for talking to the radio and the FIA/ISC tracking technology. The chassis controller also has a number of outputs to drive relays and hydraulic valves, while the engine ECU has 25 analogue inputs, 15 digital inputs, two CAN links and outputs for injectors, coils, relays and pulse width modulation, which involves switching power supply to a component (in the case of a rally car, say, a control valve) on and off very rapidly. DC voltage is converted to a square-wave signal alternating between fully on – nearly 12 volts – and zero, thereby providing a series of power 'kicks'. By adjusting the duty cycle of the signal, or the fraction of time it is 'on,' and modulating the width of the pulse, the average power supply can be varied.

The chassis controller monitors sensor input and the switch panel. If it receives information that there is a problem with fuel pressure, for example, it will deduce that there is a fault in fuel pump one and swap to fuel pump two, without the driver having to flick any switches – or even to think about it.

As an operational example, when the driver wants to switch on the heated screen, he will press the relevant switch on the membrane panel. This sends the information to the chassis controller, which decides whether it is a sensible operation to undertake; for instance, the car might have a low battery or an alternator problem. If this is the case, the chassis controller will override the driver's decision and not allow the heated screen's high current drain. The system will make the driver aware of this and if it is a safety-critical decision the driver can override the chassis controller.

Pi admits that the engine power gain provided by this new system is 'not huge', and that the smaller alternator can nevertheless drain some three horsepower. However, under wide-open throttle conditions when exiting a corner in stage mode, for example, it is highly likely that all available engine power will be needed, and so the latest system will provide this by switching non-critical circuits out of the car at that particular moment and then on again – extremely quickly.

Compact Flash cards receive information in the form of a data file, which can be translated by software in a laptop to graphical format, for assessment by engineers when the car comes in for service or at the end of a test run.

Additionally, off-car information and data are provided by a Pi-developed software package displaying stage times and results as web pages on monitors in the service area. This information and data can also be sent to the co-driver's dashboard as a text message, using a digital messaging system first developed for Ford's 2002 rally programme. Information sent can range from previous stage times to more complex instructions such as directions to adjust car settings. While this communication system evidently can provide a competitive edge, it also carries a safety function in that the driver and co-driver can be warned about incidents or accidents ahead of them in a stage.

With many chassis and engine sensors feeding multiple controllers, the car is effectively 'running itself' electronically. As Warr pointed out, 'One sensor/controller depends on the other and you can't really make an instantaneous decision at one moment in time what the car is doing, and how it's going to react to those conditions.'

Ford hasn't been alone in developing electronic control and hydraulic systems. However, Citroën Sport's system eschews complication and simply harnesses dynamic physical forces in a particularly interesting way. This is the passive anti-roll bar system fitted to the Xsara throughout 2003.

Offering 'something for almost nothing,' the system is based on a concept patented as 'RFS,' an acronym for Reverse Function Stabiliser, by the Australian company, Kinetic. Conventional anti-roll bars cannot differentiate between a true roll mode and an articulation mode, or a single wheel mode – actually a special case of articulation. Hence, they continue to provide vertical stiffness to the wheels during articulation inputs – which is precisely when such stiffness is detrimental to suspension efficiency and reliability.

Citroën's system, however, is able to distinguish between roll input and articulation input. This is referred to as 'mode decoupling' and in practical terms means that, when cornering, the system allows the anti-roll bars to react to roll forces conventionally, but if a wheel then encounters a bump during the corner, the system distributes this additional 'bump force' among all four wheels, thus ensuring that the bump has minimal disruption to the vertical tyre force of the 'bumped' wheel. This happens simultaneously and instantaneously with no computers, pumps, valves, or corresponding power drain.

The torsional resistance to wheel articulation provided by conventional anti-roll bars compromises grip. By dissipating the effects of bump forces, the Xsara's system can keep wheels on the ground more often and strongly, thereby improving grip. More equal and reduced tyre wear is a further benefit.

The anti-roll bar on each axle is split in two, and each 'half' roll bar is linked by a hydraulic circuit to the half roll bar on the same side of the other axle. There are, therefore, two hydraulic circuits in total, one linking the half roll bars on the left-hand side of the car, the other linking the half roll bars on the right-hand side of the car. Between each of these two hydraulic circuits are two double-acting piston/cylinder assemblies, one located between the two front half roll bars, the other between the two rear half roll bars. These assemblies provide a connection between the two circuits and can thus influence the behaviour of the opposite circuit. A

Photograph Martin Sharp

piston-type accumulator maintains pressure between each of the two hydraulic circuits.

Its operation is best described by example: as the Xsara travels through a smooth

left-hand corner, say, both right-hand wheels are under compression roll forces, so there is no fluid flowing in the system and the anti-roll bars are working 'conventionally'. If the right-hand front wheel hits a rock during a corner, fluid will flow in the right-hand circuit, effectively instantaneously, thereby 'alerting' the right-hand rear wheel to a change in forces. However, because that right-hand rear wheel did not experience the impact of the 'rock force,' it 'knows intuitively' that that 'rock force' cannot be part of the 'roll force'.

In a conventional system, the 'rock force' would be resisted by just the front anti-roll bar, resulting in a massive vertical tyre load variation of the right-front wheel. However, when the fluid flows through the Xsara's system, because both front and rear cylinder assemblies are double acting, the flow is reciprocal: the amount of fluid going towards the rear in one circuit is matched by the amount of fluid flowing forward in the other circuit. The rear piston/cylinder assembly must therefore move to match the movement of that in the front cylinder.

The rear assembly movement applies equal and opposite torque to the rear anti-roll bar halves as that received by the front bar's. In our example the result would be that the front right 'single wheel' rock force becomes a distributed four-wheel articulation force, effectively optimising wheel loadings; and while all this is happening the system is maintaining the original roll force. Modifying the pressure in the hydraulic circuits can also provide a certain amount of control over the way in which this ingenious system works. In the Citroën application, if required, this is achieved in the service area.

A much more complicated chassis control system appeared first on Solberg's Sanremo Impreza. Devoid

of anti-roll bars, the car was equipped with a system controlling roll and pitch through hydraulic pressure on the damper units.

Prodrive began considering controlled suspension options in 1997, deciding to commit to this system 12 months before it appeared on its first rally. By then it had been endurance-tested for some 2,000 miles, and there had been an additional 1,000 miles or so of set-up work with drivers.

In conjunction with TAG, Prodrive has developed a new electronics system for the Impreza. Packaged in two boxes, this was fitted to the controlled-suspension car at Sanremo. It controls all car functions, including the suspension, using one system, whereas the standard 2003 arrangement in Tommi Mäkinen's Impreza had three separate ECUs, controlling the engine management system, chassis and data logging. However, the latest type does not incorporate a power controller similar to the Focus's.

The Prodrive/Subaru controlled suspension has been given the acronym ECD, and it has a separate hydraulic pump providing pressure up to 150 bar. This is driven by a small shaft off the rear of the gearbox and located under the rear seat pan, necessitating a re-designed fuel tank.

When compared to earlier Lotus active suspension developments, the Subaru system cannot accurately be described as active. Springing and damping are provided by conventional shock absorbers similar to those on 2002 Imprezas, with springs on each suspension strut. Suspension links remain the same. However, by varying pressures into the bump and rebound areas of the four dampers extremely rapidly, via four accumulators, it is possible to have fine control of each corner of the car, thereby optimising roll and pitch according to driver and tyre requirements.

The system computes the required pressure in each corner from inputs from lateral g, longitudinal g and yaw sensors, plus interfacing with differential and engine activity. The driver can adjust the car balance from the cockpit.

At the time of writing, the FIA had yet to arrive at a specific definition of active suspension, which it intends to ban on WR Cars in 2005. The Citroën anti-roll bar system is entirely passive and therefore could be used

in 2005. With electronically controlled, hydraulically actuated damping, the Subaru system is most likely to be excluded, whereas some considered that Peugeot's electro-hydraulic roll bar control could well be allowed in 2005.

Peugeot Sport's Chief Engineer, Michel Nandan, explained that should his hydraulic anti-roll bars be banned, he would seriously consider a development of Citroën's passive system and that, had there been sufficient space in the 206, he would certainly have used something akin to Subaru's system in place of the hydraulic anti-roll bars.

The Fabia didn't break much new ground, but it was the first new WR Car, based on a model new to the series, to appear in the 'noughties'. It is also the first Skoda competition car to benefit fully from computer-aided design, courtesy of the recent collaboration between Skoda Motorsport and the Czech company's new technical and R & D departments. Combining these computational techniques with the talents of experienced craftsmen in the Motorsport department produced a car sporting contemporary architecture and greater sophistication than its Octavia predecessor.

The Fabia WRC was in its infancy, indeed barely teething, on its first World Championship appearance on the Deutschland in July. Such an early taste of competition was a somewhat audacious decision, but one taken on the basis that the 2003 season would be a matter of development, pure and simple.

It may also be considered brave to have introduced this new car immediately with two alternative gearboxes, thereby using up both possibilities to homologate competition transmissions for a new WR Car. One transmission option, produced by Xtrac, uses three active differentials with a semi-automatic gearchange and positions the gear cluster on the end of the crankshaft, while the alternative Swedish Carlsson 'Tractive' system features passive differentials, locating the gearbox, front and centre differentials behind the engine, driven from the crankshaft by drop gears. The Carlsson casing is machined from solid metal and the system is claimed to carry a 20-kilo weight penalty.

The Xtrac option relies on Prodrive electronics for hydraulic actuation of differentials and powered

Photograph Martin Sharp

GET A GRIP — AND IMPROVE IT

Twelve days after Henri Toivonen perished in his Delta S4 in May 1986, I was talking to the distinguished rally engineer, Wynne Mitchell, in his office at Austin Rover Group Motorsport. ARG had prepared lightweight Group B Metro 6R4s for that fateful Tour of Corsica and Wynne was baffled. Malcolm Wilson's practice 6R4 had been prepared from a loose-surface car. When the late Tony Pond drove it, he pronounced, 'That's the nicest 6R4 I've ever driven'.

On the event Pond explained that Toivonen was pulling away from his lightweight 6R4 after three kilometres, saying, perhaps a little ambitiously, 'If I had my practice car I'd be in the first three'.

Those were the days when four-wheel drive was something of a black art, and Pond considered his car's weakness was that he couldn't get the power down out of corners.

Having measured the 'good' 6R4s and the 'bad' lightweight ones, and swapped bits between them, Mitchell had nearly cracked the conundrum.

'I reckon that these cars take on a set, and once they're settled…Michelin is investigating whether the lightweight mods affected the structural rigidity. It wasn't the weight, I think it was actually the structure that was influenced by those mods,' he said.

Eighteen years later, Aimé Chatard, Rallies Manager of Michelin Competition since 1993, recalled the time in 1998, when Michelin began proposing to teams that if they increased their cars' torsional rigidity, there would be greater potential for lateral force control. Mitchell had been essentially right: on dry asphalt, where the most grip is available, generally the stiffer the car, the better the tyres can be made to grip.

Since 1998 top rally cars have been revelling in astounding levels of grip and, as Chatard says, it is increasing step by step. His company, Michelin, has been consistently involved in World Championship rallying since it began in 1973, indeed, winning the first-ever World Championship Monte with Jean-Claude Andruet's Alpine-Renault A110. Well before then, the top three finishers on the '54 Monte were on Michelin Xs bought from local dealers, and the company's first official involvement came in 1963 when Citroën asked Michelin to come up with a suitable competition tyre for the DS. Michelin has had unparalleled success in the World Championship, equipping its 200th rally winner, Markko Märtin, in Finland in 2003.

Chatard considers that the astounding grip available today came first through getting the switch from slicks to moulded tyres right, then from being able to design tyres for cars capable of guaranteeing the maintenance of the tyre's footprint, through both improved chassis stiffness and optimised suspension design and geometry.

Michelin is involved in an exceptional range of activities, from motorcycle racing and off-road competition to Formula 1, yet it has 'good partnerships,' as Chatard terms them, with its rally teams. The choice of language is significant, for the car manufacturers aren't seen purely as customers. Here's to the next 200 victories.

gearshift systems, each system having a dedicated hydraulic accumulator, both situated in the engine compartment.

The Fabia's front siderails are 90mm closer together than those of the Octavia. This requires a shorter Xtrac gearbox through using thinner gears in the cluster, which do not compromise torque capacity. Combined with improved suspension design, these closer siderails contribute to an important 20mm more front wheel travel. The car also benefits from 15mm more rear wheel travel than the Octavia.

The complex roll cage employs larger-diameter tubes, of thinner wall section, than used previously. These are shaped according to the CAD data and

TECHNICAL REVIEW

Swing low, sweet chariots: Ford laid the intercooler and radiator flat, beneath the fans, to improve weight distribution (far left), while lowering the ride height was one of the advantages of Subaru's active dampers. New rear suspension geometry (above) demonstrated Ford's innovative approach.

assembled on a CAD-designed jig. Unusually — and logically — bodyshell assembly entails the finished roll cage being fitted first to the floorpan, which has a transmission tunnel of maximum permitted size to aid access, before the side panels and roof are added to complete the basic structure. This process has been developed to ensure optimum weld quality on the roll cage, because of the improved access to cage joints. It is not necessarily a swifter process than the more conventional method of fitting the cage to a pre-assembled bodyshell.

A new regulation for 2004 dictates that, within a tolerance of minus five kilogrammes, WR Cars' bodyshell and roll cage assemblies must weigh a minimum of 320 kilos, whereas earlier regulations were free in this regard. Henceforth, front wings may be in composite materials, and bonnets and boots — or rear hatches — may be aluminium. To comply with the rules, the 2003 Fabia bodyshell (which is 50% more rigid than the Octavia shell) is all steel and the FIA decided that the new Skoda had to comply with the 320-kilo rule in 2003. The switch to lighter panels for 2004 will therefore enable the team to further optimise the car's weight distribution with ballast.

The Fabia's transverse, 20-valve engine, which derived from the Octavia's, has been optimised for the new application by Lehmann and is canted rearwards around its crankshaft axis by the maximum permitted 25 degrees. As the standard Fabia engine leans back 13 degrees, the extra lean provides a small potential weight distribution improvement.

Designed by the Austrian engineer, Kurt Chabek, and using Reiger dampers, the Fabia WRC's front suspension conforms to the MacPherson strut convention, while a similar arrangement at the rear reflects current thinking in having two transverse links per side, with a third longitudinal link attached to the upright and extending 350mm forwards to pick up on a standard mounting.

A concentration, then, in 2003, on manipulating time through controlling aerodynamic forces, applying advanced levels of control to sophisticated systems. In a year when a new generation of drivers made their presence felt, the best engineers also played a starring role.

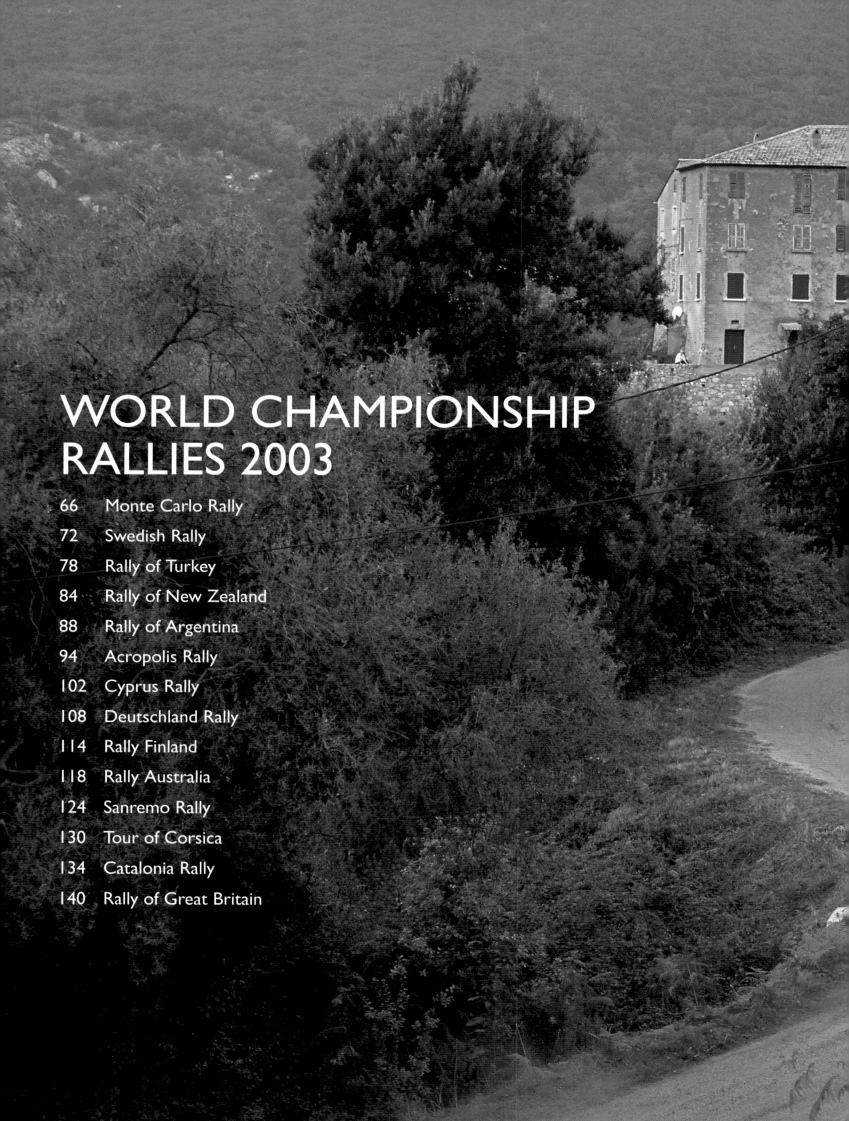

WORLD CHAMPIONSHIP RALLIES 2003

A World Championship rally is truly a circus coming to town in the 21st century, but if there wasn't much snow at Tallard, there was plenty at altitude. François Duval makes light of the slush (below), while Armin Schwarz, as ever, was in his element on the Monte for Hyundai. Portugal has gone, but its fans have not forgotten.

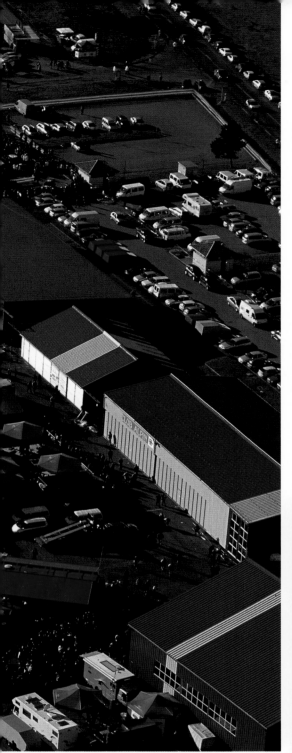

A. YOU CAN STEAL THE RALLYE
BUT NOT THE PASSION
- PORTUGAL -

MONTE CARLO RALLY

The missing front bumper – the consequence of a spin on the Col de Turini – was proof that the closing stages of the Monte Carlo Rally had been hard fought; predictably, Markko Märtin hadn't managed to fend off Carlos Sainz at the last gasp. He had squeezed ahead of the third Citroën in the first place largely because the Spaniard ran into brake trouble when a wheel bearing collapsed and once that was fixed, Sainz calmly repulsed the challenge on the last loop over the Turini to guarantee a Citroën sweep of the top three.

Given Märtin's limited Monte experience and Ford's desperately brief test on Michelins, that was no disgrace; and in truth, the Estonian had been the one cloud that scudded even momentarily across Citroën's horizon in the second half of the event. It was a result that exceeeded Guy Fréquelin's wildest dreams: the faulty wheel bearing was pretty much the only blemish on a peerless display of superb engineering and teamwork. There wasn't even a wrong tyre choice on a rally that offered more snow and consequently presented more difficult choices than usual. Fréquelin's troops couldn't have made a better start to their first full World Championship campaign. Vengeance for 2002's controversial defeat had been amply taken.

Yet without the magnificent Sébastien Loeb, the rally might easily have gone to Peugeot, for Marcus Grönholm was the early pacesetter. Even the first two stages were mostly Tarmac, but there was quite enough snow and ice to justify studs, and Grönholm was in his element. He was half a minute up after the two, while Loeb, starting ninth, drove warily, coping

with snow scattered across the road by earlier cars corner-cutting.

But the odds can veer with dizzying speed on the Monte and far from capitalising on his favourable starting position on Plan de Vitrolles, the formidable 29-miler run twice to conclude the first leg, Grönholm spun. Loeb regained time when he had expected to lose, then set a blistering pace on the second run to bring Grönholm within striking distance – and to his rivals' disbelief, he would have been quicker still if he hadn't spun.

Had the snow lingered, Grönholm might have stood a chance, but a 20-second lead against a former French Champion of Loeb's calibre was never likely to be enough in the Alpes-Maritimes on asphalt. Once he swapped studs for racers, Grönholm was never entirely at ease. Loeb mercilessly increased the pressure on the Col St. Raphaël and the rally was settled when the Finn cannoned into a wall and deranged the steering on the treacherous, snowy descent of the Col de Bleine. Peugeot made do with fifth from a dogged Richard Burns. It was a better result than Vélizy customarily achieves on the Monte, but a thumping defeat nonetheless.

Loeb appeared satisfied rather than elated. Once Grönholm dropped back, there was none of the pressure he had had to endure to win the Deutschland Rally four months previously. He had been the best part of a minute ahead of Colin McRae after the first leg and while the Scot also recorded his best Monte result, there had never been much question of challenging the victor.

RALLYCOURSE
MONTE CARLO RALLY

Sébastien Loeb's display was exemplary, the Citroëns in a league apart (top and far right) on classic mountain terrain. Petter Solberg looked threatening until he planted his Impreza into this bridge. Guy Wilks's battle-worn Puma survived near-enough everything the Alps threw at it (top right), only for the wheel studs to strip with the finish almost in sight.

MONTE CARLO RALLY

STATISTICS World Rally Championship **Round 1**

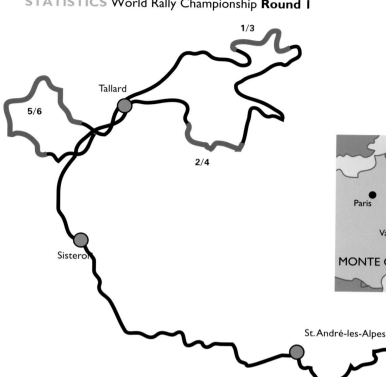

Monte Carlo Rally, January 24-26 2003,
FIA World Rally Championship Round 1

RUNNING ORDER

1	Marcus Grönholm/	Peugeot 206 WRC
	Timo Rautiainen	Gr A
7	Petter Solberg/	Subaru Impreza WRC2003
	Phil Mills	Gr A
19	Carlos Sainz/	Citroën Xsara WRC
	Marc Martí	Gr A
17	Colin McRae/	Citroën Xsara WRC
	Derek Ringer	Gr A
2	Richard Burns/	Peugeot 206 WRC
	Robert Reid	Gr A
3	Gilles Panizzi/	Peugeot 206 WRC
	Hervé Panizzi	Gr A
8	Tommi Mäkinen/	Subaru Impreza WRC2003
	Kaj Lindström	Gr A
4	Markko Märtin/	Ford Focus RS WRC02
	Michael Park	Gr A
18	Sébastien Loeb/	Citroën Xsara WRC
	Daniel Elena	Gr A
15	Toni Gardemeister/	Skoda Octavia WRC E3
	Paavo Lukander	Gr A
11	Freddy Loix/	Hyundai Accent WRC3
	Sven Smeets	Gr A
10	Armin Schwarz/	Hyundai Accent WRC3
	Manfred Hiemer	Gr A
20	Cédric Robert/	Peugeot 206 WRC
	Gérald Bedon	Gr A
22	Roman Kresta/	Peugeot 206 WRC
	Milos Hulka	Gr A
5	François Duval/	Ford Focus RS WRC02
	Jean-Marc Fortin	Gr A
14	Didier Auriol/	Skoda Octavia WRC E3
	Denis Giraudet	Gr A
6	Mikko Hirvonen/	Ford Focus RS WRC02
	Jarmo Lehtinen	Gr A
21	Anthony Warmbold/	Ford Focus RS WRC02
	Gemma Price	Gr A

SPECIAL STAGE TIMES

SS1 PRUNIERES 1 (28.36 KM)
1 M.Grönholm/T.Rautiainen (Peugeot 206 WRC) 18m07.6s;
2 P.Solberg/P.Mills (Subaru Impreza WRC2003) 18m11.8s;
3 C.McRae/D.Ringer (Citroën Xsara WRC) 18m15.9s;
4 C.Sainz/M.Martí (Citroën) 18m17.2s;
5 S.Loeb/D.Elena (Citroën Xsara WRC) 18m21.6s;
6 R.Burns/R.Reid (Peugeot 206 WRC) 18m24.4s; JWC
B.Tirabassi/J.Renucci (Renault Clio) 21m16.2s

SS2 SELONNET 1 (22.52 KM)
1 Grönholm/Rautiainen (Peugeot) 16m00.3s; 2 McRae/
Ringer (Citroën) 16m29.7s; 3 T.Mäkinen/K.Lindström
(Subaru Impreza WRC2003) 16m31.7s; 4 Solberg/Mills
(Subaru) 16m37.0s; 5 Loeb/Elena (Citroën) 16m41.5s; 6
Burns/Reid (Peugeot) 16m45.2s; JWC D.Carlsson/
M.Andersson (Suzuki Ignis) 18m12.2s

SS3 PRUNIERES 2 (28.36 KM)
1 Loeb/Elena (Citroën) 17m54.5s; 2 Solberg/Mills (Subaru)
18m01.1s; 3 McRae/Ringer (Citroën) 18m01.4s; 4 Grönholm/
Rautiainen (Peugeot) 18m08.5s; 5 Burns/Reid (Peugeot)
18m14.0s; 6 M.Märtin/M.Park (Ford Focus RS WRC02)
18m14.1s; JWC M.Baldacci/G.Bernacchini (Fiat Punto)
20m26.1s

SS4 SELONNET 2 (22.52 KM)
1 Grönholm/Rautiainen (Peugeot) 15m33.7s; 2 Solberg/Mills
(Subaru) 15m46.6s; 3 Burns/Reid (Peugeot) 15m47.9s;
4 Loeb/Elena (Citroën) 15m48.1s; 5 Sainz/Martí (Citroën)
15m54.0s; 6 R.Kresta/M.Hulka (Peugeot 206 WRC)
16m06.3s; JWC Carlsson/Andersson (Suzuki) 17m43.2s

SS5 PLAN DE VITROLLES 1 (47.27 KM)
1 Loeb/Elena (Citroën) 28m54.9; 2 Sainz/Martí (Citroën)
29m12.6s; 3 Grönholm/Rautiainen (Peugeot) 29m13.2s;
4 Märtin/Park (Ford) 29m22.2s; 5 Burns/Reid (Peugeot)
29m17.0s; 6 McRae/Ringer (Citroën) 29m37.8s; JWC
Carlsson/Andersson (Suzuki) 33m21.5s

SS6 PLAN DE VITROLLES 2 (47.27 KM)
1= Loeb/Elena (Citroën), McRae/Ringer (Citroën)
30m04.7s; 3 Sainz/Martí (Citroën) 30m21.1s; 4
Grönholm/Rautiainen (Peugeot) 30m21.4s; 5 Burns/Reid
(Peugeot) 30m40.1s; 6 Märtin/Park (Ford) 30m43.2s ;
JWC Carlsson/Andersson (Suzuki) 34m51.6s

SS7 LES 4 CHEMINS 1 (32.11 KM)
Cancelled - spectators

SS8 SAINT ANTONIN 1 (25.15 KM)
1 Loeb/Elena (Citroën) 18m08.8s; 2 McRae/Ringer (Citroën)
18m13.6s; 3 Grönholm/Rautiainen (Peugeot) 18m15.8s; 4
Märtin/Park (Ford) 18m15.9s; 5 Sainz/Martí (Citroën)
18m17.3s; 6 C.Robert/G.Bedon (Peugeot 206 WRC)
18m22.0s; JWC M.Ligato/R.Garcia (Fiat Punto) 19m52.5s

SS9 LES 4 CHEMINS 2 (32.11 KM)
1 Loeb/Elena (Citroën) 24m59.3s; 2 Sainz/Martí (Citroën)
25m09.0s; 3 Märtin/Park (Ford) 25m12.9s; 4 McRae/Ringer
(Citroën) 25m13.6s; 5 Kresta/Hulka (Peugeot) 25m22.0s;
6 Robert/Bedon (Peugeot) 25m35.3s; JWC No times

SS10 SAINT ANTONIN 2 (25.15 KM)
1 Sainz/Martí (Citroën) 17m52.3s; 2 McRae/Ringer (Citroën)
17m53.4s; 3 Märtin/Park (Ford) 17m54.2s; 4 Grönholm/
Rautiainen (Peugeot) 18m00.5s; 5 Loeb/Elena (Citroën)
18m01.4s; 16m21.4s; 6 F.Duval/J-M.Fortin (Ford Focus
WRC02) 18m01.9s; JWC No times

SS11 SOSPEL 1 (32.58 KM)
1 McRae/Ringer (Citroën) 25m30.6s; 2 Loeb/Elena (Citroën)
25m33.6s; 3 Grönholm/Rautiainen (Peugeot) 25m44.6s;
4 Robert/Bedon (Peugeot) 25m45.1s; 5 Duval/Fortin
(Ford) 25m46.5s; 6 Märtin/Park (Ford) 25m49.4s; JWC
Tirabassi/Renucci (Renault) 28m57.7s

SS12 LANTOSQUE 1 (19.52 KM)
1 Märtin/Park (Ford) 14m09.4s; 2 Duval/Fortin (Ford)
14m11.4s; 3 Burns/Reid (Peugeot) 14m15.9s; 4 A.Schwarz/
M.Hiemer (Hyundai Accent WRC3) 14m27.7s; 5 D.Auriol/
D.Giraudet (Skoda Octavia WRC E3) 14m35.4s; 6 Sainz/
Martí (Citroën) 14m46.4s; JWC K.Katajamäki/A.Niikka
(VW Polo) 15m48.7s

SS13 SOSPEL 2 (32.58 KM)
1 Sainz/Martí (Citroën) 24m52.0s; 2 Märtin/Park (Ford)
24m56.9s; 3 Duval/Fortin (Ford) 25m02.1s; 4 McRae/Ringer
(Citroën) 25m14.8s; 5 Burns/Reid (Peugeot) 25m17.5s;
6 Schwarz/Hiemer (Hyundai) 25m20.1s; JWC Tirabassi/
Renucci (Renault) 28m01.1s

SS14 LANTOSQUE 2 (19.52 KM)
1 Sainz/Martí (Citroën) 13m46.1s; 2 Märtin/Park (Ford)
13m52.8s; 3 Duval/Fortin (Ford) 13m58.5s; 4 McRae/Ringer
(Citroën) 14m02.7s; 5 Robert/Bredon (Peugeot)
14m05.8s; 6 Burns/Reid (Peugeot) 14m09.7s; JWC
Baldacci/Bernacchini (Fiat) 15m42.4s

MAJOR RETIREMENTS

7	Solberg/Mills	Subaru Impreza WRC2003
	Accident SS5	Gr A
3	Panizzi/Panizzi	Peugeot 206 WRC
	Withdrawn SS8	Gr A
8	Mäkinen/Lindström	Subaru Impreza WRC2003
	Accident SS5	Gr A
15	Gardemeister/L'der	Skoda Octavia WRC E3
	Engine SS2	Gr A
11	Loix/Smeets	Hyundai Accent WRC3
	Accident SS9	Gr A
6	Hirvonen/Lehtinen	Ford Focus RS WRC02
	Accident SS9	Gr A

FIA CLASS WINNERS

A8 Over 2000 cc	Loeb/Elena
	(Citroën Xsara WRC)
A6 1400-1600 cc	Jean-Joseph/Boyère
	Renault Clio

RALLY LEADERS

Overall: SS1-8 Grönholm; SS9-14 Loeb
JWC: SS1 Tirabassi; SS2 Carlsson; SS3-5 Tirabassi; SS6
Carlsson; SS8-14 Tirabassi (SS7 cancelled)

SPECIAL STAGE ANALYSIS

	1st	2nd	3rd	4th	5th	6th
Loeb (Citroën)	5	1	-	1	3	-
Sainz (Citroën)	3	2	1	1	2	2
Grönholm (Peugeot)	3	-	3	3	-	-
McRae (Citroën)	2	3	2	3	-	1
Märtin (Ford)	1	2	2	2	-	3
Solberg (Subaru)	-	3	-	1	-	-
Duval (Ford)	-	1	2	-	1	1
Burns (Peugeot)	-	-	2	-	4	3
Mäkinen (Subaru)	-	-	1	-	-	-
Robert (Peugeot)	-	-	-	1	1	2
Schwarz (Hyundai)	-	-	-	1	-	1
Kresta (Peugeot)	-	-	-	-	1	1
Auriol (Skoda)	-	-	-	-	1	-

WORLD CHAMPIONSHIP POINTS

Drivers
1 Loeb 10; 2 McRae 8; 3 Sainz 6; 4 Märtin 5; 5 Burns 4;
6 Robert 3; 7 Duval 2; 8 Schwarz 1

Manufacturers
1 Citroën 18; 2 Ford 10; 3 Peugeot 6; 4 Hyundai 3;
5 Skoda 2

Junior World Championship
1 Tirabassi 10; 2 Ligato 8; 3 Broccoli 6; 4 Aava 5; 5
Ceccato 4; 6 Sebalj 3; 7 Baldacci 2; 8 Harrach 1

ROUTE DETAILS

Total route of 1390.03 km of which 382.91 km were
competitive on 13 stages (1 cancelled totalling 32.11 km)

Leg 1 Friday 24 January, 6 special stages totalling 196.30 km
Leg 2 Saturday 25 January, 3 special stages totalling 82.41
km (1 cancelled totalling 32.11km)
Leg 3 Sunday 26 January, 4 special stages totalling 104.20 km

RECENT WINNERS

RESULTS

	Driver/Co-driver	Car	Time	Class
1	Sébastien Loeb/Daniel Elena	Citroën Xsara WRC	4h29m11.4s	
2	Colin McRae/Derek Ringer	Citroën Xsara WRC	4h29m49.5s	Gr A
3	Carlos Sainz/Luis Moya	Citroën Xsara WRC	4h30m03.6s	Gr A
4	Markko Märtin/Michael Park	Ford Focus RS WRC02	4h30m06.9s	
5	Richard Burns/Robert Reid	Peugeot 206 WRC	4h32m27.9s	Gr A
6	Cédric Robert/Gérald Bedon	Peugeot 206 WRC	4h34m28.1s	Gr A
7	François Duval/Jean-Marc Fortin	Ford Focus RS WRC02	4h34m28.5s	Gr A
8	Armin Schwarz/Manfred Hiemer	Hyundai Accent WRC3	4h35m53.7s	Gr A
9	Didier Auriol/Denis Giraudet	Skoda Octavia WRC E3	4h36m25.2s	Gr A
10	Roman Kresta/Milos Hulka	Peugeot 206 WRC	4h37m02.3s	Gr A

51 starters, 30 finishers

STAGE NUMBERS	1	3	4	5	6	7	8	9	10	11	12	13	14
Loeb	5	4	4	3	2	2	2	1	1	1	1	1	1
McRae	3	2	2	4	3	3	3	2	2	2	2	2	2
Sainz	4	7	7	6	5	5	4	3	3	3	4	4	3
Märtin	8	8	6	7	6	6	6	4	4	4	3	3	4
Burns	6	6	5	5	4	4	5	5	5	5	5	5	5
Robert	9	9	8	8	7	7	7	6	6	6	6	6	6
Duval	10	10	10	12	11	10	8	9	8	7	7	7	7
Schwarz	11	13	13	11	9	8	9	8	9	9	8	8	8
Auriol	13	12	11	13	10	11	11	10	10	10	10	9	9
Kresta	12	11	12	10	8	9	10	7	7	8	9	10	10
Grönholm	11	1	1	1	1	1	15	15	14	13	13	13	
Loix	14	15	14	14	12	12	12	R					
Hirvonen	15	14	15	15	13	13	13	R					
Panizzi	16	16	16	16	14	14	R						
Solberg	2	3	3	2	R								
Mäkinen	7	5	9	9	R								
G'meister	21	R											

FINISH LINES

Cédric Robert was Peugeot's star performer, catching the eye with sixth place in a customer-tune 206 WRC... François Duval finished seventh, only a whisker behind Robert, but a shade lucky to get away with spinning into a tree and ripping a rear wheel off his works Focus in the first leg... Subaru's rally was over by SS4, both Petter Solberg and Tommi Mäkinen leaving the road... Brice Tirabassi romped to a comfortable Junior Championship class victory in his Clio once Suzuki's lead driver, Daniel Carlsson, went OTL when detained for speeding by the police, but the 1600cc class was won by Tirabassi's team-mate, Simon Jean-Joseph, who is too old to qualify for the championship... Gilles Panizzi's season got off to a disastrous start, the Peugeot-driving Frenchman being penalised a minute by the stewards for practising without the regulation GPS transmitter... Mikko Hirvonen's first rally as an unofficial works driver ended with his Focus a considerable distance from the road on the Col de Bleine, the Finn outwitted by a patch of ice when driving on racers... Guy Wilks looked set for Junior points on his first Monte until his Puma stripped its wheel studs and lost a wheel with the finish in sight... Kosti Katajamäki finished second of the Juniors on the road, but was subsequently excluded when it emerged that Volkswagen had made an error on the homologation form and his Polo's rear caliper pistons were smaller than those specified...

Rallying after dusk is widely frowned on in the 21st-century World Championship, but as Marcus Grönholm demonstrates, lights gleaming, brake discs glowing, it's uniquely atmospheric.

To say that there were some angry and frustrated Peugeot drivers in Karlstad would have been a gross understatement. Under normal circumstances, Juuso Pykälisto might have achieved a respectable finish on the Swedish Rally, despite rolling his semi-works 206. Spectators soon had the car on its wheels, but then he stalled the engine and as the crowd scattered, he was struck amidships by the works driver, Harri Rovanperä. Both retired on the spot. As for Richard Burns, one needed to check the results to remind oneself that he had achieved a rare and difficult feat. He became only the sixth non-Nordic driver in the event's 50-year history to finish in the first three.

Naturally, Burns wasn't especially concerned with fusty statistics. He loves fast stages and had liked to think that he could carry the attack to Marcus Grönholm. However, he couldn't persuade his 206 to hold its line through long corners and, to his undisguised fury he discovered not only that the brake pedal lacked feel, but that Peugeot hadn't brought any of his preferred pads on the assumption that the replacements were better. It said a good deal for the 206's intrinsic qualities – and for Burns's for that matter – that he outpaced the Fords and Citroëns by a convincing margin nevertheless.

Burns's disappointment was understandable. As his third place indicated, the Peugeot was very definitely the car to have, yet there was no disguising that this had been a one-horse race. Drivers invariably recoil from any suggestion that winning is easy, but Marcus Grönholm had to rack his brains to think of any kind of setback. In the end, he suggested that perhaps he had started a little too slowly. He hadn't taken the lead until SS2. Even the weather had run in his favour, as fresh snow the night before the start meant that the first few cars had to plough tracks for the rest and therefore his poor Monte result turned to his advantage. He was 27 seconds ahead by the end of the first leg – a secure margin by Swedish standards – and experienced little difficulty in extending it to 50 by the end. He might fairly be said to have won at a canter.

Even so, there was no disguising the runner-up's delight, for Tommi Mäkinen had the demeanour of someone who has unlocked the key to a mystery. For the first time in months, he seemed at one with the Subaru. The fact that his team-mate, Petter Solberg, was plainly not at ease no doubt added to his satisfaction, but the rally had gone better than Tommi had dared hope. As he explained, Subaru hadn't put much effort into testing, on the basis that the results were unlikely to be especially good. It was a mute testimony to the expected performance of Pirelli's snow tyres and given that he had driven with such aggression, it raised the tempting idea that he might have given Grönholm real trouble if he had been on Michelins.

It was a difficult thought to sustain for long: if it hadn't been for engine failure in 2001, Grönholm would have triumphed for the fourth year running. He hadn't won single-handed, but on snow he has no peers.

SWEDISH RALLY

RALLYCOURSE World Rally Championship **Round 2**

The idea of beating Marcus Grönholm in Sweden is more fantasy than ambition, although Richard Burns (top left), out of sorts with the handling and brakes, had hoped to deny his Peugeot team-mate his third victory in four years; he was third. Tommi Mäkinen was far better pleased with second, delivering his most impressive performance for Subaru in months. Jussi Välimäki's first official outing for Hyundai (right) showed only fleeting promise.

SWEDISH RALLY

Oddly, Petter Solberg's rallycross background means that he isn't in his element at 100 mph on a narrow, snow-covered forest track. The Norwegian (top right) was thrilled that he had made progress. For Colin McRae, Sweden is a home from home (above), although like Carlos Sainz (right), he found that the Xsara needed refinement. As Kristian Kolberg demonstrates, Hyundai is gaining ground with privateers.

SWEDISH RALLY

International Swedish Rally, 8-10 February 2003,
FIA World Rally Championship Round 2

RUNNING ORDER

18	Sébastien Loeb/ Daniel Elena	Citroën Xsara WRC Gr A
17	Colin McRae/ Derek Ringer	Citroën Xsara WRC Gr A
19	Carlos Sainz/ Marc Marti	Citroën Xsara WRC Gr A
4	Markko Märtin/ Michael Park	Ford Focus RS WRC02 Gr A
2	Richard Burns/ Robert Reid	Peugeot 206 WRC Gr A
5	François Duval/ Jean-Marc Fortin	Ford Focus RS WRC02 Gr A
10	Armin Schwarz/ Manfred Hiemer	Hyundai Accent WRC3 Gr A
14	Didier Auriol/ Denis Giraudet	Skoda Octavia WRC E3 Gr A
1	Marcus Grönholm/ Timo Rautiainen	Peugeot 206 WRC Gr A
15	Toni Gardemeister/ Paavo Lukander	Skoda Octavia WRC E3 Gr A
6	Mikko Hirvonen/ Jarmo Lehtinen	Ford Focus RS WRC02 Gr A
11	Freddy Loix/ Sven Smeets	Hyundai Accent WRC3 Gr A
8	Tommi Mäkinen/ Kaj Lindström	Subaru Impreza WRC2003 Gr A
7	Petter Solberg/ Phil Mills	Subaru Impreza WRC2003 Gr A
3	Harri Rovanperä/ Risto Pietilainen	Peugeot 206 WRC Gr A
12	Jussi Välimäki/ Tero Gardemeister	Hyundai Accent WRC3 Gr A
24	Roman Kresta/ Milos Hulka	Peugeot 206 WRC Gr A
21	Janne Tuohino/ Jukka Aho	Ford Focus RS WRC02 Gr A
22	Tomasz Kuchar/ Maciek S'paniak	Ford Focus RS WRC01 Gr A
32	Juuso Pykälistö/ Esko Mertsalmi	Peugeot 206 WRC Gr A
35	Kristian Sohlberg/ Jakke Honkanen	Mitsubishi Lancer WRC2 Gr A

SPECIAL STAGE TIMES

SS1 SAGEN 1 (14.17 KM)
1 S.Loeb/D.Elena (Citroën Xsara WRC) 7m25.6s; 2 R.Burns/
R.Reid (Peugeot 206 WRC) 7m26.2s; 3 M.Grönholm/
T.Rautiainen (Peugeot 206 WRC) 7m26.7s; 4 T.Mäkinen/
K.Lindström (Subaru Impreza WRC2003) 7m32.7s;
5= H.Rovanperä/R.Pietilainen (Peugeot 206 WRC),
M.Märtin/M.Park (Ford Focus RS WRC02), C.McRae/
D.Ringer (Citroën Xsara WRC) 7m33.2s; PC T.Arai/
T.Sircombe (Subaru Impreza WRX) 8m14.2s

SS2 RAMMEN 1 (23.16 KM)
1 Grönholm/Rautiainen (Peugeot) 12m05.5s; 2 Rovanperä/
Pietilainen (Peugeot) 12m13.6s; 3 Burns/Reid (Peugeot)
12m14.2s; 4 Mäkinen/Lindström (Subaru) 12m15.4s;
5 J.Tuohino/J.Aho (Ford Focus RS WRC02) 12m17.7s;
6 Pykälistö/E.Mertsalmi (Peugeot 206 WRC) 12m18.4s;
PC No times

SS3 GRANBERGET 1 (43.69 KM)
1 Grönholm/Rautiainen (Peugeot) 21m43.9s; 2 Mäkinen/
Lindström (Subaru) 21m52.2s; 3 Rovanperä/Pietilainen
(Peugeot) 21m59.8s; 4 Burns/Reid (Peugeot) 22m01.0s;

5 Pykälistö/Mertsalmi (Peugeot) 22m02.0s; 6 McRae/Ringer
(Citroën) 22m05.6s; PC Arai/Sircombe (Subaru) 23m47.5s

SS4 MALTA (11.25 KM)
1 Grönholm/Rautiainen (Peugeot) 5m39.1s; 2 Mäkinen/
Lindström (Subaru) 5m41.2s; 3 Rovanperä/Pietilainen
(Peugeot) 5m42.7s; 4 Burns/Reid (Peugeot) 5m45.5s;
5= P.Solberg/P.Mills (Subaru Impreza WRC2003),
C.Sainz/M.Marti (Citroën Xsara WRC) 5m46.2s;
PC S.Blomqvist/A.Goni (Subaru Impreza WRX) 6m16.8s

SS5 BRUNNBERG 1 (31.50 KM)
Cancelled – Duval accident

SS6 HAGFORS SPRINT 1 (1.86 KM)
1 Burns/Reid (Peugeot) 1m58.0s; 2 Märtin/Park (Ford)
1m58.4s; 3 Sainz/Marti (Citroën) 1m58.8s; 4 Grönholm/
Rautiainen (Peugeot) 1m59.0s; 6 Mäkinen/Lindström (Subaru) 1m59.6s;
PC Blomqvist/Goni (Subaru) 2m07.5s

SS7 GRANBERGET 2 (43.69 km)
1 Rovanperä/Pietilainen (Peugeot) 21m28.0s; 2 Mäkinen/
Lindström (Subaru) 21m30.6s; 3 Grönholm/Rautiainen
(Peugeot) 21m32.1s; 4 Burns/Reid (Peugeot) 21m32.9s;
5 McRae/Ringer (Citroën) 21m34.5s; 6 Märtin/Park (Ford)
21m35.6s; PC Arai/Sircombe (Subaru) 23m28.0s

SS8 FREDRIKSBERG (18.14 KM)
Stage stopped due to Rovanperä and Pykälistö colliding.
Notional times given.

SS9 LEJEN (25.04 KM)
1 Grönholm/Rautiainen (Peugeot) 11m56.2s; 2 Mäkinen/
Lindström (Subaru) 12m01.9s; 3 Loeb/Elena (Citroën)
12m05.3s; 4= McRae/Ringer (Citroën), Märtin/Park (Ford)
12m09.3s; 6 Burns/Reid (Peugeot) 12m09.6s; PC Arai/
Sircombe (Subaru) 13m10.6s

SS10 VARGASEN (32.43 KM)
1 Grönholm/Rautiainen (Peugeot) 18m08.7s; 2 Mäkinen/
Lindström (Subaru) 18m12.7s; 3 Loeb/Elena (Citroën)
18m14.5s; 4 Burns/Reid (Peugeot) 18m16.6s; 5 McRae/
Ringer (Citroën) 18m18.3s; 6 Märtin/Park (Ford)
18m21.5s; PC Arai/Sircombe (Subaru) 19m57.6s

SS11 TORNTORP (19.21 KM)
1 Grönholm/Rautiainen (Peugeot) 10m12.7s; 2 Loeb/Elena
(Citroën) 10m14.6s; 3= Mäkinen/Lindström (Subaru),
McRae/Ringer (Citroën) 10m17.3s; 5 Märtin/Park (Ford)
10m20.4s; 6 Burns/Reid (Peugeot) 10m21.3s; PC J.Kulig/
J.Baran (Mitsubishi Lancer E6) 11m12.8s

SS12 HAGFORS SPRINT 2 (1.86 KM)
1 Mäkinen/Lindström (Subaru) 1m56.8s; 2 Burns/Reid
(Peugeot) 1m56.9s; 3 Märtin/Park (Ford) 1m57.3s; 4 Sainz/

Marti (Citroën) 1m57.5s; 5 Solberg/Mills (Subaru) 1m57.6s;
6 Grönholm/Rautiainen (Peugeot) 1m57.8s; PC Arai/
Sircombe (Subaru) 2m06.7s

SS13 Sagen 2 (14.17 km)
1 Mäkinen/Lindström (Subaru) 7m19.1s; 2 Loeb/Elena
(Citroën) 7m19.5s; 3 Grönholm/Rautiainen (Peugeot)
7m20.6s; 4 Burns/Reid (Peugeot) 7m21.4s; 5 Märtin/Park
(Ford) 7m22.5s; 6 Solberg/Mills (Subaru) 7m22.6s; PC Arai/
Sircombe (Subaru) 8m07.8s

SS14 RAMMEN 2 (23.16 KM)
1 Grönholm/Rautiainen (Peugeot) 11m41.4s; 2 Mäkinen/
Lindström (Subaru) 11m43.1s; 3 McRae/Ringer (Citroën)
11m45.7s; 4 Märtin/Park (Ford) 11m46.5s; 5 Burns/Reid
(Peugeot) 11m47.4s; 6 Solberg/Mills (Subaru) 11m47.9s;
PC Blomqvist/Goni (Subaru) 12m51.5s

SS15 HARA (11.91 KM)
1 McRae/Ringer (Citroën) 5m55.4s; 2 Grönholm/
Rautiainen (Peugeot) 5m56.4s; 3 Mäkinen/Lindström
(Subaru) 5m57.1s; 4 Märtin/Park (Ford) 5m59.0s; 5 Solberg/
Mills (Subaru) 5m59.5s; 6 Burns/Reid (Peugeot) 5m59.6s;
PC K.Singh/A.Oh (Proton Pert) 6m37.2s

SS16 BRUNNBERG 2 (31.66 KM)
1 Märtin/Park (Ford) 15m08.7s; 2 Grönholm/Rautiainen
(Peugeot) 15m11.7s; 3 Loeb/Elena (Citroën) 15m15.5s;
4 Solberg/Mills (Subaru) 15m16.0s; 5 McRae/Ringer
(Citroën) 15m18.7s; 6 Mäkinen/Lindström (Subaru)
15m18.8s; PC Kulig/Baran (Mitsubishi) 16m44.2s

SS17 HAGFORS (39.85 KM)
1 Solberg/Mills (Subaru) 19m40.0s; 2 Märtin/Park (Ford)
19m42.1s; 3 Loeb/Elena (Citroën) 19m45.7s; 4 Burns/Reid
(Peugeot) 19m46.3s; 5 McRae/Ringer (Citroën) 19m47.7s;
6 Grönholm/Rautiainen (Peugeot) 19m48.9s; PC Kulig/
Baran (Mitsubishi) 21m38.7s

MAJOR RETIREMENTS

5	Duval/Fortin	Ford Focus RS WRC02		
	Accident	SS5		Gr A
3	Rovanperä/P'lainen	Peugeot 206 WRC		
	Accident	SS8		Gr A
17	Välimäki/G'meister	Hyundai Accent WRC3		
	T'mission	SS7		Gr A
32	Pykälistö/Mertsalmi	Peugeot 206 WRC		
	Accident	SS8		Gr A

FIA CLASS WINNERS

A8 Over 2000 cc		Grönholm/Rautiainen Peugeot 206 WRC
N4 Over 2000 cc		Bäcklund/Holmstrand Mitsubishi Lancer E7
N3 1600-2000 cc		Wikström/Fredriksson Renault Clio Sport

RALLY LEADERS

Overall: SS1 Loeb; SS2-17 Grönholm
PC: SS1-15 Arai; SS16 Blomqvist; SS17 Kulig
(SS5 cancelled)

SPECIAL STAGE ANALYSIS

	1st	2nd	3rd	4th	5th	6th
Grönholm (Peugeot)	7	2	3	1	-	2
Mäkinen (Subaru)	2	6	2	2	-	2
Loeb (Citroën)	1	2	4	-	-	-
Burns (Peugeot)	1	2	1	6	1	3
Märtin (Ford)	1	2	1	3	3	2
Rovanperä (Peugeot)	1	1	2	-	1	-
McRae (Citroën)	1	-	2	1	6	1
Solberg (Subaru)	1	-	-	1	3	2
Sainz (Citroën)	-	-	1	1	1	-
Pykälistö (Peugeot)	-	-	-	1	1	1
Tuohino (Ford)	-	-	1	-	-	-

WORLD CHAMPIONSHIP POINTS

Drivers
1= Loeb, McRae 12; 3= Grönholm, Burns, Märtin 10; 6
Mäkinen 8; 7 Sainz 6; 8= Robert, Solberg 3; 10 Duval 2 etc

Manufacturers
1 Citroën 24; 2 Peugeot 22; 3 Ford 15; 4 Subaru 11; 5=
Hyundai, Skoda 3

Junior World Championship
1 Tirabassi 10; 2 Ligato 8; 3 Broccoli 6; 4 Aava 5; 5
Ceccato 4; 6 Sebalj 3; 7 Baldacci 2; 8 Harrach 1

Production Cup
1 Blomqvist 10; 2 Singh 8; 3 Rowe 6; 4 Bourne 5; 5
Holowczyc 4; 6 Roman 3; 7 Sztuka 2; 8 Richard 1

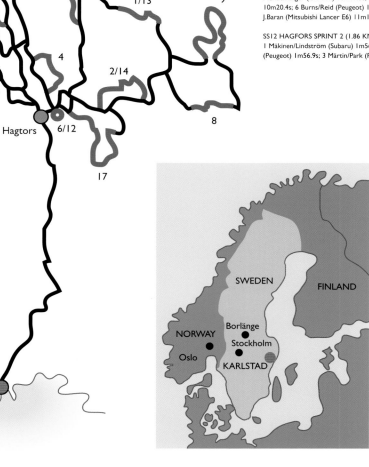

Torsby

3/7

5/16

15

11

4

1/13

9

2/14

10

Hagtors

6/12

8

17

KARLSTAD

SWEDEN

FINLAND

NORWAY

Borlänge

Stockholm

Oslo

KARLSTAD

ROUTE DETAILS

Total route of 1935.13 km of which 355.41 km were competitive on 16 stages (1 cancelled totalling 31.50 km)

Leg 1 Friday 7th February, 5 Special Stages totalling 94.29km (1 cancelled totalling 31.50km)
Leg 2 Saturday 8th February, 6 Special Stages totalling 140.37 km
Leg 3 Sunday 9th February, 5 Special Stages totalling 120.75 km

RESULTS

1	Marcus Grönholm/	Peugeot 206 WRC	
	Timo Rautiainen	3h03m28.1s	
2	Tommi Mäkinen/	Subaru Impreza WRC2003	
	Kaj Lindström	3h04m18.9s	Gr A
3	Richard Burns/	Peugeot 206 WRC	
	Robert Reid	3h04m46.0s	Gr A
4	Markko Märtin/	Ford Focus RS WRC02	
	Michael Park	3h05m13.9sGr A	
5	Colin McRae/	Citroën Xsara WRC	
	Derek Ringer	3h05m43.9s	Gr A
6	Petter Solberg/	Subaru Impreza WRC2003	
	Phil Mills	3h05m47.2s	Gr A
7	Sébastien Loeb/	Citroën Xsara WRC	
	Daniel Elena	3h06m42.8s	Gr A
8	Toni Gardemeister/	Skoda Octavia WRC E3	
	Paavo Lukander	3h06m47.3s	Gr A
9	Carlos Sainz/	Citroën Xsara WRC	
	Marc Marti	3h06m52.3s	Gr A
10	Freddy Loix/	Hyundai Accent WRC3	
	Sven Smeets	3h07m04.5s	Gr A

75 starters, 54 finishers

One of the stars the year before, François Duval made an impact once more, but of the entirely wrong kind.

RECENT WINNERS

1965	Tom Trana/Gunnar Thermenius	Volvo 544
1966	Ake Andersson/Sven-Olof Svedberg	Saab 96
1967	Bengt Soderström/Gunnar Palm	Ford Lotus Cortina
1968	Björn Waldegård/Lars Helmer	Porsche 911T
1969	Björn Waldegård/Lars Helmer	Porsche 911S
1970	Björn Waldegård/Lars Helmer	Porsche 911S
1971	Stig Blomqvist/Arne Hertz	Saab 96 V4
1972	Stig Blomqvist/Arne Hertz	Saab 96 V4
1973	Stig Blomqvist/Arne Hertz	Saab 96 V4
1975	Björn Waldegård/Hans Thorszelius	Lancia Stratos
1976	Per Eklund/Björn Cederberg	Saab 96 V4
1977	Stig Blomqvist/Hans Sylvan	Saab 99 EMS
1978	Björn Waldegård/Hans Thorszelius	Ford Escort RS
1979	Stig Blomqvist/Björn Cederberg	Saab 99 Turbo
1980	Anders Kullang/Bruno Berglund	Opel Ascona 400
1981	Hannu Mikkola/Arne Hertz	Audi Quattro
1982	Stig Blomqvist/Björn Cederberg	Audi Quattro A1
1983	Hannu Mikkola/Arne Hertz	Audi Quattro A1
1984	Stig Blomqvist/Björn Cederberg	Audi Quattro A2
1985	Ari Vatanen/Terry Harryman	Peugeot 205 Turbo 16
1986	Juha Kankkunen/Juha Piironen	Peugeot 205 Turbo 16 E2
1987	Timo Salonen/Seppo Harjanne	Mazda 323 Turbo
1988	Markku Alén/Ilkka Kivimäki	Lancia Delta HF 4x4
1989	Ingvar Carlsson/Per Carlsson	Mazda 323 Turbo
1991	Kenneth Eriksson/Staffan Parmander	
		Mitsubishi Galant VR-4
1992	Mats Jonsson/Lars Bäckman	Toyota Celica GT4
1993	Mats Jonsson/Lars Bäckman	Toyota Celica Turbo 4wd
1994	Thomas Rådström/Lars Bäckman	Toyota Celica Turbo 4wd
1995	Kenneth Eriksson/Staffan Parmander	
		Mitsubishi Lancer RS-E2
1996	Tommi Mäkinen/Seppo Harjanne	Mitsubishi Lancer RS-E3
1997	Kenneth Eriksson/Staffan Parmander	
		Subaru Impreza WRC97
1998	Tommi Mäkinen/Risto Mannisenmäki	Mitsubishi Lancer E4
1999	Tommi Mäkinen/Risto Mannisenmäki	Mitsubishi Lancer E6
2000	Marcus Grönholm/Timo Rautiainen	Peugeot 206 WRC
2001	Harri Rovanperä/Risto Pietilainen	Peugeot 206 WRC
2002	Marcus Grönholm/Timo Rautiainen	Peugeot 206 WRC

FINISH LINES

Markko Märtin won a duel with Colin McRae comfortably in the end, backing off as the finish neared and making sure of fourth place in the top Focus. He won 80 euros in the process, having taken a bet with McRae that he would be quicker on SS13... A spin during the first leg cost the Scot 20 seconds, but he was generally the quickest Citroën driver and recovered strongly to take fifth... François Duval retired on SS5 after hitting a snowbank and ripping the front wheels off his works Focus... Toni Gardemeister was highly impressive, holding a place in the top six for a while and finishing eighth in his Octavia... Janusz Kulig looked to have taken maximum Production Championship points by a whisker, only to see victory handed to Stig Blomqvist, driving a Subaru, when scrutineering revealed that the Pole's Mitsubishi had an illegal flywheel... Toshiro Arai had been well in contention for victory until his Impreza's turbo blew on SS15... Leaving aside championship registration, there had never been much doubt that a Swede would win the class, Kenneth Bäcklund sweeping to victory in his Evo VII... Freddy Loix was the pick of the Hyundai drivers, but a dire lack of testing restricted him to tenth... Jussi Välimäki retired his Accent at the beginning of the second leg with broken transmission...

STAGE NUMBERS	1	2	3	4	5	6	7	8	9	10	11	12	14	15	16	17
Grönholm	3	1	1	1	1	1	1	1	1	1	1	1	1	1	1	1
Mäkinen	4	4	2	2	2	2	2	2	2	2	2	2	2	2	2	2
Burns	2	2	3	3	3	3	3	3	3	3	3	3	3	3	3	3
Märtin	5	9	8	7	7	5	4	4	4	4	4	4	4	4	4	4
McRae	5	22	14	14	13	11	8	7	5	5	5	5	5	5	5	5
Solberg	13	12	11	8	8	7	5	5	6	6	6	6	6	6	6	
Loeb	1	6	18	18	18	15	13	12	11	10	10	10	10	9	9	7
G'meister	9	5	6	6	6	8	6	6	7	7	7	7	7	7	7	8
Sainz	8	8	13	12	12	13	10	9	8	8	8	8	8	8	8	9
Loix	15	13	9	10	9	9	7	8	9	9	9	9	9	10	10	10
Hirvonen	11	15	15	16	16	15	16	14	14	12	12	12	12	11	11	11
Sohlberg	13	11	10	11	11	12	11	11	13	16	15	13	13	12	12	
Schwarz	19	19	17	17	16	14	12	13	14	13	13	13	12	12	13	13
Tuohino	16	10	7	9	9	10	9	10	10	11	11	11	19	19	19	17
Auriol	18	18	23	23	22	20	18	18	17	17	17	17	16	17	17	18
Rovanperä	5	3	4	4	4	4	R									
Pykälisto	11	7	5	5	5	6	R									
Välimäki	17	14	12	13	14	R										
Duval	10	17	19	19	R											

RALLY OF TURKEY

RALLYCOURSE World Rally Championship **Round 3**

It would be misleading to suggest that Carlos Sainz is inclined to see the glass as half-empty; he tends to the view that it may be knocked over at any moment. After 15 years at the pinnacle of the sport, he is in no danger of taking anything for granted and even after he bounded into a secure-looking lead on Myra, the tenth of the Rally of Turkey's 18 stages, he was keen to emphasise that victory was far from assured.

Indeed, Sainz had spent much of the week radiating pessimism. His loose-surface experience in the Xsara prior to the shakedown amounted to two days in Portugal that had been badly affected by rain. He didn't feel fully attuned to the car and he didn't need to remind anyone that it was nothing like as highly developed for the loose as it was for asphalt.

Besides, the stages didn't invite complacency. New additions to the World Championship are apt to spring surprises and Turkey more than lived up to expectations. Snow in the Daglari Mountains forced last-minute re-routes and the roughness of the roads caught many drivers unawares. The Imprezas were certainly capable of winning, but Petter Solberg lost an early lead after hitting a rock that broke the steering, and Tommi Mäkinen dropped out of the reckoning when he clouted a boulder and smashed a wishbone mounting on SS10. Marcus Grönholm was soon out of contention too, power steering failure reducing the Peugeot driver to a distant tenth.

Myra was beyond question the turning point. Until then, it had looked as though Harri Rovanperä's second World Championship rally win was within range. His hopes were soon dashed: he also hit a rock, the 206 crabbing back to service in Kemer with a rear spring jutting through the strut turret. Rovanperä could barely contain his disappointment and frustration, but he knew the wound was self-inflicted.

He might have been no higher than second by then in a perfectly healthy 206. Sainz had picked his moment and a scintillating time on the 15-miler doubled his advantage over his nearest challenger, Richard Burns, to a minute. Once gearchange problems had been cured and he had gained a more favourable running position, Burns had been entitled to hope that Sainz was catchable. Instead, he was left voicing rueful admiration of the Spaniard's abilities on narrow, twisty roads; his neat driving style pays ample dividends.

Sainz professed that there was no secret. It wasn't a matter of driving with restraint, nor of preserving the car on the rough; the rally was no rougher and certainly no twistier than Cyprus. He had merely driven as fast as he could in the circumstances. Neatness comes naturally to him. It sounded as dry as an instruction manual. The secret, insofar as there was one, was that Sainz had once more appreciated what those circumstances were more quickly than his rivals, just as he had when the World Championship first visited Indonesia and Cyprus.

But Sainz was well aware that it was a momentous occasion. It was his 25th World Championship rally win, bringing him level with his out-of-sorts Citroën colleague Colin McRae. He allowed himself to dwell on the paradox that he is accused of doing well on familiar rallies through experience, while retaining a knack of winning rallies that are new to everyone. Six weeks before his 41st birthday, he was content to remind the world that he was still fast.

The mountains bordering Turkey's southern coast might have been made for rallying, and produced mixed fortunes for Peugeot and Citroën alike. While Richard Burns was second in his 206, Citroën's Director Guy Fréquelin listens mournfully as Sébastien Loeb and Daniel Elena explain how they came to run out of petrol.

RALLY OF TURKEY

There's nothing like a new challenge to bring out the best in Carlos Sainz, the Spaniard taking an emphatic victory (top left). It was a notable week for François Duval too (below left), third place being the Ford driver's best result at that point. Steering trouble made all too many hairpins a trial for Marcus Grönholm (below right), whereas Simon Jean-Joseph was an easy class winner for Renault. With a sequential gearbox (near left), it helps to know when you're in neutral. For most of the season, that's where Hyundai's campaign stayed.

RALLY OF TURKEY

STATISTICS World Rally Championship **Round 3**

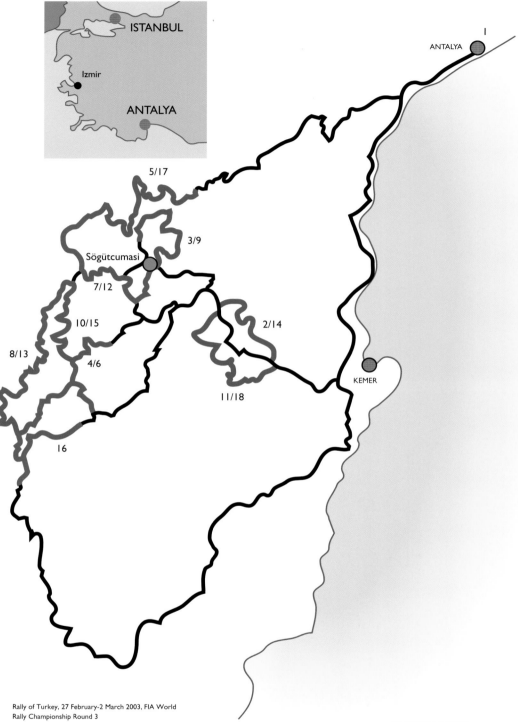

Sögütcumasi

Rally of Turkey, 27 February-2 March 2003, FIA World
Rally Championship Round 3

RUNNING ORDER

18	Sébastien Loeb / Daniel Elena	Citroën Xsara WRC / Gr A
17	Colin McRae / Derek Ringer	Citroën Xsara WRC / Gr A
1	Marcus Grönholm / Timo Rautiainen	Peugeot 206 WRC
2	Richard Burns / Robert Reid	Peugeot 206 WRC
4	Markko Märtin / Michael Park	Ford Focus RS WRC02 / Gr A
8	Tommi Mäkinen / Kaj Lindström	Subaru Impreza WRC2003
19	Carlos Sainz / Marc Martí	Citroën Xsara WRC
7	Petter Solberg / Phil Mills	Subaru Impreza WRC2003 / Gr A
5	François Duval / Stéphane Prevot	Ford Focus RS WRC02
10	Armin Schwarz / Manfred Hiemer	Hyundai Accent WRC3 / Gr A
15	Toni Gardemeister / Paavo Lukander	Skoda Octavia WRC E3 / Gr A
14	Didier Auriol / Denis Giraudet	Skoda Octavia WRC E3 / Gr A
11	Freddy Loix / Sven Smeets	Hyundai Accent WRC3 / Gr A
6	Mikko Hirvonen / Jarmo Lehtinen	Ford Focus RS WRC02 / Gr A
3	Harri Rovanperä / Risto Pietilainen	Peugeot 206 WRC / Gr A
21	Gilles Panizzi / Hervé Panizzi	Peugeot 206 WRC / Gr A
22	Juuso Pykälistö / Esko Mertsalmi	Peugeot 206 WRC / Gr A

SPECIAL STAGE TIMES

SS1 EFES PILSEN (1.55 KM)
1 M.Grönholm/T.Rautiainen (Peugeot 206 WRC)
1m12.1s; 2 P.Solberg/P.Mills (Subaru Impreza WRC2003)
1m12.2s; 3 R.Burns/R.Reid (Peugeot 206 WRC) 1m12.3s; 4=
C.McRae/ D.Ringer (Citroën Xsara WRC),
C.Sainz/M.Martí (Citroën Xsara WRC) 1m12.4s; 6
M.Märtin/M.Park (Ford Focus RS WRC02) 1m12.6s; JWC
B.Tirabassi/J.Renucci (Renault Clio) 1m22.8s

SS2 SIMENA 1 (2.73 KM)
1 H.Rovanperä/R.Pietilainen (Peugeot 206 WRC); Solberg/
Mills (Subaru) 1m52.7s; 3 J.Pykälistö/E.Mertsalmi (Peugeot
206 WRC) 1m53.5s; 4 G.Panizzi/H.Panizzi (Peugeot 206
WRC) 1m54.1s; 5 M.Hirvonen/J.Lehtinen (Ford Focus RS
WRC02) 1m54.2s; 6= Sainz/Martí (Citroën), Märtin/Park
(Ford) 1m54.3s; JWC D.Carlsson/M.Andersson (Suzuki
Ignis) 2m07.3s

SS3 PHASELIS 1 (16.42 KM)
1 Solberg/Mills (Subaru) 12m28.6s; 2 T.Mäkinen/K.Lindström
(Subaru Impreza WRC2003) 12m35.6s; 3 F.Duval/S.Prevot
(Ford Focus RS WRC02) 12m36.3s; 4 A.Schwarz/M.Hiemer
(Hyundai Accent WRC3) 12m38.3s; 5 McRae/Ringer
(Citroën) 12m40.5s; 6 Rovanperä/Pietilainen (Peugeot)
12m41.7s; JWC Carlsson/Andersson (Suzuki) 14m07.1s

SS4 SILYON 1 (29.87 KM)
1 Rovanperä/Pietilainen (Peugeot) 23m51.8s; 2 Schwarz
Hiemer (Hyundai) 23m59.6s; 3 Sainz/Martí (Citroën)
24m02.6s; 4 Panizzi/Panizzi (Peugeot) 24m04.0s; 5
Mäkinen/ Lindström (Subaru) 24m10.5s; 6 Duval/Prevot
(Ford) 24m10.7s; JWC Carlsson/Andersson (Suzuki)
26m23.8s

SS5 PERGE 1 (14.91 KM)
1 Märtin/Park (Ford) 11m50.5s; 2 Rovanperä/Pietilainen
(Peugeot) 11m51.3s; 3 Duval/Prevot (Ford) 11m51.8s;
4 Panizzi/Panizzi (Peugeot) 11m52.4s; 5 F.Loix/S.Smeets
(Hyundai Accent WRC3) 11m53.8s; 6 Mäkinen/Lindström
(Subaru) 11m54.5s; JWC Carlsson/Andersson (Suzuki)
12m44.0s

SS6 SILYON 2 (29.87 KM)
1 Rovanperä/Pietilainen (Peugeot) 23m19.1s; 2 Märtin/
Park (Ford) 23m19.7s; 3 Sainz/Martí (Citroën) 23m20.9s;
4 Duval/Prevot (Ford) 23m32.8s; 5 Mäkinen/Lindström
(Subaru) 23m34.1s; 6 Burns/Reid (Peugeot) 23m35.2s;
JWC M.Ligato/R.Garcia (Fiat Punto) 26m25.3s

SS7 OLYMPOS 1 (20.44 KM)
1 Rovanperä/Pietilainen (Peugeot) 16m45.1s; 2
Duval/Prevot (Ford) 16m48.5s; 3 Mäkinen/Lindström
(Subaru) 16m54.0s; 4 Burns/Reid (Peugeot) 16m54.5s; 5
McRae/Ringer (Citroën) 16m55.3s; 6 Sainz/Martí
(Citroën) 16m56.5s; JWC Ligato/Garcia (Fiat) 19m09.4s

SS8 KUMLUCA 1 (28.92) KM
1 Sainz/Martí (Citroën) 24m47.0s; 2 Burns/Reid (Peugeot)
24m49.6s; 3 Märtin/Park (Ford) 24m56.4s; 4 Rovanperä/
Pietilainen (Peugeot) 24m57.0s; 5 Grönholm/Rautiainen
(Peugeot) 24m57.5s; 6 Mäkinen/Lindström (Subaru)
25m05.5s; JWC P.Teuronen/H.Kaapro (Suzuki Ignis)
27m35.9s

SS9 PHASELIS 2 (15.49 KM)
1 Grönholm/Rautiainen (Peugeot) 11m51.4s; 2 Mäkinen/
Lindström (Subaru) 11m53.6s; 3 Rovanperä/Pietilainen
(Peugeot) 11m55.2s; 4 Sainz/Martí (Citroën) 11m55.9s;
5 Burns/Reid (Peugeot) 11m56.4s; 6 McRae/Ringer (Citroën)
11m58.8s; JWC Carlsson/Andersson (Suzuki) 13m29.4s

SS10 MYRA 1 (24.01 KM)
1 Sainz/Martí (Citroën) 21m45.4s; 2 Panizzi/Panizzi
(Peugeot) 22m10.3s; 3 Märtin/Park (Ford) 22m10.7s;
4 Burns/Reid (Peugeot) 22m11.1s; 5 Duval/Prevot (Ford)
22m16.2s; 6 Grönholm/Rautiainen (Peugeot) 22m18.8s;
JWC Carlsson/Andersson (Suzuki) 24m16.0s

SS11 KEMER 1 (20.30 KM)
1 Burns/Reid (Peugeot) 15m06.8s; 2 McRae/Ringer
(Citroën) 15m07.7s; 3 Grönholm/Rautiainen (Peugeot)
15m11.4s; 4 Sainz/Martí (Citroën) 15m13.1s; 5 Märtin/
Park (Ford) 15m16.9s; 6 Duval/Prevot (Ford) 15m17.7s;
JWC Carlsson/Andersson (Suzuki) 16m41.2s

SS12 OLYMPOS 2 (20.44 KM)
1 Märtin/Park (Ford) 16m29.6s; 2 Duval/Prevot (Ford)
16m32.1s; 3 Sainz/Martí (Citroën) 16m33.7s; 4 T.Garde-
meister/P.Lukander (Skoda Octavia WRC E3) 16m37.7s;
5 McRae/Ringer (Citroën) 16m39.8s; 6 Panizzi/Panizzi
(Peugeot) 16m40.9s; JWC Teuronen/Kaapro (Suzuki)
18m34.9s

SS13 KUMLUCA 2 (28.92 KM)
1 Sainz/Martí (Citroën) 24m27.1s; 2 Grönholm/Rautiainen
(Peugeot) 24m32.4s; 3 Märtin/Park (Ford) 24m36.2s;
4 Burns/Reid (Peugeot) 24m41.1s; 5 Panizzi/Panizzi
(Peugeot) 24m53.9s; 6 Gardemeister/Lukander (Skoda)
24m57.7s; JWC Teuronen/Kaapro (Suzuki) 27m39.7s

SS14 SIMENA 2 (2.73 KM)
1 McRae/Ringer (Citroën) 1m51.3s; 2 Märtin/Park (Ford)
1m51.4s; 3 Burns/Reid (Peugeot) 1m52.0s; 4 Sainz/Martí
(Citroën) 1m52.1s; 5 Grönholm/Rautiainen (Peugeot)
1m52.2s; 6 Panizzi/Panizzi (Peugeot) 1m52.9s; JWC
Carlsson/Andersson (Suzuki) 2m05.9s

SS15 MYRA 2 (24.21 KM)
1 Burns/Reid (Peugeot) 21m20.7s; 2
Grönholm/Rautiainen (Peugeot) 21m25.0s; 3 Märtin/Park
(Ford) 21m25.6s; 4 Sainz/ Martí (Citroën) 21m31.3s; 5
Mäkinen/Lindström (Subaru) 21m32.8s; 6 Panizzi/Panizzi
(Peugeot) 21m33.0s; JWC K.Katajamäki/M.Anttila (VW
Polo) 23m50.5s

SS16 ARYKANDA (12.00 KM)
1 Duval/Prevot (Ford) 8m13.4s; 2 Märtin/Park (Ford)
8m13.8s; 3 McRae/Ringer (Citroën) 8m13.9s; 4
Burns/Reid (Peugeot) 8m17.9s; 5 Grönholm/Rautiainen
(Peugeot) 8m18.2s; 6 Sainz/Martí (Citroën) 8m18.3s;
JWC G.Wilks/P.Pugh (Ford Puma) 9m19.3s

SS17 PERGE 2 (24.97 KM)
1 Grönholm/Rautiainen (Peugeot) 18m13.8s; 2
Burns/Reid (Peugeot) 18m24.0s; 3 Märtin/Park (Ford)
18m24.1s;
4 Sainz/Martí (Citroën) 18m27.2s; 5 Panizzi/Panizzi
(Peugeot) 18m27.8s; 6 McRae/Ringer (Citroën) 18m28.9s;
JWC Katajamäki/Anttila (VW) 20m55.0s

SS18 KEMER 2 (20.30 KM)
1 Grönholm/Rautiainen (Peugeot) 14m46.5s; 2 McRae/
Ringer (Citroën) 14m56.1s; 3 Burns/Reid (Peugeot)
14m58.0s; 4 Märtin/Park (Ford) 14m59.9s; 5 Duval/Prevot
(Ford) 15m03.1s; 6 Panizzi/Panizzi (Peugeot) 15m05.7s;
JWC Katajamäki/Anttila (VW) 17m24.2s

Timing beams and satellite links trigger results these days — in theory, at least — but marshals continue to supervise the process, well wrapped against the winter chill in this instance.

MAJOR RETIREMENTS

18	Loeb/Elena	Citroën Xsara WRC	
	Out of fuel	SS3	Gr A
7	Solberg/Mills	Subaru Impreza WRC2003	
	Steering	SS4	Gr A
10	Schwarz/Hiemer	Hyundai Accent WRC3	
	Suspension	SS7	Gr A
6	Hirvonen/Lehtinen	Ford Focus RS WRC02	
	Suspension	SS4	Gr A
3	Rovanperä/P'lainen	Peugeot 206 WRC	
	Rear Axle	SS13	Gr A

FIA CLASS WINNERS

A8 Over 2000 cc	Sainz/Marti	
	Citroën Xsara WRC	
A6 1400-1600cc	Jean-Joseph/Boyere	
	Renault Clio	
N4 Over 2000 cc	Girdauskas/Shoshas	
	Mitsubishi Lancer E7	

RALLY LEADERS

Overall: SS1 Grönholm, SS2-3 Solberg; SS4-9 Rovanperä; SS10-18 Sainz

JWC: SS1 Tirabassi; SS2-12 Carlsson; SS13-18 Katajamäki

SPECIAL STAGE ANALYSIS

	1st	2nd	3rd	4th	5th	6th
Grönholm (Peugeot)	4	2	1	-	4	1
Rovanperä (Peugeot)	4	1	1	1	-	-
Sainz (Citroën)	3	-	3	6	-	4
Märtin (Ford)	2	3	5	1	1	2
Burns (Peugeot)	2	2	3	4	1	1
Solberg (Subaru)	2	1	-	-	-	-
Duval (Ford)	1	2	2	1	2	2
McRae (Citroën)	1	2	1	1	3	2
Mäkinen (Subaru)	-	2	1	-	3	2
Panizzi (Peugeot)	-	1	1	2	2	4
Schwarz (Hyundai)	-	1	-	1	-	-
Hirvonen (Ford)	-	-	-	-	1	-
Loix (Hyundai)	-	-	-	1	-	-

WORLD CHAMPIONSHIP POINTS

Drivers
1 Burns 18; 2 McRae 17; 3 Sainz 16; 4 Märtin 13; 5 Loeb 12; 6 Grönholm 10; 7 Mäkinen 9, 8 Duval 8; 9 Panizzi 4; 10= Robert, Solberg, Gardemeister 3 etc

Manufacturers
1 Citroën 39; 2 Peugeot 31; 3 Ford 25; 4 Subaru 13; 5 Skoda 6; 6 Hyundai 3

Junior World Championship
1= Tirabassi, Katajamäki 10; 3= Ligato, Canellas 8; 5= Broccoli, Wilks 6; 7= Aava, Teuronen 5 etc

Production Cup
1 Blomqvist 10; 2 Singh 8; 3 Rowe 6; 4 Bourne 5; 5 Holowczyc 4; 6 Roman 3; 7 Sztuka 2; 8 Richard 1

ROUTE DETAILS

Total route of 1193.85 km of which 337.88 km were competitive on 18 stages

Leg 1 Thursday 27th-Friday 28th February, 6 Special Stages totalling 95.35 km

Leg 2 Saturday 1st March, 7 Special Stages totalling 158.52 km

Leg 3 Sunday 2nd March, 5 Special Stages totalling 84.21 km

RESULTS

1	Carlos Sainz/	Citroën Xsara WRC	
	Marc Marti	4h32m14.1s	
2	Richard Burns/	Peugeot 206 WRC	
	Robert Reid	4h33m02.0s	Gr A
3	François Duval/	Ford Focus RS WRC02	
	Stéphane Prevot	4h34m00.6s	Gr A
4	Colin McRae/	Citroën Xsara WRC	
	Derek Ringer	4h34m23.2s	Gr A
5	Gilles Panizzi/	Peugeot 206 WRC	
	Hervé Panizzi	4h34m55.7s	Gr A
6	Markko Märtin/	Ford Focus RS WRC02	
	Michael Park	4h35m39.0s	Gr A
7	Toni Gardemeister/	Skoda Octavia WRC E3	
	Paavo Lukander	4h37m27.1s	Gr A
8	Tommi Mäkinen/	Subaru Impreza WRC2003	
	Kaj Lindström	4h39m32.7s	Gr A
9	Marcus Grönholm/	Peugeot 206 WRC	
	Timo Rautiainen	4h43m06.3s	Gr A
10	Freddy Loix/	Hyundai Accent WRC3	
	Sven Smeets	4h43m54.5s	Gr A

58 starters, 27 finishers

RECENT WINNERS

First running of the event in this format, and in this location.

STAGE NUMBERS	1	2	3	4	5	6	7	8	9	10	11	12	13	14	15	16	17	18
Sainz	4	3	7	3	5	2	2	2	2	2	1	1	1	1	1	1	1	1
Burns	3	8	12	8	8	6	6	5	5	2	2	2	2	2	2	2	2	2
Duval	9	8	3	5	2	3	3	4	4	3	3	3	3	3	3	3	3	3
McRae	4	5	4	7	6	7	7	7	7	6	4	4	4	4	4	4	4	4
Panizzi	13	10	8	6	4	5	5	6	6	4	5	5	5	5	5	5	5	5
Märtin	6	4	16	12	12	12	10	10	10	9	8	7	7	7	6	6	6	6
G'meister	12	15	10	10	10	10	9	9	9	7	6	6	6	7	7	7	7	
Mäkinen	7	6	2	4	3	4	4	3	3	5	9	9	8	8	8	8	8	8
Grönholm	1	7	11	16	18	19	15	13	12	12	11	11	11	11	10	10	9	9
Loix	16	13	13	9	9	9	8	8	8	7	9	9	9	9	9	9	10	10
Pykälisto	20	17	45	17	16	13	11	11	11	11	10	10	10	10	11	11	11	11
Rovanperä	10	2	6	1	1	1	1	1	1	1	10	12	12	R				
Schwarz	11	12	5	2	7	8	R											
Auriol	15	14	14	11	11	11	R											
Solberg	2	1	1	R														
Loeb	7	16	9	R														
Hirvonen	13	11	15	R														

FINISH LINES

On his first rally with Stéphane Prevot navigating in place of Jean-Marc Fortin, François Duval put in the drive of his career, taking third in his works Focus... Chronic gearbox problems in the first leg wrecked his team-mate Markko Märtin's prospects, although the Estonian recovered to finish sixth... Freddy Loix survived two stages with a blown turbo and a bout of damper trouble to coax his works Hyundai home in tenth place... Rear suspension failure forced Armin Schwarz to retire the other works Accent on SS7... Juuso Pykälisto managed 11th place, delayed by power steering problems and a roll when driving in the dust of Balazs Benik's Focus... Sébastien Loeb's retirement was particularly agonising: his co-driver Daniel Elena missed an awkward turning and their Xsara ran out of petrol as they retraced their steps... Mikko Hirvonen ran into trouble with his Focus's hydraulics almost at once, then lost concentration momentarily, hit a rock and broke the rear suspension... Kosti Katajamäki made up for his Monte disappointment by taking maximum Junior Championship points in his Polo... Daniel Carlsson had looked on course for victory until he got a front puncture in his Suzuki... Martin Stenshorne withdrew his Puma at the end of the first leg, as his co-driver Clive Jenkins had gastroenteritis...

For three days, Marcus Grönholm successfully conveyed the impression that leading the Rally of New Zealand was about as taxing – and exciting – as a milk round. But towards the end of the second leg, there was a flutter of something close to panic in the number-one 206.

The Finn misjudged his braking for a T-junction early in Parahi and after slithering towards the outside of the bend, the Peugeot tipped on to its side. Although there were only two spectators on hand, the car was soon back on its wheels, but Grönholm and Timo Rautiainen didn't know how much time they had lost. The driver feared the worst and as his navigator had forgotten to press the 'split' button on his stopwatch, he couldn't offer much reassurance.

It had echoes of Richard Burns's spectacular exit from the rally the year before. He had amassed a healthy lead, but couldn't afford to ease off and hand the initiative to Grönholm; a stage or two from safety, he had rolled the car at considerable speed and the Finn, his team-mate and arch-rival, had cruised to victory. They were merely echoes, for within a stage, Grönholm was indeed cruising to another New Zealand victory. The T-junction mishap cost him precisely 35 seconds to Markko Märtin and halved his lead, but the 206 was in robust health and on SS14, a broken cambelt halted the Focus a mile or so after Märtin had spun. The pressure was off. With a day to run, maintaining a minute's lead over Burns was pretty much the rallying equivalent of a milk round.

It had been an accomplished performance, in which Grönholm had led from start to finish. He had been quickest on the first stage, even though rain had ensured that the gravel sank into the mud and a lower starting position therefore offered no advantage, capitalised to good effect when it did turn dry and gravelly on SS4, then added ten seconds to his lead on the crucial 36-miler combining Parahi and Ararua at the beginning of the second leg.

Yet Grönholm's nonchalant superiority had been expected and the upstart challenger was the talk of the rally. Before the start, Ford had blended optimism and pessimism. No one at M-Sport questioned that Christian Loriaux's re-engineered Focus was quick, but there was some doubt that it was reliable. In any case, it was unfair to expect too much of the drivers, whose knowledge of the event was limited or non-existent. In the event, Märtin and the Focus were a revelation. Prior knowledge is usually most precious at high average speeds, yet on the quickest Rally of New Zealand ever, Märtin kept the all-conquering Grönholm just about in sight. He set an astoundingly good time considering that the hydraulics went sick and sent the differential programming haywire for most of Parahi-Ararua, and as he gained confidence in the Ford's beautifully balanced handling, he began to chip away at the Finn's lead. He hadn't gained much, but three consecutive fastest times obliged Grönholm to take the challenge seriously.

It would be misleading to proclaim that Grönholm was rattled, far less that Märtin was poised to stage the upset of the season, but the victor left New Zealand with food for thought. A businesslike success had brought him only two points closer to the championship lead, thanks to a dogged drive from Burns, who had minimised the disadvantage of running first on the road to take second. As for Märtin, he had planted the idea that perhaps the Focus had become the car to beat.

For Marcus Grönholm, New Zealand was an exercise in seeing through a glass clearly (above), at least once Markko Märtin and the new Focus (top right) were out of the way. New Zealand remains Peugeot country, Petter Solberg unable to haul his Subaru past Richard Burns (left). Even Colin McRae's virtuosity couldn't make the Xsara competitive.

RALLY OF NEW ZEALAND

RALLYCOURSE World Rally Championship **Round 4**

RALLY OF NEW ZEALAND

STATISTICS World Rally Championship **Round 4**

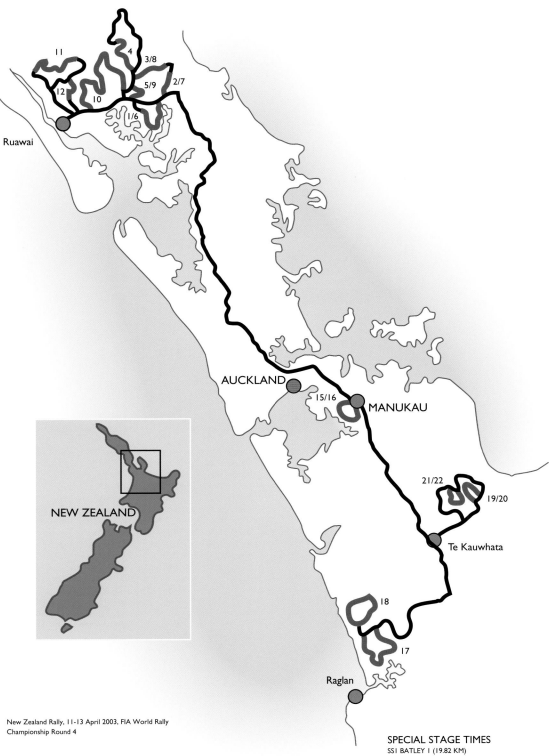

Ruawai

AUCKLAND

15/16

MANUKAU

21/22

19/20

Te Kauwhata

18

17

Raglan

NEW ZEALAND

New Zealand Rally, 11-13 April 2003, FIA World Rally
Championship Round 4

RUNNING ORDER

2	Richard Burns/	Peugeot 206 WRC
	Robert Reid	Gr A
17	Colin McRae/	Citroën Xsara WRC
	Derek Ringer	Gr A
19	Carlos Sainz/	Citroën Xsara WRC
	Marc Marti	Gr A
4	Markko Märtin/	Ford Focus RS WRC03
	Michael Park	Gr A
18	Sébastien Loeb/	Citroën Xsara WRC
	Daniel Elena	Gr A
1	Marcus Grönholm/	Peugeot 206 WRC
	Timo Rautiainen	Gr A
8	Tommi Mäkinen/	Subaru Impreza WRC2003
	Kaj Lindström	Gr A
5	François Duval/	Ford Focus RS WRC03
	Stéphane Prevot	Gr A
7	Petter Solberg/	Subaru Impreza WRC2003
	Phil Mills	Gr A
15	Toni Gardemeister/	Skoda Octavia WRC E3
	Paavo Lukander	Gr A
10	Armin Schwarz/	Hyundai Accent WRC3

	Manfred Hiemer	Gr A
14	Didier Auriol/	Skoda Octavia WRC E3
	Denis Giraudet	Gr A
11	Freddy Loix/	Hyundai Accent WRC3
	Sven Smeets	Gr A
6	Mikko Hirvonen/	Ford Focus WRC02
	Jarmo Lehtinen	Gr A
3	Harri Rovanperä/	Peugeot 206 WRC
	Risto Pietilainen	Gr A
12	Jussi Välimäki/	Hyundai Accent WRC3
	Tero Gardemeister	Gr A
32	Alister McRae/	Mitsubishi Lancer WRC2
	David Senior	Gr A
33	Kristian Sohlberg/	Mitsubishi Lancer WRC2
	Jakke Honkanen	Gr A
34	Tomasz Kuchar/	Ford Focus WRC02
	Maciej S'paniak	Gr A
35	Manfred Stohl/	Peugeot 206 WRC
	Ilka Minor	Gr A

SPECIAL STAGE TIMES

SS1 BATLEY 1 (19.82 KM)
1 M.Grönholm/T.Rautiainen (Peugeot 206 WRC) 10m45.2s;
2 M.Märtin/M.Park (Ford Focus RS WRC03) 10m51.3s;
3 H.Rovanperä/R.Pietilainen (Peugeot 206 WRC) 10m54.4s;
4 P.Solberg/P.Mills (Subaru Impreza WRC2003) 10m54.9s;
5 R.Burns/R.Reid (Peugeot 206 WRC) 11m01.1s; 6 M.Stohl/
I.Minor (Peugeot 206 WRC) 11m01.3s; PC T.Arai/
T.Sircombe (Subaru Impreza WRX) 11m44.7s

SS2 WAIPU GORGE 1 (11.24 KM)
1 Burns/Reid (Peugeot) 6m37.0s; 2 Märtin/Park (Ford)
6m37.7s; 3 Grönholm/Rautiainen (Peugeot) 6m37.9s;
4 Solberg/Mills (Subaru) 6m39.7s; 5 T.Mäkinen/K.Lindström
(Subaru Impreza WRC2003) 6m43.6s; 6 C.Sainz/M.Martí
(Citroën Xsara WRC) 6m45.2s; PC H.Al Wahaibi/
N.Beech (Mitsubishi Lancer E7) 7m07.7s

SS3 BROOKS 1 (16.03 KM)
1 Grönholm/Rautiainen (Peugeot) 9m46.3s; 2 Solberg/Mills
(Subaru) 9m51.4s; 3 Rovanperä/Pietilainen (Peugeot)
9m52.9s; 4= Märtin/Park (Ford), Loeb/Elena (Citroën
Xsara WRC) 9m53.8s; 6 Burns/Reid (Peugeot) 9m54.1s;
PC Arai/Sircombe (Subaru) 10m31.5s

SS4 NEW CASSIDY (21.64 KM)
1 Grönholm/Rautiainen (Peugeot) 12m13.7s; 2 Rovanperä/
Pietilainen (Peugeot) 12m15.2s; 3 Solberg/Mills (Subaru)
12m16.6s; 4 K.Sohlberg/J.Honkanen (Mitsubishi Lancer
WRC2) 12m18.1s; 5 Märtin/Park (Ford) 12m18.7s;
6 Mäkinen/Lindström (Subaru) 12m20.5s; PC P.Bourne/
M.Stacey (Subaru Impreza WRX) 13m03.6s

SS5 PAPAROA STATION 1 (11.64 KM)
1 Grönholm/Rautiainen (Peugeot) 6m18.2s; 2 C.McRae/
D.Ringer (Citroën Xsara WRC) 6m19.7s; 3 Burns/Reid
(Peugeot) 6m19.9s; 4 Solberg/Mills (Subaru) 6m21.1s;
5 Märtin/Park (Ford) 6m21.5s; 6 Mäkinen/Lindström
(Subaru) 6m24.1s; PC Arai/Sircombe (Subaru) 6m49.0s

SS6 BATLEY 2 (19.82 KM)
1 Grönholm/Rautiainen (Peugeot) 10m33.0s; 2 Märtin/Park
(Ford) 10m35.9s; 3 Rovanperä/Pietilainen (Peugeot)
10m37.5s; 4 Burns/Reid (Peugeot) 10m41.2s; 5 Loeb/Elena
(Citroën) 10m41.4s; 6 Solberg/Mills (Subaru) 10m41.5s;
PC R.Ferreyros/J.Marin (Mitsubishi Lancer E7) 11m26.1s

SS7 WAIPU GORGE 2 (11.24 KM)
1 Burns/Reid (Peugeot) 6m34.9s; 2 Grönholm/Rautiainen
(Peugeot) 6m36.6s; 3 Märtin/Park (Ford) 6m37.1s; 4 Loeb/
Elena (Citroën) 6m38.7s; 5 Solberg/Mills 6m38.8s; 6 Sainz/
Martí (Citroën) 6m39.4s; PC Arai/Sircombe (Subaru)
7m10.3s

SS8 BROOKS 2 (16.03 KM)
1 Grönholm/Rautiainen (Peugeot) 9m22.9s; 2 Burns/Reid
(Peugeot) 9m29.5s; 3 Solberg/Mills (Subaru) 9m30.8s;
4 Loeb/Elena (Citroën) 9m31.7s; 5 Rovanperä/Pietilainen
(Peugeot) 9m32.9s; 6 Märtin/Park (Ford) 9m33.2s;
PC Ferreyros/Marin (Mitsubishi) 10m11.6s

SS9 PAPAROA STATION 2 (11.64 KM)
1 Grönholm/Rautiainen (Peugeot) 6m11.7s; 2 Burns/Reid
(Peugeot) 6m12.5s; 3 Solberg/Mills (Subaru) 6m14.3s;
4 Märtin/Park (Ford) 6m14.4s; 5 Loeb/Elena (Citroën)
6m15.8s; 6 Sainz/Martí (Citroën) 6m18.6s; PC Ferreyros/
Marin (Mitsubishi) 6m39.6s

SS10 PARAHI / ARARUA (59.00 KM)
1 Grönholm/Rautiainen (Peugeot) 33m20.5s; 2 Burns/Reid
(Peugeot) 33m31.0s; 3 Rovanperä/Pietilainen (Peugeot)
33m41.1s; 4 Märtin/Park (Ford) 33m44.8s; 5 Loeb/Elena
(Citroën) 33m54.4s; 6 Solberg/Mills (Subaru) 33m58.0s;
PC Arai/Sircombe (Subaru) 35m52.4s

SS11 MITITAI FINISH (20.15 KM)
1 Märtin/Park (Ford) 10m03.0s; 2 Grönholm/Rautiainen
(Peugeot) 10m03.7s; 3 Rovanperä/Pietilainen (Peugeot)
10m12.5s; 4 Burns/Reid (Peugeot) 10m14.1s; 5 Solberg/
Mills (Subaru) 10m14.5s; 6 Loeb/Elena (Citroën)
10m21.7s; PC Al Wahaibi/Beech (Mitsubishi) 11m06.8s

SS12 TOKATOKA (10.15 KM)
1 Märtin/Park (Ford) 5m07.1s; 2 Grönholm/Rautiainen
(Peugeot) 5m07.6s; 3 Burns/Reid (Peugeot) 5m09.6s;
4 Rovanperä/Pietilainen (Peugeot) 5m11.2s; 5 Solberg/Mills
(Subaru) 5m12.8s; 6 Loeb/Elena (Citroën) 5m14.6s;
PC N.McShea/C.Patterson (Mitsubishi Lancer E6) 5m34.1s

SS13 PARAHI (25.18 KM)
1 Märtin/Park (Ford) 12m42.6s; 2 Burns/Reid (Peugeot)
12m45.6s; 3 Rovanperä/Pietilainen (Peugeot) 12m49.1s;
4 Loeb/Elena (Citroën) 12m52.3s; 5 Sainz/Martí (Citroën)
12m56.1s; 6 Mäkinen/Lindström (Subaru) 13m00.2s;
PC Arai/Sircombe (Subaru) 13m50.0s

SS14 ARARUA (31.75 KM)
1 Grönholm/Rautiainen (Peugeot) 19m01.3s; 2 Burns/Reid
(Peugeot) 19m17.9s; 3 Loeb/Elena (Citroën) 19m20.7s;
4 Solberg/Mills (Subaru) 19m22.7s; 5 Mäkinen/Lindström
(Subaru) 19m29.0s; 6 Sainz/Martí (Citroën) 19m33.7s;
PC No times

SS15 MANUKAU SUPER 1 (2.10 KM)
1 F.Duval/S.Prevot (Ford Focus RS WRC03) 1m36.4s;
2= M.Ligato/R.Garcia (PC Mitsubishi Lancer E7), Arai/
Sircombe (PC Subaru) 1m37.7s; 4= F.Loix/S.Smeets
(Hyundai Accent WRC3), B.Herbert/R.Ryan (Subaru
Impreza WRX-N) 1m38.2s; 6 Mäkinen/Lindström (Subaru)
1m38.4s

SS16 MANUKAU SUPER 2 (2.10 KM)
1 Solberg/Mills (Subaru) 1m40.2s; 2 Loix/Smeets (Hyundai)
1m41.8s; 3= A.McRae/D.Senior (Mitsubishi Lancer
WRC2), Sainz/Martí (Citroën) 1m42.0s; 5 Mäkinen/
Lindström (Subaru) 1m42.2s; 6 Grönholm/Rautiainen
(Peugeot) 1m42.3s; PC K.Singh/A.Oh (Proton Pert) 1m50.7s

SS17 TE AKAU SOUTH (27.34 KM)
1 Grönholm/Rautiainen (Peugeot) 15m49.7s; 2 Solberg/Mills
(Subaru) 15m54.2s; 3 Burns/Reid (Peugeot) 16m02.5s; 4
Loeb/Elena (Citroën) 16m08.1s; 5 T.Gardemeister/
P.Lukander (Skoda Octavia WRC E3) 16m21.3s;
6 Mäkinen/Lindström (Subaru) 16m22.4s; PC D.Sola/
A.Romani (Mitsubishi Lancer E7) 17m01.9s

SS18 TE AKAU NORTH (32.37 KM)
1 Burns/Reid (Peugeot) 17m43.0s; 2 Grönholm/Rautiainen (Peugeot) 17m43.2s; 3 Solberg/Mills (Subaru) 17m45.1s; 4 Mäkinen/Lindström (Subaru) 18m12.6s; 5 D.Auriol/D.Giraudet (Skoda Octavia WRC E3) 18m14.5s; 6 Gardemeister/Lukander (Skoda) 18m14.6s; PC Sola/Romani (Mitsubishi) 18m50.6s

SS19 RIDGE / CAMPBELL 1 (16.45 KM)
1 Burns/Reid (Peugeot) 8m53.7s; 2 Grönholm/Rautiainen (Peugeot) 8m54.3s; 3 Solberg/Mills (Subaru) 8m55.5s; 4 Mäkinen/Lindström (Subaru) 9m04.1s; 5 Loeb/Elena (Citroën) 9m05.3s; 6 Gardemeister/Lukander (Skoda) 9m07.1s; PC Arai/Sircombe (Subaru) 9m34.8s

SS20 RIDGE / CAMPBELL 2 (16.45 KM)
1 Burns/Reid (Peugeot) 8m46.9s; 2 Grönholm/Rautiainen (Peugeot) 8m48.3s; 3 Solberg/Mills (Subaru) 8m49.1s; 4 Loeb/Elena (Citroën) 8m53.2s; 5 Mäkinen/Lindström (Subaru) 8m53.6s; 6 Gardemeister/Lukander (Skoda) 8m55.7s; PC Arai/Sircombe (Subaru) 9m33.6s

SS21 FYFE 1 (10.60 KM)
1 Burns/Reid (Peugeot) 5m42.3s; 2 Grönholm/Rautiainen (Peugeot) 5m43.0s; 3 Loeb/Elena (Citroën) 5m47.5s; 4 Mäkinen/Lindström (Subaru) 5m49.8s; 5 Auriol/Giraudet (Skoda) 5m50.2s; 6 Solberg/Mills (Subaru) 5m51.9s; PC Al Wahaibi/Beech (Mitsubishi) 6m07.3s

SS22 FYFE 2 (10.60 KM)
1 Burns/Reid (Peugeot) 5m36.9s; 2 Grönholm/Rautiainen (Peugeot) 5m39.0s; 3 Solberg/Mills (Subaru) 5m40.8s; 4 Loeb/Elena (Citroën) 5m42.2s; 5 Mäkinen/Lindström (Subaru) 5m42.4s; 6 Sainz/Martí (Citroën) 5m44.4s; PC Sola/Romani (Mitsubishi) 6m02.8s

MAJOR RETIREMENTS
17	McRae/Grist	Citroën Xsara WRC		
	Suspension	SS6		Gr A
4	Märtin/Park	Ford Focus RS WRC03		
	Engine	SS14		Gr A
10	Schwarz/Hiemer	Hyundai Accent WRC3		
	Accident	SS1		Gr A
11	Loix/Smeets	Hyundai Accent WRC3		
	Accident	SS18		Gr A
3	Rovanperä/P'lainen	Peugeot 206 WRC		
	Accident	SS14		Gr A
12	Välimäki/G'meister	Hyundai Accent WRC3		
	Accident	SS7		Gr A
33	Sohlberg/Honkanen	Mitsubishi Lancer WRC2		
	Accident	SS17		Gr A
35	Stohl/Minor	Peugeot 206 WRC		
	Accident	SS10		

FIA CLASS WINNERS
A8 Over 2000 cc — Grönholm/Rautiainen Peugeot 206 WRC
N4 Over 2000 cc — Arai/Sircombe Subaru Impreza WRX

RALLY LEADERS
Overall: SS1-22 Grönholm
PC: SS1-3; SS4 Bourne; SS5-22 Arai

SPECIAL STAGE ANALYSIS
	1st	2nd	3rd	4th	5th	6th
Grönholm (Peugeot)	10	8	1	-	-	1
Burns (Peugeot)	7	5	3	2	1	1
Märtin (Ford)	3	3	1	3	2	1
Solberg (Subaru)	1	2	7	4	3	3
Duval (Ford)	1	-	-	1	-	-
Rovanperä (Peugeot)	-	1	6	1	1	-
Loix (Hyundai)	-	1	-	1	-	-
C.McRae (Citroën)	-	1	-	-	-	-
Arai (Subaru)	-	1	-	-	-	-
Ligato (Mitsubishi)	-	1	-	-	-	-
Loeb (Citroën)	-	-	2	7	4	2
Sainz (Citroën)	-	-	1	-	1	5
A.McRae (Mitsubishi)	-	-	1	-	-	-
Mäkinen (Subaru)	-	-	-	3	5	5
Sohlberg (Mitsubishi)	-	-	-	1	-	-
Herbert (Subaru)	-	-	-	1	-	-
Auriol (Skoda)	-	-	-	-	2	-
Gardemeister (Skoda)	-	-	-	-	1	3
Stohl (Peugeot)	-	-	-	-	-	1

WORLD CHAMPIONSHIP POINTS
Drivers
1 Burns 26; 2 Grönholm 20; 3= McRae, Loeb 17; 5 Sainz 16; 6 Märtin 13; 7 Mäkinen 11; 8 Solberg 9; 9 Duval 8; 10 Gardemeister 7 etc

Manufacturers
1 Peugeot 44; 2 Citroën 39; 3 Ford 25; 4 Subaru 22; 5 Skoda 12; 6 Hyundai 3

Junior World Championship
1= Tirabassi, Katajamäki 10; 3= Ligato, Canellas 8; 5= Broccoli, Wilks 6; 7= Aava, Teuronen 5 etc

Production Cup
1= Blomqvist, Rowe, Singh 11; 4 Arai 10; 5 Ligato 8; 6 Al Wahaibi 6 etc

ROUTE DETAILS
Total route of 1297.81 kms of which 403.52 km were competitive on 22 stages

Leg 1 Friday 11th April, 9 special stages totalling 139.10 km
Leg 2 Saturday 12th April, 7 special stages totalling 150.35 km
Leg 3 Sunday 13th April, 6 special stages totalling 114.07 km

RESULTS
1	Marcus Grönholm/Timo Rautiainen	Peugeot 206 WRC	3h45m21.2s	Gr A
2	Richard Burns/Robert Reid	Peugeot 206 WRC	3h46m29.9s	Gr A
3	Petter Solberg/Phil Mills	Subaru Impreza WRC2003	3h47m31.0s	Gr A
4	Sebastian Loeb/Daniel Elena	Citroën Xsara WRC	3h49m36.6s	Gr A
5	Toni Gardemeister/Paavo Lukander	Skoda Octavia WRC E3	3h53m35.0s	Gr A
6	Alister McRae/David Senior	Mitsubishi Lancer WRC2	3h54m35.4s	Gr A
7	Tommi Mäkinen/Kaj Lindström	Subaru Impreza WRC2003	3h55m11.4s	Gr A
8	Didier Auriol/Denis Giraudet	Skoda Octavia WRC E3	3h55m29.8s	Gr A
9	François Duval/Stephane Prevot	Ford Focus RS WRC03	3h56m32.9s	Gr A
10	Mikko Hirvonen/Jarmo Lehtinen	Ford Focus RS WRC02	3h59m05.5s	Gr A

80 starters, 46 finishers

STAGE NUMBERS	1	2	3	4	5	6	7	8	9	10	11	12	13	14	15	16	17	18	19	20	21	22
Grönholm	1	1	1	1	1	1	1	1	1	1	1	1	1	1	1	1	1	1	1	1	1	1
Burns	5	4	4	6	5	5	5	4	3	3	3	3	2	2	2	2	2	2	2	2	2	2
Solberg	4	3	3	3	3	4	4	5	5	3	3	3	3	3	3	3	3	3	3	3	3	3
Loeb	11	10	9	8	7	7	7	7	6	6	6	4	4	4	4	4	4	4	4	4	4	4
G'meister	9	13	14	14	14	13	13	13	9	9	9	9	9	8	7	7	6	5	5	5	5	5
A.McRae	16	16	15	15	14	14	14	14	11	11	11	11	7	6	6	7	6	6	6	6	6	6
Mäkinen	7	6	6	5	6	6	6	6	7	7	7	7	5	10	9	9	8	8	8	8	8	7
Auriol	10	9	10	11	10	11	10	10	10	12	12	12	12	9	8	8	7	7	7	7	7	8
Duval	13	11	12	16	17	17	15	16	15	15	13	13	13	13	13	10	9	10	10	9	9	9
Hirvonen	17	18	18	18	18	18	16	16	15	15	15	15	15	11	11	11	10	10	10	10	10	10
Loix	15	12	13	12	13	12	12	12	12	10	10	10	6	5	5	5	R					
Sohlberg	12	14	11	10	11	10	11	11	8	8	8	4	4	4	4	R						
Märtin	2	2	2	2	2	2	2	2	2	2	2	2	2	R								
Rovanperä	3	5	5	4	4	4	4	5	5	5	5	5	4	4	R							
Stohl	6	8	7	7	9	9	9	9	9	R												
Välimäki	18	17	17	17	16	15	R															
C.McRae	14	15	15	13	12	R																

FINISH LINES
Petter Solberg had hoped to beat Richard Burns for second, but was obliged to make do with third, partly thanks to a chronic tyre vibration that slowed his Impreza in the closing stages... Alister McRae put in a measured performance to take sixth on Mitsubishi's first outing of the season... His older brother, Colin, fared nothing like as well, crippling his Xsara's front suspension when he clipped a bank on SS6... François Duval ensured that one of the new Focuses finished its first rally, recovering from a major hydraulic failure that disabled the differentials and demoted him to 17th in the first leg to finish ninth... Tommi Mäkinen was out of sorts on the stages, but drove with a little too much gusto on the road sections. An encounter with the police earned Subaru's Finn a five-minute penalty... Carlos Sainz had a 41st birthday to forget: he slid off while trying to pass Didier Auriol's misfiring Skoda on SS10, doing little damage to his Xsara, but losing 14 minutes and any chance of a finish in the points... Freddy Loix had looked on course for fifth place until he crashed his Accent on SS18... Harri Rovanperä was holding fourth when he crashed his 206 towards the end of the second leg...

Making up for lost time: Richard Burns fought back to take second after sweeping gravel running first on the opening day.

RALLY OF ARGENTINA

'The TGV has arrived,' noted Corrado Provera contentedly, as the radio disclosed that Marcus Grönholm had completed SS13; another stage, another fastest time. It was an appealing metaphor, the Finn overhauling his rivals rather like a train in northern France thundering past cars on the motorway to Paris.

Yet Grönholm's weekend entirely lacked the timetabled progress of a TGV, much like the event itself. It had been a tortured route to his final destination. For the second rally in a row, he was the quickest driver, but the 206 bore the scars of a small but potentially catastrophic misjudgement. This time, the event had looked to be running very much in his favour when he squirted the car wide on the first run at Ascochinga-La Cumbre, clouted a rock embedded in a bank and all but took the left rear wheel off; but the wheel stayed on and while he had dropped close to two minutes, he coaxed the crippled 206 to service. There was at least a chance that he might win yet. By SS13, Peugeot's TGV was pulling strongly once more.

Winning had seemed an uncertain thing even earlier in the first leg when the satellite-based timing equipment proved so capricious that Grönholm threatened to go home – indeed, he felt it had contributed to the loss of concentration on Ascochinga – and when long delays followed spectator problems the next morning, the Finn voiced the fear that too many stages would be cancelled to allow him to make up lost ground. When he was allowed to attempt a stage, it was promptly stopped and his shattering time was awarded to his opponents too. He treated it not so much as a setback as a fresh challenge. It was an awe-inspiring, inexorable performance. On Capilla del Monte, the final stage of a wearisome, much-protracted second leg, even Carlos Sainz conceded six seconds. Markko Märtin looked a beaten man, resigned to losing his slender lead at some time of Grönholm's choosing the next morning. As for Richard Burns, he was thrashed by almost a second a kilometre, 20 seconds slower in a notionally identical car. Grönholm had smacked the same wall as he had in 2000, but the wheel had stood up to the impact and 206 rear bumpers aren't expected to last.

No doubt Grönholm would have caught the fleeing Ford anyway, although Märtin was putting up stern resistance when the oil pressure vanished on the re-scheduled re-run of Capilla del Monte on the final morning. After that, he could afford to slacken his pace a fraction while keeping an eye on the dogfight between Sainz and Burns.

It was an epic, extraordinary victory and a fitting culmination to an extraordinary rally, but Grönholm had been lucky: lucky that the Focus had proved fragile (Märtin would have been further ahead it hadn't been for two bouts of gear selection trouble) and lucky above all that Marc Marti's casual hand signal had prompted Sainz to ease his Citroën into a time control early. But for the minute's penalty after SS19, even Grönholm's virtuosity would have been to no avail.

Sainz accepted defeat with characteristic dignity. He was made to fight tooth and nail for second. Provera had been quick to add that, like a French railway company, Peugeot had many fast trains and if it wasn't for turbo failure on the final stage, Burns would have given the 206 its 14th one-two. That turbo looked to have done Grönholm's title prospects no harm at all.

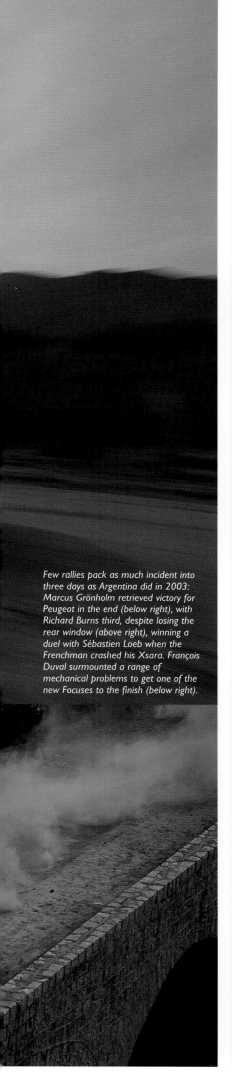

Few rallies pack as much incident into three days as Argentina did in 2003: Marcus Grönholm retrieved victory for Peugeot in the end (below right), with Richard Burns third, despite losing the rear window (above right), winning a duel with Sébastien Loeb when the Frenchman crashed his Xsara. François Duval surmounted a range of mechanical problems to get one of the new Focuses to the finish (below right).

RALLY OF ARGENTINA

Carlos Sainz made a splash, but a momentary oversight by Marc Martí cost the Citroën crew a minute and victory (centre right). Didier Auriol took a stirring sixth in the twilight of the Octavia's career (below). The works Subaru drivers struggled a little with new dampers, Tommi Mäkinen (top right) the quicker of the two, although Petter Solberg (top left) got the better result. In common with many crews, both carried a tribute to the late 'Possum' Bourne.

RALLY OF ARGENTINA

Rally Argentina, 8-11 May 2003,
FIA World Rally Championship Round 5

RUNNING ORDER

2	Richard Burns/	Peugeot 206 WRC
	Robert Reid	Gr A
1	Marcus Grönholm/	Peugeot 206 WRC
	Timo Rautiainen	Gr A
18	Sébastien Loeb/	Citroën Xsara WRC
	Daniel Elena	Gr A
17	Colin McRae/	Citroën Xsara WRC
	Derek Ringer	Gr A
19	Carlos Sainz/	Citroën Xsara WRC
	Marc Marti	Gr A
4	Markko Märtin/	Ford Focus RS WRC03
	Michael Park	Gr A
8	Tommi Mäkinen/	Subaru Impreza WRC2003
	Kaj Lindström	Gr A
7	Petter Solberg/	Subaru Impreza WRC2003
	Phil Mills	Gr A
5	François Duval/	Ford Focus RS WRC03
	Stéphane Prevot	Gr A
15	Toni Gardemeister/	Skoda Octavia WRC E3
	Paavo Lukander	Gr A
14	Didier Auriol/	Skoda Octavia WRC E3
	Denis Giraudet	Gr A
10	Armin Schwarz/	Hyundai Accent WRC3
	Manfred Hiemer	Gr A
11	Freddy Loix/	Hyundai Accent WRC3
	Sven Smeets	Gr A
6	Mikko Hirvonen/	Ford Focus RS WRC02
	Jarmo Lehtinen	Gr A
3	Harri Rovanperä/	Peugeot 206 WRC
	Risto Pietilainen	Gr A
21	Antony Warmbold/	Ford Focus RS WRC02
	Gemma Price	Gr A
32	Gabriel Pozzo/	Skoda Octavia WRC E3
	Daniel Stillo	Gr A
33	Gabriel Raies/	Toyota Corolla WRC
	Jorge Peres	Gr A
51	Karamjit Singh/	Proton Pert
	Allen Oh	Gr N
54	Toshihiro Arai/	Subaru Impreza WRX
	Tony Sircombe	Gr N

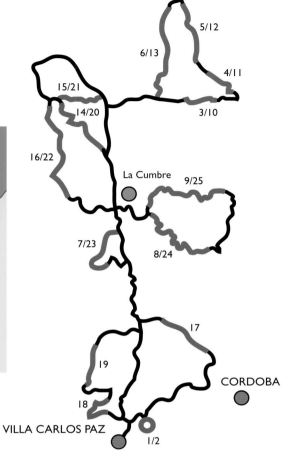

La Cumbre

5/12
6/13
4/11
15/21
14/20
3/10
16/22
9/25
7/23
8/24
17
19
CORDOBA
18
1/2
VILLA CARLOS PAZ

SPECIAL STAGE TIMES

SS1 PRO RACING A (3.02 KM)
1 M.Grönholm/T.Rautiainen (Peugeot 206 WRC)
2m09.7s; 2 P.Solberg/P.Mills (Subaru Impreza WRC2003)
2m11.0s; 3 C.McRae/D.Ringer (Citroën Xsara WRC)
2m11.4s; 4 C.Sainz/M.Marti (Citroën Xsara WRC)
2m12.7s; 5 R.Burns/R.Reid (Peugeot 206 WRC) 2m13.7s;
6 M.Hirvonen/J.Lehtinen (Ford Focus RS WRC02)
2m13.9s; PC M.Ligato/R.Garcia (Mitsubishi Lancer E7)
2m19.4s

SS2 PRO RACING B (3.02 KM)
1 Burns/Reid (Peugeot) 2m09.4s; 2 Sainz/Marti (Citroën)
2m10.3s; 3 Grönholm/Rautiainen (Peugeot) 2m10.5s; 4
T.Mäkinen/K.Lindström (Subaru Impreza WRC2003)
2m11.4s; 5 Solberg/Mills (Subaru) 2m11.5s; 6
M.Märtin/M.Park (Ford Focus RS WRC03) 2m11.6s; PC
Ligato/Garcia (Mitsubishi) 2m18.3s

SS3 EL ROPOSO 1 (10.03 KM)
1 Grönholm/Rautiainen (Peugeot) 5m44.9s; 2 Märtin/Park
(Ford) 5m48.0s; 3 Solberg/Mills (Subaru) 5m48.3s; 4
H.Rovanperä/R.Pietilainen (Peugeot 206 WRC) 5m48.5s;
5 Sainz/Marti (Citroën) 5m49.6s; 6 S.Loeb/D.Elena
(Citroën Xsara WRC) 5m49.7s; PC Ligato/Garcia
(Mitsubishi) 6m04.4s

SS4 CANADA DE RIO PINTO 1 (10.91 KM)
1 Grönholm/Rautiainen (Peugeot) 7m43.4s; 2 Burns/Reid
(Peugeot) 7m46.5s; 3 Mäkinen/Lindström (Subaru)
7m46.6s; 4 Solberg/Mills (Subaru) 7m47.1s; 5 Sainz/Marti
(Citroën) 7m48.0s; 6 Märtin/Park (Ford) 7m48.7s; PC
Ligato/Garcia (Mitsubishi) 8m14.8s

SS5 VILLA ALBERTINA 1 (15.17 KM)
1 Mäkinen/Lindström (Subaru) 8m54.5s; 2
Grönholm/Rautiainen (Peugeot) 8m54.7s; 3 Märtin/Park
(Ford) 8m57.7s; 4 Burns/Reid (Peugeot) 8m58.8s; 5
McRae/Ringer (Citroën) 8m59.3s; 6 Sainz/Marti (Citroën)
8m59.7s; PC N.McShea/C.Patterson (Mitsubishi Lancer
E6) 9m48.9s

SS6 MUSEO FADER 1 (18.49 KM)
1 Sainz/Marti (Citroën) 10m12.7s; 2 Märtin/Park (Ford)
10m14.2s; 3 Grönholm/Rautiainen (Peugeot) 10m14.9s; 4
Mäkinen/Lindström (Subaru) 10m15.5s; 5
Rovanperä/Pietilainen (Peugeot) 10m16.0s; 6
McRae/Ringer (Citroën) 10m17.5s; PC
G.Manfrinato/C.Condotta (Mitsubishi Lancer E6)
11m04.5s

SS7 LA FALDA 1 (9.37 KM)
1 Sainz/Marti (Citroën) 6m25.1s; 2 Loeb/Elena (Citroën)
6m27.6s; 3 Grönholm/Rautiainen (Peugeot) 6m28.0s; 4
Märtin/Park (Ford) 6m29.3s; 5= Mäkinen/Lindström
(Subaru), Solberg/Mills (Subaru) 6m29.7s; PC
McShea/Patterson (Mitsubishi) 7m04.9s

SS8 LA CUMBRE 1 (23.46 KM)
1 Rovanperä/Pietilainen (Peugeot) 18m47.6s; 2
Grönholm/Rautiainen (Peugeot) 18m50.0s; 3 Solberg/Mills
(Subaru) 18m50.9s; 4 Märtin/Park (Ford) 18m53.7s; 5
Sainz/Marti (Citroën) 18m57.5s; 6 Loeb/Elena (Citroën)
18m57.7s; PC T.Arai/T.Sircombe (Subaru Impreza WRX)
19m47.1s

SS9 ASCOCHINGA 1 (28.83 KM)
1 Sainz/Marti (Citroën) 19m07.4s; 2 Loeb/Elena (Citroën)
19m07.6s; 3 Solberg/Mills (Subaru) 19m10.0s; 4
Rovanperä/Pietilainen (Peugeot) 19m12.1s; 5 Burns/Reid
(Peugeot) 19m18.7s; 6 F.Duval/S.Prevot (Ford Focus RS
WRC03) 19m21.3s; PC McShea/Patterson (Mitsubishi)
20m11.2s

SS10 EL ROPOSO 2 (10.03 KM)
1 Märtin/Park (Ford) 5m38.4s; 2 Grönholm/Rautiainen
(Peugeot) 5m40.0s; 3 Rovanperä/Pietilainen (Peugeot)
5m43.7s; 4 Loeb/Elena (Citroën) 5m43.9s; 5= Sainz/Marti
(Citroën), Mäkinen/Lindström (Subaru) 5m44.9s; PC
McShea/Patterson (Mitsubishi) 6m06.2s

SS11 CANADA DE RIO PINTO 2 (10.91 KM)
1 Grönholm/Rautiainen (Peugeot) 7m38.2s; 2
Mäkinen/Lindström (Subaru) 7m41.1s; 3 Märtin/Park
(Ford) 7m42.3s; 4 Solberg/Mills (Subaru) 7m44.6s; 5
Loeb/Elena (Citroën) 7m44.9s; 6 Burns/Reid (Peugeot)
7m45.0s; PC K.Singh/A.Oh (Proton Pert) 8m23.8s

SS12 VILLA ALBERTINA 2 (15.17 KM)
1 Grönholm/Rautiainen (Peugeot) 8m47.5s; 2
Mäkinen/Lindström (Subaru) 8m51.5s; 3 Märtin/Park
(Ford) 8m53.0s; 4 Burns/Reid (Peugeot) 8m54.7s; 5
Sainz/Marti (Citroën) 8m56.0s; 6 Solberg/Mills (Subaru)
8m58.1s; PC McShea/Patterson (Mitsubishi) 9m49.7s

SS13 MUSEO FADER 2 (18.49 KM)
1 Märtin/Park (Ford) 9m49.6s; 2 Grönholm/Rautiainen
(Peugeot) 9m51.3s; 3 Sainz/Marti (Citroën) 9m51.6s; 4
Mäkinen/Lindström (Subaru) 9m54.8s; 5
Rovanperä/Pietilainen (Peugeot) 9m56.7s; 6 Burns/Reid
(Peugeot) 9m57.0s; 6; PC Arai/Sircombe (Subaru)
10m48.0s

SS14 CAPILLA DEL MONTE 1 (23.02 KM)
Cancelled due to spectators

SS15 SAN MARCOS SIERRA 1 (9.61 KM)
Stage stopped after 8 cars. Notional times given to
remaining crews, therefore no representative fastest
times

SS16 CUCHI CORRAL 1 (22.57 KM)
1 Sainz/Martí (Citroën) 13m13.6s; 2 Grönholm/Rautiainen
(Peugeot) 13m14.8s; 3 Burns/Reid (Peugeot) 13m16.7s; 4
Märtin/Park (Ford) 13m18.2s; 5 Solberg/Mills (Subaru)
13m20.2s; 6 Mäkinen/Lindström (Subaru) 13m30.6s; PC
McShea/Patterson (Mitsubishi) 14m32.9s

SS17 COSQUIN (19.19 KM)
1 Grönholm/Rautiainen (Peugeot) 13m17.0s; 2
Märtin/Park (Ford) 13m18.1s; 3 Loeb/Elena (Citroën)
13m20.1s; 4 Sainz/Marti (Citroën) 13m24.1s; 5 Burns/Reid
(Peugeot) 13m25.1s; 6 Rovanperä/Pietilainen (Peugeot)
13m31.6s; PC Arai/Sircombe (Subaru) 14m24.0s

SS18 CARLOS PAZ (14.81 KM)
1 Grönholm/Rautiainen (Peugeot) 10m08.3s; 2 Sainz/Marti
(Citroën) 10m08.4s; 3 Loeb/Elena (Citroën) 10m09.5s; 4
Burns/Reid (Peugeot) 10m13.5s; 5 Solberg/Mills (Subaru)
10m13.9s; 6 Märtin/Park (Ford) 10m16.2s; PC
McShea/Patterson (Mitsubishi) 11m00.0s

SS19 TANTI (9.50 KM)
1 Sainz/Marti (Citroën) 5m52.1s; 2 Grönholm/Rautiainen
(Peugeot) 5m52.3s; 3 Burns/Reid (Peugeot) 5m52.6s; 4
Loeb/Elena (Citroën) 5m54.0s; 5 Märtin/Park (Ford)
5m55.6s; 6 Solberg/Mills (Subaru) 5m56.1s; PC
Arai/Sircombe (Subaru) 6m21.0s

SS20 CAPILLA DEL MONTE 2 (23.02 KM)
1 Grönholm/Rautiainen (Peugeot) 17m06.5s; 2 Sainz/Marti
(Citroën) 17m12.8s; 3 Märtin/Park (Ford) 17m17.2s; 4
Solberg/Mills (Subaru) 17m22.8s; 5 Burns/Reid (Peugeot)
17m26.3s; 6 Mäkinen/Lindström (Subaru) 17m36.4s; PC
Arai/Sircombe (Subaru) 18m20.3s

SS21 CAPILLA DEL MONTE 3 (23.02 KM)
1 Grönholm/Rautiainen (Peugeot) 16m49.2s; 2 Burns/Reid
(Peugeot) 16m58.5s; 3 Solberg/Mills (Subaru) 17m00.6s; 4
Sainz/Marti (Citroën) 17m01.3s; 5 Rovanperä/Pietilainen
(Peugeot) 17m07.3s; 6 Hirvonen/Lehtinen (Ford)
17m30.1s; PC Arai/Sircombe (Subaru) 18m09.9s

SS22 CUCHI CORRAL 1 (22.57 KM)
1 Sainz/Marti (Citroën) 13m04.6s; 2 Grönholm/Rautiainen
(Peugeot) 13m06.3s; 3 Burns/Reid (Peugeot) 13m08.2s; 4
Solberg/Mills (Subaru) 13m13.6s; 5 Hirvonen/Lehtinen
(Ford) 13m23.4s; 6 Rovanperä/Pietilainen (Peugeot)
13m24.4s; PC McShea/Patterson (Mitsubishi) 14m21.4s

SS23 LA FALDA 2 (9.37 KM)
1 Grönholm/Rautiainen (Peugeot) 6m24.4s; 2
Solberg/Mills (Subaru) 6m25.8s; 3 Sainz/Marti (Citroën)
6m25.9s; 4 Burns/Reid (Peugeot) 6m26.5s; 5
D.Auriol/D.Giraudet (Skoda Octavia WRC E3) 6m33.5s; 6
Rovanperä/Pietilainen (Peugeot) 6m33.6s; PC
D.Sola/A.Romani (Mitsubishi Lancer E7) 7m02.9s

SS24 LA CUMBRE 2 (23.46 KM)
1 Grönholm/Rautiainen (Peugeot) 18m23.6s; 2 Burns/Reid
(Peugeot) 18m27.4s; 3 Solberg/Mills (Subaru) 18m33.0s; 4
Sainz/Marti (Citroën) 18m37.4s; 5 Rovanperä/Pietilainen
(Peugeot) 18m38.4s; 6 Auriol/Giraudet (Skoda) 18m57.8s;
PC Sola/Romani (Mitsubishi) 19m42.1s

SS25 ASCOCHINGA 2 (28.83 KM)
1 Sainz/Marti (Citroën) 18m36.5s; 2 Grönholm/Rautiainen
(Peugeot) 18m43.7s; 3 Solberg/Mills (Subaru) 18m51.5s; 4
Rovanperä/Pietilainen (Peugeot) 18m56.6s; 5 Duval/Fortin
(Ford) 19m13.0s; 6 T.Gardemeister/P.Lukander (Skoda
Octavia WRC E3) 19m23.3s; PC Sola/Romani (Mitsubishi)
20m00.0s

Don't try this at home: split seconds later, Marcos Ligato's Lancer gave up the ghost on landing.

MAJOR RETIREMENTS

18	Loeb/Elena	Citroën Xsara WRC		
	Accident	SS20	Gr A
17	McRae/Ringer	Citroën Xsara WRC		
	Fire	SS9	Gr A
4	Märtin/Park	Ford Focus RS WRC03		
	ngine	SS21	Gr A
8	Mäkinen/Lindström	Subaru Impreza WRC2003		
	Withdrawn	SS20		
10	Schwarz/Hiemer	Hyundai Accent WRC3		
	Engine	SS24	Gr A
11	Loix/Smeets	Hyundai Accent WRC3		
	Engine	SS6	Gr A
32	Pozzo/Stillo	Skoda Octavia WRC E3		
	Withdrawn	SS0	Gr A

FIA CLASS WINNERS

A8	Over 2000 cc	Grönholm/Rautiainen
		Peugeot 206 WRC
A7	1600-2000 cc	Aguirre/Lavalle
		Renault Clio Williams
N4	Over 2000 cc	Arai/Sircombe
		Subaru Impreza WRX
N3	1600-2000cc	Angeloni/Angeloni
		Seat Ibiza GTI-16v
N2	1400-1600 cc	Bottazzini/Coronel
		Honda Civic

RALLY LEADERS

Overall: SS1-6 Grönholm; SS7-19 Sainz; SS20 Märtin; SS21-25 Grönholm
PC: SS1-4 Ligato; SS5-25 Arai (SS14 Cancelled)

SPECIAL STAGE ANALYSIS

	1st	2nd	3rd	4th	5th	6th
Grönholm (Peugeot)	11	9	2	-	-	-
Sainz (Citroën)	7	4	2	4	5	1
Märtin (Ford)	2	3	6	2	1	3
Burns (Peugeot)	1	3	3	4	5	2
Mäkinen (Subaru)	1	2	1	4	1	3
Rovanperä (Peugeot)	1	-	1	3	4	3
Solberg (Subaru)	-	2	6	6	3	2
Loeb (Citroën)	-	2	2	2	1	2
McRae (Citroën)	-	-	1	-	1	-
Hirvonen (Ford)	-	-	-	-	1	1
Duval (Ford)	-	-	-	-	1	1
Auriol (Skoda)	-	-	-	-	1	1
Gardemeister (Skoda)	-	-	-	-	-	1

WORLD CHAMPIONSHIP POINTS

Drivers
1 Burns 32; 2 Grönholm 30; 3 Sainz 24; 4= McRae, Loeb 17; 6= Solberg, Märtin 13; 8= Mäkinen 11; 9= Duval, Gardemeister 9 etc

Manufacturers
1 Peugeot 65; 2 Citroën 52; 3 Ford 29; 4 Subaru 27; 5 Skoda 19; 6 Hyundai 3

Junior World Championship
1= Tirabassi, Katajamäki 10; 3= Ligato, Canellas 8; 5= Broccoli, Wilks 6; 7= Aava, Teuronen 5 etc

Production Cup
1= Arai 20; 2 Singh 17; 3= Blomqvist, Rowe 11; 5= Ligato, Sola 8 etc.

ROUTE DETAILS

Original total route of 1376.84 km of which 392.46 km were competitive on 25 stages.
During the event, leg 2 was shortened due to spectator congestion and extra stages were added to leg 3. The following reflect this.

Leg 1 Thursday 8th May – Friday 9th May, 13 Special Stages totalling 176.90 km

Leg 2 Saturday 10th May, 6 Special Stages totalling 98.70 km (1 cancelled totalling 23.02 km)

Leg 3 Sunday 11th May, 5 Special Stages totalling 107.25 km

RESULTS

1	Marcus Grönholm/	Peugeot 206 WRC	
	Timo Rautiainen	4h14m45.0s	Gr A
2	Carlos Sainz/	Citroën Xsara WRC	
	Marc Marti	4h15m11.6s	Gr A
3	Richard Burns/	Peugeot 206 WRC	
	Robert Reid	4h15m57.8s	Gr A
4	Harri Rovanperä/	Peugeot 206 WRC	
	Risto Pietilainen	4h17m04.3s	Gr A
5	Petter Solberg/	Subaru Impreza WRC2003	
	Phil Mills	4h17m56.4s	Gr A
6	Didier Auriol/	Skoda Octavia WRC E3	
	Denis Giraudet	4h22m43.5s	Gr A
7	Toni Gardemeister/	Skoda Octavia WRC E3	
	Paavo Lukander	4h23m18.7s	Gr A
8	François Duval/	Ford Focus RS WRC03	
	Stephane Prevot	4h26m40.3s	Gr A
9	Toshihiro Arai/	Subaru Impreza WRX	
	Tony Sircombe	4h34m46.7s	Gr N
10	Gabriel Raies/	Toyota Corolla WRC	
	Jorge Perez	4h34m48.4s	Gr A

78 starters, 33 finishers

STAGE NUMBERS	1	2	3	4	5	6	7	8	9	10	11	12	13	15	16	17	18	19	20	21	22	23	24	25
Grönholm	1	1	1	1	1	1	4	2	7	6	6	6	6	6	5	4	4	4	2	1	1	1	1	1
Sainz	4	3	3	3	4	2	1	1	1	1	1	1	1	1	1	1	1	3	2	2	2	3	2	
Burns	5	4	4	4	3	5	5	4	4	5	5	3	3	3	3	3	3	4	3	3	3	2	3	
Rovanperä	10	8	6	8	8	7	8	5	2	2	4	4	4	4	5	6	6	5	5	5	5	5	5	
Solberg	2	2	2	2	2	14	13	13	12	8	8	8	8	9	7	7	7	7	6	5	5	5	5	
Auriol	11	13	12	11	10	9	10	9	11	10	11	11	11	11	10	10	10	10	9	8	7	7	6	6
G'meister	9	14	10	10	9	9	9	9	8	6	7	7	7	7	11	11	11	11	11	10	9	8	8	7
Duval	14	9	15	13	12	12	12	11	9	9	9	9	9	8	8	8	8	8	7	6	9	9	8	8
Arai	20	18	19	17	16	14	14	13	12	12	12	12	12	12	12	13	13	11	10	10	11	9	9	
Raies	16	16	17	17	15	22	18	16	15	15	14	14	14	13	13	12	12	12	11	11	10	10	10	
Hirvonen	6	11	13	36	33	26	47	45	39	37	36	32	30	30	28	28	26	26	23	20	20	20	17	16
Schwarz	8	11	11	12	11	11	11	10	10	10	10	10	10	9	9	9	9	9	8	7	6	6	R	
Märtin	12	7	5	6	5	4	3	3	5	3	2	2	2	2	2	2	2	2	1	R				
Mäkinen	7	6	6	5	2	3	2	21	24	23	21	20	19	19	19	19	16	15	13	R				
Loeb	15	15	9	7	7	8	7	6	3	4	3	5	5	5	6	6	5	5	5	R				
McRae	3	5	8	9	6	6	6	7	R															
Loix	13	10	14	14	13	R																		

FINISH LINES

Punctures dogged Harri Rovanperä in the early stages, but he finally scored his first points of the season, taking fourth in his works 206... Subaru's rally had all but run off the rails by the end of the first leg, Petter Solberg eventually salvaging fifth after parking his Impreza on its side in a ditch for two minutes, then spinning at 115 mph, while gearbox trouble on the same corner as in 2002 knocked Tommi Mäkinen out of the reckoning... Subaru's Group N revival continued to gather pace, Toshihiro Arai claiming maximum Production points without much difficulty... Despite wrenching his wrist when the steering kicked in the second leg, Didier Auriol was the top Skoda driver, taking sixth; Toni Gardemeister would have beaten him, however, if it wasn't for a minute's road penalty inflicted before the start for a recce infringement... Colin McRae's rally came to a fiery end on SS9, the crew quelling the blaze a number of times before it eventually destroyed their Xsara... Sébastien Loeb recorded some impressive times in the second leg before crashing his Citroën on SS20...Engine trouble accounted for both works Hyundais, Freddy Loix's damaged by a faulty boost control sensor, Armin Schwarz's blowing out water two stages from the finish with sixth place in sight... François Duval wasn't expected to match Märtin's pace and didn't, but suffered a range of mechanical problems in his works Focus anyway, notably a jammed gearbox towards the finish... Turbocharger and gearbox trouble in the first leg ensured that Mikko Hirvonen was always likely to be the last works finisher, but he scored a point for Ford nevertheless... Dani Solá was the Production class runner-up in his Lancer Evo VII, hampered by a puncture, a temporary loss of power and transmission trouble... Like many drivers, Karamjit Singh was appalled at the roughness of the roads. He was third in the Production class in the works Proton, surviving a bent propshaft, suspension damage and a puncture... Niall McShea looked on course for second in Group N until a heavy landing smashed the Jardine Lloyd Thompson Lancer's oil filter...

PREVIOUS WINNERS

1979	Jean Guichet/Jean Todt	Peugeot 504
1980	Walter Röhrl/Christian Geistdörfer	Fiat 131 Abarth
1981	Guy Fréquelin/Jean Todt	Talbot Sunbeam Lotus
1983	Hannu Mikkola/Arne Hertz	Audi Quattro A1
1984	Stig Blomqvist/Björn Cederberg	Audi Quattro A2
1985	Timo Salonen/Seppo Harjanne	Peugeot 205 Turbo 16
1986	Miki Biasion/Tiziano Siviero	Lancia Delta S4
1987	Miki Biasion/Tiziano Siviero	Lancia Delta HF 4x4
1988	Jorge Recalde/Jorge Del Buono	Lancia Delta Integrale
1989	Mikael Ericsson/Claes Billstam	Lancia Delta Integrale
1990	Miki Biasion/Tiziano Siviero	Lancia Delta Integrale 16v
1991	Carlos Sainz/Luis Moya	Toyota Celica GT4
1992	Didier Auriol/Bernard Occelli	Lancia Delta HF Integrale
1993	Juha Kankkunen/Nicky Grist	Toyota Celica Turbo 4wd
1994	Didier Auriol/Bernard Occelli	Toyota Celica Turbo 4wd
1995	Jorge Recalde/Mārtin Christie	Lancia Delta HF Integrale
1996	Tommi Mäkinen/Seppo Harjanne	Mitsubishi Lancer E3
1997	Tommi Mäkinen/Seppo Harjanne	Mitsubishi Lancer E4
1998	Tommi Mäkinen/Risto Mannisenmäki	Mitsubishi Lancer E5
1999	Juha Kankkunen/Juha Repo	Subaru Impreza WRC99
2000	Richard Burns/Robert Reid	Subaru Impreza WRC2000
2001	Colin McRae/Nicky Grist	Ford Focus RS WRC
2002	Carlos Sainz/Luis Moya	Ford Focus RS WRC02

As the crews headed back to Lamia for the last service of the first leg, the odds had tilted perceptibly in favour of Marcus Grönholm. True, he was only third, but he had recorded some ominously rapid stage times, he was only 15.8 seconds behind the overnight leader, Markko Märtin, and had incontestably made the best of unfavourable circumstances,. Running second on gravel-strewn roads, Ford and its Estonian star looked in danger of letting a glorious opportunity slither from their grasp.

Nothing had gone disastrously wrong – Märtin was leading, after all – but the first casualty had been the plan. Starting seventh, Märtin should have exploited relatively gravel-free stages to romp clear of his most dangerous adversaries. Instead, he had attempted the first loop with tyres that were too hard, he hadn't liked the handling until he reverted to his original choice of anti-roll bars and he had lost time late in the afternoon when the wipers entangled themselves and jammed on one side of the windscreen. Most dramatically of all, the bonnet had flown open on Elatia – the stage on which a puncture had cost him his chance of winning in 2002. Markko was still pink with exertion half an hour later, having driven for 12 miles peering through a slit at the base of the windscreen, as the bonnet had blocked the roof vent and the cockpit temperature rocketed; the following morning, he confessed that he was still feeling the effects.

He had revealed considerable reserves of determination to drop just six seconds to the fastest car, yet the Peugeots were very much within striking distance and Markko himself had described the first leg as 'crucial'. Those were not the only reasons for putting money on Grönholm. From the outset, Märtin hadn't seemed nervous exactly, but ill at ease.

M-Sport's Director, Malcolm Wilson, had been describing the Acropolis as the first real chance of winning with the 2003 Focus for weeks and Märtin had loaded more pressure on himself by lauding the car to the skies. He is a formidable underdog, but he looked far from assured when success was anticipated. It was easy to view him as Grönholm's prey.

The threat from Peugeot evaporated along with the available petrol in Grönholm's fuel tank as he cruised to service, yet Märtin looked just as vulnerable on Saturday morning, losing a few more seconds in Harri Rovanperä's dust when the Finn's 206 fell victim to gearbox trouble. The Ford man admitted to pouring cold water over his head to wake himself up as Petter Solberg closed in. The rally was finely poised, Märtin's first World Championship win far from assured. Defeat would have revived the accusation that he was a gifted driver who lacked the killer instinct; it was too awful to contemplate. And then, with the Focus on song, Märtin began to drive fluently. Unwilling to commence the final leg with the outcome in the balance, he unleashed a salvo of devastating stage times that left his opponents trailing in his wake. In theory, Carlos Sainz should have been contemplating a fourth Acropolis victory. In practice, he knew the last leg was very much a matter of defending second place from Solberg.

Sure enough, aside from a scare when he misheard a pace note, Märtin's chief concern in the closing miles was coping with a World Rally Car's tendency to become more difficult to tame when driven slowly. It had been very much a triumph for Ford as well: unreliability had cost Peugeot dearly, Richard Burns also running into gearbox problems, while a broken driveshaft undid Solberg in the second leg. Märtin's drive that same afternoon brooked no criticism.

The pursuit of Märtin's Ford was unflagging, but unavailing, Petter Solberg (below) and Carlos Sainz (centre) fighting for a distant second place, the Spaniard ultimately taking the verdict. The carnage among the Juniors was predictable. Their senior yardstick, Simon Jean-Joseph, was never seriously troubled (top right). Tyres take enormous punishment on the back roads of Greece; Subaru's Pirellis were equal to the strain.

ACROPOLIS RALLY
RALLYCOURSE World Rally Championship **Round 6**

ACROPOLIS RALLY

Eat dust! Markko Märtin rose to the occasion, leaving his opponents trailing in his wake. It was one of Richard Burns's finest performances of the season, the Reading man grappling with gearbox problems for much of the rally yet still finishing fourth (above). Hyundai endured a soul-destroying week, clutch trouble defeating Jussi Välimäki (top right), whereas Jari-Matti Latvala must have wondered what all the fuss was about, the 18-year-old Finn claiming tenth on his first attempt at the Acropolis (near right). Reliability was Citroën's strongest suit (previous page) and not to be sneezed at in such conditions.

ACROPOLIS RALLY

STATISTICS World Rally Championship **Round 6**

Rendina

17/20 18/21 19/22

ATHENS

LAMIA

1/6

3/9

2/7

8/16

4/12

5/13

Elatia

11-15

Amfissa

10-14

ITEA

Acropolis Rally, 6-8 June 2003,
FIA World Rally Championship Round 6

RUNNING ORDER

2	Richard Burns/	Peugeot 206 WRC
	Robert Reid	Gr A
1	Marcus Grönholm/	Peugeot 206 WRC
	Timo Rautiainen	Gr A
19	Carlos Sainz/	Citroën Xsara WRC
	Marc Marti	Gr A
18	Sébastien Loeb/	Citroën Xsara WRC
	Daniel Elena	Gr A
17	Colin McRae/	Citroën Xsara WRC
	Derek Ringer	Gr A
7	Petter Solberg/	Subaru Impreza WRC2003
	Phil Mills	Gr A
4	Markko Märtin/	Ford Focus RS WRC03
	Michael Park	Gr A
8	Tommi Mäkinen/	Subaru Impreza WRC2003
	Kaj Lindström	Gr A
5	François Duval/	Ford Focus RS WRC03
	Stéphane Prevot	Gr A
15	Toni Gardemeister/	Skoda Octavia WRC E3
	Paavo Lukander	Gr A
3	Harri Rovanperä/	Peugeot 206 WRC
	Risto Pietilainen	Gr A
21	Gilles Panizzi/	Peugeot 206 WRC
	Hervé Panizzi	Gr A
14	Didier Auriol/	Skoda Octavia WRC E3
	Denis Giraudet	Gr A
10	Armin Schwarz/	Hyundai Accent WRC3
	Manfred Hiemer	Gr A
11	Freddy Loix/	Hyundai Accent WRC3
	Sven Smeets	Gr A
6	Mikko Hirvonen/	Ford Focus RS WRC02
	Jarmo Lehtinen	Gr A
22	Roman Kresta/	Peugeot 206 WRC
	Jan Tomanek	Gr A
24	Juuso Pykälistö/	Peugeot 206 WRC
	Esko Mertsalmi	Gr A
25	Daniel Sola/	Citroën Xsara WRC
	Alex Romani	Gr A
12	Jussi Välimäki/	Hyundai Accent WRC3
	Tero Gardemeister	Gr A
26	Manfred Stohl/	Hyundai Accent WRC3
	Ilka Minor	Gr A
20	Jari-Matti Latvala/	Ford Focus RS WRC02
	Carl Williamson	Gr A

SPECIAL STAGE TIMES

SS1 PAVLIANI 1 (24.45 KM)
1 F.Duval/S.Prevot (Ford Focus RS WRC03) 19m54.7s;
2 M.Märtin/M.Park (Ford Focus RS WRC03) 19m56.6s;
3 C.McRae/D.Ringer (Citroën Xsara WRC) 19m58.8s;
4 C.Sainz/M.Marti (Citroën Xsara WRC) 20m03.3s;
5 M.Grönholm/T.Rautiainen (Peugeot 206 WRC) 20m04.4s;
6 T.Mäkinen/K.Lindström (Subaru Impreza WRC2003) 20m05.7s; JWC B.Tirabassi/J.Renucci (Renault Clio) 21m50.4s

SS2 STROMI 1 (14.61 KM)
1 Märtin/Park (Ford) 11m40.2s; 2 McRae/Ringer (Citroën) 11m42.9s; 3 Duval/Prevot (Ford) 11m44.6s; 4 G.Panizzi/H.Panizzi (Peugeot 206 WRC) 11m44.9s; 5 Mäkinen/Lindström (Subaru) 11m46.4s; 6 D.Auriol/D.Giraudet (Skoda Octavia WRC E3) 11m46.9s; JWC D.Carlsson/M.Andersson (Suzuki Ignis) 12m57.0s

SS3 ELEFTHEROHORI (18.67 KM)
1 H.Rovanperä/R.Pietilainen (Peugeot 206 WRC) 11m28.2s; 2 Märtin/Park (Ford) 11m31.0s; 3 Duval/Prevot (Ford) 11m31.6s; 4 Grönholm/Rautiainen (Peugeot) 11m31.7s; 5 McRae/Ringer (Citroën) 11m32.1s; 6 P.Solberg/P.Mills (Subaru Impreza WRC2003) 11m34.2s; JWC Carlsson/Andersson (Suzuki) 12m45.3s

SS4 RENGINI 1 (11.84 KM)
1 Rovanperä/Pietilainen (Peugeot) 8m41.8s; 2 McRae/Ringer (Citroën) 8m42.9s; 3 Duval/Prevot (Ford) 8m46.4s; 4 Märtin/Park (Ford) 8m48.1s; 5 Panizzi/Panizzi (Peugeot) 8m49.4s; 6 Mäkinen/Lindström (Subaru) 8m51.1s; JWC Tirabassi/Renucci (Renault) 9m52.4s

SS5 ELATIA – ZELI 1 (34.68 KM)
1 Rovanperä/Pietilainen (Peugeot) 24m21.9s; 2 McRae/Ringer (Citroën) 24m24.4s; 3 Grönholm/Rautiainen (Peugeot) 24m26.1s; 4 Märtin/Park (Ford) 24m27.9s; 5 Sainz/Marti (Citroën) 24m32.5s; 6 Solberg/Mills (Subaru) 24m37.2s; JWC Tirabassi/Renucci (Renault) 27m17.5s

SS6 PAVLIANI 2 (24.45 KM)
1 Solberg/Mills (Subaru) 19m29.5s; 2 Grönholm/Rautiainen (Peugeot) 19m36.7s; 3 Rovanperä/Pietilainen (Peugeot) 19m40.1s; 4 Mäkinen/Lindström (Subaru) 19m40.6s; 5 Märtin/Park (Ford) 19m42.7s; 6 Sainz/Marti (Citroën) 19m46.3s; JWC Tirabassi/Renucci (Renault) 21m36.6s

SS7 STROMI 2 (14.61 KM)
1 Grönholm/Rautiainen (Peugeot) 11m25.6s; 2 Solberg/Mills (Subaru) 11m25.8s; 3 Rovanperä/Pietilainen (Peugeot) 11m26.7s; 4 Sainz/Marti (Citroën) 11m28.1s; 5 Panizzi/Panizzi (Peugeot) 11m28.2s; 6 Märtin/Park (Ford) 11m28.5s; JWC Tirabassi/Renucci (Renault) 12m47.5s

SS8 LILEA 1 (2.25 KM)
Cancelled – due to excessive dust at the super-special !

SS9 MENDENITSA (17.34 KM)
1 Solberg/Mills (Subaru) 10m55.0s; 2 Sainz/Marti (Citroën) 10m59.6s; 3 Rovanperä/Pietilainen (Peugeot) 11m00.9s; 4 Märtin/Park (Ford) 11m01.7s; 5 Mäkinen/Lindström (Subaru) 11m03.8s; 6 R.Burns/R.Reid (Peugeot 206 WRC) 11m05.2s; JWC Tirabassi/Renucci (Renault) 12m30.5s

SS10 BAUXITES 1 (23.45 KM)
1 Solberg/Mills (Subaru) 14m14.8s; 2 Sainz/Marti (Citroën) 14m16.7s; 3= McRae/Ringer (Citroën), Burns/Reid (Peugeot) 14m18.8s; 5 Märtin/Park (Ford) 14m25.3s; 6 Mäkinen/Lindström (Subaru) 14m29.9s; JWC Tirabassi/Renucci (Renault) 16m01.7s

SS11 DROSOHORI 1 (17.76 KM)
1 Märtin/Park (Ford) 14m48.6s; 2 Sainz/Marti (Citroën) 14m52.4s; 3 Burns/Reid (Peugeot) 14m53.7s; 4 McRae/Ringer (Citroën) 14m57.9s; 5 Mäkinen/Lindström (Subaru) 15m05.2s; 6 Auriol/Giraudet (Skoda) 15m10.2s; JWC Tirabassi/Renucci (Renault) 16m28.7s

SS12 RENGINI 2 (11.84 KM)
1 Rovanperä/Pietilainen (Peugeot) 8m30.2s; 2 Burns/Reid (Peugeot) 8m31.3s; 3 Solberg/Mills (Subaru) 8m34.4s; 4 McRae/Ringer (Citroën) 8m34.7s; 5 Sainz/Marti (Citroën) 8m36.2s; 6 Märtin/Park (Ford) 8m37.5s; JWC Tirabassi/Renucci (Renault) 9m45.0s

SS13 ELATIA – ZELI 2 (34.68 KM)
1 Märtin/Park (Ford) 23m44.2s; 2 Solberg/Mills (Subaru) 23m49.2s; 3 Rovanperä/Pietilainen (Peugeot) 23m49.7s; 4= McRae/Ringer (Citroën), Sainz/Marti (Citroën) 23m55.0s; 6 Burns/Reid (Peugeot) 23m57.8s; JWC Carlsson/Andersson (Suzuki) 27m04.4s

SS14 BAUXITES 2 (23.45 KM)
1 Märtin/Park (Ford) 13m51.9s; 2 Solberg/Mills (Subaru) 13m53.0s; 3 McRae/Ringer (Citroën) 13m55.5s; 4 Burns/Reid (Peugeot) 13m59.0s; 5 Panizzi/Panizzi (Peugeot) 13m59.8s; 6 Sainz/Marti (Citroën) 14m00.9s; JWC Carlsson/Andersson (Suzuki) 15m39.6s

SS15 DROSOHORI 2 (17.76 KM)
1 Märtin/Park (Ford) 14m23.6s; 2 Solberg/Mills (Subaru) 14m27.3s; 3 Sainz/Marti (Citroën) 14m30.3s; 4 Rovanperä/Pietilainen (Peugeot) 14m33.7s; 5 Burns/Reid (Peugeot) 14m35.6s; 6 Panizzi/Panizzi (Peugeot) 14m39.4s; JWC Tirabassi/Renucci (Renault) 16m05.3s

SS16 LILEA 2 (2.25 KM)
1 Sainz/Marti (Citroën) 1m57.6s; 2= Märtin/Park (Ford), Auriol/Giraudet (Skoda) 1m58.0s; 4 Rovanperä/Pietilainen (Peugeot) 1m58.3s; 5 Solberg/Mills (Subaru) 1m58.6s; 6 McRae/Ringer (Citroën) 1m59.2s; JWC Carlsson/Andersson (Suzuki) 2m08.9s

SS17 DIKASTRO 1 (18.40 KM)
1 Solberg/Mills (Subaru) 16m08.7s; 2 Märtin/Park (Ford) 16m18.6s; 3 McRae/Ringer (Citroën) 16m19.7s; 4= Burns/Reid (Peugeot), Mäkinen/Lindström (Subaru) 16m20.1s; 6 Rovanperä/Pietilainen (Peugeot) 16m22.0s; JWC Tirabassi/Renucci (Renault) 17m59.8s

SS18 NEW TARZAN 1 (20.65 KM)
1 Solberg/Mills (Subaru) 15m27.8s; 2 McRae/Ringer (Citroën) 15m29.5s; 3 Burns/Reid (Peugeot) 15m30.4s; 4 Sainz/Marti (Citroën) 15m32.1s; 5 Märtin/Park (Ford) 15m32.5s; 6 Mäkinen/Lindström (Subaru) 15m35.7s; JWC Carlsson/Andersson (Suzuki) 16m58.0s

SS19 AGIOS STEFANOS 1 (13.47 KM)
1 Mäkinen/Lindström (Subaru) 10m02.6s; 2 Sainz/Marti (Citroën) 10m03.1s; 3 McRae/Ringer (Citroën) 10m03.4s; 4 Solberg/Mills (Subaru) 10m03.6s; 5 Burns/Reid (Peugeot) 10m04.6s; 6 Märtin/Park (Ford) 10m07.7s; JWC Tirabassi/Renucci (Renault) 11m04.8s

SS20 DIKASTRO 2 (18.40 KM)
1 Solberg/Mills (Subaru) 15m58.3s; 2 Panizzi/Panizzi (Peugeot) 16m04.1s; 3 Sainz/Marti (Citroën) 16m04.8s; 4 Mäkinen/Lindström (Subaru) 16m06.6s; 5 Rovanperä/Pietilainen (Peugeot) 16m11.2s; 6 Burns/Reid (Peugeot) 16m11.8s; JWC Tirabassi/Renucci (Renault) 17m47.0s

SS21 NEW TARZAN 2 (20.65 KM)
1 Sainz/Martí (Citroën) 15m10.3s; 2 Panizzi/Panizzi (Peugeot) 15m13.1s; 3 Märtin/Park (Ford) 15m13.6s; 4 Burns/Reid (Peugeot) 15m14.5s; 5 Rovanperä/Pietilainen (Peugeot) 15m14.9s; 6 Mäkinen/Lindström (Subaru) 15m22.0s; JWC Carlsson/Andersson (Suzuki) 16m51.6s

SS22 AGIOS STEFANOS 2 (13.47 KM)
1 Solberg/Mills (Subaru) 9m46.7s; 2 Burns/Reid (Peugeot) 9m49.2s; 3 Sainz/Martí (Citroën) 9m49.4s; 4 Märtin/Park (Ford) 9m50.1s; 5 Panizzi/Panizzi (Peugeot) 9m51.8s; 6 Rovanperä/Pietilainen (Peugeot) 9m54.2s; WC Carlsson/Andersson (Suzuki) 10m56.4s

MAJOR RETIREMENTS

1	Grönholm/R'iainen	Peugeot 206 WRC		
	Fuel feed	SS7	Gr A
18	Loeb/Elena	Citroën Xsara WRC		
	Engine	SS1	Gr A
5	Duval/Prevot	Ford Focus RS WRC03		
	Accident	SS5	Gr A
15	Gardemeister/L'der	Skoda Octavia WRC E3		
	Engine	SS6	Gr A
10	Schwarz/Hiemer	Hyundai Accent WRC3		
	Engine	SS1	Gr A
11	Loix/Smeets	Hyundai Accent WRC3		
	Suspension	SS3	Gr A
6	Hirvonen/Lehtinen	Ford Focus RS WRC02		
	Suspension	SS6	Gr A
22	Kresta/Tomanek	Peugeot 206 WRC		
	Mechanical	SS17	Gr A
24	Pykälistö/Mertsalmi	Peugeot 206 WRC		
	Accident	SS3	Gr A
12	Välimäki/G'meister	Hyundai Accent WRC3		
	Clutch	SS9	

FIA CLASS WINNERS

A8 Over 2000 cc	Märtin/Park
	Ford Focus RS WRC03
A6 1400-1600 cc	Jean-Joseph/Boyere
	Renault Clio
N4 Over 2000 cc	Petalidis/Samartzis
	Mitsubishi Lancer E7

RALLY LEADERS
Overall: SS1 Duval; SS2-22 Märtin
JWC: SS1-22 Tirabassi

SPECIAL STAGE ANALYSIS

	1st	2nd	3rd	4th	5th	6th
Solberg (Subaru)	7	4	1	1	1	2
Märtin (Ford)	5	4	1	4	3	3
Rovanperä (Peugeot)	4	-	4	2	2	2
Sainz (Citroën)	2	5	2	4	2	2
Grönholm (Peugeot)	1	1	1	1	1	-
Duval (Ford)	1	-	3	-	-	-
Mäkinen (Subaru)	1	-	-	3	3	5
McRae (Citroën)	-	4	5	3	1	2
Burns (Peugeot)	-	2	3	3	2	3
Panizzi (Peugeot)	-	2	-	1	4	1
Auriol (Skoda)	-	1	-	-	-	2

WORLD CHAMPIONSHIP POINTS
Drivers
1 Burns 37; 2 Sainz 32; 3 Grönholm 30; 4 Märtin 23; 5 Solberg 19; 6 McRae 18; 7 Loeb 17; 8 Mäkinen 15; 9= Duval, Gardemeister 9 etc

Manufacturers
1 Peugeot 73; 2 Citroën 62; 3 Ford 39; 4 Subaru 37; 5 Skoda 20; 6 Hyundai 3

Junior World Championship
1= Tirabassi 20; 2 Canellas 13; 3 Aava 11; 4 Katajamäki 10; 5 Wilks 9; 6= Ligato, Carlsson 8 etc

Production Cup
1= Arai 20; 2 Singh 17; 3= Blomqvist, Rowe 11; 5= Ligato, Sola 8 etc

ROUTE DETAILS
Total route of 1443.44 km of which 396.88 km were competitive on 21 stages (1 cancelled totalling 2.25 km)

Leg 1 Friday 6th June, 7 Special Stages totalling 143.31 km (1 cancelled totalling 2.25 km)

Leg 2 Saturday 7th June, 8 Special Stages totalling 148.53 km

Leg 3 Sunday 8th June, 6 Special Stages totalling 105.04 km

RESULTS

1	Markko Märtin/	Ford Focus RS WRC03		
	Michael Park	4h53m40.5s	Gr A
2	Carlos Sainz/	Citroën Xsara WRC		
	Marc Marti	4h54m26.5s	Gr A
3	Petter Solberg/	Subaru Impreza WRC2003		
	Phil Mills	4h54m33.2s	
4	Richard Burns/	Peugeot 206 WRC		
	Robert Reid	4h55m47.1s	Gr A
5	Tommi Mäkinen/	Subaru Impreza WRC2003		
	Kaj Lindström	4h55m52.8s	Gr A
6	Harri Rovanperä/	Peugeot 206 WRC		
	Risto Pietilainen	4h57m25.2s	
7	Gilles Panizzi/	Peugeot 206 WRC		
	Hervé Panizzi	4h57m34.8s	Gr A
8	Colin McRae/	Citroën Xsara WRC		
	Derek Ringer	4h57m45.5s	GrA
9	Didier Auriol/	Skoda Octavia WRC E3		
	Denis Giraudet	5h00m07.7s	Gr A
10	Jari-Matti Latvala/	Fors Focus RS WRC02		
	Carl Williamson	5h05m13.9s	

82 starters, 37 finishers

STAGE NUMBERS

STAGE NUMBERS	1	2	3	4	5	6	7	8	9	10	11	12	13	15	16	17	18	19	20	21	22
Märtin	2	1	1	1	1	1	1	1	1	1	1	1	1	1	1	1	1	1	1	1	1
Sainz	4	7	8	7	4	6	4	4	3	2	2	2	2	2	2	2	2	2	3	2	2
Solberg	7	6	5	8	6	4	3	3	5	4	3	3	3	3	3	3	3	3	2	3	3
Burns	12	12	10	12	11	10	9	8	7	7	6	6	6	6	6	6	6	6	6	5	4
Mäkinen	6	3	4	4	5	5	5	5	4	3	4	5	5	5	5	5	5	5	5	4	5
Rovanperä	8	8	6	3	2	2	2	2	9	9	8	7	8	7	7	7	7	7	7	6	6
Panizzi	10	5	7	5	7	7	6	7	6	6	7	9	9	9	8	8	8	8	8	7	7
McRae	3	16	14	9	8	8	7	6	5	4	3	3	4	4	4	4	4	4	4	8	8
Auriol	13	10	9	10	9	9	8	9	8	8	9	9	9	9	9	9	9	9	9	9	9
Latvala	18	18	17	16	14	13	12	12	13	13	12	12	12	12	11	11	10	10	10	10	10
Stohl	11	9	12	13	12	11	10	10	10	10	11	11	11	10	10	11	11	11	11	11	
Sola	16	15	16	17	15	14	13	13	12	11	13	13	13	13	12	12	12	12	12		
Kresta	14	14	13	14	13	12	11	11	11	11	10	10	10	10	R						
Välimäki	34	25	23	23	16	15	14	R													
Grönholm	5	4	3	6	3	3	R														
G'meister	17	17	15	15	18	R															
Hirvonen	9	11	11	11	10	R															
Duval	1	2	2	2	R																
Pykälistö	15	13	R																		
Loix	67	63	R																		

FINISH LINES
Having battled against brake problems for much of the rally, Colin McRae slumped from fourth to eighth thanks to an electrical problem in his Xsara on the penultimate stage... Petter Solberg lost a few seconds in McRae's dust, but a spin also ensured that the Norwegian Subaru driver was third rather than second... Sébastien Loeb didn't even complete the first stage, retiring his Xsara with a blown engine... Jari-Matti Latvala celebrated his first World Championship rally for Ford by finishing tenth... It was a disastrous rally for Hyundai, Freddy Loix retiring with front suspension damage on SS3; his Accent also caught fire briefly when a shock absorber reservoir burst and sprayed oil on to the turbo... Armin Schwarz didn't get that far, the cambelt breaking on SS1... Jussi Välimäki looked on course for a finish until the clutch failed and he went OTL... François Duval led briefly, only to retire when he slid his Focus into a ditch and got stuck... Toni Gardemeister dropped out when his Octavia blew its turbo in the first leg... Brice Tirabassi survived a minor excursion and overheating to take a fine Junior Championship class win in his Clio... Two of the Super 1600 front runners didn't survive the first stage, Marcos Ligato retiring his Fiat on the same corner as Kris Meeke abandoned his Opel, both cars with broken steering... Ville-Pertti Teuronen lasted only one more stage before his Ignis snapped a driveshaft... Guy Wilks survived all kinds of steering problems to struggle home seventh in class, sixth in World Championship classification in his Puma... Simon Jean-Joseph was in excellent form once more, taking his fourth successive 1600 class win at World Championship level in his Clio...

RECENT WINNERS

1965	Carl-Magnus Skogh/'Tandlakare'	Volvo 122S
1966	Bengt Söderstrom/Gunnar Palm	Ford Lotus Cortina
1967	Paddy Hopkirk/Ron Crellin	Mini Cooper S
1968	Roger Clark/Jim Porter	Ford Escort TC
1969	Pauli Toivonen/Matti Kolari	Porsche 911S
1970	Jean-Luc Thérier/Marcel Callewaert	Alpine Renault A110
1971	Ove Andersson/Arne Hertz	Alpine Renault A110
1972	Håkan Lindberg/Helmut Eisendle	Fiat 124 Spyder
1973	Jean-Luc Thérier/Christian Delferrier	Alpine Renault A110
1975	Walter Röhrl/Jochen Berger	Opel Ascona
1976	Harry Kallström/Claes-Goran Andersson	Datsun 160J
1977	Björn Waldegård/Hans Thorszelius	Ford Escort RS
1978	Walter Röhrl/Christian Geistdörfer	Fiat 131 Abarth
1979	Björn Waldegård/Hans Thorszelius	Ford Escort RS
1980	Ari Vatanen/David Richards	Ford Escort RS
1981	Ari Vatanen/David Richards	Ford Escort RS
1982	Michèle Mouton/Fabrizia Pons	Audi Quattro
1983	Walter Röhrl/Christian Geistdörfer	Lancia Rally 037
1984	Stig Blomqvist/Björn Cederberg	Audi Quattro A2
1985	Timo Salonen/Seppo Harjanne	Peugeot 205 Turbo 16
1986	Juha Kankkunen/Juha Piironen	Peugeot 205 Turbo 16 E2
1987	Markku Alén/Ilkka Kivimäki	Lancia Delta HF 4x4
1988	Miki Biasion/Tiziano Siviero	Lancia Delta Integrale
1989	Miki Biasion/Tiziano Siviero	Lancia Delta Integrale
1990	Carlos Sainz/Luis Moya	Toyota Celica GT4
1991	Juha Kankkunen/Juha Piironen	Lancia Delta Integrale 16v
1992	Didier Auriol/Bernard Occelli	Lancia Delta HF Integrale
1993	Miki Biasion/Tiziano Siviero	Ford Escort RS Cosworth
1994	Carlos Sainz/Luis Moya	Subaru Impreza 555
1995	Aris Vovos/Kostas Stefanis	Lancia Delta HF Integrale
1996	Colin McRae/Derek Ringer	Subaru Impreza 555
1997	Carlos Sainz/Luis Moya	Ford Escort WRC
1998	Colin McRae/Nicky Grist	Subaru Impreza WRC98
1999	Richard Burns/Robert Reid	Subaru Impreza WRC99
2000	Colin McRae/Nicky Grist	Ford Focus WRC
2001	Colin McRae/Nicky Grist	Ford Focus RS WRC01
2002	Colin McRae/Nicky Grist	Ford Focus RS WRC02

Younger rivals recoil from getting out of shape. To the fans' delight, Colin McRae adheres to traditional methods.

CYPRUS RALLY

Mohammed Ali in his prime couldn't have played Harri Rovanperä with more gusto; while most of his opponents looked dejected – even punch drunk – Petter Solberg appeared to be revelling in every moment of one of the most punishing World Championship rallies of recent times. He was driving to a plan, he declared, he had something in hand and Rovanperä could beat him only on the handful of stages that were predominantly uphill. The intention was plain enough: Rovanperä was to conclude that Peugeot power was his sole asset against sheer driving ability and Prodrive's engineers were given a little reminder that the Impreza's flat-four was short of muscle. With a day of the Cyprus Rally to run and 25 seconds in hand, Solberg announced that the fight was on and that he was ready to attack.

Few were disposed to bet on Rovanperä. It had been an admirable performance, in which the slender Finn had overcome major gearbox problems in the first leg and a bout of overheating in the second. He alone had sustained any kind of challenge to the Subaru driver, but every time he inched a little closer, Solberg had been able to retaliate. The Norwegian had driven flawlessly. It wasn't difficult to believe that he could go quicker if necessary.

In the event, Rovanperä's assault never came. By Saturday night, Peugeot Sport's management had seen and suffered enough. They had fared no worse than the bulk of their rivals – there were just 18 of the 51 starters left by then – but they were entirely dependent on Rovanperä after the loss of Marcus Grönholm thanks to a broken propshaft and then Richard Burns, after a prolonged battle with overheating. If Rovanperä retired in pursuit of Solberg, Citroën would sweep the next three

places and the precious manufacturers' championship lead would be in jeopardy; better to settle for second.

Had Burns coaxed his 206 the last mile to service on Saturday afternoon, Rovanperä might have been permitted to seek a gap in Solberg's defences. There didn't seem much doubt that Petter was ready for a fight – even when a hapless bird managed to fly through the roof vent – but there were at least some grounds for thinking that the Impreza was taking real punishment. As the ambient temperature soared to 36 degrees Celsius, the engineers were obliged to reduce hydraulic pressure in the transmission and differential swaps became almost a matter of routine, not because they were giving immediate cause for alarm, but simply to ensure that the car left the service area with cold oil in the stifling heat. A small, tank tape 'fence' appeared in the radiator opening midway through the rally as well, a hastily contrived modification to lower the air intake temperature.

While Rovanperä manfully contained his disappointment, Peugeot's decision turned out to be academic. A broken driveshaft hamstrung its surviving car on Sunday morning and although the four minutes separating the first two did Rovanperä no justice, he was a shade lucky to remain runner-up. With three Xsaras running strongly, Citroën might have been expected to order Sébastien Loeb to press home the attack. Instead, he maintained his defensive pace and fell 2.8 seconds short after more than five hours of competitive driving. The only hint of last-stage exuberance came from Solberg, of all people, who relaxed and shot off the road momentarily. Cyprus had knocked the stuffing out of everyone else.

Heat and dust suited the unquenchable Petter Solberg down to the ground (top left), but the Norwegian was made to work hard for his victory, Harri Rovanperä dogging him until the dying kilometres in the last Peugeot. The Limassol service area, variously dubbed 'Camp X-ray' or 'Sangatte,' provided a debilitating environment for the mechanics.

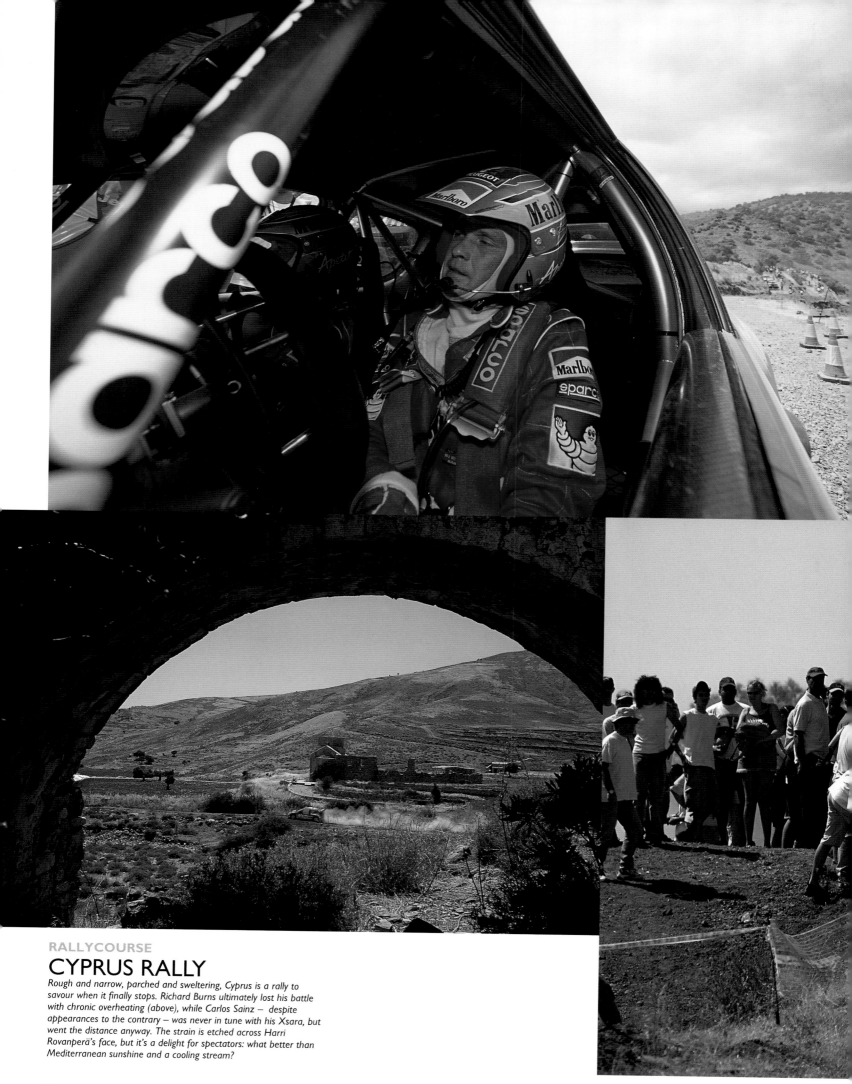

CYPRUS RALLY

Rough and narrow, parched and sweltering, Cyprus is a rally to
savour when it finally stops. Richard Burns ultimately lost his battle
with chronic overheating (above), while Carlos Sainz – despite
appearances to the contrary – was never in tune with his Xsara, but
went the distance anyway. The strain is etched across Harri
Rovanperä's face, but it's a delight for spectators: what better than
Mediterranean sunshine and a cooling stream?

CYPRUS RALLY

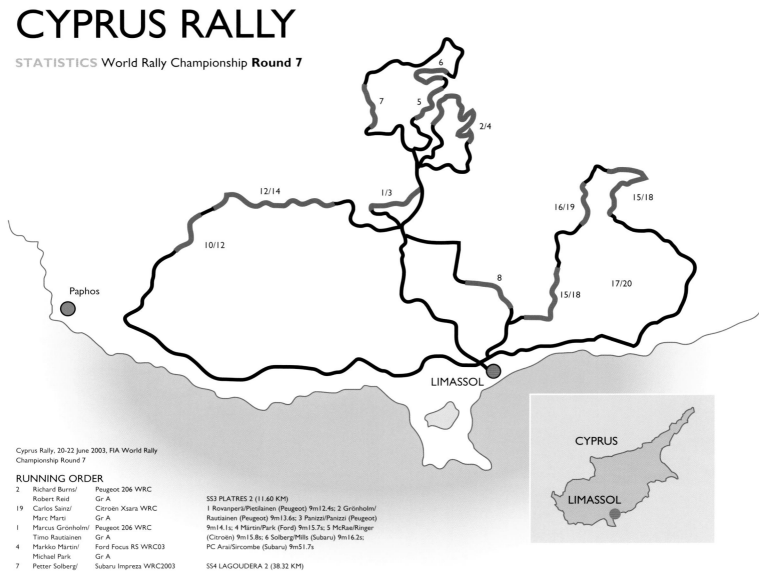

Cyprus Rally, 20-22 June 2003, FIA World Rally
Championship Round 7

RUNNING ORDER

2	Richard Burns/	Peugeot 206 WRC
	Robert Reid	Gr A
19	Carlos Sainz/	Citroën Xsara WRC
	Marc Marti	Gr A
1	Marcus Grönholm/	Peugeot 206 WRC
	Timo Rautiainen	Gr A
4	Markko Märtin/	Ford Focus RS WRC03
	Michael Park	Gr A
7	Petter Solberg/	Subaru Impreza WRC2003
	Phil Mills	Gr A
17	Colin McRae/	Citroën Xsara WRC
	Derek Ringer	Gr A
18	Sébastien Loeb/	Citroën Xsara WRC
	Daniel Elena	Gr A
8	Tommi Mäkinen/	Subaru Impreza WRC2003
	Kaj Lindström	Gr A
5	François Duval/	Ford Focus RS WRC03
	Stéphane Prevot	Gr A
15	Toni Gardemeister/	Skoda Octavia WRC E3
	Paavo Lukander	Gr A
3	Harri Rovanperä/	Peugeot 206 WRC
	Risto Pietilainen	Gr A
20	Gilles Panizzi/	Peugeot 206 WRC
	Hervé Panizzi	Gr A
14	Didier Auriol/	Skoda Octavia WRC E3
	Denis Giraudet	Gr A
10	Armin Schwarz/	Hyundai Accent WRC3
	Manfred Hiemer	Gr A
11	Freddy Loix/	Hyundai Accent WRC3
	Sven Smeets	Gr A
6	Mikko Hirvonen/	Ford Focus RS WRC02
	Jarmo Lehtinen	Gr A
22	Juuso Pykälistö	Peugeot 206 WRC
	Esko Mertsalmi	Gr A
21	Antony Warmbold/	Ford Focus RS WRC02
	Gemma Price	Gr A
12	Justin Dale/	Hyundai Accent WRC3
	Andrew Bargery	Gr A

SPECIAL STAGE TIMES

SS1 PLATRES 1 (11.60 KM)
1 H.Rovanperä/R.Pietilainen (Peugeot 206WRC) 9m27.1s;
2 P.Solberg/P.Mills (Subaru Impreza WRC2003) 9m32.9s;
3 D.Auriol/D.Giraudet (Skoda Octavia WRC E3) 9m33.9s;
4 C.McRae/D.Ringer (Citroën Xsara WRC) 9m35.3s;
5 G.Panizzi/H.Panizzi (Peugeot 206 WRC) 9m35.5s;
6 M.Hirvonen/J.Lehtinen (Ford Focus WRC02) 9m37.3s;
PC T.Arai/T.Sircombe (Subaru Impreza WRX) 9m58.0s

SS2 LAGOUDERA 1 (38.32 KM)
1 Rovanperä/Pietilainen (Peugeot) 35m18.4s; 2 T.Mäkinen/
K.Lindström (Subaru Impreza WRC2002) 35m21.0s;
3 Panizzi/Panizzi (Peugeot) 35m25.4s; 4 M.Grönholm/
T.Rautiainen (Peugeot 206 WRC) 35m26.2s; 5 Solberg/
Mills (Subaru) 35m32.7s; 6 M.Märtin/M.Park (Ford Focus
RS WRC03) 35m41.3s; PC Arai/Sircombe (Subaru)
38m11.4s

SS3 PLATRES 2 (11.60 KM)
1 Rovanperä/Pietilainen (Peugeot) 9m12.4s; 2 Grönholm/
Rautiainen (Peugeot) 9m13.6s; 3 Panizzi/Panizzi (Peugeot)
9m14.1s; 4 Märtin/Park (Ford) 9m15.7s; 5 McRae/Ringer
(Citroën) 9m15.8s; 6 Solberg/Mills (Subaru) 9m16.2s;
PC Arai/Sircombe (Subaru) 9m51.7s

SS4 LAGOUDERA 2 (38.32 KM)
1 Grönholm/Rautiainen (Peugeot) 34m30.3s; 2 S.Loeb/
D.Elena (Citroën Xsara WRC) 34m31.8s; 3 Solberg/Mills
(Subaru) 34m38.3s; 4 C.Sainz/M.Marti (Citroën Xsara
WRC) 34m40.5s; 5 McRae/Ringer (Citroën) 34m48.3s;
6 Panizzi/Panizzi (Peugeot) 34m49.6s; PC J.Kulig/J.Baran
(Mitsubishi Lancer E6) 39m13.7s

SS5 KOURDALI (15.00 KM)
1 Mäkinen/Lindström (Subaru) 15m48.5s; 2 Solberg/Mills
(Subaru) 15m56.8s; 3 Rovanperä/Pietilainen (Peugeot)
16m03.3s; 4 Loeb/Elena (Citroën) 16m15.6s; 5 R.Burns/
R.Reid (Peugeot 206 WRC) 16m20.0s; 6 Panizzi/Panizzi
(Peugeot) 16m22.8s; PC M.Ligato/R.Garcia (Mitsubishi
Lancer E7) 17m13.1s

SS6 ASINOU (25.61 KM)
1 Solberg/Mills (Subaru) 26m28.3s; 2 Rovanperä/Pietilainen
(Peugeot) 26m34.1s; 3 Sainz/Marti (Citroën) 26m54.1s;
4 Loeb/Elena (Citroën) 26m54.6s; 5 Burns/Reid (Peugeot)
27m01.3s; 6 McRae/Ringer (Citroën) 27m02.4s;
PC D.Sola/A.Romani (Mitsubishi Lancer E7) 28m30.3s

SS7 ORKONDAS (17.99 KM)
1 Mäkinen/Lindström (Subaru) 19m02.7s; 2 Solberg/Mills
(Subaru) 19m11.0s; 3 Rovanperä/Pietilainen (Peugeot)
19m15.6s; 4 McRae/Ringer (Citroën) 19m28.1s; 5 Sainz/
Martí (Citroën) 19m32.8s; 6 Loeb/Elena (Citroën)
19m33.3s; PC Ligato/Garcia (Mitsubishi) 20m33.4s

SS8 AKROUNDA (7.99 KM)
1 Mäkinen/Lindström (Subaru) 8m01.4s; 2 Rovanperä/
Pietilainen (Peugeot) 8m03.5s; 3 Solberg/Mills (Subaru)
8m06.5s; 4 Loeb/Elena (Citroën) 8m15.2s; 5 McRae/Ringer
(Citroën) 8m15.3s; 6 Burns/Reid (Peugeot) 8m17.1s;
PC Ligato/Garcia (Mitsubishi) 8m32.7s

SS9 FOINI 1 (30.33 KM)
1 Rovanperä/Pietilainen (Peugeot) 27m23.4s; 2 Mäkinen/
Lindström (Subaru) 27m25.4s; 3 Solberg/Mills (Subaru)
27m28.9s; 4 McRae/Ringer (Citroën) 27m45.7s; 5 Loeb/
Elena (Citroën) 27m51.6s; 6 Sainz/Martí (Citroën)
27m56.9s; PC Ligato/Garcia (Mitsubishi) 29m36.7s

SS10 GALATAREIA 1 (15.55 KM)
1 Mäkinen/Lindström (Subaru) 11m14.7s; 2 Solberg/Mills
(Subaru) 11m15.8s; 3 Rovanperä/Pietilainen (Peugeot)
11m25.3s; 4 Loeb/Elena (Citroën) 11m25.7s; 5 Sainz/Martí
(Citroën) 11m32.8s; 6 McRae/Ringer (Citroën) 11m45.7s;
PC Ligato/Garcia (Mitsubishi) 12m30.3s

SS11 FOINI 2 (30.33 KM)
1 Rovanperä/Pietilainen (Peugeot) 26m54.4s; 2 Solberg/
Mills (Subaru) 26m55.6s; 3 McRae/Ringer (Citroën)
27m07.1s; 4 Loeb/Elena (Citroën) 27m08.4s; 5 Sainz/Martí
(Citroën) 27m18.6s; 6 Hirvonen/Lehtinen (Ford)
27m50.0s; PC Ligato/Garcia (Mitsubishi) 29m25.2s

SS12 GALATAREIA 2 (15.55 KM)
1 Solberg/Mills (Subaru) 10m58.6s; 2 Rovanperä/Pietilainen
(Peugeot) 11m10.7s; 3 Loeb/Elena (Citroën) 11m11.6s;
4 McRae/Ringer (Citroën) 11m15.7s; 5 Hirvonen/Lehtinen
(Ford) 11m14.1s; 6 Sainz/Martí (Citroën) 11m28.0s;
PC Ligato/Garcia (Mitsubishi) 12m27.2s

SS13 VAVATSINIA 1 (19.00 KM)
1 Solberg/Mills (Subaru) 17m00.3s; 2 Rovanperä/Pietilainen
(Peugeot) 17m04.1s; 3 McRae/Ringer (Citroën) 17m18.5s;
4 Loeb/Elena (Citroën) 17m18.9s; 5 Sainz/Martí (Citroën)
17m28.0s; 6 Hirvonen/Lehtinen (Ford) 17m36.9s; P
C Ligato/Garcia (Mitsubishi) 18m18.5s

SS14 MACHERAS 1 (12.94 KM)
1 Solberg/Mills (Subaru) 11m26.5s; 2 Rovanperä/Pietilainen
(Peugeot) 11m34.6s; 3 McRae/Ringer (Citroën) 11m44.7s;
4 Loeb/Elena (Citroën) 11m48.0s; 5 Sainz/Martí (Citroën)
11m50.5s; 6 Hirvonen/Lehtinen (Ford) 11m53.0s;
PC Arai/Sircombe (Subaru) 12m36.7s

SS15 KELLAKI 1 (9.49 KM)
1 Solberg/Mills (Subaru) 8m29.2s; 2 Sainz/Martí (Citroën)
8m38.6s; 3 Rovanperä/Pietilainen (Peugeot) 8m39.6s;
4 McRae/Ringer (Citroën) 8m43.7s; 5 Hirvonen/Lehtinen
(Ford) 8m46.0s; 6 A.Ginlay/R.Kennedy (Ford Focus RS
WRC01) 8m48.7s; PC Arai/Sircombe (Subaru) 9m11.7s

SS16 VAVATSINIA 2 (19.00 KM)
1 Solberg/Mills (Subaru) 16m45.3s; 2 Sainz/Martí (Citroën)
17m00.1s; 3= McRae/Ringer (Citroën), Loeb/Elena
(Citroën) 17m05.2s; 5 Hirvonen/Lehtinen (Ford)
17m19.6s; 6 A.Schwarz/M.Hiemer (Hyundai Accent
WRC3) 17m34.2s; PC Arai/Sircombe (Subaru) 18m30.6s

SS17 MACHERAS 2 (12.94 KM)
1 Sainz/Martí (Citroën) 11m32.8s; 2 McRae/Ringer (Citroën)
11m37.1s; 3 Loeb/Elena (Citroën) 11m38.8s; 4 Solberg/
Mills (Subaru) 11m41.0s; 5 Hirvonen/Lehtinen (Ford)
11m45.7s; 6 Schwarz/Hiemer (Hyundai) 12m00.5s;
PC Arai/Sircombe (Subaru) 12m50.3s

SS18 KELLAKI 2 (9.49 KM)
1 Solberg/Mills (Subaru) 8m28.7s; 2 Sainz/Martí (Citroën)
8m30.3s; 3 Loeb/Elena (Citroën) 8m35.5s; 4 McRae/Ringer
(Citroën) 8m38.1s; 5 Hirvonen/Lehtinen (Ford) 8m39.1s;
6 Schwarz/Hiemer (Hyundai) 8m49.4s; PC Arai/Sircombe
(Subaru) 9m08.1s

MAJOR RETIREMENTS

2	Burns/Reid	Peugeot 206 WRC	
	Engine	SS11	Gr A
1	Grönholm/R'iainen	Peugeot 206 WRC	
	Propshaft	SS6	Gr A
4	Märtin/Park	Ford Focus RS WRC03	
	Engine	SS5	Gr A
8	Mäkinen/Lindström	Subaru Impreza WRC2003	
	OTL	SS10	Gr A
5	Duval/Prevot	Ford Focus RS WRC03	
	Engine	SS5	Gr A
15	Gardemeister/L'der	Skoda Octavia WRC E3	
	Accident	SS9	Gr A
20	Panizzi/Panizzi	Peugeot 206 WRC	
	Engine	SS6	Gr A
14	Auriol/Giraudet	Skoda Octavia WRC E3	
	Alternator	SS11	Gr A
11	Loix/Smeets	Hyundai Accent WRC3	
	Engine	SS6	Gr A
22	Pykälistö/Mertsalmi	Peugeot 206 WRC	
	Mechanical	SS12	Gr A
21	Warmbold/Price	Ford Focus RS WRC02	
	Mechanical	SS7	Gr A
12	Dale/Bargery	Hyundai Accent WRC3	
	Engine	SS2	

FIA CLASS WINNERS

A8	Over 2000 cc	Solberg/Mills
		Subaru Impreza WRC2003
N4	Over 2000 cc	Arai/Sircombe
		Subaru Impreza WRX

RALLY LEADERS

Overall: SS1-3 Rovanperä; SS4 Grönholm; SS5-18 Solberg
PC: SS1-18 Arai

RESULTS

1	Petter Solberg/ Phil Mills	Subaru Impreza WRC2003 5h09m12.6s		Gr A
2	Harri Rovanperä/ Risto Pietilainen	Peugeot 206 WRC 5h13m26.6s		Gr A
3	Sébastien Loeb/ Daniel Elena	Citroën Xsara WRC 5h13m29.4s		Gr A
4	Colin McRae/ Derek Ringer	Citroën Xsara WRC 5h13m57.9s		Gr A
5	Carlos Sainz/ Marc Martí	Citroën Xsara WRC 5h14m54.8s		Gr A
6	Mikko Hirvonen/ Jarmo Lehtinen	Ford Focus RS WRC02 5h18m11.3s		Gr A
7	Armin Schwarz/ Manfred Hiemer	Hyundai Accent WRC3 5h22m41.6s		Gr A
8	Alister Ginley/ Rory Kennedy	Ford Focus RS WRC01 5h33m09.9s		Gr A
9	Toshihiro Arai/ Tony Sircombe	Subaru Impreza WRX 5h39m13.7s		Gr N
10	Martin Rowe/ Trevor Agnew	Subaru Impreza WRX 5h42m56.7s		Gr N

54 starters, 17 finishers

SPECIAL STAGE ANALYSIS

	1st	2nd	3rd	4th	5th	6th
Solberg (Subaru)	7	5	3	1	1	1
Rovanperä (Peugeot)	5	5	4	-	-	-
Mäkinen (Subaru)	4	2	-	-	-	-
Sainz (Citroën)	1	3	1	1	5	2
Grönholm (Peugeot)	1	1	-	1	-	-
Loeb (Citroën)	-	1	4	7	1	1
McRae (Citroën)	-	1	4	6	3	2
Panizzi (Peugeot)	-	-	2	-	1	2
Auriol (Skoda)	-	-	1	-	-	-
Märtin (Ford)	-	-	-	1	-	1
Hirvonen (Ford)	-	-	-	-	5	4
Burns (Peugeot)	-	-	-	-	2	1
Schwarz (Hyundai)	-	-	-	-	-	3
Ginlay (Ford)	-	-	-	-	-	1

WORLD CHAMPIONSHIP POINTS

Drivers
1 Burns 37; 2 Sainz 36; 3 Grönholm 30; 4 Solberg 29; 5= Märtin, McRae, Loeb 23; 8 Rovanperä 16; 9 Mäkinen 15; 10= Duval, Gardemeister 9 etc

Manufacturers
1 Peugeot 81; 2 Citroën 73; 3 Subaru 47; 4 Ford 43; 5 Skoda 20; 6 Hyundai 6

Junior World Championship
1= Tirabassi 20; 2 Canellas 13; 3 Aava 11; 4 Katajamäki 10; 5 Wilks 9; 6= Ligato, Carlsson 8 etc

Production Cup
1= Arai 30; 2 Rowe 19; 3= Singh, Blomqvist 17; 5 Ligato 13; 6 Sola 8 etc

ROUTE DETAILS

Total route of 1188.03 km of which 341.05 km were competitive on 18 stages

Leg 1 Friday 20th June, 4 Special Stages totalling 99.84 km
Leg 2 Saturday 21st June, 8 Special Stages totalling 158.35 km
Leg 3 Sunday 22nd June, 6 Special Stages totalling 82.86 km

PREVIOUS WINNERS

1971	Chris Kirmitsis/P. Lawrence	Ford Escort TC
1972	Lefteris Makrides/P. Erotokritou	Mercedes-Benz 250CE
1973	Stig Blomqvist/Arne Hertz	Saab 96 V4
1974 & 1975 Cancelled		
1976	Shekhar Mehta/Yvonne Pratt	Datsun 160J
1977	Kypros Kyprianou/A. Longinos	Hillman Avenger
1978	Roger Clark/Jim Porter	Ford Escort RS
1979	Ari Vatanen/David Richards	Ford Escort RS
1980	Roger Clark/Neil Wilson	Ford Escort RS
1981	Vahan Terzian/Theophanous	Mitsubishi Lancer Turbo
1982	Tony Fassina/'Rudy'	Opel Ascona 400
1983	Jim McRae/Ian Grindrod	Opel Manta 400
1984	John Buffum/Fred Gallagher	Audi Quattro
1985	Mauro Pregliasco/Daniele Cianci	Lancia 037
1986	Patrick Snijers/Dany Colebunders	Lancia 037
1987	David Llewellin/Phil Short	Audi Quattro Coupe
1988	Björn Waldegård/Fred Gallagher	Toyota Celica GT4
1989	Yves Loubet/Jean-Marc Andrié	Lancia Delta Integrale
1990	Dimi Mavropoulos/Nicos Antoniades	Audi Quattro Coupe
1991	A. Jeropoulos/M.Michael	Mitsubishi Galant VR-4
1992	Alex Fiorio/Vittorio Brambilla	Lancia Delta HF Integrale
1993	Alex Fiorio/Vittorio Brambilla	Lancia Delta HF Integrale
1994	Alex Fiorio/Vittorio Brambilla	Lancia Delta HF Integrale
1995	'Bagheera'/N.Stephan	Lancia Delta HF Integrale
1996	Armin Schwarz/Denis Giraudet	Toyota Celica GT-Four
1997	Krzysztof Holowczyc/Maciej Wislawski	Subaru Impreza 555
1998	Andrea Navarra/A. Materazzeti	Subaru Impreza WRC97
1999	Jean-Pierre Richelmi/Stéphane Prévot	Subaru Impreza WRC98
2000	Carlos Sainz/Luis Moya	Ford Focus WRC
2001	Colin McRae/Nicky Grist	Ford Focus RS WRC
2002	Marcus Grönholm/Timo Rautiainen	Peugeot 206 WRC

STAGE NUMBERS

STAGE NUMBERS	1	2	3	4	5	6	7	8	9	10	11	12	13	14	15	16	17	18
Solberg	2	4	4	3	1	1	1	1	1	1	1	1	1	1	1	1	1	1
Rovanperä	1	1	1	2	2	2	2	2	2	2	2	2	2	2	2	2	2	2
Loeb	19	8	9	5	5	3	3	3	3	3	3	3	3	3	3	3	3	3
McRae	4	9	7	6	6	4	4	4	4	4	4	4	4	4	4	4	4	4
Sainz	13	15	14	9	8	6	5	5	5	5	5	5	5	5	5	5	5	5
Hirvonen	6	11	11	12	9	7	7	7	7	7	6	6	6	6	6	6	6	6
Schwarz	17	13	15	14	12	10	10	10	9	9	7	7	7	7	7	7	7	7
Ginlay	18	17	17	16	14	11	11	11	10	10	8	8	8	8	8	8	8	8
Arai	21	20	20	18	17	13	12	12	11	11	9	9	9	9	9	9	9	9
Rowe	27	26	25	21	19	14	13	13	12	12	10	10	10	10	10	10	10	10
Burns	11	10	10	8	7	5	6	6	6	6	R							
Auriol	3	7	8	13	11	8	8	8	8	8	R							
Pykälistö	10	19	19	30	26	21	20	19	14	14	R							
Mäkinen	8	3	4	19	16	29	27	27	20	R								
G'meister	7	14	13	15	13	9	9	9	R									
Grönholm	9	5	3	1	4	R												
Panizzi	5	2	2	4	3	R												
Loix	16	12	12	10	10	R												
Märtin	12	6	6	7	R													
Duval	15	16	16	11	R													
Dale	20	35	R															

FINISH LINES

Neither Colin McRae nor Carlos Sainz quite came to grips with their Xsaras, losing ground badly at first with dire handling problems. Sainz fared worst and therefore had to cope with an unfavourably high starting position for the second leg... Ford's one survivor was its number three, Mikko Hirvonen, who drove with exemplary restraint to score his best World Championship result to date... It was an unmitigated disaster for the full works cars, both Markko Märtin and François Duval retiring on SS5 when the spoilers scooped dust into the air intakes and clogged the filters, grinding the engines to destruction... Armin Schwarz did Hyundai proud, labouring tirelessly against wilting shock absorbers and an overheating engine to seventh place... The Yorkshire privateer Alistair Ginley exceeded all expectations with a brave drive to eighth in his Focus, pressing on even when the oil pressure dived in the second leg... Toshihiro Arai was in fine form once more, cantering to a masterly Production victory in his Prodrive-run Impreza... A broken plastic lug caused Didier Auriol's retirement. It allowed the alternator to work loose, then to cease charging. His Skoda ground to a halt with a dead battery... Toni Gardemeister retired his Octavia after hitting a tree stump... Tommi Mäkinen battled long but in vain. Power steering trouble and suspension damage finally accounted for the works Impreza... MSD soon lowered boost and softened the anti-lag systems to withstand the heat, but Freddy Loix retired his Accent with engine trouble nevertheless... Justin Dale was one of the earliest casualties, his Accent WRC3 succumbing to engine failure... Hamed Al Wahaibi's decision to retire from the sport in mid-season although registered for the Production Championship earned him a $20,000 fine... Niall McShea retired his Jardine Lloyd Thompson Lancer with transmission trouble... Janusz Kulig crashed his Lancer Evo VI in the closing stages...Karamjit Singh also made a rare driving error, clipping a log on the inside of a hairpin and knocking a front wheel off his Proton...

Stig Blomqvist suffered from brake problems in the early stages, but on a rally that tore the heart out of the entry, the Swede got off lightly.

Plenty of drivers turn up their noses at the Deutschland's stages, but they remind Sébastien Loeb of his native Alsace and he handled his Xsara (left) as though he was on home ground. Markko Märtin was the surprise of the rally in the Castrol Focus. Petter Solberg was too ill to make full use of his Impreza (below).

DEUTSCHLAND RALLY

Marcus Grönholm was in a mood to kick himself. 3.5 seconds were all he had needed to gain his first Tarmac victory. No wonder he was inclined to regard a superb second place as an exasperating, tantalising failure.

The Finn had been the pick of Peugeot's drivers on the Deutschland Rally, swiftly making up for a somnolent first leg, revelling in Baumholder's lumpy concrete as he barged the opposition aside to hound Sébastien Loeb by the halfway point. In contrast, Gilles Panizzi was a wan shadow of his usual self and Richard Burns hadn't been able to capitalise on a good start. The lanky Briton felt ill at ease with the 206's damping on the military roads and he had made matters worse with a couple of 'schoolboy errors,' ignoring his pace notes and turning right rather than left at one of the Panzerplatte's innumerable junctions, following Friday's route rather than Saturday's, then overshooting another junction on the same stage. He had dropped to fifth by the end of the second leg and left himself far too much to do to think of winning.

A characteristic display of consistency and determination paid dividends as the rain lashed down on Sunday and by the finish, Burns was not only up to third, but only 19.7 seconds short of victory. It wouldn't have taken much – only a clean run through SS11, in fact – to put him in contention. In such treacherous conditions, who was to say what another stage might have brought, for that matter? He had at least protected his championship lead and got the better of Colin McRae. The Scot hadn't driven with such assurance for months, but dropped time thanks to a loose sumpguard, a messy spin and a poor, Michelin-inspired tyre choice in the second leg on Baumholder, then spun twice in the final leg, once at 100 mph into a pile of wood shavings. To his mind, a clean run could have brought him victory too.

But Grönholm had become unaccustomed to losing much sleep over the British drivers. On asphalt, Loeb had been the target. Picking intermediates for what turned out to be an entirely dry loop of the tank testing range hadn't helped, but tyre choice hadn't done for Grönholm's chances. There had been everything to play for at the start of the final leg. Accordingly, he had redoubled the attack in the Mosel vineyards and promptly granted Loeb a breathing space by slithering

wide at one junction, then belting a kerb and knocking the 206's tracking out. He had managed to straighten it himself after a fashion for the two stages remaining prior to service, but it had been an unnecessary error; he hadn't met his own high standards.

Thanks in part to unpredictable and often downright hostile weather, it had been an error-strewn rally. Loeb, precise as ever, had made few mistakes. He had recovered well from knocking a tyre off the rim on SS2 and on Saturday afternoon, he had profited handsomely from raising the suspension a little and staying on dry rubber when Grönholm had chosen intermediates.

Grönholm never gave up. Sensing that the rain was heavy enough to lure even Loeb into an error, he attacked the final stage with renewed ferocity and was making up ground hand over fist until Citroën, spotting the tumbling gap from sector times, warned Loeb that he was on the brink of a humiliating defeat.

Loeb kept his composure and his lead. The legions of fans returned to Alsace happy: Citroën had secured its third successive victory in Germany and could wish only that its star Frenchman was sometimes less placid under pressure; but if the Focus's transmission had been reliable, the French teams would never have seen which way Markko Märtin went.

DEUTSCHLAND RALLY

A gritty drive from Armin Schwarz (below) ensured that Hyundai got the better of Toni Gardemeister's unproven Fabia (near right). Few major rallies still offer such contrasting terrain, as Richard Burns, François Duval (top right) and the Saxo driver, Rainer Jostes, demonstrate.

DEUTSCHLAND RALLY

TRIER

GERMANY
Trier

FRANCE

ITALY

17/20

18/21

2/6

1/5

3

4

11/13

10/12

9/14
Bostalsee

19/22

8/15

7/16

Deutschland Rally, 25-27 July 2003,
FIA World Rally Championship Round 8

RUNNING ORDER

2	Richard Burns/	Peugeot 206 WRC	
	Robert Reid	Gr A	
19	Carlos Sainz/	Citroën Xsara WRC	
	Marc Marti	Gr A	
1	Marcus Grönholm/	Peugeot 206 WRC	
	Timo Rautiainen	Gr A	
7	Petter Solberg/	Subaru Impreza WRC2003	
	Phil Mills	Gr A	
18	Sébastien Loeb/	Citroën Xsara WRC	
	Daniel Elena	Gr A	
4	Markko Märtin/	Ford Focus RS WRC03	
	Michael Park	Gr A	
17	Colin McRae/	Citroën Xsara WRC	
	Derek Ringer	Gr A	
8	Tommi Mäkinen/	Subaru Impreza WRC2003	
	Kaj Lindström	Gr A	
5	François Duval/	Ford Focus RS WRC03	
	Stéphane Prevot	Gr A	
15	Toni Gardemeister/	Skoda Fabia WRC	
	Paavo Lukander	Gr A	
3	Gilles Panizzi/	Peugeot 206 WRC	
	Hervé Panizzi	Gr A	
14	Didier Auriol/	Skoda Fabia WRC	
	Denis Giraudet	Gr A	
6	Mikko Hirvonen/	Ford Focus RS WRC02	
	Jarmo Lehtinen	Gr A	
21	Cédric Robert/	Peugeot 206 WRC	
	Gérald Bedon	Gr A	
10	Armin Schwarz/	Hyundai Accent WRC3	
	Manfred Hiemer	Gr A	
11	Freddy Loix/	Hyundai Accent WRC3	
	Sven Smeets	Gr A	
23	Roman Kresta/	Peugeot 206 WRC	
	Jan Tomanek	Gr A	
24	Jari-Matti Latvala/	Ford Focus RS WRC02	
	Miikka Anttila	Gr A	
26	Antony Warmbold/	Ford Focus RS WRC02	
	Gemma Price	Gr A	
12	Manfred Stohl/	Hyundai Accent WRC3	
	Ilka Minor	Gr A	
20	Philippe Bugalski/	Citroën Xsara WRC	
	Jean-Paul Chiaroni	Gr A	
22	Matthias Kahle/	Skoda Octavia WRC E3	
	Peter Gobel	Gr A	
25	Justin Dale/	Hyundai Accent WRC3	
	Andrew Bargery	Gr A	
34	Kristian Sohlberg/	Mitsubishi Lancer WRC2	
	Jakke Honkanen	Gr A	
32	Jani Paasonen/	Mitsubishi Lancer WRC2	
	Arto Kapanen	Gr A	

SPECIAL STAGE TIMES

SS1 RUTWERTAL 1 (17.21 KM)
1 R.Burns/R.Reid (Peugeot 206 WRC) 9m37.5s; 2 M.Märtin/
M.Park (Ford Focus RS WRC03) 9m38.4s; 3 C.McRae/
D.Ringer (Citroën Xsara WRC) 9m39.4s; 4 S.Loeb/D.Elena
(Citroën Xsara WRC) 9m40.8s; 5 F.Duval/S.Prevot (Ford
Focus RS WRC03) 9m41.3s; 6 C.Sainz/M.Martí (Citroën
Xsara WRC) 9m42.7s; PC D.Sola/A.Romani (Mitsubishi
Lancer E7) 10m39.2s

SS2 DHRONTAL 1 (12.81 KM)
1 Burns/Reid (Peugeot) 8m08.1s; 2 McRae/Ringer
(Citroën) 8m08.7s; 3 Loeb/Elena (Citroën) 8m11.4s;
4 Märtin/Park (Ford) 8m11.5s; 5 Duval/Prevot (Ford)
8m11.9s; 6 M.Grönholm/T.Rautiainen (Peugeot 206
WRC) 8m12.3s; PC Sola/Romani (Mitsubishi) 8m53.9s

SS3 MAIWALD (15.61 KM)
1 Märtin/Park (Ford) 9m01.4s; 2 Burns/Reid (Peugeot)
9m04.0s; 3 G.Panizzi/H.Panizzi (Peugeot 206 WRC)
9m07.1s; 4= Grönholm/Rautiainen (Peugeot),
Duval/Prevot (Ford) 9m07.8s; 6 C.Robert/G.Bedon
(Peugeot 206 WRC) 9m09.9s; PC Sola/Romani
(Mitsubishi) 9m50.1s

SS4 PANZERPLATTE OST (35.42 KM)
1 Märtin/Park (Ford) 20m34.7s; 2 Loeb/Elena (Citroën)
20m44.2s; 3 Grönholm/Rautiainen (Peugeot) 20m44.3s;
4 Burns/Reid (Peugeot) 20m48.7s; 5 McRae/Ringer (Citroën)
20m54.3s; 6 P.Solberg/P.Mills (Subaru Impreza WRC2003)
20m55.2s; PC Sola/Romani (Mitsubishi) 22m09.2s

SS5 RUTWERTAL 2 (17.21 KM)
1 Burns/Reid (Peugeot) 9m37.8s; 2 Loeb/Elena (Citroën)
9m38.6s; 3 Grönholm/Rautiainen (Peugeot) 9m40.1s;
4 McRae/Ringer (Citroën) 9m41.2s; 5= Sainz/Martí
(Citroën), Robert/Bedon (Peugeot) 9m42.7s;
PC Sola/Romani (Mitsubishi) 10m29.9s

SS6 DHRONTAL 2 (12.81 KM)
1 Loeb/Elena (Citroën) 8m00.7s; 2 Grönholm/Rautiainen
(Peugeot) 8m01.1s; 3 McRae/Ringer (Citroën) 8m03.6s;
4 Burns/Reid (Peugeot) 8m04.3s; 5 Robert/Bedon
(Peugeot) 8m07.4s; 6 Sainz/Martí (Citroën) 8m07.7s;
PC N.McShea/C.Patterson (Mitsubishi Lancer E6) 8m50.0s

SS7 ST WENDEL 1 (6.24 KM)
1 Burns/Reid (Peugeot) 3m24.7s; 2 Grönholm/Rautiainen
(Peugeot) 3m25.4s; 3 Panizzi/Panizzi (Peugeot) 3m25.7s;
4 Märtin/Park (Ford) 3m26.1s; 5 McRae/Ringer (Citroën)
3m26.7s; 6 Robert/Bedon (Peugeot) 3m26.8s;
PC Sola/Romani (Mitsubishi) 3m46.8s

SS8 BOSENBERG 1 (17.02 KM)
1 Grönholm/Rautiainen (Peugeot) 9m16.8s; 2 Duval/Prevot
(Ford) 9m20.7s; 3 Märtin/Park (Ford) 9m23.0s; 4 R.Kresta/
J.Tomanek (Peugeot 206 WRC) 9m24.4s; 5 Burns/Reid
(Peugeot) 9m25.5s; 6 Solberg/Mills (Subaru) 9m26.3s;
PC McShea/Patterson (Mitsubishi) 10m11.1s

SS9 PETERBERG 1 (10.55 KM)
1 Märtin/Park (Ford) 6m09.5s; 2 Loeb/Elena (Citroën)
6m12.6s; 3 Grönholm/Rautiainen (Peugeot) 6m12.7s;
4 Solberg/Mills (Subaru) 6m14.6s; 5 McRae/Ringer
(Citroën) 6m15.6s; 6 Robert/Bedon (Peugeot) 6m16.3s;
PC McShea/Patterson (Mitsubishi) 6m44.1s

SS10 ERZWEILER 1 (19.98 KM)
1 Märtin/Park (Ford) 11m45.6s; 2 McRae/Ringer (Citroën)
11m48.3s; 3 Loeb/Elena (Citroën) 11m49.4s; 4 Grönholm/
Rautiainen (Peugeot) 11m54.2s; 5 Burns/Reid (Peugeot)
11m56.0s; 6 Sainz/Martí (Citroën) 11m56.7s;
PC Sola/Romani (Mitsubishi) 12m53.5s

SS11 PANZERPLATTE WEST 1 (34.02 KM)
1 Märtin/Park (Ford) 19m31.9s; 2 Kresta/Tomanek
(Peugeot) 19m47.9s; 3 McRae/Ringer (Citroën) 19m54.2s;
4= Grönholm/Rautiainen (Peugeot), Loeb/Elena (Citroën)
19m56.8s; 6 Sainz/Martí (Citroën) 19m57.3s; PC McShea/
Patterson (Mitsubishi) 21m40.4s

SS12 ERZWEILER 2 (19.98 KM)
1 Loeb/Elena (Citroën) 11m40.6s; 2 Märtin/Park (Ford)
11m42.7s; 3 Grönholm/Rautiainen (Peugeot) 11m43.8s;
4 McRae/Ringer (Citroën) 11m45.3s; 5 Duval/Prevot
(Ford) 11m50.1s; 6 Sainz/Martí (Citroën) 11m53.9s;
PC Sola/Romani (Mitsubishi) 12m47.2s

SS13 PANZERPLATTE WEST 2 (34.02 KM)
1 Märtin/Park (Ford) 19m01.6s; 2 Loeb/Elena (Citroën)
19m01.8s; 3 McRae/Ringer (Citroën) 19m06.1s; 4 Burns/
Reid (Peugeot) 19m07.1s; 5 Grönholm/Rautiainen
(Peugeot) 19m09.8s; 6 Sainz/Martí (Citroën) 19m14.9s;
PC Sola/Romani (Mitsubishi) 20m51.8s

SS14 PETERBERG 2 (10.55 KM)
1 Grönholm/Rautiainen (Peugeot) 6m25.4s; 2 Loeb/Elena
(Citroën) 6m25.7s; 3 Panizzi/Panizzi (Peugeot) 6m26.2s;
4 McRae/Ringer (Citroën) 6m27.4s; 5 F.Loix/S.Smeets
(Hyundai Accent WRC3) 6m29.0s; 6 Solberg/Mills
(Subaru) 6m30.8s; PC M.Ligato/R.Garcia (Mitsubishi
Lancer E7) 7m07.9s

SS15 BOSENBERG 2 (17.02 KM)
1 Märtin/Park (Ford) 8m56.5s; 2 Duval/Prevot (Ford)
9m00.0s; 3 Loeb/Elena (Citroën) 9m05.1s; 4 Kresta/
Tomanek (Peugeot) 9m08.0s; 5 Robert/Bedon (Peugeot)
9m10.0s; 6 Burns/Reid (Peugeot) 9m10.7s; PC Sola/
Romani (Mitsubishi) 10m27.5s

SS16 ST WENDEL 2 (6.24 KM)
1 Kresta/Tomanek (Peugeot) 3m38.0s; 2 A.Schwarz/
M.Hiemer (Hyundai Accent WRC3) 3m39.2s; 3 Loix/
Smeets (Hyundai) 3m39.8s; 4 Solberg/Mills (Subaru)
3m40.3s; 5 McRae/Ringer (Citroën) 3m40.4s; 6 Märtin/
Park (Ford) 3m40.8s; PC A.De Dominics /G.Bernacchini
(Mitsubishi Lancer E7) 4m04.2s

SS17 SCHONES MOSELLAND 1 (15.29 KM)
1 McRae/Ringer (Citroën) 9m03.6s; 2 Loeb/Elena
(Citroën) 9m06.8s; 3 Burns/Reid (Peugeot) 9m08.3s; 4
Duval/Prevot (Ford) 9m09.1s; 5 Märtin/Park (Ford)
9m11.4s; 6 Robert/ Bedon (Peugeot) 9m12.8s; PC
M.Rowe/T.Agnew (Subaru Impreza WRX) 10m10.1s

SS18 MOSELWEIN 1 (16.55 KM)
1 McRae/Ringer (Citroën) 10m04.5s; 2 Burns/Reid
(Peugeot) 10m07.5s; 3 Loeb/Elena (Citroën) 10m12.5s;
4 Solberg/Mills (Subaru) 10m12.6s; 5 Duval/Prevot (Ford)
10m14.2s; 6 Grönholm/Rautiainen (Peugeot) 10m14.9s;
PC Ligato/Garcia (Mitsubishi) 11m20.3s

SS19 ST WENDELER LAND 1 (18.93 KM)
1 Sainz/Martí (Citroën) 9m52.6s; 2 Solberg/Mills (Subaru)
9m54.1s; 3 Duval/Prevot (Ford) 9m57.9s; 4 Burns/Reid
(Peugeot) 9m58.0s; 5 Robert/Bedon (Peugeot) 9m59.1s;
6 Schwarz/Hiemer (Hyundai) 10m06.4s; PC Märtin/Park
(Mitsubishi) 12m30.5s

SS20 SCHÖNES MOSELLAND 2 (15.29 KM)
1 Märtin/Park (Ford) 9m25.7s; 2 Duval/Prevot (Ford)
9m29.0s; 3 Loeb/Elena (Citroën) 9m30.8s; 4 Burns/Reid
(Peugeot) 9m31.0s; 5= Solberg/Mills (Subaru),
McRae/Ringer (Citroën) 9m31.7s; PC Ligato/Garcia
(Mitsubishi) 10m38.4s

SS21 MOSELWEIN 2 (16.55 KM)
1 Märtin/Park (Ford) 10m31.2s; 2 Loeb/Elena (Citroën)
10m33.5s; 3 Grönholm/Rautiainen (Peugeot) 10m35.9s;
4 Solberg/Mills (Subaru) 10m37.2s; 5 McRae/Ringer
(Citroën) 10m37.7s; 6= Sainz/Martí (Citroën), Burns/Reid
(Peugeot) 10m40.3s; PC J.Kulig/M.Szczepaniak (Mitsubishi
Lancer E6) 11m57.5s

SS22 ST WENDELER LAND 2 (18.93 KM)
1 Märtin/Park (Ford) 10m32.3s; 2 Grönholm/Rautiainen
(Peugeot) 10m32.7s; 3 Solberg/Mills (Subaru) 10m34.5s;
4 Sainz/Martí (Citroën) 10m35.1s; 5 Burns/Reid (Peugeot)
10m35.4s; 6 McRae/Ringer (Citroën) 10m40.1s; PC
Kulig/Szczepaniak (Mitsubishi) 12m05.2s

MAJOR RETIREMENTS

8	Mäkinen/Lindström	Subaru Impreza WRC2003		
	Alternator	SS6		Gr A
15	Gardemeister/L'der	Skoda Fabia WRC		
	Suspension	SS13		Gr A
14	Auriol/Giraudet	Skoda Fabia WRC		
	Engine	SS7		Gr A
23	Kresta/Tomanek	Peugeot 206 WRC		
	Mechanical	SS21		Gr A
20	Bugalski/Chiaroni	Citroën Xsara WRC		
	Engine	SS11		Gr A
32	Paasonen/Kapanen	Mitsubishi Lancer WRC2		
	Accident	SS11		Gr A

ROUTE DETAILS

Total Route of 1737.57 km of which 388.23 km were
competitive on 22 stages
Leg 1 Friday 25th July, 7 special stages totalling 117.31 km
Leg 2 Saturday 26th July, 9 special stages totalling 169.38 km
Leg 3 Sunday 27th July, 6 special stages totalling 101.54 km

FIA CLASS WINNERS

A8	Over 2000 cc	Loeb/Elena	
		Citroën Xsara WRC	
A6	1400-1600 cc	Jostes/Enderle	
		Citroën Saxo	
A5	Upto 1400 cc	Hohlheimer/Kippe	
		Fiat Seicento Sporting	
N4	Over 2000 cc	Sola/Romani	
		Mitsubishi Lancer E7	
N2	Upto 1400cc	Fahrner/Poschner	
		VW Polo Gti-16v	

RALLY LEADERS

Overall: SS1-3 Burns; SS4 Märtin; SS5-8 Burns; SS9-12
Grönholm; SS13-22 Loeb
PC: SS1-22 Sola

SPECIAL STAGE ANALYSIS

	1st	2nd	3rd	4th	5th	6th
Märtin (Ford)	10	2	1	2	1	1
Burns (Peugeot)	4	2	1	5	3	2
Loeb (Citroën)	2	7	5	2	-	-
Grönholm (Peugeot)	2	3	5	2	2	-
McRae (Citroën)	2	2	4	3	6	1
Kresta (Peugeot)	1	1	-	2	-	-
Sainz (Citroën)	1	-	-	1	1	7
Duval (Ford)	-	3	1	2	4	-
Solberg (Subaru)	-	1	1	4	1	3
Schwarz (Hyundai)	-	1	-	-	-	-
Loix Hyundai	-	-	1	-	1	-
Robert (Peugeot)	-	-	-	-	4	4

WORLD CHAMPIONSHIP POINTS

Drivers
1 Burns 43; 2 Sainz 39; 3 Grönholm 38; 4 Loeb 33; 5
Solberg 30; 6 McRae 28; 7 Märtin 27; 8 Rovanperä 16; 9
Mäkinen 15; 10 Duval 11 etc

Manufacturers
1 Peugeot 95; 2 Citroën 88; 3 Ford 50; 4 Subaru 49; 5
Skoda 20; 6 Hyundai 6

Junior World Championship
1= Tirabassi 20; 2 Canellas 13; 3 Aava 11; 4 Katajamäki
10; 5 Wilks 9; 6= Ligato, Carlsson 8 etc

Production Cup
1 Arai 30; 2 Rowe 27; 3 Singh 22; 4 Blomqvist 21; 5 Sola
18; 6 Ligato 13 etc

RESULTS

1	Sébastien Loeb/	Citroën Xsara WRC	
	Daniel Elena	3h46m50.4s	Gr A
2	Marcus Grönholm/	Peugeot 206 WRC	
	Timo Rautiainen	3h46m54.0s	Gr A
3	Richard Burns/	Peugeot 206 WRC	
	Robert Reid	3h47m10.1s	Gr A
4	Colin McRae/	Citroën Xsara WRC	
	Derek Ringer	3h47m21.8s	Gr A
5	Markko Märtin/	Ford Focus RS WRC03	
	Michael Park	3h47m48.3s	Gr A
6	Carlos Sainz/	Citroën Xsara WRC	
	Marc Marti	3h48m29.0s	Gr A
7	François Duval/	Ford Focus RS WRC03	
	Stéphane Prevot	3h48m38.5s	Gr A
8	Petter Solberg/	Subaru Impreza WRC2003	
	Phil Mills	3h49m20.6s	Gr A
9	Cédric Robert/	Peugeot 206 WRC	
	Gérald Bedon	3h50m03.2s	Gr A
10	Gilles Panizzi/	Peugeot 206 WRC	
	Hervé Panizzi	3h50m30.0s	Gr A

79 starters, 44 finishers

RECENT WINNERS

1970	Hannu Mikkola/Gunnar Palm	Ford Escort TC
1982	Erwin Weber/Matthias Berg	Opel Ascona 400
1983	Walter Röhrl/Christian Geistdörfer	Lancia 037
1984	Hannu Mikkola/Christian Geistdörfer	Audi Sport Quattro
1985	Kalle Grundel/Peter Diekmann	Peugeot 205T16
1986	Michèle Mouton/Terry Harryman	Peugeot 205T16
1987	Jochi Kleint/Manfred Hiemer	VW Golf GTI
1988	Robert Droogmans/Ronny Joosten	Ford Sierra Cosworth
1989	Patrick Snijers/Dany Colebunders	Toyota Celica GT4
1990	Robert Droogmans/Ronny Joosten	Lancia Delta HF Integrale
1991	Piero Liatti/Luciano Tedeschini	
		Lancia Delta HF Integrale 16V
1992	Erwin Weber/Manfred Hiemer	Mitsubishi Galant VR-4
1993	Patrick Snijers/Dany Colebunders	Ford Escort Cosworth
1994	Dieter Depping/Peter Thul	Ford Escort Cosworth
1995	Enrico Bertone/Massimo Chiapponi	
		Toyota Celica Turbo 4WD
1996	Dieter Depping/Fred Berssen	Ford Escort Cosworth
1997	Dieter Depping/Dieter Hawranke	Ford Escort Cosworth
1998	Matthias Kahle/Dieter Schneppenheim	Toyota Corolla WRC
1999	Armin Kremer/Fred Berßen	Subaru Impreza WRC97
2000	Henrik Lundgaard/Jens Christian Anker	
		Toyota Corolla WRC
2001	Philippe Bugalski/Jean-Paul Chiaroni	Citroën Xsara WRC
2002	Sébastien Loeb/Daniel Elena	Citroën Xsara WRC

STAGE NUMBERS

STAGE NUMBERS	1	2	3	4	5	6	8	9	10	11	12	13	14	15	16	17	18	19	20	21	22	23
Loeb	4	4	5	4	2	2	3	3	3	3	2	2	1	1	1	1	1	1	1	1	1	1
Grönholm	7	6	4	3	3	3	2	2	1	1	1	2	2	2	2	2	2	2	2	2	2	2
Burns	1	1	1	2	1	1	1	2	2	3	3	3	3	4	5	5	5	5	3	3	3	3
McRae	3	2	6	5	4	4	4	5	4	4	4	4	3	4	4	4	3	4	4	4		
Märtin	2	3	2	1	6	10	10	10	10	8	5	5	5	3	3	3	4	5	5	5	5	
Sainz	6	7	9	7	7	6	6	7	7	7	7	7	6	7	7	6	7	6	6	6		
Duval	5	5	3	8	8	7	7	4	5	5	6	6	6	7	6	7	6	6	7	6	7	7
Solberg	10	12	12	11	11	9	9	9	10	10	10	10	10	10	9	8	8	8	8			
Robert	8	8	7	10	9	8	8	8	7	9	8	9	9	9	9	9	10	9	9	9		
Panizzi	9	9	8	6	5	5	5	5	6	6	8	9	8	8	8	8	8	10	10	10	10	
Loix	16	16	15	15	14	13	13	13	13	12	13	12	12	12	12	12	12	11	11	11		
Schwarz	15	15	16	16	16	15	15	14	14	14	13	13	13	13	13	13	15	13	12	12		
Hirvonen	17	19	18	18	18	18	16	16	16	15	14	14	14	14	14	14	14	14	13	13		
Kresta	11	11	11	12	13	13	14	12	12	11	11	11	11	11	11	11	11	11	R			
G'meister	14	14	13	13	12	12	12	15	15	12	26	26	R									
Bugalski	18	17	17	14	14	11	11	11	11	16	R											
Auriol	13	13	14	17	17	16	R															
Mäkinen	12	10	10	9	10	R																

FINISH LINES

Dani Solá became the first Mitsubishi driver to win the Production World Championship class all
year, the Spaniard setting the pace from the start and escaping lightly from a brush with a
Hinkelstein, putting a gouge in one of the doors... Neither of the new Fabias went the distance,
Didier Auriol's was slowed by a hydraulic leak before the engine failed, while Toni Gardemeister
was forced to retire when the rear suspension collapsed for the second stage running and a
driveshaft broke... Tommi Mäkinen had a short but intensely frustrating rally. The belt driving the
Impreza's power steering pump and alternator jumped off, and as the spare proved impossible to
fit, the battery went flat scarcely a mile from service... Petter Solberg salvaged a point in the
other works Subaru, but it was uphill progress, for the Norwegian was almost too ill to drive in
the first leg and slowed when a rear suspension link snapped in the second... A broken gear
lever hampered Martin Rowe in the final leg, but the Manxman still took second in Group N in his
David Sutton-run Impreza... Cédric Robert drove cautiously in the wet on his first rally in a
works-specification 206, but still managed to beat a below-par Gilles Panizzi in the third works
machine... Turbo failure in the closing stages badly delayed Armin Schwarz's works Accent... Jani
Paasonen and Arto Kapanen were hospitalised after crashing their works Lancer WRC2;
Kapanen was the more severely injured of the two, breaking several ribs and fracturing a
shoulder... Justin Dale endured all kinds of setbacks, ranging from gearbox trouble to a jammed
handbrake, soldiering home in 28th place in his works-run Accent...

Tourists are warmly welcomed at the
Mosel's numerous vineyards. For one
weekend a year, the visitors have
other priorities.

RALLY FINLAND

RALLYCOURSE World Rally Championship **Round 9**

To Markko Märtin, a steepling Finnish forest road is a home from home and he made short work of the opposition once Marcus Grönholm had retired. Petter Solberg snatched a brilliant, last-gasp second, while Grönholm was the most prominent victim of Peugeot's faulty wheel bearings. Even Simon Jean-Joseph and his Clio were off target for once (clockwise from above).

As he braked to a halt at the service point, Markko Märtin looked across, smiled and mimed hitting the Focus's steering wheel in frustration. It was, to put it mildly, an unexpected gesture. It's not unknown for drivers battling for the lead in Finland to utter scarcely an intelligible sentence to the press throughout the rally. The will to win is all consuming, the pressure relentless; the fun and games wait until afterwards. Märtin should have been in no mood for fun and games. Over the previous three stages, he had conceded 30 seconds thanks to an electronic fault that prevented the differentials from locking, with dire consequences for the car's handling. Possibly he didn't appreciate that the problem had also foxed the data logger and that his service crew therefore had no clear idea of what they were trying to fix, far less whether they could do so in the 20-minute service allocation, but he certainly knew that Richard Burns was only 13 seconds behind, driving with the precision of a Swiss watch and closing in.

When Märtin emerged from the car, there was a trace of irritation along with the humour in the observation that he was getting used to driving with open differentials – a tart reference to the fact that the 2003 Focus might be quick, but far from trouble-free. Yet it was plain that he no longer felt under great pressure. Marcus Grönholm's retirement half an hour previously, on the second run at Ouninpohja, had placed the rally in an entirely different light. While Märtin didn't dismiss the threat from Burns, he said that he could now drive at 100% – on the limit, but not over it.

The duel with Grönholm had taken the two men into a different realm. Even Burns had agreed that it was a 'two-horse race.' Grönholm made the striking admission for a Finn on home soil that he wasn't sure that he could beat the visitor,

while Märtin, smiling shyly, said that he had had 'a few scary moments' and whenever the Peugeot driver made up time, blamed himself for not taking enough risks.

It was impossible to tell who might have won in a straight fight. Märtin himself doubted that the two could have sustained such a pace for three days. Yet just when the electronic glitch put him at Grönholm's mercy, he made his escape. One of the 206's wheel bearings collapsed and a front wheel bounded free. Once Burns dropped a minute nursing his Peugeot back to service with a similar fault, Märtin would have been pressed to pluck defeat from the jaws of victory. Burns had his hands full fending off Petter Solberg and Subaru, narrowly losing a last-gasp battle for second.

But Märtin's demeanour had suggested that Grönholm would have had no respite. When their duel was at its fiercest, whereas Grönholm had said that he was driving too quickly to enjoy himself, Märtin had given the impression that he was thriving rather than wilting under pressure. Finland is a kind of home from home. He first attended the rally when he was 15, he had contested it five times previously and the countryside resembles Estonia. Hostile territory had been something like a preferred battleground.

The thousands of flag-waving Estonian fans weren't bothered that suspect wheel bearings had derailed Peugeot's challenge. The details were unimportant. What mattered was that their hero had become the first Estonian to win the rally, that he had done so from the front and inflicted a defeat so crushing that for the first time there wasn't a Finn in the top five. No wonder the Estonian Prime Minister, Juhan Parts, flew in for the celebrations. It was an occasion on which sport and politics were bound to coincide.

RALLY FINLAND

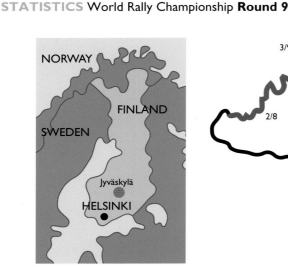

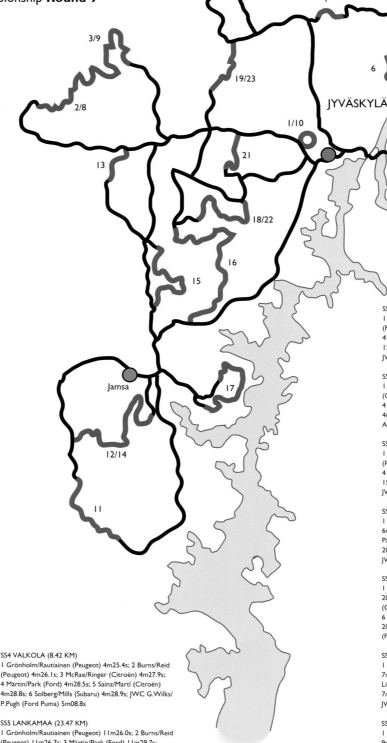

Finland Rally, 7-10 August 2003,
FIA World Rally Championship Round 9

RUNNING ORDER

2	Richard Burns/	Peugeot 206 WRC
	Robert Reid	Gr A
19	Carlos Sainz/	Citroën Xsara WRC
	Marc Martí	Gr A
1	Marcus Grönholm/	Peugeot 206 WRC
	Timo Rautiainen	Gr A
18	Sébastien Loeb/	Citroën Xsara WRC
	Daniel Elena	Gr A
7	Petter Solberg/	Subaru Impreza WRC2003
	Phil Mills	Gr A
17	Colin McRae/	Citroën Xsara WRC
	Derek Ringer	Gr A
4	Markko Märtin/	Ford Focus RS WRC03
	Michael Park	Gr A
3	Harri Rovanperä/	Peugeot 206 WRC
	Risto Pietiläinen	Gr A
8	Tommi Mäkinen/	Subaru Impreza WRC2003
	Kaj Lindström	Gr A
5	François Duval/	Ford Focus RS WRC03
	Stéphane Prevot	Gr A
15	Toni Gardemeister/	Skoda Fabia WRC
	Paavo Lukander	Gr A
14	Didier Auriol/	Skoda Fabia WRC
	Denis Giraudet	Gr A
6	Mikko Hirvonen/	Ford Focus RS WRC02
	Jarmo Lehtinen	Gr A
10	Armin Schwarz/	Hyundai Accent WRC3
	Manfred Hiemer	Gr A
11	Freddy Loix/	Hyundai Accent WRC3
	Sven Smeets	Gr A
20	Jari-Matti Latvala/	Ford Focus WRC02
	Miikka Anttila	Gr A
22	Juuso Pykälistö/	Peugeot 206 WRC
	Esko Mertsalmi	Gr A
23	Janne Tuohino/	Ford Focus WRC02
	Jukka Aho	Gr A
24	Sebastian Lindholm/	Peugeot 206 WRC
	Timo Hantunen	Gr A
12	Jussi Välimäki/	Hyundai Accent WRC3
	Jakke Honkanen	Gr A
26	Ari Vatanen/	Peugeot 206 WRC
	Juha Repo	Gr A

SPECIAL STAGE TIMES

SS1 KILLERI 1 (2.06 KM)
1 M.Märtin/M.Park (Ford Focus RS WRC03) 1m18.6s;
2 M.Grönholm/T.Rautiainen (Peugeot 206 WRC) 1m19.0s;
3 P.Solberg/P.Mills (Subaru Impreza WRC2003) 1m19.2s;
4 F.Duval/S.Prevot (Ford Focus RS WRC03) 1m19.3s;
5 S.Loeb/D.Elena (Citroën Xsara WRC) 1m19.4s;
6 H.Rovanperä/R.Pietiläinen (Peugeot 206 WRC) 1m19.5s;
JWC D.Carlsson/M.Andersson (Suzuki Ignis) 1m27.3s

SS2 JUKOJARVI 1 (22.31 KM)
1= Grönholm/Rautiainen (Peugeot), Märtin/Park (Ford)
10m50.8s; 3 Solberg/Mills (Subaru) 10m56.7s; 4 R.Burns/
R.Reid (Peugeot 206 WRC) 10m59.0s; 5 C.McRae/D.Ringer
(Citroën Xsara WRC) 11m01.1s; 6 J.Pykälistö/E.Mertsalmi
(Peugeot 206 WRC) 11m01.2s; JWC V.Teuronen/H.Kaapro
(Suzuki Ignis) 12m12.7s

SS3 KRUUNUNPERA 1 (20.17 KM)
1 Märtin/Park (Ford) 9m12.4s; 2 Grönholm/Rautiainen
(Peugeot) 9m16.1s; 3 McRae/Ringer (Citroën) 9m19.8s;
4 Burns/Reid (Peugeot) 9m22.6s; 5= Solberg/Mills (Subaru),
C.Sainz/M.Martí (Citroën Xsara WRC) 9m24.4s;
JWC Carlsson/Andersson (Suzuki) 10m26.9s

SS4 VALKOLA (8.42 KM)
1 Grönholm/Rautiainen (Peugeot) 4m25.4s; 2 Burns/Reid
(Peugeot) 4m26.1s; 3 McRae/Ringer (Citroën) 4m27.9s;
4 Märtin/Park (Ford) 4m28.5s; 5 Sainz/Martí (Citroën)
4m28.8s; 6 Solberg/Mills (Subaru) 4m28.9s; JWC G.Wilks/
P.Pugh (Ford Puma) 5m08.8s

SS5 LANKAMAA (23.47 KM)
1 Grönholm/Rautiainen (Peugeot) 11m26.0s; 2 Burns/Reid
(Peugeot) 11m26.7s; 3 Märtin/Park (Ford) 11m29.7s;
4 Sainz/Martí (Citroën) 11m34.0s; 5 Solberg/Mills (Subaru)
11m36.1s; 6 Rovanperä/Pietiläinen (Peugeot) 11m36.6s;
JWC Carlsson/Andersson (Suzuki) 13m10.5s

SS6 LAUKAA (11.82 KM)
1 Märtin/Park (Ford) 5m46.1s; 2 Grönholm/Rautiainen
(Peugeot) 5m48.3s; 3 Burns/Reid (Peugeot) 5m50.8;
4 McRae/Ringer (Citroën) 5m53.1s; 5 Sainz/Martí (Citroën)
5m53.2s; 6 M.Hirvonen/J.Lehtinen (Ford Focus RS WRC02)
5m55.7s; JWC Teuronen/Kaapro (Suzuki) 6m40.6s

SS7 RUUHIMAKI (7.57 KM)
1 Burns/Reid (Peugeot) 4m03.4s; 2 Grönholm/Rautiainen
(Peugeot) 4m06.2s; 3 Märtin/Park (Ford) 4m08.1s; 4 Sainz/
Martí (Citroën) 4m08.5s; 5 Solberg/Mills (Subaru) 4m09.3s;
6 Loeb/Elena (Citroën) 4m10.9s; JWC Carlsson/Andersson
(Suzuki) 4m41.7s

SS8 JUKOJARVI 2 (22.31 KM)
1 Märtin/Park (Ford) 10m40.1s; 2= Grönholm/Rautiainen
(Peugeot), Burns/Reid (Peugeot) 10m41.7s; 4 Solberg/Mills
(Subaru) 10m44.8s; 5 Sainz/Martí (Citroën) 10m46.6s;
6 McRae/Ringer (Citroën) 10m47.5s; JWC B.Tirabassi/
J.Renucci (Renault Clio) 12m31.8s

SS9 PAIJALA (20.17 KM)
1 Märtin/Park (Ford) 9m03.0s; 2 Grönholm/Rautiainen
(Peugeot) 9m06.5s; 3 McRae/Ringer (Citroën) 9m08.6s;
4 Loeb/Elena (Citroën) 9m09.3s; 5 Burns/Reid (Peugeot)
9m11.2s; 6 Solberg/Mills (Subaru) 9m11.8s; JWC Carlsson/
Andersson (Suzuki) 10m30.3s

SS10 KILLERI 2 (2.06 KM)
1 Grönholm/Rautiainen (Peugeot) 1m19.1s; 2 Märtin/Park
(Ford) 1m19.2s; 3 Solberg/Mills (Subaru) 1m19.4s;
4= Burns/Reid (Peugeot), Rovanperä/Pietiläinen (Peugeot)
1m19.7s; 6 McRae/Ringer (Citroën) 1m19.8s;
JWC Carlsson/Andersson (Suzuki) 1m30.1s

SS11 TALVIAINEN (21.95 KM)
1 Grönholm/Rautiainen (Peugeot) 11m21.4s; 2 Märtin/
Park (Ford) 11m23.2s; 3 Rovanperä/Pietiläinen (Peugeot)
11m24.2s; 4 Burns/Reid (Peugeot) 11m26.5s; 5 McRae/
Ringer (Citroën) 11m26.8s; 6 Solberg/Mills (Subaru)
11m31.5s; JWC Wilks/Pugh (Ford) 12m55.6s

SS12 OUNINPOHJA 1 (33.24 KM)
1 Grönholm/Rautiainen (Peugeot) 15m31.0s; 2 Märtin/Park
(Ford) 15m35.4s; 3 McRae/Ringer (Citroën) 15m39.8s;
4 Burns/Reid (Peugeot) 15m41.8s; 5 Sainz/Martí (Citroën)
15m45.9s; 6 Solberg/Mills (Subaru) 15m47.1s;
JWC K.Katajamäki/J.Laaksonen (VW Polo) 17m39.2s

SS13 URRIA (10.00 KM)
1 Burns/Reid (Peugeot) 4m48.4s; 2= McRae/Ringer
(Citroën), Grönholm/Rautiainen (Peugeot) 4m50.5s;
4 Sainz/Martí (Citroën) 4m50.7s; 5 Solberg/Mills (Subaru)
4m51.3s; 6 Märtin/Park (Ford) 4m51.4s; JWC Carlsson/
Andersson (Suzuki) 5m25.3s

SS14 OUNINPOHJA 2 (33.24 KM)
1 McRae/Ringer (Citroën) 15m25.1s; 2 Burns/Reid
(Peugeot) 15m31.5s; 3 Loeb/Elena (Citroën) 15m32.0s;
4 Sainz/Martí (Citroën) 15m37.8s; 5 Märtin/Park (Ford)
15m42.9s; 6 Solberg/Mills (Subaru) 15m43.3s;
JWC Carlsson/Andersson (Suzuki) 17m30.6s

SS15 EHIKKI (14.91 KM)
1 Burns/Reid (Peugeot) 6m52.6s; 2 Sainz/Martí (Citroën)
6m54.4s; 3 McRae/Ringer (Citroën) 6m55.4s; 4 Märtin/
Park (Ford) 6m58.9s; 5 S.Lindholm/T.Hantunen (Peugeot
206WRC) 6m59.0s; 6 Solberg/Mills (Subaru) 7m01.3s;
JWC Carlsson/Andersson (Suzuki) 7m49.6s

SS16 MOKSI-LEUSTU (40.96 KM)
1 Märtin/Park (Ford) 20m39.2s; 2 Solberg/Mills (Subaru)
20m41.2s; 3 Burns/Reid (Peugeot) 20m42.9s; 4 Sainz/Martí
(Citroën) 20m43.5s; 5 Loeb/Elena (Citroën) 20m48.0s;
6 T.Mäkinen/K.Lindström (Subaru Impreza WRC2003)
20m49.4s; JWC Carlsson/Andersson (Suzuki), Wilks/Pugh
(Ford) 23m53.5s

SS17 HIMOS (13.62 KM)
1 Solberg/Mills (Subaru) 7m30.1s; 2 Märtin/Park (Ford)
7m31.4s; 3 Sainz/Martí (Citroën) 7m33.9s; 4 Mäkinen/
Lindström (Subaru) 7m35.5s; 5 Loeb/Elena (Citroën)
7m35.6s; 6 Lindholm/Hantunen (Peugeot) 7m36.9s;
JWC Carlsson/Andersson (Suzuki) 8m35.2s

SS18 PARKKOLA 1 (19.88 KM)
1 Märtin/Park (Ford) 9m53.0s; 2 Solberg/Mills (Subaru)
9m54.3s; 3 Burns/Reid (Peugeot) 9m55.5s; 4 Sainz/Martí
(Citroën) 9m56.5s; 5 Mäkinen/Lindström (Subaru)
9m58.4s; 6 Loeb/Elena (Citroën) 9m58.5s; JWC Wilks/
Pugh (Ford) 11m14.1s

SS19 MOKKIPERA 1 (13.96 KM)
1 Burns/Reid (Peugeot) 6m56.0s; 2 Solberg/Mills (Subaru)
6m56.3s; 3 Märtin/Park (Ford) 6m56.5s; 4 Loeb/Elena
(Citroën) 7m01.9s; 5 Sainz/Martí (Citroën) 7m03.6s;
6 J.Tuohino/J.Aho (Ford Focus RS WRC02) 7m03.7s;
WC Carlsson/Andersson (Suzuki) 7m57.0s

SS20 PALSANKYLA (25.46 KM)
1 Burns/Reid (Peugeot) 13m31.2s; 2 Solberg/Mills (Subaru)
13m33.4s; 3 Märtin/Park (Ford) 13m42.5s; 4 Tuohino/Aho
(Ford) 13m48.9s; 5= Pykälistö/Mertsalmi (Peugeot),
Lindholm/Hantunen (Peugeot) 13m51.8s; JWC Tirabassi/
Renucci (Renault) 14m42.5s

SS21 KUOHU (7.76 KM)
1 Burns/Reid (Peugeot) 3m45.3s; 2 Märtin/Park (Ford)
3m46.4s; 3 Solberg/Mills (Subaru) 3m46.6s; 4 Sainz/Martí
(Citroën) 3m50.2s; 5 Mäkinen/Lindström (Subaru)
3m50.3s; 6 Lindholm/Hantunen (Peugeot) 3m50.7s;
JWC O.Svedlund/B.Nilsson (VW Polo) 4m16.7s

SS22 PARKKOLA 2 (19.88)
I Solberg/Mills (Subaru) 9m39.7s; 2 Burns/Reid (Peugeot)
9m41.0s; 3 Märtin/Park (Ford) 9m41.9s; 4 Loeb/Elena
(Citroën) 9m50.4s; 5 Sainz/Martí (Citroën) 9m50.9s;
6 Mäkinen/Lindström (Subaru) 9m51.5s; JWC Carlsson/
Andersson (Suzuki) 11m07.1s

SS23 MOKKIPERA 2 (13.96 KM)
I Solberg/Mills (Subaru) 6m47.8s; 2 Burns/Reid (Peugeot)
6m50.8s; 3 Märtin/Park (Ford) 6m52.4s; 4 Pykälistö/
Mertsalmi (Peugeot) 6m56.3s; 5 Tuohino/Aho (Ford)
6m58.4s; 6 Loeb/Elena (Citroën) 6m58.5s; JWC Carlsson/
Andersson (Suzuki) 7m51.2s

MAJOR RETIREMENTS

I	Grönholm/R'iainen	Peugeot 206 WRC		
	Suspension	SS14	Gr A
17	McRae/Ringer	Citroën Xsara WRC		
	Accident	SS16	Gr A
3	Rovanperä/P'lainen	Peugeot 206 WRC		
	Accident	SS12	Gr A
5	Duval/Prevot	Ford Focus RS WRC03		
	Lost wheel	SS19	Gr A
15	Gardemeister/L'der	Skoda Fabia WRC		
	Engine	SS12	Gr A
14	Auriol/Giraudet	Skoda Fabia WRC		
	Driver injury	SS2	Gr A
6	Hirvonen/Lehtinen	Ford Focus RS WRC02		
	Fire	SS12	Gr A
12	Välimäki/Honkanen	Hyundai Accent WRC3		
	Lost wheel	SS19	Gr A

FIA CLASS WINNERS

A8 Over 2000 cc	Märtin/Park
	Ford Focus RS WRC03
A7 1600-2000cc	Klemets/Nattiaho
	Honda Civic Type-R
A6 1400-1600 cc	Carlsson/Andersson
	Suzuki Ignis
N4 Over 2000 cc	Salo/Stenberg
	Mitsubishi Lancer E7

RALLY LEADERS

Overall: SS1-4 Märtin; SS5-8 Grönholm; SS9-11 Märtin;
SS12-13 Grönholm; SS14-23 Märtin

JWC: SS1-7 Carlsson; SS8-13 Tirabassi; SS14-23 Carlsson

SPECIAL STAGE ANALYSIS

	1st	2nd	3rd	4th	5th	6th
Märtin (Ford)	8	5	6	2	1	1
Grönholm (Peugeot)	6	7	-	-	-	-
Burns (Peugeot)	6	6	3	5	1	1
Solberg (Subaru)	3	4	4	1	4	6
McRae (Citroën)	1	1	5	1	2	2
Sainz (Citroën)	-	1	1	7	7	-
Loeb (Citroën)	-	-	1	3	3	3
Rovanperä (Peugeot)	-	-	1	1	-	3
Mäkinen (Subaru)	-	-	-	1	2	2
Tuohino (Ford)	-	-	-	1	1	1
Pykälistö (Peugeot)	-	-	-	1	1	1
Duval (Ford)	-	-	-	1	-	-
Lindholm (Peugeot)	-	-	-	-	2	2
Hirvonen (Ford)	-	-	-	-	-	1

WORLD CHAMPIONSHIP POINTS

DRIVERS
1 Burns 49; 2 Sainz 44; 3= Grönholm, Solberg 38; 5= Loeb,
Märtin 37; 7 McRae 28; 8 Mäkinen 18; 9 Rovanperä 16;
10 Duval 11 etc

MANUFACTURERS
1 Peugeot 101; 2 Citroën 97; 3= Ford, Subaru 60;
5 Skoda 20; 6 Hyundai 10

JUNIOR WORLD CHAMPIONSHIP
1= Tirabassi 28; 2 Carlsson 18; 3 Canellas 17; 4 Aava 16;
5 Wilks 15; 6= Ligato, Katajamäki 10 etc

PRODUCTION CUP
1 Arai 30; 2 Rowe 27; 3 Singh 22; 4 Blomqvist 21;
5 Solá 18; 6 Ligato 13 etc

ROUTE DETAILS

Total Route of 1727.70 km of which 409.18 km were
competitive on 23 stages

LEG 1 Friday 8th August, 10 special stages
totalling 140.36 km
LEG 2 Saturday 10th August, 7 special stages
totalling 167.92 km
LEG 3 Sunday 11th August, 6 special stages
totalling 100.90 km

The Focus was in its element in Finland, but François
Duval couldn't begin to match Markko Märtin's
exploits, the Belgian's tentative performance ending
with an accident near the finish.

RESULTS

1	Markko Märtin/	Ford Focus RS WRC03		
	Michael Park	3h21m51.7s		Gr A
2	Petter Solberg/	Subaru Impreza WRC2003		
	Phil Mills	3h22m50.6s		Gr A
3	Richard Burns/	Peugeot 206 WRC		
	Robert Reid	3h22m51.8s		Gr A
4	Carlos Sainz/	Citroën Xsara WRC		
	Marc Martí	3h23m50.7s		Gr A
5	Sébastien Loeb/	Citroën Xsara WRC		
	Daniel Elena	3h24m40.4s		Gr A
6	Tommi Mäkinen/	Subaru Impreza WRC2003		
	Kaj Lindström	3h25m16.9s		Gr A
7	Janne Tuohino/	Ford Focus RS WRC02		
	Jukka Aho	3h26m14.6s		Gr A
8	Sebastian Lindholm/	Peugeot 206 WRC		
	Timo Hantunen	3h26m31.2s		Gr A
9	Juuso Pykälistö/	Peugeot 206 WRC		
	Esko Mertsalmi	3h28m15.1s		Gr A
10	Freddy Loix/	Hyundai Accent WRC3		
	Sven Smeets	3h30m11.6s		Gr A

71 starters, 35 finishers

PREVIOUS WINNERS

1970	Hannu Mikkola/Gunnar Palm	Ford Escort TC
1971	Stig Blomqvist/Arne Hertz	Saab 96 V4
1972	Simo Lampinen/Klaus Sohlberg	Saab 96 V4
1973	Timo Mäkinen/Henry Liddon	Ford Escort RS1600
1974	Hannu Mikkola/John Davenport	Ford Escort RS1600
1975	Hannu Mikkola/Atso Aho	Toyota Corolla
1976	Markku Alén/Ilkka Kivimäki	Fiat Abarth 131
1977	Kyosti Hämäläinen/Martí Tiukkanen	Ford Escort RS
1978	Markku Alén/Ilkka Kivimäki	Fiat Abarth 131
1979	Markku Alén/Ilkka Kivimäki	Fiat Abarth 131
1980	Markku Alén/Ilkka Kivimäki	Fiat Abarth 131
1981	Ari Vatanen/David Richards	Ford Escort RS
1982	Hannu Mikkola/Arne Hertz	Audi Quattro
1983	Hannu Mikkola/Arne Hertz	Audi Quattro A1
1984	Ari Vatanen/Terry Harryman	Peugeot 205 Turbo 16
1985	Timo Salonen/Seppo Harjanne	Peugeot 205 Turbo 16 E2
1986	Timo Salonen/Seppo Harjanne	Peugeot 205 Turbo 16 E2
1987	Markku Alén/Ilkka Kivimäki	Lancia Delta HF 4x4
1988	Markku Alén/Ilkka Kivimäki	Lancia Delta Integrale
1989	Mikael Ericsson/Claes Billstam	Mitsubishi Galant VR-4
1990	Carlos Sainz/Luis Moya	Toyota Celica GT4
1991	Juha Kankkunen/Juha Piironen	Lancia Delta Integrale 16v
1992	Didier Auriol/Bernard Occelli	Lancia Delta HF Integrale
1993	Juha Kankkunen/Denis Giraudet	Toyota Celica Turbo 4wd
1994	Tommi Mäkinen/Seppo Harjanne	Ford Escort RS Cosworth
1995	Tommi Mäkinen/Seppo Harjanne	Mitsubishi Lancer RS-E3
1996	Tommi Mäkinen/Seppo Harjanne	Mitsubishi Lancer RS-E3
1997	Tommi Mäkinen/Seppo Harjanne	Mitsubishi Lancer E4
1998	Tommi Mäkinen/Seppo Harjanne	Mitsubishi Lancer E5
1999	Juha Kankkunen/Juha Repo	Subaru Impreza WRC99
2000	Marcus Grönholm/Timo Rautiainen	Peugeot 206 WRC
2001	Marcus Grönholm/Timo Rautiainen	Peugeot 206 WRC
2002	Marcus Grönholm/Timo Rautiainen	Peugeot 206 WRC

FINISH LINES

It was a hideous weekend for the Finns: the top local driver was Tommi Mäkinen, who finished a distant sixth, beset by a succession of niggling problems in his Subaru, ranging from loose EMI puncture-free inserts to intercom failure and centre differential problems... The one Finnish success was in Group N, which fell to Juha Salo, driving a Lancer Evo VII... Carlos Sainz was the top Citroën driver. He was in the running for second as the last leg began, but a brush with the scenery and a leaking damper – the two were probably connected – left him a secure but slightly distant fourth... Sébastien Loeb put in a measured, low-risk drive to take fifth in his Xsara... There was nothing low-risk about Colin McRae's performance, the Scot closing in on Richard Burns for second until he collected a minute's road penalty for booking in early at a time control. His attempts to recover ended when his Xsara skipped wide and flipped on a sixth-gear corner... Daniel Carlsson finally delivered Suzuki's first, long-awaited victory in the Junior class, fighting back strongly to dispatch Brice Tirabassi's Clio, despite stopping to change a puncture on a stage... Guy Wilks was highly impressive, recovering well from a puncture and a visit to a ditch in the first leg to be third Junior finisher in his Birkbeck-run Puma... Michelin reached another landmark, becoming the first tyre manufacturer to win 200 World Championship rallies... Kosti Katajamäki was in the running for Junior victory until he put his Polo off on Ouninpohja 2... For once, Simon Jean-Joseph didn't take the 1600 class, the Martinique driver sliding off and breaking his Renault's rear suspension... Mark Higgins retired his RED Clio in the first leg, as an engine mount broke and allowed the cambelt to jump a tooth, with disastrous consequences for the engine...

STAGE NUMBERS	1	2	3	4	5	6	7	8	9	10	11	12	13	14	15	16	17	18	19	20	21	22	23
Märtin	1	1	1	1	2	2	2	1	1	1	1	2	2	1	1	1	1	1	1	1	1	1	1
Solberg	3	3	3	5	5	5	5	4	5	5	5	5	5	3	4	4	2	2	3	3	3	3	2
Burns	6	4	5	3	3	3	3	3	3	3	3	3	3	2	2	2	2	3	2	2	2	2	3
Sainz	9	9	6	6	6	6	6	6	6	6	6	6	4	3	3	3	4	4	4	4	4	4	4
Loeb	5	12	11	11	10	8	7	7	7	7	7	7	7	6	5	5	5	5	5	5	5	5	5
Mäkinen	10	10	8	8	8	7	8	8	8	8	8	8	8	7	6	6	6	6	6	6	6	6	6
Tuohino	11	7	7	9	10	9	9	9	9	9	10	10	10	9	8	7	7	7	7	7	7	7	7
Lindholm	16	8	9	10	11	11	13	13	13	13	12	11	11	10	9	8	8	8	8	8	8	8	8
Pykälisto	13	6	10	9	7	9	10	10	10	10	9	9	11	10	9	9	9	9	9	9	9		
Loix	15	13	15	14	14	14	14	14	14	14	13	12	12	11	10	10	10	10	10	10	10	10	
Vatanen	28	19	19	20	20	20	19	19	19	19	16	15	15	13	12	12	11	11	11	11	11	11	
Schwarz	17	18	20	20	18	18	18	18	18	18	17	16	16	15	14	14	14	12	12	12	12	12	
Duval	4	14	17	15	15	16	16	15	15	15	14	13	13	12	11	11	11	R					
McRae	8	5	4	4	4	4	4	5	4	4	4	4	4	6	5	R							
Grönholm	2	2	2	2	1	1	1		2	2	2	1	1	5	R								
Rovanperä	6		68	68	66	64	62	62	59	55	54	52	R										
Hirvonen	12	17	13	13	13	13	13	11	11	11	11	11	13	R									
G'meister	14	11	12	12	12	12	12	12	12	12	11	R											
Auriol	23	R																					

117

RALLY AUSTRALIA

RALLYCOURSE World Rally Championship **Round 10**

Traditionally, Australia falls to north Europeans and it was no surprise that Petter Solberg was in his element (above) remorselessly stepping up the pace in a prolonged duel with Loeb. Toni Gardemeister displayed real determination in driving his Skoda with a broken wrist. Western Australia's ballbearing gravel is inescapable and an intrinsic part of the event's character.

Sébastien Loeb didn't hesitate: it was more important to finish. With three stages to run, it was as though he still couldn't quite believe that winning was within his grasp. For two days, he had impressed, even amazed. He had contested the Rally Australia only once before and by his own admission he had found it difficult. Sixth or seventh place was the target, a realistic goal for an exercise in refining the pace notes.

Instead, he had been among the leaders from the start, revelling in the Xsara's improved handling, in his element as grip changed constantly from dry to damp on the opening forest stages south of Perth. Once Marcus Grönholm beached his 206 on the inside of a hairpin, Loeb became the leader. No quarter had been given in a ferocious duel with Petter Solberg, the two never separated by more than 5.4 seconds during the second leg. Loeb was carefully amending his notes stage by stage, but driving the revised Xsara was a pleasure. As the final leg in Sotico began, a sensational win was a distinct possibility.

But after the first of Sotico's four long, rutted, gravel-caked stages, Loeb had slumped to second. The deficit was eight seconds – the greatest margin between the two since early on Friday. He confessed that he hadn't driven especially well on the first stage, whereas Solberg had stepped up the pace. There was no mistaking the Norwegian's jauntiness as he swapped the Subaru's tyres around a few yards away.

Would it be better to throw everything into a counter-attack or settle for a worthy second? A stage later, Loeb was back in front. Solberg had slithered off twice, doing no damage to speak of, but restoring the advantage to the Frenchman.

Loeb's defiance was admirable, but futile and after the third Sotico stage, the battle was as good as over. Anticipating plenty of gravel, Citroën had put him on the narrower Michelin ZEs, but in the harder compound. Prodrive had correctly divined that rain was a strong possibility and had left Solberg on the softer Pirelli KMs. He had barged Loeb aside by almost ten seconds and as the rain intensified, both sides were only too aware of the likely outcome. Citroën advised Loeb to maintain the pressure, but to do nothing silly. When he learnt that he had dropped another four seconds in the first six miles of the final stage, he backed off altogether. Eight World Championship points would do very well.

Loeb wasn't at all sure that tyres had made the difference. Whereas Citroën had urged caution, the notion that there might be a distinction between finishing and winning never seemed to cross Solberg's mind. Once Grönholm was out of the way, he had predicted that it would be settled in Sotico and he had been utterly convinced that he was the man to settle it. He had learnt the hard way that rallies were won on Sunday, not Friday. Although it wasn't easy – there were occasional half-spins – he promised that he had something in reserve and seemed almost disappointed to take the lead at once in Sotico. He much prefers to be the pursuer and wanted to dispatch Loeb at a moment of his choosing.

Loeb had driven magnificently, banishing any remaining doubts that he isn't capable of winning on dirt, but as Phil Mills said, Solberg had driven the 'textbook rally.' It had been tighter than the winning margin suggested, but always under control. Solberg was delighted rather than elated: finishing third in Finland had demanded more of him.

RALLY AUSTRALIA

*It turned out to be Hyundai's swansong,
Freddy Loix doing his level best with
underfunded, underpowered machinery
(top left). He made a somewhat better
impression than his fellow Belgian, François
Duval, who finished behind Mikko
Hirvonen's older Focus (top right). Even
Markko Märtin failed to do full justice to
the Ford on this occasion, but Sébastien
Loeb was a revelation (centre left),
comfortably outpacing his Citroën
colleagues, Colin McRae included, to take
a close second.*

RALLY AUSTRALIA

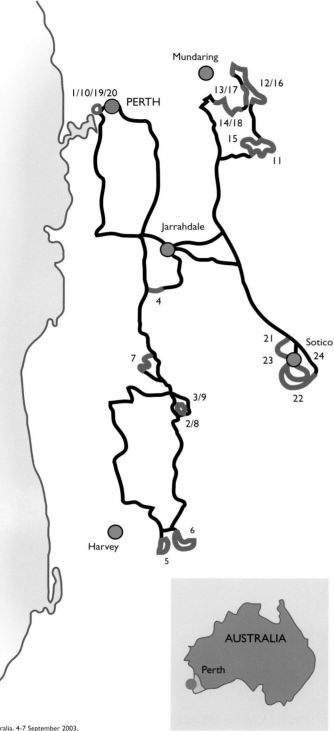

Mundaring

12/16

1/10/19/20   13/17

PERTH   14/18

15

11

Jarrahdale

4

21   Sotico

23   24

7   22

3/9

2/8

6

Harvey

5

AUSTRALIA

Perth

Rally Australia, 4-7 September 2003,
FIA World Rally Championship Round 10

RUNNING ORDER

2	Richard Burns/	Peugeot 206 WRC
	Robert Reid	Gr A
19	Carlos Sainz/	Citroën Xsara WRC
	Marc Martí	Gr A
1	Marcus Grönholm/	Peugeot 206 WRC
	Timo Rautiainen	Gr A
7	Petter Solberg/	Subaru Impreza WRC2003
	Phil Mills	Gr A
18	Sébastien Loeb/	Citroën Xsara WRC
	Daniel Elena	Gr A
4	Markko Märtin/	Ford Focus RS WRC03
	Michael Park	Gr A
17	Colin McRae/	Citroën Xsara WRC
	Derek Ringer	Gr A
8	Tommi Mäkinen/	Subaru Impreza WRC2003
	Kaj Lindström	Gr A
3	Harri Rovanperä/	Peugeot 206 WRC
	Risto Pietiläinen	Gr A
5	François Duval/	Ford Focus RS WRC03
	Stéphane Prevot	Gr A

15	Toni Gardemeister/	Skoda Fabia WRC
	Paavo Lukander	Gr A
14	Didier Auriol/	Skoda Fabia WRC
	Denis Giraudet	Gr A
6	Mikko Hirvonen/	Ford Focus RS WRC02
	Jarmo Lehtinen	Gr A
10	Armin Schwarz/	Hyundai Accent WRC3
	Manfred Hiemer	Gr A
11	Freddy Loix/	Hyundai Accent WRC3
	Sven Smeets	Gr A
21	Antony Warmbold/	Ford Focus RS WRC02
	Gemma Price	Gr A
23	Balazs Benik/	Ford Focus RS WRC01
	Bence Racz	Gr A
54	Toshihiro Arai/	Subaru Impreza WRX
	Tony Sircombe	Gr N
55	Martin Rowe/	Subaru Impreza WRX
	Trevor Agnew	Gr N
51	Karamjit Singh/	Proton Pert
	Allen Oh	Gr N

SPECIAL STAGE TIMES

SS1 PERTH CITY SUPER 1 (2.45 KM)
1 P.Solberg/P.Mills (Subaru Impreza WRC2003) 1m31.9s;
2 C.Sainz/M.Martí (Citroën Xsara WRC) 1m32.2s;
3 M.Märtin/M.Park (Ford Focus RS WRC03) 1m32.6s;
4 T.Mäkinen/K.Lindström (Subaru Impreza WRC2003)
1m32.8s; 5= H.Rovanperä/R.Pietilainen (Peugeot 206
WRC), C.McRae/D.Ringer (Citroën Xsara WRC),
S.Loeb/D.Elena (Citroën Xsara WRC), R.Burns/R.Reid
(Peugeot 206 WRC) 1m33.0s; PC M.Ligato/R.Garcia
(Mitsubishi Lancer E7) 1m39.9s

SS2 MURRAY NORTH 1 (18.49 KM)
1 M.Grönholm/T.Rautiainen (Peugeot 206 WRC) 10m29.1s;
2 Solberg/Mills (Subaru) 10m31.5s; 3 Märtin/Park (Ford)
10m35.5s; 4 Loeb/Elena (Citroën) 10m36.3s; 5 Mäkinen/
Lindström (Subaru) 10m41.4s; 6 Burns/Reid (Peugeot)
10m42.2s; PC Ligato/Garcia (Mitsubishi) 11m25.8s

SS3 MURRAY SOUTH 1 (20.12 KM)
1 Grönholm/Rautiainen (Peugeot) 11m51.8s; 2 Sainz/Martí
(Citroën) 12m00.9s; 3 Solberg/Mills (Subaru) 12m01.5s;
4 Burns/Reid (Peugeot) 12m02.0s; 5 Mäkinen/Lindström
(Subaru) 12m07.6s; 6 Loeb/Elena (Citroën) 12m09.9s;
PC Ligato/Garcia (Mitsubishi) 12m57.7s

SS4 GOBBYS (5.20 KM)
1 Märtin/Park (Ford) 2m29.6s; 2 Solberg/Mills (Subaru)
2m31.2s; 3 M.Hirvonen/J.Lehtinen (Ford Focus RS WRC02)
2m31.4s; 4 Loeb/Elena (Citroën) 2m31.5s; 5 Grönholm/
Rautiainen (Peugeot) 2m31.7s; 6 Mäkinen/Lindström
(Subaru) 2m32.4s; PC Ligato/Garcia (Mitsubishi) 2m45.2s

SS5 STIRLING WEST (15.89 KM)
1 Loeb/Elena (Citroën) 9m15.3s; 2 Solberg/Mills (Subaru)
9m15.8s; 3 Grönholm/Rautiainen (Peugeot) 9m17.5s;
4 Burns/Reid (Peugeot) 9m20.6s; 5 Märtin/Park (Ford)
9m22.8s; 6 Rovanperä/Pietilainen (Peugeot) 9m24.0s;
PC Ligato/Garcia (Mitsubishi) 10m06.1s

SS6 STIRLING LONG (34.99 KM)
1 Loeb/Elena (Citroën) 20m02.1s; 2 Grönholm/Rautiainen
(Peugeot) 20m10.1s; 3 Burns/Reid (Peugeot) 20m19.7s;
4 Solberg/Mills (Subaru) 20m22.0s; 5 Rovanperä/Pietilainen
(Peugeot) 20m23.0s; 6 Mäkinen/Lindström (Subaru)
20m25.0s; PC M.Rowe/T.Agnew (Subari Impreza WRX)
21m54.6s

SS7 TURNER HILL (7.00 KM)
1 Solberg/Mills (Subaru) 4m22.2s; 2 Grönholm/Rautiainen
(Peugeot) 4m24.5s; 3 Burns/Reid (Peugeot) 4m25.4s;
4 Loeb/Elena (Citroën) 4m25.9s; 5 Sainz/Martí (Citroën)
4m26.9s; 6= Mäkinen/Lindström (Subaru), McRae/Ringer
(Citroën) 4m28.5s; PC K.Singh/A.Oh (Proton Pert)
4m51.7s

SS8 MURRAY NORTH 2 (18.49 KM)
1= Solberg/Mills (Subaru), Loeb/Elena (Citroën) 10m14.4s;
3 Märtin/Park (Ford) 10m15.3s; 4 Mäkinen/Lindström
(Subaru) 10m19.6s; 5 Burns/Reid (Peugeot) 10m19.8s;
6 McRae/Ringer (Citroën) 10m22.7s; PC N.McShea/
C.Patterson (Mitsubishi Lancer E6) 11m12.7s

SS9 MURRAY SOUTH 2 (20.12 KM)
1 Loeb/Elena (Citroën) 11m30.0s; 2 Solberg/Mills (Subaru)
11m33.1s; 3 Märtin/Park (Ford) 11m35.7s; 4 Grönholm/
Rautiainen (Peugeot) 11m38.9s; 5 Sainz/Martí (Citroën)
11m39.8s; 6 Burns/Reid (Peugeot) 11m40.4s; PC T.Arai/
T.Sircombe (Subaru Impreza WRX) 12m52.0s

SS10 PERTH CITY SUPER 2 (2.45 KM)
1 F.Duval/S.Prevot (Ford Focus RS WRC03) 1m33.5s;
2= Märtin/Park (Ford), Mäkinen/Lindström (Subaru)
1m33.7s; 4= Solberg/Mills (Subaru), McRae/Ringer
(Citroën) 1m33.9s; 6 Loeb/Elena (Citroën) 1m34.0s;
PC S.Blomqvist/R.Scott (Subaru Impreza WRX) 1m40.7s

SS11 BERAKING EAST (8.88 KM)
1 Solberg/Mills (Subaru) 5m09.6s; 2 Loeb/Elena (Citroën)
5m10.8s; 3 Burns/Reid (Peugeot) 5m13.5s; 4 Rovanperä/
Pietilainen (Peugeot) 5m15.4s; 5= Mäkinen/Lindström
(Subaru), McRae/Ringer (Citroën) 5m17.0s; PC Arai/
Sircombe (Subaru) 5m40.1s

SS12 HELENA EAST 1 (20.49 KM)
1 Solberg/Mills (Subaru) 11m38.2s; 2 Loeb/Elena (Citroën)
11m40.9s; 3 Burns/Reid (Peugeot) 11m45.5s; 4 Märtin/Park
(Ford) 11m48.8s; 5 Rovanperä/Pietilainen (Peugeot)
11m49.6s; 6 McRae/Ringer (Citroën) 11m50.3s; PC Rowe/
Agnew (Subaru) 12m43.4s

SS13 HELENA WEST 1 (12.60 KM)
1 Loeb/Elena (Citroën) 7m18.4s; 2 Solberg/Mills (Subaru)
7m21.0s; 3 McRae/Ringer (Citroën) 7m24.1s; 4 Burns/Reid
(Peugeot) 7m24.9s; 5 Mäkinen/Lindström (Subaru) 7m25.5s;
6 Sainz/Martí (Citroën) 7m27.2s; PC Arai/Sircombe
(Subaru) 8m00.5s

SS14 HELENA SOUTH 1 (17.31 KM)
1 Solberg/Mills (Subaru) 8m55.2s; 2 Loeb/Elena (Citroën)
8m55.7s; 3 Burns/Reid (Peugeot) 9m00.0s; 4 Märtin/Park
(Ford) 9m00.3s; 5 McRae/Ringer (Citroën) 9m00.4s;
6 Mäkinen/Lindström (Subaru) 9m02.2s; PC Rowe/Agnew
(Subaru) 9m52.6s

SS15 BERAKING WEST (9.42 KM)
1 Solberg/Mills (Subaru) 4m38.7s; 2 Loeb/Elena (Citroën)
4m39.9s; 3 Märtin/Park (Ford) 4m42.3s; 4 Burns/Reid
(Peugeot) 4m42.5s; 5 Sainz/Martí (Citroën) 4m45.3s;
6 Mäkinen/Lindström (Subaru) 4m46.1s; PC D.Solá/
A.Romani (Mitsubishi Lancer E7) 5m05.1s

SS16 HELENA EAST 2 (20.49 KM)
1 Loeb/Elena (Citroën) 11m23.8s; 2 Solberg/Mills (Subaru)
11m25.4s; 3 Märtin/Park (Ford) 11m30.7s; 4 Rovanperä/
Pietilainen (Peugeot) 11m31.3s; 5 Burns/Reid (Peugeot)
11m32.7s; 6 McRae/Ringer (Citroën) 11m33.8s; PC Solá/
Romani (Mitsubishi) 12m31.0s

SS17 HELENA WEST 2 (12.60 KM)
1 Loeb/Elena (Citroën) 7m10.6s; 2 Solberg/Mills (Subaru)
7m10.9s; 3 Märtin/Park (Ford) 7m16.9s; 4 Rovanperä/
Pietilainen (Peugeot) 7m17.2s; 5 Sainz/Martí (Citroën)
7m17.7s; 6 McRae/Ringer (Citroën) 7m19.3s; PC Solá/
Romani (Mitsubishi) 7m53.2s

SS18 HELENA SOUTH 2 (17.31 KM)
1 Loeb/Elena (Citroën) 8m46.6s; 2 Solberg/Mills (Subaru)
8m49.0s; 3 McRae/Ringer (Citroën) 8m49.3s; 4 Märtin/Park
(Ford) 8m51.3s; 5 Rovanperä/Pietilainen (Peugeot)
8m51.8s; 6 Sainz/Martí (Citroën) 8m52.2s; PC Solá/Romani
(Mitsubishi) 9m40.5s

SS19 PERTH CITY SUPER 3 (2.45 KM)
1 Märtin/Park (Ford) 1m31.7s; 2 Mäkinen/Lindström
(Subaru) 1m32.4s; 3 Solberg/Mills (Subaru) 1m32.5s; 4 Loeb/
Elena (Citroën) 1m32.7s; 5 McRae/Ringer (Citroën)
1m33.2s; 6 Burns/Reid (Peugeot) 1m33.4s; PC Blomqvist/
Scott (Subaru) 1m39.1s

SS20 PERTH CITY SUPER 4 (2.45 KM)
1 Märtin/Park (Ford) 1m31.8s; 2 McRae/Ringer (Citroën)
1m32.3s; 3 Solberg/Mills (Subaru) 1m32.6s; 4= Sainz/Martí
(Citroën), Loeb/Elena (Citroën) 1m32.8s; 6 Mäkinen/
Lindström (Subaru) 1m33.1s; PC Blomqvist/Scott (Subaru)
1m38.7s

SS21 BANNISTER NORTH (21.81 KM)
1 Solberg/Mills (Subaru) 13m11.9s; 2 Loeb/Elena (Citroën)
13m17.6s; 3 Sainz/Martí (Citroën) 13m18.5s; 4 Burns/Reid
(Peugeot) 13m21.3s; 5 McRae/Ringer (Citroën) 13m22.9s;
6 Rovanperä/Pietilainen (Peugeot) 13m25.7s; PC Rowe/
Agnew (Subaru) 14m36.6s

SS22 BANNISTER SOUTH (34.16 KM)
1 Loeb/Elena (Citroën) 16m00.1s; 2 Solberg/Mills (Subaru)
16m02.0s; 3 Burns/Reid (Peugeot) 16m09.1s; 4 Sainz/Martí
(Citroën) 16m11.9s; 5 McRae/Ringer (Citroën) 16m12.8s;
6 Rovanperä/Pietilainen (Peugeot) 16m16.4s; PC Rowe/
Agnew (Subaru) 17m36.1s

SS23 BANNISTER WEST (24.69 KM)
1 Solberg/Mills (Subaru) 12m22.6s; 2 McRae/Ringer
(Citroën) 12m28.1s; 3 Sainz/Martí (Citroën) 12m28.6s;
4 Mäkinen/Lindström (Subaru) 12m28.9s; 5 Loeb/Elena
(Citroën) 12m31.9s; 6 Burns/Reid (Peugeot) 12m32.7s;
PC McShea/Patterson (Mitsubishi) 13m48.8s

SS24 BANNISTER CENTRAL (33.45 KM)
1 McRae/Ringer (Citroën) 18m10.0s; 2 Sainz/Martí (Citroën)
18m14.0s; 3 Solberg/Mills (Subaru) 18m20.9s; 4 Hirvonen/
Lehtinen (Ford) 18m23.7s; 5 Mäkinen/Lindström (Subaru)
18m24.4s; 6 Burns/Reid (Peugeot) 18m26.6s; PC McShea/
Patterson (Mitsubishi) 20m07.5s

MAJOR RETIREMENTS

1	Grönholm/R'iainen	Peugeot 206 WRC		
	Withdrawn	SS10	Gr A	
4	Märtin/Park	Ford Focus RS WRC03		
	Excluded	SS20	Gr A	

FIA CLASS WINNERS

A8 Over 2000 cc	Solberg/Mills
	Subaru Impreza WRC2003
N4 Over 2000 cc	Rowe/Agnew
	Subaru Impreza WRX

RALLY LEADERS

Overall: SS1 Solberg; SS2-7 Grönholm; SS8-11 Loeb; SS12 Loeb, Solberg; SS13-20 Loeb; SS21 Solberg; SS22 Loeb; SS23-24 Solberg

PC: SS1-7 Ligato; SS8-24 Rowe

SPECIAL STAGE ANALYSIS

	1st	2nd	3rd	4th	5th	6th
Solberg (Subaru)	9	9	4	2	-	-
Loeb (Citroën)	9	5	-	5	2	2
Märtin (Ford)	3	1	7	3	1	-
Grönholm (Peugeot)	2	2	1	1	1	-
McRae (Citroën)	1	2	2	1	5	6
Duval (Ford)	1	-	-	-	-	-
Sainz (Citroën)	-	3	2	2	4	2
Mäkinen (Subaru)	-	2	-	3	5	6
Burns (Peugeot)	-	-	6	5	3	5
Hirvonen (Ford)	-	-	1	1	-	-
Rovanperä (Peugeot)	-	-	-	3	4	3

WORLD CHAMPIONSHIP POINTS

DRIVERS
1 Burns 55; 2= Solberg, Sainz 48; 4 Loeb 45; 5 Grönholm 38; 6 Märtin 37; 7 McRae 33; 8 Mäkinen 21; 9 Rovanperä 18; 10 Duval 11 etc

MANUFACTURERS
1= Peugeot, Citroën 110; 3 Subaru 74; 4 Ford 61; 5 Skoda 20; 6 Hyundai 12

JUNIOR WORLD CHAMPIONSHIP
1= Tirabassi 28; 2 Carlsson 18; 3 Canellas 17; 4 Aava 16; 5 Wilks 15; 6= Ligato, Katajamäki 10 etc

PRODUCTION CUP
1 Rowe 37; 2= Arai, Singh 30; 4 Blomqvist 26; 5 Solá 22; 6 Ligato 13 etc

ROUTE DETAILS

Total route of 1795.16 km of which 396.31 km were competitive on 24 stages

LEG 1 Thursday 4th September – Friday 5th September, 10 special stages totalling 145.20 km

LEG 2 Saturday 6th September, 10 special stages totalling 124.00 km

LEG 3 Sunday 7th September, 4 special stages totalling 117.11 km

RESULTS

1	Petter Solberg/	Subaru Impreza WRC2003	
	Phil Mills	3h32m07.1s	Gr A
2	Sébastien Loeb/	Citroën Xsara WRC	
	Daniel Elena	3h32m33.7s	Gr A
3	Richard Burns/	Peugeot 206 WRC	
	Robert Reid	3h34m00.1s	Gr A
4	Colin McRae/	Citroën Xsara WRC	
	Derek Ringer	3h34m37.8s	Gr A
5	Carlos Sainz/	Citroën Xsara WRC	
	Marc Martí	3h34m44.3s	Gr A
6	Tommi Mäkinen/	Subaru Impreza WRC2003	
	Kaj Lindström	3h35m08.6s	Gr A
7	Harri Rovanperä/	Peugeot 206 WRC	
	Risto Pietilainen	3h36m11.0s	Gr A
8	Freddy Loix/	Hyundai Accent WRC3	
	Sven Smeets	3h39m07.8s	Gr A
9	Mikko Hirvonen/	Ford Focus RS WRC02	
	Jarmo Lehtinen	3h39m17.7s	Gr A
10	François Duval/	Ford Focus RS WRC03	
	Stéphane Prevot	3h39m59.3s	Gr A

49 starters, 32 finishers

PREVIOUS WINNERS

1989	Juha Kankkunen/Juha Piironen	Toyota Celica GT4
1990	Juha Kankkunen/Juha Piironen	Lancia Delta Integrale-16v
1991	Juha Kankkunen/Juha Piironen	Lancia Delta Integrale-16v
1992	Didier Auriol/Bernard Occelli	Lancia Delta HF Integrale
1993	Juha Kankkunen/Nicky Grist	Toyota Celica Turbo 4WD
1994	Colin McRae/Derek Ringer	Subaru Impreza 555
1995	Kenneth Eriksson/Staffan Parmander	
		Mitsubishi Lancer RS -E2
1996	Tommi Mäkinen/Seppo Harjanne	Mitsubishi Lancer RS-E3
1997	Colin McRae/Nicky Grist	Subaru Impreza WRC97
1998	Tommi Mäkinen/Risto Mannisenmaki	Mitsubishi Lancer E5
1999	Richard Burns/Robert Reid	Subaru Impreza WRC99
2000	Marcus Grönholm/Timo Rautiainen	Peugeot 206 WRC
2001	Marcus Grönholm/Timo Rautiainen	Peugeot 206 WRC
2002	Marcus Grönholm/Timo Rautiainen	Peugeot 206 WRC

STAGE NUMBERS	1	2	3	4	5	6	7	8	9	10	11	12	13	14	15	16	17	18	19	20	21	22	23	24
Solberg	1	2	2	2	3	3	2	2	2	2	1	2	2	2	2	2	2	2	2	1	2	1	1
Loeb	5	4	4	3	3	2	2	1	1	1	1	1	1	1	1	1	1	1	1	1	2	1	2	2
Burns	5	6	3	4	4	4	4	3	3	3	3	3	3	3	3	3	3	3	3	3	3	3	3	3
McRae	5	8	8	8	8	9	9	7	7	7	7	7	7	7	6	6	5	5	5	4	4	4	4
Sainz	2	7	5	5	6	6	5	6	6	6	6	6	6	6	7	7	7	7	5	5	5	5
Mäkinen	4	5	6	5	5	5	4	4	4	4	4	4	5	5	5	6	6	6	6	6	6	6
Rovanperä	5	10	9	9	9	8	8	8	8	8	8	8	8	8	8	8	8	8	7	7	7
Loix	12	9	10	12	10	11	9	9	9	9	9	9	9	9	9	9	9	9	10	8	8	8
Hirvonen	11	11	11	10	11	13	11	11	11	11	11	11	11	11	11	11	11	11	10	9	9
Duval	9	12	13	13	13	12	12	11	12	12	11	10	10	10	10	10	10	10	9	9	10	10
G'meister	14	15	14	14	14	14	14	14	14	13	13	13	13	13	13	13	13	12	11	11	11
Auriol	13	13	12	11	12	11	10	10	10	10	12	12	12	12	12	12	12	11	12	12	12
Schwarz	15	14	14	15	15	15	15	14	13	13	14	14	14	14	14	14	14	13	13	13
Märtin	3	3	7	7	7	7	7	5	5	5	5	5	5	5	4	4	4	4	4	R
Grönholm	9	1	1	1	1	1	1	31	R

FINISH LINES

Richard Burns completed his 2003 stint ploughing gravel from running first with a flawless drive to third place in the top Peugeot, hampered a little by a faulty front differential towards the end of the second leg, but never quite able to match the leading duo... Colin McRae spent the longest leg of the rally manhandling a Xsara without front brakes. A gritty recovery earned him fourth, despite two minor excursions in Sotico... Carlos Sainz made it three Citroëns in the top five, dissatisfied with the handling for much of the rally... Martin Rowe put in one of the finest drives of his career to take Group N victory and the Production World Championship lead in his David Sutton Impreza... Freddy Loix was in sparkling form for Hyundai, taking a deserved eighth... Markko Märtin was excluded from fourth place when caught using a rock as ballast; it turned out that his Focus was comfortably above the minimum weight limit. François Duval drove with unusual hesitancy to finish tenth in the second 2003 car, but Mikko Hirvonen gave Ford some encouragement by taking ninth at the first attempt in his 2002 machine... Toni Gardemeister drove circumspectly, handicapped by a broken wrist which prevented him from steering properly, but got the better of his Skoda team-mate, Didier Auriol, when the Frenchman ran into hydraulic problems in the last leg... Toshihiro Arai never looked like exercising his usual Group N dominance, as the works Impreza's engine was down on power at first, then blew its gearbox in the second leg... Ed Ordynski had looked on course for his ninth Group N victory in Perth until he rolled his Lancer Evo VII on the spectator stage at Gloucester Park... Dean Herridge took a fine second in Group N, leading Rowe until he hit rocks and bent his Impreza's steering in the final leg... Niall McShea lost time when a stone split the rear differential and later from changing a puncture in Sotico, but still took fourth in Group N in his Allport-tuned Lancer Evo VI... Marcos Ligato was one of the Group N pacesetters before his Lancer broke a driveshaft and later retired with broken transmission...

An outsider for most of the season, Martin Rowe put in another finely judged drive in Australia to make himself the overwhelming favourite for the Group N world title

Had he been two minutes longer in service, Gilles Panizzi was convinced that he could have won. If only he had made his tyre choice earlier, there would have been time to cut a few more grooves in the tread and then he would have devoured Sébastien Loeb along with Carlos Sainz, Marcus Grönholm and Markko Märtin. It was a bold claim, but the Peugeot driver was in exuberant form after rocketing from fifth to second in two stages. He alone had dared to take intermediates when all his rivals had chosen dry-weather tyres and it had paid off handsomely when the clouds burst over Monte Ceppo.

Panizzi had made his choice having rung a friend in the mountains, ascertaining that the sky was the colour of slate and that the wind was a weakening easterly. No one other than Peugeot's Sports Director, Jean-Pierre Nicolas, had supported his decision whole-heartedly. Even his brother, Hervé, had had misgivings.

At the post-event press conference, a casual observer might have assumed that the beaming Panizzi had won, not Loeb, but the truth was that the older man's demeanour was an indication of relief as much pride and delight: while adroit tactics had restored Peugeot's self-esteem, the all-conquering 206 had looked thoroughly ordinary for most of the rally and if

it hadn't been for the rain, Panizzi wouldn't have troubled Sainz, far less Loeb and Märtin.

Panizzi's spectacular gamble nearly cost Loeb his victory, but it couldn't disguise the fact that his brilliance had made it a somewhat processional rally until the rain arrived. It's taken as read that the Xsara is a superb Tarmac car, but without Loeb, Citroën would have been sunk. Sainz put in a brave but below-par drive – as well he might, less than a week after an operation to remove kidney stones – while Colin McRae began steadily and continued in the same vein. He had nothing but admiration for Loeb's searing pace in the fog on the first two stages, and once the Alsace man had established a 20-second lead, he defended it with a peerless blend of speed and judgement.

Yet the contest was far from one-sided and the Citroën was the car to have solely because it was reliable. Loeb gained a morale-boosting advantage at once thanks to the Focus's aerodynamics, which drew every leaf on the road into Märtin's radiator, sending coolant temperatures soaring and power plummeting. Loeb stemmed the Estonian's counter-attack with a blistering attack on Friday's final loop across Monte Ceppo, but he made his escape for good before even attempting a stage the following morning. The 'Hoover,' as the mechanics nicknamed the Ford, had

functioned perfectly once holes had been drilled to allow the leaves to escape from the radiator duct, but it started misfiring shortly before it was due to leave Saturday's first service. It turned out that the main ECU was at fault and changing it involved removing the driver's seat. By the time he was mobile, Märtin had incurred 30 seconds in road penalties and Loeb was more or less out of reach.

The leader wasn't especially perturbed when it began to rain. He was comfortably ahead of Märtin, who was also on medium-compound Michelins, and Panizzi gained only 30 seconds on the penultimate stage, which was partially dry. Loeb's elation at extending his lead over the Ford driver on the final test momentarily gave way to astonishment when he saw Panizzi's time, for he had never imagined that he was in danger of losing. Citroën had kept him fully informed of Märtin's split times by radio, but reasoning that Panizzi was no threat in championship terms, had decided not to risk unsettling him by letting him know that his lead was tumbling.

Loeb is a level-headed man. Sanremo confirmed his view that a rally is never won until the car is over the finish ramp and that the real danger came not from Panizzi, but Märtin – and even he was no great threat in championship terms.

SANREMO RALLY

RALLYCOURSE World Rally Championship **Round 11**

Sébastien Loeb's victory was as meticulously planned as a military campaign, although he was nearly outmanoeuvred by a newly inspired Gilles Panizzi (top) on the final stage. Sanremo's compact route doesn't make life easy for spectators; it takes dedication to be this cheerful.

SANREMO RALLY

The Focus (top left) rarely looks as though it is being driven hard, but there was no denying its speed and Markko Märtin could have won had it been reliable. Carlos Sainz and the Xsara might have been made for each other, their combined reliability netting a solid fourth place (above). Mirco Baldacci was in a class of his own in the Junior contest, scoring a rare win for Fiat (far left), whereas it was all muck and bullets for Subaru.

SANREMO RALLY

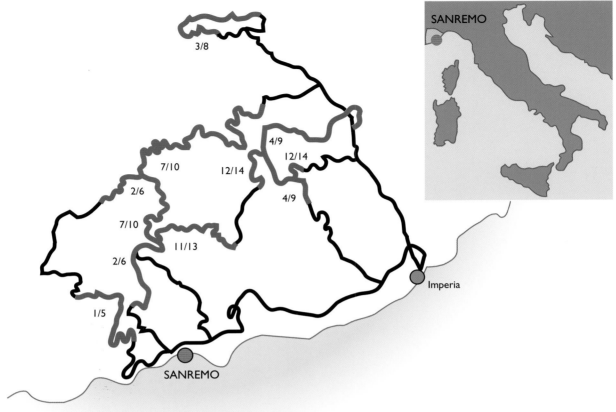

Sanremo Rally, 3-5 October 2003,
FIA World Rally Championship Round 11

RUNNING ORDER

2	Richard Burns/	Peugeot 206 WRC
	Robert Reid	Gr A
7	Petter Solberg/	Subaru Impreza WRC2003
	Phil Mills	Gr A
19	Carlos Sainz/	Citroën Xsara WRC
	Marc Martí	Gr A
18	Sébastien Loeb/	Citroën Xsara WRC
	Daniel Elena	Gr A
1	Marcus Grönholm/	Peugeot 206 WRC
	Timo Rautiainen	Gr A
4	Markko Märtin/	Ford Focus RS WRC03
	Michael Park	Gr A
17	Colin McRae/	Citroën Xsara WRC
	Derek Ringer	Gr A
8	Tommi Mäkinen/	Subaru Impreza WRC2003
	Kaj Lindström	Gr A
5	François Duval/	Ford Focus RS WRC03
	Stéphane Prevot	Gr A
15	Toni Gardemeister/	Skoda Fabia WRC
	Paavo Lukander	Gr A
3	Gilles Panizzi/	Peugeot 206 WRC
	Hervé Panizzi	Gr A
14	Didier Auriol/	SkodaFabia WRC
	Denis Giraudet	Gr A
6	Mikko Hirvonen/	Ford Focus WRC02
	Jarmo Lehtinen	Gr A
23	Cédric Robert/	Peugeot 206 WRC
	Gerald Bedon	Gr A
22	Roman Kresta/	Peugeot 206 WRC
	Jan Tomanek	Gr A
20	Philippe Bugalski/	Citroën Xsara WRC
	Jean-Paul Chiaroni	Gr A

SPECIAL STAGE TIMES

SS1 PERINALDO 1 (12.40 KM)
1 S.Loeb/D.Elena (Citroën Xsara WRC) 7m56.2s; 2 F.Duval/
S.Prevot (Ford Focus RS WRC03) 7m56.7s; 3 M.Grönholm/
T.Rautiainen (Peugeot 206 WRC) 7m57.5s; 4 G.Panizzi/
H.Panizzi (Peugeot 206 WRC) 7m57.6s; 5 C.Sainz/M.Martí
(Citroën Xsara WRC) 7m58.7s; 6 P.Solberg/P.Mills
(Subaru Impreza WRC2003) 8m01.8s; JWC B.Tirabassi/
J.Renucci (Renault Clio) 8m42.1s

SS2 CEPPO 1 (36.42 KM)
1 Loeb/Elena (Citroën) 24m05.5s; 2 Grönholm/Rautiainen
(Peugeot) 24m20.2s; 3 Duval/Prevot (Ford) 24m25.6s;
4 M.Märtin/M.Park (Ford Focus RS WRC03) 24m26.0s;
5 Sainz/Martí (Citroën) 24m30.1s; 6 C.McRae/D.Ringer
(Citroën Xsara WRC) 24m34.5s; JWC M.Baldacci/
G.Bernacchini (Fiat Punto) 26m34.0s

SS3 COSIO 1 (19.19 KM)
1 Märtin/Park (Ford) 11m56.3s; 2 Loeb/Elena (Citroën)
12m01.3s; 3= Duval/Prevot (Ford), Panizzi/Panizzi
(Peugeot) 12m02.0s; 5 Grönholm/Rautiainen (Peugeot)
12m05.1s; 6 McRae/Ringer (Citroën) 12m07.9s;
JWC Tirabassi/Renucci (Renault) 13m19.9s

SS4 SAN BARTOLOMEO 1 (25.31 KM)
1 Märtin/Park (Ford) 14m47.2s; 2 Loeb/Elena (Citroën)
14m48.4s; 3 Panizzi/Panizzi (Peugeot) 14m56.1s;
4 Grönholm/Rautiainen (Peugeot) 14m57.3s; 5
Duval/Prevot (Ford) 15m01.9s; 6 McRae/Ringer (Citroën)
15m03.0s; JWC Baldacci/Bernacchini (Fiat) 16m20.1s

SS5 PERINALDO 2 (12.40 KM)
1 Loeb/Elena (Citroën) 7m45.6s; 2 Märtin/Park (Ford)
7m46.1s; 3 Grönholm/Rautiainen (Peugeot) 7m50.2s;
4 Panizzi/Panizzi (Peugeot) 7m50.8s; 5 Sainz/Martí
(Citroën) 7m51.2s; 6 Duval/Prevot (Ford) 7m52.9s;
JWC Baldacci/Bernacchini (Fiat) 8m37.2s

SS6 CEPPO 2 (36.42 KM)
1 Loeb/Elena (Citroën) 23m38.7s; 2 Märtin/Park (Ford)
23m49.1s; 3 Grönholm/Rautiainen (Peugeot) 23m55.0s;
4 Sainz/Martí (Citroën) 23m55.6s; 5 McRae/Ringer
(Citroën) 24m14.3s; 6 Duval/Prevot (Ford) 24m15.6s;
JWC Baldacci/Bernacchini (Fiat) 26m49.6s

SS7 TEGLIA 1 (52.30 KM)
1 Märtin/Park (Ford) 35m01.7s; 2 Loeb/Elena (Citroën)
35m02.4s; 3 Grönholm/Rautiainen (Peugeot) 35m19.0s;
4 Panizzi/Panizzi (Peugeot) 35m24.1s; 5 Sainz/Martí
(Citroën) 35m25.1s; 6 Duval/Prevot (Ford) 35m31.5s;
JWC M.Ceccato/M.Dotta (Fiat Punto) 39m06.4s

SS8 COSIO 2 (19.19 KM)
1 Märtin/Park (Ford) 11m51.3s; 2 Panizzi/Panizzi (Peugeot)
11m57.3s; 3 Grönholm/Rautiainen (Peugeot) 11m57.6s;
4 Duval/Prevot (Ford) 11m57.8s; 5 Sainz/Martí (Citroën)
11m59.2s; 6 P.Bugalski/J-P.Chiaroni (Citroën Xsara WRC)
12m00.4s; JWC S.Canellas/X.Amigo (Suzuki Ignis) 13m15.8s

SS9 SAN BARTOLOMEO 2 (25.31 KM)
1 Märtin/Park (Ford) 14m44.2s; 2 Loeb/Elena (Citroën)
14m46.2s; 3 Grönholm/Rautiainen (Peugeot) 14m48.3s;
4 Panizzi/Panizzi (Peugeot) 14m48.8s; 5 Sainz/Martí
(Citroën) 14m50.1s; 6 Duval/Prevot (Ford) 14m52.7s;
JWC Baldacci/Bernacchini (Fiat) 16m22.0s

SS10 TEGLIA 2 (52.30 KM)
1 Märtin/Park (Ford) 34m48.6s; 2 Loeb/Elena (Citroën)
34m55.5s; 3 Sainz/Martí (Citroën) 34m58.1s; 4 Grönholm/
Rautiainen (Peugeot) 35m01.0s; 5 Panizzi/Panizzi (Peugeot)
35m04.3s; 6 Bugalski/Chiaroni (Citroën) 35m21.1s;
JWC Baldacci/Bernacchini (Fiat) 38m54.6s

SS11 VIGNAI 1 (26.54 KM)
1 Loeb/Elena (Citroën) 18m00.7s; 2 Märtin/Park (Ford)
18m04.2s; 3 Duval/Prevot (Ford) 18m07.5s; 4 Sainz/Martí
(Citroën) 18m07.6s; 5 Grönholm/Rautiainen (Peugeot)
18m08.2s; 6 Panizzi/Panizzi (Peugeot) 18m12.4s;
JWC No times

SS12 COLLE D'OGGIA 1 (21.52 KM)
1 Märtin/Park (Ford) 14m03.8s; 2 Grönholm/Rautiainen
(Peugeot) 14m03.8s; 3 Sainz/Martí (Citroën) 14m04.4s;
4 Loeb/Elena (Citroën) 14m05.1s; 5 Duval/Prevot (Ford)
14m05.6s; 6 Panizzi/Panizzi (Peugeot) 14m07.6s;
JWC No times

SS13 VIGNAI 2 (26.54 KM)
1 Panizzi/Panizzi (Peugeot) 19m42.6s; 2 Grönholm/
Rautiainen (Peugeot) 20m02.6s; 3 Loeb/Elena (Citroën)
20m10.9s; 4 Märtin/Park (Ford) 20m13.0s; 5 N.Bernardi/
B.Brissart (Renault Clio Super) 20m33.1s; 6 Sainz/Martí
(Citroën) 20m44.4s; JWC Canellas/Amigo (Suzuki)
21m45.6s

SS14 SS12 COLLE D'OGGIA 2 (21.52 KM)
1 Panizzi/Panizzi (Peugeot) 15m59.6s; 2 P.Tarantino/
F.Colombo (Renault Clio Williams) 16m16.9s; 3 Bernardi/
Brissart (Renault) 16m50.8s; 4 M.Higgins/M.Gibson (Gr N
Subaru Impreza WRX) 16m51.9s; 5 P.Liatti/V.Geminatti
(Peugeot 206 Super) 16m54.1s; 6 G.Corona/F.Florean (Gr
N Renault Clio RS) 17m02.5s; JWC A.Feghali/J.Matar
(Ford Puma) 17m21.3s

MAJOR RETIREMENTS

1	Grönholm/R'iainen	Peugeot 206 WRC		
	Accident	SS14		Gr A
7	Solberg/Mills	Subaru Impreza WRC2003		
	Fuel System	SS6		Gr A
15	Gardemeister/L'der	Skoda Fabia WRC		
	Accident	SS2		Gr A
6	Hirvonen/Lehtinen	Ford Focus RS WRC02		
	Engine	SS3		Gr A

FIA CLASS WINNERS

A8 Over 2000cc	Loeb/Elena
	Citroën Xsara WRC
A7 1600-2000cc	Tarantino/Colombo
	Renault Clio Williams
A6 1400-1600cc	Bernardi/Brissart
	Renault Clio
N4 Over 2000cc	Higgins/Gibson
	Subaru Impreza WRX
N3 1600-2000cc	Corona/Florean
	Renault Clio RS
N1 Upto 1400cc	Gai/Gai
	MG ZR 105

RALLY LEADERS

Overall: SS1-14 Loeb

JWC: SS1 Tirabassi; SS2-14 Baldacci

SPECIAL STAGE ANALYSIS

	1st	2nd	3rd	4th	5th	6th
Märtin (Ford)	7	3	-	2	-	-
Loeb (Citroën)	5	5	1	1	-	-
Panizzi (Peugeot)	2	1	2	4	1	2
Grönholm (Peugeot)	-	3	6	2	2	-
Duval (Ford)	-	1	3	1	2	4
Tarantino (Renault)	-	1	-	-	-	-
Sainz (Citroën)	-	-	2	2	6	1
Bernardi (Renault)	-	-	2	-	-	-
Higgins (Subaru)	-	-	-	1	-	-
McRae (Citroën)	-	-	-	-	1	3
Liatti (Peugeot)	-	-	-	-	1	-
Bugalski (Citroën)	-	-	-	-	-	2
Solberg (Subaru)	-	-	-	-	-	1
Corona (Renault)	-	-	-	-	-	1

WORLD CHAMPIONSHIP POINTS

DRIVERS
1 Burns 57; 2 Loeb 55; 3 Sainz 53; 4 Solberg 48; 5 Märtin
43; 6 Grönholm 38; 7 McRae 36; 8 Mäkinen 21; 9
Rovanperä 18; 10 Duval 15 etc

MANUFACTURERS
1 Citroën 125; 2 Peugeot 121; 3 Subaru 76; 4 Ford 71; 5
Skoda 21; 6 Hyundai 12

JUNIOR WORLD CHAMPIONSHIP
1 Tirabassi 28; 2 Canellas 25; 3= Carlsson, Wilks 18; 5
Aava 16; 6 Baldacci 12 etc

PRODUCTION CUP
1 Rowe 37; 2= Arai, Singh 30; 4 Blomqvist 26; 5 Solá 22; 6
Ligato 13 etc

STAGE NUMBERS	1	2	3	4	5	6	7	8	9	10	11	12	13	14
Loeb	1	1	1	1	1	1	1	1	1	1	1	1	1	1
Panizzi	4	6	5	5	5	6	6	6	5	5	5	5	4	2
Märtin	8	5	4	2	2	2	2	2	2	2	2	2	2	3
Sainz	5	4	6	6	6	4	4	4	4	4	4	4	5	4
Duval	2	3	3	4	4	5	5	5	6	6	6	6	6	5
McRae	7	7	7	7	7	7	7	7	7	7	7	7	7	6
Burns	10	12	12	10	10	11	11	11	10	9	9	9	9	10
Bugalski	11	11	9	9	9	10	8	8	8	8	8	8	8	8
Robert	15	10	11	12	12	12	10	11	11	10	10	10	9	9
Mäkinen	9	9	10	11	10	9	9	9	10	11	11	11	11	10
Kresta	12	15	13	13	13	13	12	12	12	12	12	12	12	11
Auriol	14	14	14	14	14	14	13	13	13	13	13	13	13	12
Grönholm	3	2	2	3	3	3	3	3	3	3	3	3	3	R
Solberg	6	8	8	8	8	8	8	R						
Hirvonen	13	13	15	R										
Gardemeister	16	R												

ROUTE DETAILS

Total route of 1375.86 km of which 387.36 km were competitive on 14 stages

LEG 1 Friday 3rd October, 6 special stages totalling 142.14 km
LEG 2 Saturday 4th October, 4 special stages totalling 149.10 km
LEG 3 Sunday 5th October, 4 special stages totalling 96.12 km

RESULTS

1 Sébastain Loeb/ — Citroën Xsara WRC
   Daniel Elena — 4h16m33.7s — Gr A
2 Gilles Panizzi/ — Peugeot 206 WRC
   Hervé Panizzi — 4h17m02.0s — Gr A
3 Markko Märtin/ — Ford Focus RS WRC03
   Michael Park — 4h17m28.3s — Gr A
4 Carlos Sainz/ — Citroën Xsara WRC
   Marc Martí — 4h19m06.9s — Gr A
5 François Duval/ — Ford Focus RS WRC03
   Stéphane Prevot — 4h20m32.6s — Gr A
6 Colin McRae/ — Citroën Xsara WRC
   Derek Ringer — 4h20m57.5s — Gr A
7 Richard Burns/ — Peugeot 206 WRC
   Robert Reid — 4h23m43.2s — Gr A
8 Philippe Bugalski/ — Citroën Xsara WRC
   Jean-Paul Chiaroni — 4h23m46.3s — Gr A
9 Cédric Robert/ — Peugeot 206 WRC
   Gerald Bedon — 4h23m59.4s — Gr A
10 Tommi Mäkinen/ — Subaru Impreza WRC2003
   Kaj Lindström — 4h24m05.9s — Gr A

54 starters, 36 finishers

RECENT WINNERS

Year		Car
1970	Jean-Luc Thérier/Marcel Callewaert	Alpine Renault A110
1971	Ove Andersson/Arne Hertz	Alpine Renault A110
1972	Amilcare Ballestrieri/Arnaldo Bernacchini	Lancia Fulvia
1973	Jean-Luc Thérier/Jacques Jaubert	Alpine Renault A110
1975	Björn Waldegård/Hans Thorszelius	Lancia Stratos
1976	Björn Waldegård/Hans Thorszelius	Lancia Stratos
1977	Jean Claude Andruet/Christian Delferrier	Fiat 131 Abarth
1978	Markku Alén/Ilkka Kivimäki	Lancia Stratos
1979	Tony Fassina/Mauro Mannini	Lancia Stratos
1980	Walter Röhrl/Christian Geistdörfer	Fiat 131 Abarth
1981	Michèle Mouton/Fabrizia Pons	Audi Quattro
1982	Stig Blomqvist/Björn Cederberg	Audi Quattro A2
1983	Markku Alen/Ilkka Kivimaki	Lancia Rallye 037
1984	Ari Vatanen/Terry Harryman	Peugeot 205 Turbo 16
1985	Walter Röhrl/Christian Geistdörfer	Audi Sport Quattro S1
1986	Annulled	
1987	Miki Biasion/Tiziano Siviero	Lancia Delta HF 4x4
1988	Miki Biasion/Tiziano Siviero	Lancia Delta Integrale
1989	Miki Biasion/Tiziano Siviero	Lancia Delta Integrale 16v
1990	Didier Auriol/Bernard Occelli	Lancia Delta Integrale 16v
1991	Didier Auriol/Bernard Occelli	Lancia Delta Integrale 16v
1992	Andrea Aghini/Sauro Farnocchia	Lancia Delta HF Integrale
1993	Franco Cunico/Steve Evangelisti	Ford Escort RS Cosworth
1994	Didier Auriol/Bernard Occelli	Toyota Celica Turbo 4wd
1995	Piero Liatti/Alex Alessandrini	Subaru Impreza 555
1996	Colin McRae/Derek Ringer	Subaru Impreza 555
1997	Colin McRae/Nicky Grist	Subaru Impreza WRC97
1998	Tommi Mäkinen/Risto Mannisenmäki	Mitsubishi Lancer E5
1999	Tommi Mäkinen/Risto Mannisenmäki	Mitsubishi Lancer E6
2000	Gilles Panizzi/Hervé Panizzi	Peugeot 206 WRC
2001	Gilles Panizzi/Hervé Panizzi	Peugeot 206 WRC
2002	Gilles Panizzi/Hervé Panizzi	Peugeot 206 WRC

FINISH LINES

Richard Burns's rally was a three-day nightmare, in which he couldn't come to grips with his 206's handling at all and he moved into the points only on the final stage... Last-minute gearbox problems in his Bozian 206 cost Cédric Robert his chance of beating Burns, while Philippe Bugalski was all at sea in his Xsara, having picked the hardest dry-weather Michelins for the deluge... Subaru endured a bitterly disappointing rally: Tommi Mäkinen finished an ignominious 11th, beset by tyre problems, while Petter Solberg ran out of petrol two miles from service at the end of the first leg. The real concern was that he was no higher than eighth, despite using the much-vaunted active dampers for the first time... Toni Gardemeister became the first major retirement, crashing his Fabia in fog on SS2... Didier Auriol limped home with major hydraulic problems, but the Fabia had been consistently off the pace... The works Hyundais failed to appear, as Hyundai and Motor Sport Developments failed to resolve their financial dispute... Mirco Baldacci romped to a clear Junior class win, Fiat's second Super 1600 success at World Championship level... Salvador Canellas fought back to take second in his Suzuki, despite stopping on one stage to change a puncture... The 1600 class win, ignoring championship considerations, was taken very comfortably by Nicolas Bernardi in a Clio funded by the French motorsport federation; it was his first rally in almost a year... For once, Simon Jean-Joseph wasn't the 1600 pacesetter, brake problems hampering the Martinique Clio driver's progress... Brice Tirabassi slithered into a wall in his Renault on the second stage and subsequently retired with electrical trouble, but retained the Junior Championship lead when Daniel Carlsson crashed his Ignis while driving on a puncture... Kris Meeke had been on course for a highly impressive second until he crashed his Corsa in the final leg... Kosti Katajamäki retired his Polo with transmission failure...

The undisputed kings of Sanremo, the Peugeot men got a rude awakening in Italy, for the 206 was horribly off the pace until the rain came.

TOUR OF CORSICA

Asked if there was any chance of beating a car on Pirellis in such conditions, Carlos Sainz didn't hesitate before answering, 'No'.

He had probably reached the conclusion the moment he had looked out of the bedroom window that morning. The eastern side of Corsica was overcast and gloomy, the roads were damp and Pirellis, the tyres that no right-thinking rally driver would touch on dry asphalt, were worth their weight in kevlar. Barring the unforeseen, Petter Solberg was poised to claim an extraordinary victory on the Tour of Corsica for Subaru.

Sainz must have been reminded of his vain pursuit of Colin McRae in 1997, when Pirelli rubber had helped the Scot trump the Spaniard's Michelin-shod Escort. It is hard to tell whether even Pirelli knows precisely what mixture of physics and chemistry makes its tyres so effective in the damp, but despite constant development and considerable expenditure, it remains an iron law of rally tyre design.

Sainz had to be content with second place and a splendid consolation prize in the form of the World Championship lead. It was a superb, rightly applauded effort in which he beat François Duval in the sprint for the line after a brave gamble on hand-cut, dry-weather tyres. Yet it was naturally overshadowed by Solberg's wildly improbable triumph.

Subaru had gone to Corsica very much on the back foot. Prodrive had decided to shelve its 'active' dampers after a thoroughly demoralising foray to Sanremo, concluding that it was better to accept that miracles were unlikely on Tarmac, concentrating on reliability and hoping to snatch enough points to give Solberg an outside chance of staying in contention for the World Championship; rain might even restore a little pride. The driver promised that the car had improved, but made no bones about the fact that he would be thrashed nevertheless if it was dry.

Then, as if to snuff out his championship prospects once and for all, Solberg crashed violently 18 hours before the start, cutting a telegraph pole in two. The impact disconnected the neighbouring village, brought the shakedown to a premature conclusion and all but wrecked the Impreza. Indeed, the team attempted to repair the car only because all the alternatives, including flying a replacement in from Banbury, were illegal. One of the front chassis legs was an inch out of line, the other two inches. Mere inches didn't do justice to the damage at the rear, the rear crossmember and C-post badly crushed by the impact. The bodyshell straightened surprisingly readily in the course of a long, laborious night, but Solberg's state of mind was another matter. On Friday, there wasn't a hint

of his usual ebullience. The Norwegian didn't mind admitting that he was scared, sobered by the thought that bad as the crash was, the alternative had been tumbling down a 600-foot drop.

Of course, Subaru had been lucky: lucky that the Impreza could be repaired at all; lucky that the only dry day of the rally was the shortest, with fewer than 60 miles of stages; lucky that Solberg's most dangerous rivals, Sébastien Loeb and Markko Märtin, both contrived to leave the road within a few minutes of each other on the first, soaking ascent of the Col Saint Georges on Saturday morning.

But the team had made the most of its luck. Solberg confronted and conquered his misgivings with astonishing speed, bounding from eighth to first in six stages. In contrast to many of his rivals, he never made a poor tyre choice and his sole conspicuous error once the rally began was a spin on the Col Saint Georges. By Sunday morning, an unlikely victory looked all but inevitable. He had more than made amends.

At the shakedown, some fans had persuaded Loeb to sign a banner reading, 'Sébastien sur une nuage Corse' – 'Sébastien on a Corsican cloud'. In the event, Citroën and its short-odds favourite had been given a brutal reminder that success can never be taken for granted, whereas Solberg had found the silver lining.

Petter Solberg's victory was one of the least expected in Corsica's long history and owed a great deal to Prodrive's mechanics (far left). The Norwegian (below left, in conversation with David Richards) recovered his usual ebullience with remarkable speed. François Duval put in one of his most convincing performances to take third in his Focus (near left), while Martin Rowe calmly made sure of the Production World title in his Impreza.

TOUR OF CORSICA

STATISTICS World Rally Championship **Round 12**

Tour de Corse, 17-19 October 2003,
FIA World Rally Championship Round 12

RUNNING ORDER

2	Richard Burns/	Peugeot 206 WRC
	Robert Reid	Gr A
18	Sébastien Loeb/	Citroën Xsara WRC
	Daniel Elena	Gr A
19	Carlos Sainz/	Citroën Xsara WRC
	Marc Martí	Gr A
7	Petter Solberg/	Subaru Impreza WRC2003
	Phil Mills	Gr A
4	Markko Märtin/	Ford Focus RS WRC03
	Michael Park	Gr A
1	Marcus Grönholm/	Peugeot 206 WRC
	Timo Rautiainen	Gr A
17	Colin McRae/	Citroën Xsara WRC
	Derek Ringer	Gr A
8	Tommi Mäkinen/	Subaru Impreza WRC2003
	Kaj Lindström	Gr A

5	François Duval/	Ford Focus RS WRC03
	Stéphane Prevot	Gr A
3	Gilles Panizzi/	Peugeot 206 WRC
	Hervé Panizzi	Gr A
15	Toni Gardemeister/	Skoda Fabia WRC
	Paavo Lukander	Gr A
14	Didier Auriol/	SkodaFabia WRC
	Denis Giraudet	Gr A
6	Mikko Hirvonen/	Ford Focus RS WRC02
	Jarmo Lehtinen	Gr A
24	Cédric Robert/	Peugeot 206 WRC
	Gerald Bedon	Gr A
20	Philippe Bugalski/	Citroën Xsara WRC
	Jean-Paul Chiaroni	Gr A
22	Antony Warmbold/	Ford Focus RS WRC02
	Gemma Price	Gr A
21	Alexandre Bengue/	Peugeot 206 WRC
	Caroline Escudero	Gr A
32	Manfred Stohl/	Peugeot 206 WRC
	Ilka Minor	Gr A

SPECIAL STAGE TIMES

SS1 CARGESE 1 (14.64 KM)
1 C.Sainz/M.Martí (Citroën Xsara WRC) 9m49.6s;
2 R.Burns/R.Reid (Peugeot 206 WRC) 9m50.5s; 3 M.Märtin/
M.Park (Ford Focus RS WRC03) 9m51.2s; 4 C.McRae/
D.Ringer (Citroën Xsara WRC) 9m51.5s; 5 M.Grönholm/
T.Rautiainen (Peugeot 206 WRC) 9m51.8s; 6 F.Duval/
S.Prevot (Ford Focus RS WRC03) 9m52.0s; PC D.Solá/
A.Romani (Mitsubishi Lancer E8) 10m35.8s

SS2 VICO 1 (15.49 KM)
1 S.Loeb/D.Elena (Citroën Xsara WRC) 10m04.6s;
2 Märtin/Park (Ford) 10m05.4s; 3 Grönholm/Rautiainen
(Peugeot) 10m06.2s; 4 Sainz/Martí (Citroën) 10m07.1s;
5 Duval/Prevot (Ford) 10m07.7s; 6 P.Solberg/P.Mills
(Subaru Impreza WRC2003) 10m08.0s; PC Solá/Romani
(Mitsubishi) 10m58.3s

SS3 GOLFE DE LA LISCIA 1 (17.52 KM)
1 Märtin/Park (Ford) 10m43.6s; 2 Loeb/Elena (Citroën)
10m46.7s; 3 Sainz/Martí (Citroën) 10m48.6s; 4 Burns/ Reid
(Peugeot) 10m49.0s; 5 Grönholm/Rautiainen (Peugeot)
10m49.2s; 6 Solberg/Mills (Subaru) 10m52.0s; PC
Solá/Romani (Mitsubishi) 11m53.8s

SS4 CARGESE 2 (14.64 KM)
1 Duval/Prevot (Ford) 9m45.3s; 2 Grönholm/Rautiainen
(Peugeot) 9m48.9s; 3 Loeb/Elena (Citroën) 9m49.6s;
4 McRae/Ringer (Citroën) 9m51.1s; 5 Sainz/Martí
(Citroën) 9m52.2s; 6 G.Panizzi/H.Panizzi (Peugeot)
9m53.0s; PC Solá/Romani (Mitsubishi) 10m34.6s

SS5 VICO 2 (15.49 KM)
1 Märtin/Park (Ford) 10m03.6s; 2 Loeb/Elena (Citroën)
10m06.2s; 3 Duval/Prevot (Ford) 10m06.6s; 4 A.Bengue/
C.Escudero (Peugeot 206 WRC) 10m07.4s; 5 Grönholm/
Rautiainen (Peugeot) 10m08.3s; 6 Burns/Reid (Peugeot)
10m10.0s; PC Solá/Romani (Mitsubishi) 10m54.0s

SS6 GOLFE DE LA LISCIA 2 (17.52 KM)
1 Märtin/Park (Ford) 10m43.2s; 2 Duval/Prevot (Ford)
10m43.7s; 3= Loeb/Elena (Citroën), Sainz/Martí (Citroën)
10m45.3s; 5 Grönholm/Rautiainen (Peugeot) 10m45.6s;
6 Burns/Reid (Peugeot) 10m49.6s; PC Solá/Romani
(Mitsubishi) 11m51.1s

SS7 AMPAZA 1 (38.64 KM)
1 Märtin/Park (Ford) 25m32.2s; 2 Solberg/Mills (Subaru)
25m36.6s; 3 Loeb/Elena (Citroën) 25m41.1s; 4 Sainz/Martí
(Citroën) 25m42.2s; 5 Panizzi/Panizzi (Peugeot) 25m45.3s;
6 Duval/Prevot (Ford) 25m47.6s; PC Solá/Romani
(Mitsubishi) 28m02.5s

SS8 PONT DE LA MASINA 1 (15.42) KM
1 M.Hirvonen/J.Lehtinen (Ford Focus RS WRC02)
10m31.5s; 2 P.Bugalski/J-P.Chiaroni (Citroën Xsara WRC)
10m40.0s; 3 T.Gardemeister/P.Lukander (Skoda Fabia
WRC) 10m40.7s; 4 Panizzi/Panizzi (Peugeot) 10m41.2s; 5
C.Robert/G.Bedon (Peugeot 206 WRC) 10m42.9s; 6
T.Mäkinen/K.Lindström (Subaru Impreza WRC2003)
10m46.9s; PC Solá/Romani (Mitsubishi) 11m52.1s

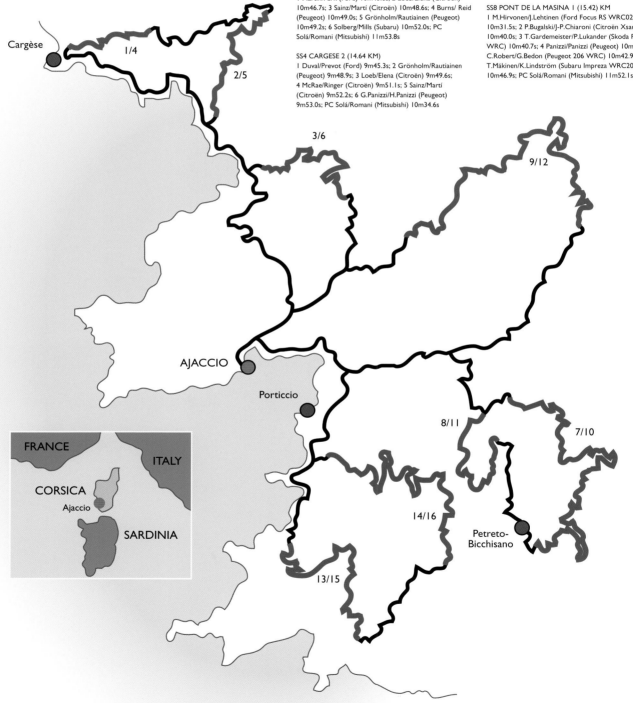

Cargèse

1/4

2/5

3/6

9/12

AJACCIO

Porticcio

8/11

7/10

FRANCE

ITALY

CORSICA

Ajaccio

SARDINIA

14/16

Petreto-
Bicchisano

13/15

SS9 COL DE CARAZZI 1 (40.93 KM)
1 Panizzi/Panizzi (Peugeot) 27m23.5s; 2 Loeb/Elena (Citroën) 27m25.3s; 3 Duval/Prevot (Ford) 27m30.9s; 4 Sainz/Marti (Citroën) 27m31.9s; 5 Grönholm/Rautiainen (Peugeot) 27m40.5s; 6 Solberg/Mills (Subaru) 27m42.0s; PC Solá/Romani (Mitsubishi) 30m01.1s

SS10 AMPAZA 2 (38.64 KM)
1 Solberg/Mills (Subaru) 25m20.7s; 2 Märtin/Park (Ford) 25m33.6s; 3 Sainz/Marti (Citroën) 25m34.1s; 4 Duval/Prevot (Ford) 25m40.6s; 5 Panizzi/Panizzi (Peugeot) 25m43.5s; 6 McRae/Ringer (Citroën) 25m45.5s; PC Solá/Romani (Mitsubishi) 27m44.8s

SS11 PONT DE LA MASINA 2 (15.42 KM)
1 Solberg/Mills (Subaru) 10m22.3s; 2 Märtin/Park (Ford) 10m25.5s; 3 Duval/Prevot (Ford) 10m25.6s; 4 Sainz/Marti (Citroën) 10m28.3s; 5 McRae/Ringer (Citroën) 10m30.8s; 6 Burns/Reid (Peugeot) 10m32.2s ; PC N.McShea/C.Patterson (Mitsubishi Lancer E6) 11m36.6s

SS12 COL DE CARAZZI 2 (40.93 KM)
1 Solberg/Mills (Subaru) 27m15.6s; 2 Mäkinen/Lindström (Subaru) 27m24.8s; 3 Märtin/Park (Ford) 27m33.2s; 4 Sainz/Marti (Citroën) 27m33.4s; 5 Loeb/Elena (Citroën) 27m33.6s; 6 McRae/Ringer (Citroën) 27m34.4s; PC Solá/Romani (Mitsubishi) 30m08.4s

SS13 PENITENCIER COTI CHIAVARI 1 (24.23 KM)
1 Loeb/Elena (Citroën) 15m19.0s; 2 Solberg/Mills (Subaru) 15m22.3s; 3 Duval/Prevot (Ford) 15m26.6s; 4 Grönholm/Rautiainen (Peugeot) 15m28.6s; 5 Mäkinen/Lindström (Subaru) 15m29.6s; 6 Sainz/Marti (Citroën) 15m29.7s; PC T.Arai/T.Sircombe (Subaru Impreza WRX) 17m04.6s

SS14 PONT DE CALZOLA 1 (31.80 KM)
1 Loeb/Elena (Citroën) 19m47.2s; 2 Solberg/Mills (Subaru) 19m51.9s; 3 Grönholm/Rautiainen (Peugeot) 19m53.5s; 4 Panizzi/Panizzi (Peugeot) 19m53.9s; 5 Burns/Reid (Peugeot) 19m58.3s; Sainz/Marti (Citroën) 19m58.7s; PC Arai/Sircombe (Subaru) 22m01.8s

SS15 PENITENCIER COTI CHIAVARI 2 (24.23 KM)
1 Loeb/Elena (Citroën) 15m25.4s; 2 Grönholm/Rautiainen (Peugeot) 15m26.0s; 3 McRae/Ringer (Citroën) 15m27.2s; 4 Solberg/Mills (Subaru) 15m32.1s; 5= Bugalski/Chiaroni (Citroën), Duval/Prevot (Ford) 15m34.1s; PC J.Kulig/M.Szcepaniak (Mitsubishi Lancer E6) 17m11.8s

SS16 PONT DE CALZOLA 1 (31.80 KM)
1 Loeb/Elena (Citroën) 19m56.4s; 2 Grönholm/Rautiainen (Peugeot) 19m59.2s; 3 Sainz/Marti (Citroën) 20m02.9s; 4 Bugalski/Chiaroni (Citroën) 20m04.3s; 5 Mäkinen/Lindström (Subaru) 20m07.3s; 6 Burns/Reid (Peugeot) 20m07.8s; PC Kulig/Szcepaniak (Mitsubishi) 22m13.6s

MAJOR RETIREMENTS

4	Märtin/Park	Ford Focus RS WRC02		
	Accident	SS15		Gr A
14	Auriol/Giraudet	Skoda Fabia WRC		
	Hydraulics	SS1		Gr A
21	Bengue/Escudero	Peugeot 206 WRC		
	Accident	SS7		Gr A
32	Stohl/Minor	Peugeot 206 WRC		
	Accident	SS11		Gr A

FIA CLASS WINNERS

A8 Over 2000 cc	Solberg/Mills	
	Subaru Impreza WRC2003	
A6 1600cc-2000cc	Habani/Baunel	
	Renault Clio Super	
N4 Over 2000 cc	Higgins/Gibson	
	Subaru Impreza WRX	
N3 1600-2000cc	Mercier/Lemay	
	Renault Clio RS	
N1 Upto 1400cc	Rocard/Berthat	
	Peugeot 106 Rallye	

RALLY LEADERS

Overall: SS1 Sainz; SS2-3 Märtin; SS4-7 Loeb; SS8-11 Duval; SS12-16 Solberg

PC: SS1-12 Sola; SS13-16 McShea

SPECIAL STAGE ANALYSIS

	1st	2nd	3rd	4th	5th	6th
Loeb (Citroën)	5	3	3	-	1	-
Märtin (Ford)	4	3	2	-	-	-
Solberg (Subaru)	3	3	-	1	-	3
Duval (Ford)	1	1	4	1	2	2
Sainz (Citroën)	1	-	3	6	1	2
Panizzi (Peugeot)	1	-	-	2	2	1
Hirvonen (Ford)	1	-	-	-	-	-
Grönholm (Peugeot)	-	3	2	1	5	-
Burns (Peugeot)	-	1	1	-	-	4
Bugalski (Citroën)	-	1	-	1	1	-
Mäkinen (Subaru)	-	1	-	-	2	1
McRae (Citroën)	-	-	1	2	1	2
Gardemeister (Skoda)	-	-	1	-	-	-
Bengue (Peugeot)	-	-	-	1	-	-
Robert (Peugeot)	-	-	-	-	-	1

Skoda raised the sparks, but on this occasion, it was Subaru that raised the storm.

WORLD CHAMPIONSHIP POINTS

DRIVERS
1 Sainz 61; 2= Burns, Solberg 58; 4 Loeb 55; 5= Märtin, Grönholm 43; 7 McRae 40; 8 Mäkinen 23; 9 Duval 21; 10 Rovanperä 18 etc

MANUFACTURERS
1 Citroën 137; 2 Peugeot 129; 3 Subaru 88; 4 Ford 78; 5 Skoda 21; 6 Hyundai 12

JUNIOR WORLD CHAMPIONSHIP
1 Tirabassi 28; 2 Canellas 25; 3= Carlsson, Wilks 18; 5 Aava 16; 6 Baldacci 12 etc

PRODUCTION CUP
1 Rowe 43; 2 Arai 38; 3= Singh, Blomqvist 30; 5 Solá 22; 6 McShea 18 etc

ROUTE DETAILS

Total route of 971.75 km of which 397.40 km were competitive on 16 stages

LEG 1 Friday 17th October, 6 Special Stages totalling 95.30 km

LEG 2 Saturday 18th October, 6 Special Stages totalling 190.00 km

LEG 3 Sunday 19th October, 4 Special Stages totalling 112.10 km

RESULTS

1	Petter Solberg/ Phil Mills	Subaru Impreza WRC2003 4h20m15.3s	Gr A
2	Carlos Sainz/ Marc Marti	Citroën Xsara WRC 4h20m51.9s	Gr A
3	François Duval/ Stéphane Prevot	Ford Focus RS WRC03 4h20m57.0s	Gr A
4	Marcus Grönholm/ Timo Rautiainen	Peugeot 206 WRC 4h21m24.5s	Gr A
5	Colin McRae/ Derek Ringer	Citroën Xsara WRC 4h21m41.3s	Gr A
6	Gilles Panizzi/ Hervé Panizzi	Peugeot 206 WRC 4h22m14.0s	Gr A
7	Tommi Mäkinen/ Kaj Lindström	Subaru Impreza WRC2003 4h22m41.1s	Gr A
8	Richard Burns/ Robert Reid	Peugeot 206 WRC 4h22m52.0s	Gr A
9	Philippe Bugalski/ Jean-Paul Chiaroni	Citroën Xsara WRC 4h23m02.1s	Gr A
10	Mikko Hirvonen/ Jarmo Lehtinen	Mitsubishi Lancer WRC 4h24m10.7s	Gr A

62 starters, 34 finishers

FINISH LINES

Peugeot endured another troubled rally: each of its drivers displayed a knack for choosing the wrong tyres, and even Marcus Grönholm couldn't improve on fourth place; Gilles Panizzi complained bitterly about the handling at first and came sixth, while Richard Burns conceded ground in the wet and briefly suffered a loss of power, finishing eighth... It was the worst French performance in Corsica in 20 years, Panizzi being the best of the bunch... The 1998 British Rally Champion, Martin Rowe, became the first Subaru driver to win the Production World Championship, guiding his David Sutton Impreza to a measured third in class, content to leave the spoils on the day to Niall McShea and the Jardine Lloyd Thompson Lancer Evo VI... Sticking rear brakes hampered Colin McRae at first, but the Citroën driver might have staved off Grönholm for fourth if it hadn't been for a poor tyre choice near the end... Tommi Mäkinen didn't like his Impreza's handling at all in the early stages, but managed to hold off Burns in the end, despite a spin on the last stage... Alexandre Bengue showed real promise in his customer-tune Yacco 206, holding ninth place until he crashed on SS7... Didier Auriol was the first retirement, the Frenchman's Fabia expiring at the start of the first stage, thanks to a water leak that disabled the ECU controlling the clutch and gearbox. It made it impossible to select a gear without wrecking the clutch... Dani Solá looked on course for Group N victory until in quick succession his Lancer Evo VIII's turbo pipe worked loose and the rear differential expired... Mark Higgins played a starring role on his first attempt at the rally, winning Group N, albeit outside the World Championship classification, in his RED Impreza...

RECENT WINNERS

1970	Bernard Darniche/Guy Demange	Alpine Renault A110
1972	Jean-Claude Andruet/'Biche'	Alpine Renault A110
1973	Jean-Pierre Nicolas/Michel Vial	Alpine Renault A110
1974	Jean-Claude Andruet/'Biche'	Lancia Stratos
1975	Bernard Darniche/Alain Mahé	Lancia Stratos
1976	Sandro Munari/Silvio Maiga	Lancia Stratos
1977	Bernard Darniche/Alain Mahé	Fiat Abarth 131
1978	Bernard Darniche/Alain Mahé	Fiat Abarth 131
1979	Bernard Darniche/Alain Mahé	Lancia Stratos
1980	Jean-Luc Thérier/Michel Vial	Porsche 911SC
1981	Bernard Darniche/Alain Mahé	Lancia Stratos
1982	Jean Ragnotti/Jean-Marc Andrié	Renault 5 Turbo
1983	Markku Alén/Ilkka Kivimäki	Lancia 037 Rally
1984	Markku Alén/Ilkka Kivimäki	Lancia 037 Rally
1985	Jean Ragnotti/Jean-Marc Andrié	Renault 5 Maxi Turbo
1986	Bruno Saby/Jean-François Fauchille	Peugeot 205 Turbo 16 E2
1987	Bernard Béguin/Jean-Jacques Lenne	BMW M3
1988	Didier Auriol/Bernard Occelli	Ford Sierra RS Cosworth
1989	Didier Auriol/Bernard Occelli	Lancia Delta Integrale
1990	Didier Auriol/Bernard Occelli	Lancia Delta Integrale 16v
1991	Carlos Sainz/Luis Moya	Toyota Celica GT4
1992	Didier Auriol/Bernard Occelli	Lancia Delta HF Integrale
1993	François Delecour/Daniel Grataloup	Ford Escort RS Cosworth
1994	Didier Auriol/Bernard Occelli	Toyota Celica Turbo 4wd
1995	Didier Auriol/Denis Giraudet	Toyota Celica GT-Four
1996	Philippe Bugalski/Jean-Paul Chiaroni	Renault Maxi Mégane
1997	Colin McRae/Nicky Grist	Subaru Impreza WRC97
1998	Colin McRae/Nicky Grist	Subaru Impreza WRC98
1999	Philippe Bugalski/Jean-Paul Chiaroni	Citroën Xsara Kit
2000	Gilles Panizzi/Hervé Panizzi	Peugeot 206 WRC
2001	Jesus Puras/Marc Marti	Citroën Xsara WRC
2002	Gilles Panizzi/Hervé Panizzi	Peugeot 206 WRC

STAGE NUMBERS	1	2	3	4	5	6	7	8	9	10	11	12	13	14	15	16
Solberg	8	7	7	8	8	6	3	3	3	2	1	1	1	1	1	1
Sainz	1	2	3	4	4	4	2	2	2	3	3	3	3	3	3	2
Duval	6	5	6	4	3	2	3	1	1	1	1	2	2	2	2	3
Grönholm	5	4	4	3	2	3	5	4	3	5	6	5	4	4	4	4
McRae	4	8	8	6	7	7	7	5	6	6	5	4	4	5	5	5
Panizzi	9	9	9	9	9	10	11	10	8	5	4	4	6	6	6	6
Mäkinen	11	11	11	12	12	12	11	9	9	9	9	7	7	7	7	7
Burns	2	6	5	5	5	6	8	6	8	8	7	8	8	8	8	8
Bugalski	12	13	12	10	11	10	9	7	7	7	8	9	9	9	9	9
Hirvonen	15	15	14	14	15	16	14	10	10	10	10	10	10	10	10	10
G'meister	13	12	13	13	13	13	13	11	11	11	11	11	11	11	11	11
Robert	14	14	16	16	16	15	12	12	13	13	13	13	13	13	12	12
Loeb	7	3	1	1	1	1	1	8	12	12	14	12	14	12	13	13
Märtin	3	1	1	7	6	5	2	14	14	13	12	12	12	12	12R	
Bengue	10	10	10	11	9	9	R									
Auriol	R															

133

CATALONIA RALLY

Gilles Panizzi couldn't believe his luck. As he drew up at the startline of the final stage, nothing had been further from his mind than victory, for Sébastien Loeb was surely out of reach. The Citroën driver had led the Catalonia Rally from the start and while he had lost ground on the two previous stages, he had time in hand – still 40 seconds, in fact – with 22 competitive miles to go. Unflappable as ever, the Alsace man was on his way to yet another win secured with minimum risk and maximum economy. An ill-advised tyre choice at the beginning of the rally had done for Panizzi, the ultra-soft, Monte Carlo-compound Michelins wearing all too quickly, despite the mountain chill. It was some consolation that the 206 was back on song after two distinctly chequered Tarmac forays, but holding off Markko Märtin's Focus for second was the limit of his ambitions – a tall enough order on its own, in fact.

Even when Peugeot radioed split times indicating that he was gaining quickly, Panizzi refused to believe that victory was within his grasp. The Citroën man was running four minutes behind and would no doubt speed up, just as he had when Marcus Grönholm launched a final counter-attack in Germany. But Loeb was in trouble and whereas Panizzi discounted the radio message, the leader recognised at the same moment that the rally was lost.

In similar circumstances, Panizzi would have been incandescent with rage and disappointment. Loeb's anguish was contained, but undisguised. He had been undone by a poor tyre choice and he was angry enough to suggest that he didn't know there was a better Michelin available. He had picked the standard wet, whereas Panizzi and Märtin had gambled on the softer Monte Carlo compound. Peugeot and Ford had concluded that they had no choice, for on the previous loop Petter Solberg had used Pirelli's intermediates to devastating effect, catching them hand over fist. If the softer, more deeply treaded Michelins didn't work, he looked on course for second place – an astonishing achievement considering that the Subaru driver had been a distant tenth that morning. Loeb had the security of a two-minute buffer; Citroën knew that the stickiest rubber had done Panizzi and Marcus Grönholm no good in the first leg, that the ambient temperature was well above its usual operating range and, above all, that it was untested. There was no need for recklessness at this point – not with Loeb's fourth

victory of the season and the World Championship in sight. It was a forgiveable, if serious misjudgement.

Loeb had had grounds for concern but not for alarm when he lost a chunk of time on the first stage of the loop. There wasn't much grip with the harder rubber, but he had something in hand. When he pushed to the limit on the second and conceded seven seconds in three miles, however, he had suspected the worst. The split times on the final run at Viladrau confirmed his fears. It was hard to take after two and a half near-flawless days; in the dry, even Märtin, nursing a strained neck after his substantial accident in Corsica the week before, had had no answer to him.

Downcast by Carlos Sainz's plunge to seventh after his engine mysteriously cut out for 40 seconds on the final stage, probably when water seeped into the electrics, the Citroën men might have taken some convincing that it could have been worse. Yet Märtin might easily have deprived Loeb of second. The Estonian fell only 0.6 seconds short, and if the gearchange and differential hydraulics hadn't reported sick on the penultimate stage, Panizzi might also have struggled to stay in front. Caution had done Loeb no good; reliability offered a crumb of comfort.

Gilles Panizzi's recovery from a poor tyre choice in the first leg was impressive, his use of ultrasoft wets in Sunday's deluge inspired; Peugeot's drought was ended in triumphal fashion (left). For Petter Solberg, the rain came a little too late, whereas for a disenchanted Colin McRae (top) the rally couldn't end soon enough.

CATALONIA RALLY

Markko Märtin came tantalisingly close to victory for Ford, whereas Luca Cecchettini never looked like repeating Fiat's Sanremo success. While Carlos Sainz's event steadily deteriorated, Toni Gardemeister's spirits rose as the Skoda thrived in worsening conditions (clockwise from near left).

CATALONIA RALLY

Rally Catalunya, 24-26 October 2003,
FIA World Rally Championship Round 13

RUNNING ORDER

19	Carlos Sainz/	Citroën Xsara WRC
	Marc Martí	Gr A
7	Petter Solberg/	Subaru Impreza WRC2003
	Phil Mills	Gr A
2	Richard Burns/	Peugeot 206 WRC
	Robert Reid	Gr A
18	Sébastien Loeb/	Citroën Xsara WRC
	Daniel Elena	Gr A
1	Marcus Grönholm/	Peugeot 206 WRC
	Timo Rautiainen	Gr A
4	Markko Märtin/	Ford Focus RS WRC03
	Michael Park	Gr A
17	Colin McRae/	Citroën Xsara WRC
	Derek Ringer	Gr A
8	Tommi Mäkinen/	Subaru Impreza WRC2003
	Kaj Lindström	Gr A
5	François Duval/	Ford Focus RS WRC03
	Stéphane Prevot	Gr A
3	Gilles Panizzi/	Peugeot 206 WRC
	Hervé Panizzi	Gr A
15	Toni Gardemeister/	Skoda Fabia WRC
	Paavo Lukander	Gr A
14	Didier Auriol/	SkodaFabia WRC
	Denis Giraudet	Gr A
6	Mikko Hirvonen/	Ford Focus RS WRC02
	Jarmo Lehtinen	Gr A
21	Cédric Robert/	Peugeot 206 WRC
	Gerald Bedon	Gr A
20	Philippe Bugalski/	Citroën Xsara WRC
	Jean-Paul Chiaroni	Gr A
22	Roman Kresta/	Peugeot 206 WRC
	Jan Tomanek	Gr A
23	Antony Warmbold/	Ford Focus RS WRC02
	Gemma Price	Gr A
33	Alister Ginlay/	Ford Focus RS WRC02
	Rory Kennedy	Gr A

SPECIAL STAGE TIMES

SS1 LA TRONA 1 (13.17 KM)
1 P.Solberg/P.Mills (Subaru Impreza WRC2003) 8m23.6s;
2 F.Duval/S.Prevot (Ford Focus RS WRC03) 8m23.7s;
3 M.Märtin/M.Park (Ford Focus RS WRC03) 8m23.9s;
4 S.Loeb/D.Elena (Citroën Xsara WRC) 8m25.4s;
5 G.Panizzi/H.Panizzi (Peugeot 206 WRC) 8m26.4s;
6 C.McRae/D.Ringer (Citroën Xsara WRC) 8m26.7s;
JWC B.Tirabassi/J.Renucci (Renault Clio) 9m14.4s

SS2 ALPENS – LES LLOSSES 1 (21.80 KM)
1 Loeb/Elena (Citroën) 13m07.3s; 2 C.Sainz/M.Martí
(Citroën Xsara WRC) 13m11.8s; 3 Märtin/Park (Ford)
13m14.2s; 4 McRae/Ringer (Citroën) 13m16.4s; 5 R.Burns/
R.Reid (Peugeot 206 WRC) 13m17.8s; 6 Solberg/Mills
(Subaru) 13m21.6s; JWC Tirabassi/Renucci (Renault)
14m32.9s

SS3 LA POBLA DE LILLET 1 (22.55 KM)
1 Loeb/Elena (Citroën) 15m03.5s; 2 Sainz/Martí (Citroën)
15m06.9s; 3 Solberg/Mills (Subaru) 15m11.0s; 4 Burns/Reid
(Peugeot) 15m17.0s; 5 McRae/Ringer (Citroën) 15m18.3s;
6 Märtin/Park (Ford) 15m19.0s; JWC Tirabassi/Renucci
(Renault) 16m37.8s

SS4 SANT JULIA 1 (26.27 KM)
1 Loeb/Elena (Citroën) 15m35.3s; 2 Panizzi/Panizzi (Peugeot)
15m35.8s; 3 Duval/Prevot (Ford) 15m37.1s; 4 Sainz/Martí
(Citroën) 15m37.8s; 5 Märtin/Park (Ford) 15m38.3s;
6 Burns/Reid (Peugeot) 15m39.8s; JWC S.Canellas/
X.Amigo (Suzuki Ignis) 17m22.9s

SS5 TARADELL 1 (5.05 KM)
1 Märtin/Park (Ford) 2m56.2s; 2= Sainz/Martí (Citroën),
Panizzi/Panizzi (Peugeot) 2m57.4s; 4 Loeb/Elena (Citroën)
2m58.4s; 5 Burns/Reid (Peugeot) 2m58.5s; 6 Duval/Prevot
(Ford) 2m58.6s; JWC K.Meeke/C.Patterson (Opel Corsa)
3m16.8s

SS6 LA TRONA 2 (13.17 KM)
1 Panizzi/Panizzi (Peugeot) 8m15.7s; 2 Märtin/Park (Ford)
8m18.6s; 3 Duval/Prevot (Ford) 8m18.8s; 4 Burns/Reid
(Peugeot) 8m20.2s; 5 Loeb/Elena (Citroën) 8m20.7s;
6 Sainz/Martí (Citroën) 8m22.8s; JWC Tirabassi/Renucci
(Renault) 9m06.9s

SS7 ALPENS – LES LLOSSES 2 (21.80 KM)
1 Panizzi/Panizzi (Peugeot) 13m10.6s; 2 Duval/Prevot (Ford)
13m11.6s; 3 Loeb/Elena (Citroën) 13m11.9s; 4 Märtin/Park
(Ford) 13m14.0s; 5 Sainz/Martí (Citroën) 13m16.5s;
6 P.Bugalski/J-P.Chiaroni (Citroën Xsara WRC) 13m17.7s;
JWC Tirabassi/Renucci (Renault) 14m23.6s

SS8 LA POBLA DE LILLET 1 (22.55 KM)
1 Loeb/Elena (Citroën) 14m55.3s; 2 Panizzi/Panizzi (Peugeot)
14m57.5s; 3 Burns/Reid (Peugeot) 15m00.9s; 4 Bugalski/
Chiaroni (Citroën) 15m03.2s; 5 Duval/Prevot (Ford)
15m03.5s; 6 Sainz/Martí (Citroën) 15m03.8s;
JWC Tirabassi/Renucci (Renault) 16m31.5s

SS9 OLOST 1 (23.08 KM)
1 Panizzi/Panizzi (Peugeot) 11m39.4s; 2 Märtin/Park (Ford)
11m39.9s; 3 Loeb/Elena (Citroën) 11m41.7s; 4 Duval/Prevot
(Ford) 11m44.1s; 5 M.Grönholm/T.Rautiainen (Peugeot
206 WRC) 11m47.5s; 6 Burns/Reid (Peugeot) 11m50.0s;
JWC Meeke/Patterson (Opel) 12m52.7s

SS10 LLUCA 1 (14.04 KM)
1 Märtin/Park (Ford) 8m15.9s; 2 Duval/Prevot (Ford)
8m16.1s; 3 Burns/Reid (Peugeot) 8m18.5s; 4 Panizzi/Panizzi
(Peugeot) 8m18.8s; 5 Loeb/Elena (Citroën) 8m19.1s;
6 Sainz/Martí (Citroën) 8m22.0s; JWC Canellas/Amigo
(Suzuki) 9m07.6s

SS11 SANT BOI DE LLUCANES 1 (12.85 KM)
1 Panizzi/Panizzi (Peugeot) 8m06.7s; 2= Märtin/Park (Ford),
Loeb/Elena (Citroën) 8m07.2s; 4 Burns/Reid (Peugeot)
8m08.8s; 5 Duval/Prevot (Ford) 8m10.2s; 6 Solberg/Mills
(Subaru) 8m10.9s; JWC Tirabassi/Renucci (Renault) 8m55.4s

SS12 SANT JULIA 2 (26.27 KM)
1 Duval/Prevot (Ford) 15m30.4s; 2 Panizzi/Panizzi (Peugeot)
15m31.1s; 3 Grönholm/Rautiainen (Peugeot) 15m31.4s;
4 Loeb/Elena (Citroën) 15m33.2s; 5= McRae/Ringer
(Citroën), Märtin/Park (Ford) 15m35.4s; JWC Tirabassi/
Renucci (Renault) 17m07.9s

SS13 TARADELL 2 (5.05 KM)
1 Burns/Reid (Peugeot) 2m58.3s; 2 Märtin/Park (Ford)
2m58.4s; 3 Sainz/Martí (Citroën) 2m58.8s; 4 Panizzi/Panizzi
(Peugeot) 2m59.0s; 5= Solberg/Mills (Subaru), Loeb/Elena
(Citroën) 2m59.1s; JWC Meeke/Patterson (Opel) 3m14.6s

SS14 OLOST 2 (23.08 KM)
1 Märtin/Park (Ford) 11m37.0s; 2 Loeb/Elena (Citroën)
11m40.4s; 3 Grönholm/Rautiainen (Peugeot) 11m41.9s;
4 Panizzi/Panizzi (Peugeot) 11m43.2s; 5 Duval/Prevot
(Ford) 11m44.1s; 6 Burns/Reid (Peugeot) 11m47.0s;
JWC Tirabassi/Renucci (Renault) 12m50.4s

SS15 LLUCA 2 (14.04 KM)
1 Märtin/Park (Ford) 8m19.5s; 2 Duval/Prevot (Ford)
8m21.7s; 3 Sainz/Martí (Citroën) 8m23.4s; 4 Solberg/Mills
(Subaru) 8m23.9s; 5 Loeb/Elena (Citroën) 8m24.6s;
6 C.Robert/G.Bedon (Peugeot 206 WRC) 8m25.2s;
JWC V.Teuronen/M.Markkula (Suzuki Ignis) 9m08.9s

SS16 SANT BOI DE LLUCanes 2 (12.85 KM)
1 Loeb/Elena (Citroën) 8m05.5s; 2 Märtin/Park (Ford)
8m07.1s; 3 Panizzi/Panizzi (Peugeot) 8m07.4s; 4 Duval/
Prevot (Ford) 8m08.4s; 5 Grönholm/Rautiainen (Peugeot)
8m08.5s; 6 Sainz/Martí (Citroën) 8m10.1s; JWC Tirabassi/
Renucci (Renault) 8m55.4s

SS17 SANT BARTOMEU DEL GR 1 (11.55 KM)
1 Solberg/Mills (Subaru) 6m27.2s; 2 T.Mäkinen/K.Lindström
(Subaru Impreza WRC2003) 6m29.4s; 3 Sainz/Martí
(Citroën) 6m43.7s; 4 Grönholm/Rautiainen (Peugeot)
6m44.1s; 5 McRae/Ringer (Citroën) 6m45.6s; 6 Loeb/Elena
(Citroën) 6m45.9s; JWC Canellas/Amigo (Suzuki) 7m03.4s

3/8

2/7

10/15

1/6/11/16

9/14/17/20

4/12/19/22

5/13/18/21

FRANCE

SPAIN

Lloret de Mar

Barcelona

MADRID

PORTUGAL

LLORET
DE MAR

Barcelona

For over 300 days a year, it's merely a bridge on the C25, but when the Catalonia Rally is on, it becomes a superb vantage point with panoramic views of the Santa Julia and Viladrau stages. Sébastien Loeb entertains the legions of fans in his Citroën.

SS18 LA ROCA 1 (5.05 KM)
1 R.Kresta/J.Tomanek (Peugeot 206 WRC) 3m16.2s;
2 Mäkinen/Lindström (Subaru) 3m19.4s; 3 Solberg/Mills (Subaru) 3m19.8s; 4 Panizzi/Panizzi (Peugeot) 3m21.3s;
5= Burns/Reid (Peugeot), Sainz/Martí (Citroën) 3m21.7s;
JWC Tirabassi/Renucci (Renault) 3m35.1s

SS19 VILADRAU 1 (35.18 KM)
1 Mäkinen/Lindström (Subaru) 23m19.8s; 2 Solberg/Mills (Subaru) 23m26.7s; 3 Grönholm/Rautiainen (Peugeot) 24m00.3s; 4 Loeb/Elena (Citroën) 24m06.4s; 5 Panizzi/Panizzi (Peugeot) 24m11.9s; 6 McRae/Ringer (Citroën) 24m13.4s; JWC Meeke/Patterson (Opel) 25m29.4s

SS20 SANT BARTOMEU DEL GR 2 (11.55 KM)
1 Märtin/Park (Ford) 6m29.4s; 2 Solberg/Mills (Subaru) 6m32.0s; 3 Duval/Prevot (Ford) 6m33.6s; 4 Mäkinen/Lindström (Subaru) 6m34.7s; 5 Panizzi/Panizzi (Peugeot) 6m35.4s; 6 Sainz/Martí (Citroën) 6m37.0s; JWC Tirabassi/Renucci (Renault) 7m04.2s

SS21 LA ROCA 1 (5.05 KM)
1 Grönholm/Rautiainen (Peugeot) 3m22.2s; 2 Duval/Prevot (Ford) 3m22.4s; 3 Panizzi/Panizzi (Peugeot) 3m23.0s; 4 T.Gardemeister/P.Lukander (Skoda Fabia WRC) 3m23.5s; 5 Robert/Bedon (Peugeot) 3m24.2s; 6 Kresta/Tomanek (Peugeot) 3m24.8s; JWC Tirabassi/Renucci (Renault) 3m39.7s

SS22 VILADRAU 2 (35.18 KM)
1 Panizzi/Panizzi (Peugeot) 23m38.4s; 2 Grönholm/Rautiainen (Peugeot) 23m39.2s; 3 Märtin/Park (Ford) 23m41.7s; 4 Duval/Prevot (Ford) 23m50.7s; 5 Mäkinen/Lindström (Subaru) 23m57.0s; 6 Solberg/Mills (Subaru) 24m00.5s; JWC Tirabassi/Renucci (Renault) 25m45.1s

MAJOR RETIREMENTS

2	Burns/Reid	Peugeot 206 WRC	
	Accident	SS19	Gr A
14	Auriol/Giraudet	Skoda Fabia WRC	
	Clutch	SS9	Gr A

FIA CLASS WINNERS

A8 Over 2000 cc	Panizzi/Panizzi	
	Peugeot 206 WRC	
A6 1400-1600 cc	Jean-Joseph/Boyere	
	Renault Clio	
N4 Over 2000 cc	Pons/Julia	
	Mitsubishi Lancer E7	

RALLY LEADERS
Overall: SS1 Solberg; SS2-21 Loeb; SS22 Panizzi
JWC : SS1-22 Tirabassi

SPECIAL STAGE ANALYSIS

	1st	2nd	3rd	4th	5th	6th
Märtin (Ford)	5	5	3	1	2	1
Panizzi (Peugeot)	5	4	2	4	3	-
Loeb (Citroën)	5	2	2	4	4	1
Solberg (Subaru)	2	2	2	1	1	3
Duval (Ford)	1	5	3	3	3	1
Mäkinen (Subaru)	1	2	-	1	1	-
Grönholm (Peugeot)	1	1	3	1	2	-
Burns (Peugeot)	1	-	2	3	3	3
Kresta (Peugeot)	1	-	-	-	-	1
Sainz (Citroën)	-	3	3	1	2	5
McRae (Citroën)	-	-	-	1	3	2
Bugalski (Citroën)	-	-	-	1	1	1
Gardemeister (Skoda)	-	-	-	1	-	-
Robert (Peugeot)	-	-	-	-	1	1

WORLD CHAMPIONSHIP POINTS
DRIVERS
1= Loeb, Sainz 63; 3 Solberg 62; 4 Burns 58; 5 Märtin 49; 6 Grönholm 46; 7 McRae 40; 8 Panizzi 27; 9 Duval 26; 10 Mäkinen 24 etc

MANUFACTURERS
1 Citroën 147; 2 Peugeot 142; 3 Subaru 93; 4 Ford 89; 5 Skoda 21; 6 Hyundai 12

JUNIOR WORLD CHAMPIONSHIP
1 Tirabassi 38; 2 Canellas 31; 3 Carlsson 23; 4 Aava 20; 5 Wilks 18; 6 Teuronen 13 etc

PRODUCTION CUP
1 Rowe 43; 2 Arai 38; 3= Singh, Blomqvist 30; 5 Solá 22; 6 McShea 18 etc

ROUTE DETAILS
Total route of 1553.72 km of which 381.18 km were competitive on 22 stages

LEG 1 Friday 24th October, 8 Special Stages totalling 146.36 km

LEG 2 Saturday 25th October, 8 Special Stages totalling 131.26 km

LEG 3 Sunday 26th October, 6 Special Stages totalling 103.56 km

FINISH LINES
François Duval overcame brake problems and a fogged windscreen to take fourth place for the second rally in succession in his works Focus... The latest Pirellis were still no match for Michelins on a dry stage of any length, but Petter Solberg would certainly have improved on fifth in his Subaru if it wasn't for an alternator failure in the first leg that cost 50 seconds in road penalties... Tommi Mäkinen survived power steering problems and last-minute clutch trouble to finish eighth in his works Impreza... Richard Burns retired for only the second time all season, skating off on a patch of mud and breaking one of the 206's steering arms when in sixth place in the last leg... Colin McRae was a distant ninth, hampered a little by brake trouble in his Xsara, but chiefly by a struggle for motivation... Broken rear anti-roll bars slowed Toni Gardemeister once more, but the Finn was delighted with his Skoda's handling in the wet... Didier Auriol retired early in the second leg when his Fabia's clutch expired; he had lost time in the first leg with a faulty wastegate... Brice Tirabassi laid one hand on the Junior world title with an accomplished victory in his Clio, trouble-free aside from intercom failure on the last stage. He was comfortably quicker than the Suzukis... Kris Meeke was an excellent second in the Team Palmer Corsa, despite a jammed throttle on the last stage of the second leg... Neither Polo finished, Kosti Katajamäki pulling out with a dead alternator, while Oscar Svedlund was sidelined when the differential broke... Guy Wilks gained experience rather than points, losing 20 minutes in the first leg when he spun off and had to rebuild his Puma's suspension in the stage, then more time with spins, a cracked exhaust manifold and power steering failure... Mirco Baldacci was the first Junior retirement, the Punto's engine blowing on SS2...

STAGE NUMBERS	1	2	3	4	5	6	7	8	9	10	11	12	13	14	15	16	17	18	19	20	21	22
Panizzi	5	7	8	5	5	5	4	4	3	3	3	2	3	3	3	3	3	3	2	2	2	1
Loeb	4	1	1	1	1	1	1	1	1	1	1	1	1	1	1	1	1	1	1	1	1	2
Märtin	3	2	4	3	3	3	3	2	2	2	3	2	2	2	2	2	2	2	3	3	3	3
Duval	2	9	9	7	7	6	5	5	5	5	5	5	5	5	5	5	5	5	5	5	5	4
Solberg	1	6	3	10	10	10	10	11	11	11	11	10	10	10	10	9	8	6	6	6	6	5
Grönholm	14	14	14	12	11	11	11	10	9	9	9	8	8	8	8	8	9	8	8	7	6	
Sainz	8	3	2	2	2	2	2	4	4	4	4	4	4	4	4	4	4	4	4	4	7	
Mäkinen	9	8	7	8	8	8	8	9	10	10	10	11	11	11	11	11	11	10	7	7	8	
McRae	6	4	5	6	6	7	6	7	7	7	7	7	7	7	7	7	7	9	9	9	9	
Bugalski	11	10	10	9	9	9	9	8	8	8	9	9	9	9	9	10	11	10	10	10	10	
Robert	12	11	11	11	12	12	12	12	12	12	12	12	12	12	12	12	12	12	11	11	11	
G'meister	13	14	15	15	15	14	13	13	13	13	13	13	13	13	13	13	14	13	13	12		
Kresta	16	16	16	16	16	15	14	14	14	14	14	14	14	14	14	14	12	12	12	13		
Hirvonen	15	13	13	13	16	16	16	15	15	15	15	15	15	15	15	15	14	14	14			
Burns	7	5	6	4	4	4	7	6	6	6	6	6	6	6	6	6	6	6	R			
Auriol	10	12	12	14	14	13	15	15	R													

RESULTS

1	Gilles Panizzi/	Peugeot 206 WRC	
	Hervé Panizzi	3h55m09.4s	Gr A
2	Sébastien Loeb/	Citroën Xsara WRC	
	Daniel Elena	3h55m22.4s	Gr A
3	Markko Märtin/	Ford Focus RS WRC03	
	Michael Park	3h55m23.0s	Gr A
4	François Duval/	Ford Focus RS WRC03	
	Stéphane Prevot	3h56m04.8s	Gr A
5	Petter Solberg/	Subaru Impreza WRC2003	
	Phil Mills	3h56m20.2s	Gr A
6	Marcus Grönholm/	Peugeot 206 WRC	
	Timo Rautiainen	3h56m38.5s	Gr A
7	Carlos Sainz/	Citroën Xsara WRC	
	Marc Martí	3h56m52.4s	Gr A
8	Tommi Mäkinen/	Subaru Impreza WRC2003	
	Kaj Lindström	3h57m04.5s	Gr A
9	Colin McRae/	Citroën Xsara WRC	
	Derek Ringer	3h58m24.6s	Gr A
10	Philippe Bugalski/	Citroën Xsara WRC	
	Jean-Paul Chiaroni	4h00m23.0s	Gr A
47 starters, 33 finishers			

RECENT WINNERS

1980	Antonio Zanini/Jordi Sabater	Porsche 911SC
1981	Eugenio Ortiz/Guillermo Barreras	Renault 5 Turbo
1982	Antonio Zanini/Victor Sabater	Talbot Sunbeam Lotus
1983	Adartico Vudafieri/Tiziano Siviero	Lancia 037 Rally
1984	Salvador Servia/Jordi Sabater	Opel Manta 400
1985	Fabrizio Tabaton/Luciano Tedeschini	Lancia 037 Rally
1986	Fabrizio Tabaton/Luciano Tedeschini	Lancia Delta S4
1987	Dario Cerrato/Giuseppe Cerri	Lancia Delta HF 4x4
1988	Bruno Saby/Jean-François Fauchille	Lancia Delta HF 4x4
1989	Yves Loubet/Jean-Marc Andrié	Lancia Delta Integrale
1990	Dario Cerrato/Giuseppe Cerri	Lancia Delta Integrale 16v
1991	Armin Schwarz/Arne Hertz	Toyota Celica GT4
1992	Carlos Sainz/Luis Moya	Toyota Celica Turbo 4wd
1993	François Delecour/Daniel Grataloup	Ford Escort RS Cosworth
1994	Enrico Bertone/Massimo Chiapponi	Toyota Celica Turbo 4wd
1995	Carlos Sainz/Luis Moya	Subaru Impreza 555
1996	Colin McRae/Derek Ringer	Subaru Impreza 555
1997	Tommi Mäkinen/Seppo Harjanne	Mitsubishi Lancer E4
1998	Didier Auriol/Denis Giraudet	Toyota Corolla WRC
1999	Philippe Bugalski/Jean-Paul Chiaroni	Citroën Xsara Kit
2000	Colin McRae/Nicky Grist	Ford Focus WRC
2001	Didier Auriol/Denis Giraudet	Peugeot 206 WRC
2002	Gilles Panizzi/Hervé Panizzi	Peugeot 206 WRC

Asked how he felt, David Lapworth paused while he sought the appropriate phrase and admitted to 'a reasonable level of apprehension given the circumstances'. Prodrive had left nothing to chance, even the requisite level of apprehension. In truth, with two stages of the Rally of Great Britain to run, only the desire not to appear complacent seemed to justify any level of apprehension at all. Petter Solberg had led since the fourth of the 18 stages. There was nothing left to conquer but the nagging fear that no rally can go entirely according to plan.

Solberg had driven beautifully, modulating his pace from the start to split times relayed by radio, remorselessly outrunning, then subduing Sébastien Loeb. Like the Frenchman, he made the occasional poor tyre choice in the second leg, failing to realise how slippery the Welsh forests became once earlier cars had polished the surface in relatively dry conditions. He got a scare too when the Impreza landed viciously in a hole on Resolfen on Saturday afternoon, little more than a mile into a 27-mile stage. It turned out that there was no damage other than a bent steering link, but his heart was in his mouth until he discovered that he had gained rather than lost time at the first split; by the end of the stage, his lead had swelled to 40 seconds, and Loeb was running out of time and distance to take the rally and the World Championship.

Solberg remained wary, insisting that his adversary was keeping him under pressure, reminding his audience that Carlos Sainz had lost the World Championship 300 yards from the end of the final stage in 1998. He was ready for a last-gasp sprint for the line if necessary. While the Impreza had run strongly, he was all too aware that it had ground to a halt at the shakedown when a gearbox oil union fell apart. But there was no cause for alarm, no need for a charge. Even he admitted that it had nothing in common with the high-tension duel with Loeb in Australia.

RALLY OF GREAT BRITAIN

RALLYCOURSE World Rally Championship **Round 14**

For a World Championship showdown between two drivers seeking their first world titles, it was conspicuously lacking in drama: circumstances had contrived to occasion Subaru the lowest possible level of apprehension. Richard Burns had been very much the championship outsider in any case, but his blackout the week beforehand had removed him from the rally and the reckoning. Then the fateful decision to rush new in-car cameras into service over two months before the original date contributed to a series of fires in Sainz's Xsara. After a fraught morning, in which he had been required to repair the wiring after the car filled with smoke just as he prepared to start the first forest stage, the Spaniard ended his rally down a bank on SS3, having lost concentration and ignored a pace note.

Brechfa did for the two drivers most likely to deprive Solberg of victory too, Marcus Grönholm's season continuing its downward spiral with another accident and an encounter with the police when trying to coax the stricken 206 to service, 14 minutes down. Markko Märtin's agony was prolonged only a few miles further, the Focus's engine on its last legs after losing water on both Brechfa and Trawscoed. However, it was Sainz's retirement that changed the complexion of the rally. Under pressure from Citroën's chairman, Claude Satinet, Guy Fréquelin had no choice but to order Loeb to slow immediately: Citroën wanted the World Championship for Manufacturers above all else and once Sainz had gone, both Loeb and Colin McRae needed to finish to prevent Peugeot turning the tables at the 11th hour.

It was heavy-handed – exceptionally cautious too, when Peugeot had been deprived of Grönholm and Burns – and a test of obedience that strained even Loeb's self-control. It tied one arm behind McRae's back besides, although a puncture in Margam would probably have handed third to Tommi Mäkinen on his final World Championship appearance regardless. However, Solberg's victory was in no sense hollow. On the contrary, Loeb himself conceded that in such conditions, the Norwegian had always been the likely winner. Lapworth described it as the sort of anti-climax that Subaru wanted, but it was an anti-climax nonetheless.

Subaru and Solberg were an irresistible force, the Norwegian (below left) taking an impeccable victory, while Tommi Mäkinen rounded off his World Championship career with his best British result. François Duval (top right) and Freddy Loix, making his first appearance for Peugeot, were also impressive. Manfred Stohl (far right) put in another excellent performance in his private 206, whereas Skoda didn't thrive on Epynt's chilly wastes.

THINK AUTOMOTIVE
WALES

RALLY OF GREAT BRITAIN

Rally of Great Britain, 6-9 November 2003,
FIA World Rally Championship Round 14

RUNNING ORDER

18	Sébastien Loeb/	Citroën Xsara WRC
	Daniel Elena	Gr A
19	Carlos Sainz/	Citroën Xsara WRC
	Marc Martí	Gr A
7	Petter Solberg/	Subaru Impreza WRC2003
	Phil Mills	Gr A
4	Markko Märtin/	Ford Focus RS WRC03
	Michael Park	Gr A
1	Marcus Grönholm/	Peugeot 206 WRC
	Timo Rautiainen	Gr A
17	Colin McRae/	Citroën Xsara WRC
	Derek Ringer	Gr A
21	Gilles Panizzi/	Peugeot 206 WRC
	Hervé Panizzi	Gr A
5	François Duval/	Ford Focus RS WRC03
	Stéphane Prevot	Gr A
8	Tommi Mäkinen/	Subaru Impreza WRC2003
	Kaj Lindström	Gr A
3	Harri Rovanperä/	Peugeot 206 WRC
	Risto Pietilainen	Gr A
15	Toni Gardemeister/	Skoda Fabia WRC
	Paavo Lukander	Gr A
14	Didier Auriol/	Skoda Fabia WRC
	Denis Giraudet	Gr A
6	Mikko Hirvonen/	Ford Focus RS WRC02
	Jarmo Lehtinen	Gr A
2	Freddy Loix/	Peugeot 206 WRC
	Sven Smeets	Gr A
24	Juuso Pykälisto/	Peugeot 206 WRC
	Risto M'nisenmäki	Gr A
22	Roman Kresta/	Peugeot 206 WRC
	Jan Tomanek	Gr A
20	Jari-Matti Latvala/	Ford Focus RS WRC02
	Mika Anttila	Gr A
23	Antony Warmbold/	Ford Focus RS WRC02
	Gemma Price	Gr A
25	Daniel Solá/	Citroën Xsara WRC
	Alex Romani	Gr A
33	Alistair Ginley/	Ford Focus RS WRC02
	Rory Kennedy	Gr A
34	Manfred Stohl/	Peugeot 206 WRC
	Ilka Minor	Gr A

SPECIAL STAGE TIMES

SS1 CARDIFF 1 (2.45 KM)
1 P.Solberg/P.Mills (Subaru Impreza WRC2003) 2m08.7s; 2 M.Märtin/M.Park (Ford Focus RS WRC03) 2m10.1s; 3= M.Grönholm/T.Rautiainen (Peugeot 206 WRC), T.Mäkinen/K.Lindström (Subaru Impreza WRC2003) 2m10.5s; 5 C.Sainz/M.Martí (Citroën Xsara WRC) 2m11.1s; 6= F.Loix/S.Smeets (Peugeot 206 WRC), S.Loeb/D.Elena (Citroën Xsara WRC) 2m12.0s; JWC K.Meeke/C.Patterson (Opel Corsa), M.Baldacci/ G.Bernacchini (Fiat Punto) 2m25.0s

SS2 BRECHFA (23.12 KM)
1 Loeb/Elena (Citroën) 13m19.6s; 2 Solberg/Mills (Subaru) 13m24.2s; 3 Märtin/Park (Ford) 13m28.0s; 4 Grönholm/ Rautiainen (Peugeot) 13m30.0s; 5 Sainz/Martí (Citroën) 13m38.5s; 6 Mäkinen/Lindström (Subaru) 13m44.2s; JWC Meeke/Patterson (Opel) 15m45.5s

SS3 TRAWSCOED (27.97 KM)
1 Loeb/Elena (Citroën) 16m23.4s; 2 Solberg/Mills (Subaru) 16m25.9s; 3 Märtin/Park (Ford) 16m29.0s; 4 Mäkinen/ Lindström (Subaru) 16m45.2s; 5 C.McRae/D.Ringer (Citroën Xsara WRC) 16m54.9s; 6 H.Rovanperä/ R.Pietilainen (Peugeot 206 WRC) 16m55.8s; JWC D.Carlsson/M.Andersson (Suzuki Ignis) 19m11.2s

SS4 RHEOLA 1 (32.58 KM)
1 Solberg/Mills (Subaru) 17m58.6s; 2 Loeb/Elena (Citroën) 18m07.1s; 3 Mäkinen/Lindström (Subaru) 18m15.8s; 4 McRae/Ringer (Citroën) 18m19.9s; 5 G.Panizzi/H.Panizzi (Peugeot 206 WRC) 18m26.6s; 6 Rovanperä/Pietilainen (Peugeot) 18m33.7s; JWC Carlsson/Andersson (Suzuki) 20m28.2s

SS5 RESOLFEN 1 (43.09 KM)
1 Solberg/Mills (Subaru) 22m40.9s; 2 Loeb/Elena (Citroën) 22m44.0s; 3 Mäkinen/Lindström (Subaru) 23m02.8s; 4 McRae/Ringer (Citroën) 23m06.7s; 5 Rovanperä/ Pietilainen (Peugeot) 23m17.3s; 6 Panizzi/Panizzi (Peugeot) 23m24.6s; JWC Carlsson/Andersson (Suzuki) 25m48.7s

SS6 RHEOLA 2 (32.58 KM)
1 Loeb/Elena (Citroën) 17m50.9s; 2 Solberg/Mills (Subaru) 17m52.5s; 3 McRae/Ringer (Citroën) 17m53.2s; 4 Mäkinen/ Lindström (Subaru) 18m03.4s; 5 Rovanperä/Pietilainen (Peugeot) 18m12.0s; 6 Loix/Smeets (Peugeot) 18m15.9s; JWC B.Tirabassi/J.Renucci (Renault Clio) 20m09.7s

SS7 CARDIFF 2 (2.45 KM)
1 Solberg/Mills (Subaru) 2m06.4s; 2 Mäkinen/Lindström (Subaru) 2m07.5s; 3 McRae/Ringer (Citroën) 2m08.1s; 4 Loeb/Elena (Citroën) 2m08.2s; 5 F.Duval/S.Prevot (Ford Focus RS WRC03) 2m08.6s; 6 J.Pykälisto/R.Mannisenmäki (Peugeot 206 WRC) 2m09.4s; JWC Baldacci/Bernacchini (Fiat) 2m21.4s

SS8 CRYCHAN 1 (13.05 KM)
1 Solberg/Mills (Subaru) 7m10.6s; 2 Loeb/Elena (Citroën) 7m14.6s; 3 McRae/Ringer (Citroën) 7m15.6s; 4 Mäkinen/ Lindström (Subaru) 7m16.0s; 5 Rovanperä/Pietilainen (Peugeot) 7m20.4s; 6 Duval/Prevot (Ford) 7m21.5s; JWC Carlsson/Andersson (Suzuki) 8m06.1s

SS9 HALFWAY 1 (18.53 KM)
1 Solberg/Mills (Subaru) 10m15.7s; 2 Loeb/Elena (Citroën) 10m18.4s; 3 Mäkinen/Lindström (Subaru) 10m20.7s; 4 McRae/Ringer (Citroën) 10m21.1s; 5 Rovanperä/ Pietilainen (Peugeot) 10m30.5s; 6 Loix/Smeets (Peugeot) 10m31.4s; JWC Carlsson/Andersson (Suzuki) 11m26.0s

SS10 CRYCHAN 2 (13.05 KM)
1 Solberg/Mills (Subaru) 7m08.0s; 2 McRae/Ringer (Citroën) 7m10.9s; 3 Loeb/Elena (Citroën) 7m13.6s; 4 Mäkinen/ Lindström (Subaru) 7m13.7s; 5 Loix/Smeets (Peugeot) 7m16.7s; 6 Duval/Prevot (Ford) 7m17.7s; JWC Carlsson/ Andersson (Suzuki) 8m02.6s

SS11 HALFWAY 2 (18.53 KM)
1 Solberg/Mills (Subaru) 10m11.0s; 2 Loeb/Elena (Citroën) 10m15.4s; 3 Mäkinen/Lindström (Subaru) 10m16.3s; 4 McRae/Ringer (Citroën) 10m19.5s; 5 Duval/Prevot (Ford) 10m25.5s; 6 Rovanperä/Pietilainen (Peugeot) 10m25.7s; JWC Meeke/Patterson (Opel) 11m18.6s

SS12 MARGAM FOREST (17.37 KM)
1 Solberg/Mills (Subaru) 9m57.7s; 2 Loeb/Elena (Citroën) 9m57.8s; 3 McRae/Ringer (Citroën) 10m00.3s; 4 Mäkinen/ Lindström (Subaru) 10m02.2s; 5 Rovanperä/Pietilainen (Peugeot) 10m09.9s; 6 Duval/Prevot (Ford) 10m10.6s; JWC Carlsson/Andersson (Suzuki) 11m13.7s

SS13 MARGAM PARK 1 (12.64 KM)
1 Solberg/Mills (Subaru) 7m08.8s; 2 Mäkinen/Lindström (Subaru) 7m14.6s; 3 McRae/Ringer (Citroën) 7m14.9s; 4 Loeb/Elena (Citroën) 7m15.3s; 5 Duval/Prevot (Ford) 7m23.3s; 6 Rovanperä/Pietilainen (Peugeot) 7m25.2s; JWC Meeke/Patterson (Opel) 8m05.0s

SS14 RESOLFEN 2 (43.09 KM)
1 Solberg/Mills (Subaru) 22m21.3s; 2 Loeb/Elena (Citroën) 22m30.8s; 3 McRae/Ringer (Citroën) 22m37.3s; 4 Mäkinen/Lindström (Subaru) 22m41.1s; 5 Rovanperä/ Pietilainen (Peugeot) 22m52.5s; 6 Loix/Smeets (Peugeot) 22m57.3s; JWC Carlsson/Andersson (Suzuki) 25m18.6s

SS15 CARDIFF 3 (2.45 KM)
1 Solberg/Mills (Subaru) 2m05.1s; 2 Loeb/Elena (Citroën) 2m05.5s; 3 McRae/Ringer (Citroën) 2m06.4s; 4 Mäkinen/ Lindström (Subaru) 2m06.6s; 5 Duval/Prevot (Ford) 2m06.8s; 6 Loix/Smeets (Peugeot) 2m07.7s; JWC Meeke/ Patterson (Opel) 2m18.5s

SS16 RHONDDA 1 (30.61 KM)
1 Loeb/Elena (Citroën) 16m25.5s; 2 Solberg/Mills (Subaru) 16m30.7s; 3 Mäkinen/Lindström (Subaru) 16m35.6s; 4 McRae/Ringer (Citroën) 16m37.9s; 5 M.Stohl/I.Minor (Peugeot 206 WRC) 16m49.7s; 6 R.Kresta/J.Tomanek (Peugeot 206 WRC) 16m56.2s; JWC Meeke/Patterson (Opel) 18m27.2s

SS17 RHONDDA 2 (30.61 KM)
1 Loeb/Elena (Citroën) 16m21.1s; 2 Solberg/Mills (Subaru) 16m24.6s; 3 Mäkinen/Lindström (Subaru) 16m34.1s; 4 McRae/Ringer (Citroën) 16m35.8s; 5 Stohl/Minor (Peugeot) 16m59.1s; 6 Kresta/Tomanek (Peugeot) 17m02.7s; JWC Carlsson/Andersson (Suzuki) 18m24.9s

SS18 MARGAM PARK 2 (12.64 KM)
1 Solberg/Mills (Subaru) 7m07.4s; 2 Loeb/Elena (Citroën) 7m18.5s; 3 Duval/Prevot (Ford) 7m22.9s; 4 Stohl/Minor (Peugeot) 7m26.5s; 5 Mäkinen/Lindström (Subaru) 7m26.6s; 6 Kresta/Tomanek (Peugeot) 7m29.9s; JWC Carlsson/Andersson (Suzuki) 8m09.4s

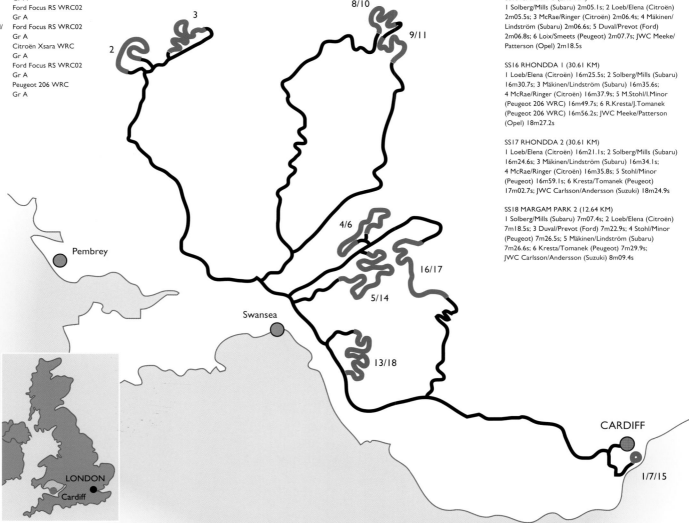

Pembrey

Swansea

CARDIFF

LONDON
Cardiff

3
2
8/10
9/11
4/6
16/17
5/14
13/18
1/7/15

Sébastien Loeb gave a glimpse of what he might have achieved in the opening stages, before dutifully helping Citroën take the manufacturers' championship.

MAJOR RETIREMENTS

19	Sainz/Martí	Citroën Xsara WRC	
	Accident	SS3	Gr A
4	Märtin/Park	Ford Focus RS WRC03	
	Engine	SS3	Gr A
1	Grönholm/R'iainen	Peugeot 206 WRC	
	Suspension	SS3	Gr A
21	Panizzi/Panizzi	Peugeot 206 WRC	
	T'mission	SS8	Gr A
3	Rovanperä/P'lainen	Peugeot 206 WRC	
	T'mission	SS16	Gr A
15	Gardemeister/L'der	Skoda Fabia WRC	
	Accident	SS16	Gr A
6	Hirvonen/Lehtinen	Ford Focus RS WRC02	
	Accident	SS3	Gr A
25	Solá/Romani	Citroën Xsara WRC	
	Fire	SS14	Gr A

FIA CLASS WINNERS

A8	Over 2000 cc	Solberg/Mills
		Subaru Impreza WRC2003
A6	1400-1600 cc	Carlsson/Andersson
		Suzuki Ignis
A5	Upto 1400cc	Burgess/Holder
		Rover Mini Cooper
N4	Over 2000cc	Jones/Lewis
		Subaru Impreza WRX
N3	1600-2000cc	Evans/Mole
		MG ZR

RALLY LEADERS

Overall: SS1 Solberg; SS2-3 Loeb; SS4-18 Solberg
JWC: SS1 Baldacci, Meeke; SS2-4 Meeke; SS5-18 Carlsson

SPECIAL STAGE ANALYSIS

	1st	2nd	3rd	4th	5th	6th
Solberg (Subaru)	13	5	-	-	-	-
Loeb (Citroën)	5	9	1	2	-	1
Mäkinen (Subaru)	-	2	7	7	1	1
McRae (Citroën)	-	1	7	6	1	-
Märtin (Ford)	-	1	2	-	-	-
Grönholm (Peugeot)	-	-	1	1	-	-
Duval (Ford)	-	-	1	-	4	3
Stohl (Peugeot)	-	-	-	1	2	-
Rovanperä (Peugeot)	-	-	-	-	6	4
Sainz (Citroën)	-	-	-	-	2	-
Loix (Peugeot)	-	-	-	-	1	5
Panizzi (Peugeot)	-	-	-	-	1	1
Kresta (Peugeot)	-	-	-	-	-	3
Pykälistö (Peugeot)	-	-	-	-	-	1

WORLD CHAMPIONSHIP POINTS

DRIVERS
1 Solberg 72; 2 Loeb 71; 3 Sainz 63; 4 Burns 58;
5 Märtin 49; 6 Grönholm 46; 7 McRae 45;
8= Duval, Mäkinen 30; 10 Panizzi 27 etc

MANUFACTURERS
1 Citroën 160; 2 Peugeot 145; 3 Subaru 109; 4 Ford 93;
5 Skoda 23; 6 Hyundai 12

JUNIOR WORLD CHAMPIONSHIP
1 Tirabassi 38; 2 Canellas 36; 3 Carlsson 33;
4= Aava, Baldacci 20; 6 Teuronen 19 etc

PRODUCTION CUP
1 Rowe 43; 2 Arai 38; 3= Singh, Blomqvist 30; 5 Solá 22;
6 McShea 18 etc

ROUTE DETAILS

Total route of 1553.72 km of which 376.81 km were competitive on 18 special stages

LEG 1 Thursday 6th November – Friday 7th November, 7 special stages totalling 166.69 km

LEG 2 Saturday 8th November, 8 special stages totalling 138.71 km

LEG 3 Sunday 9th November, 3 special stages totalling 73.86 km

RESULTS

1	Petter Solberg/	Subaru Impreza WRC2003	
	Phil Mills	3h28m58.1s	Gr A
2	Sébastien Loeb/	Citroën Xsara WRC	
	Daniel Elena	3h29m41.7s	Gr A
3	Tommi Mäkinen/	Subaru Impreza WRC2003	
	Kaj Lindström	3h31m56.9s	Gr A
4	Colin McRae/	Citroën Xsara WRC	
	Derek Ringer	3h34m26.2s	Gr A
5	François Duval/	Ford Focus RS WRC03	
	Stéphane Prevot	3h36m14.2s	Gr A
6	Freddy Loix/	Peugeot 206 WRC	
	Sven Smeets	3h37m04.6s	Gr A
7	Manfred Stohl/	Peugeot 206 WRC	
	Ilka Minor	3h37m46.4s	Gr.A
8	Roman Kresta/	Peugeot 206 WRC	
	Jan Tomanek	3h38m00.7s	Gr A
9	Juuso Pykälisto/	Peugeot 206 WRC	
	Risto M'nisenmäki	3h38m51.7s	Gr A
10	Jari-Matti Latvala/	Ford Focus RS WRC02	
	Mika Antilla	3h41m23.4s	Gr A

75 starters, 39 finishers

FINISH LINES

François Duval won the battle of the Belgians, securing fifth in the surviving works Focus... Freddy Loix stepped in to replace Richard Burns at the last minute and took sixth on his first rally in a 206, hampered by limited testing; it emerged that he wanted the same changes to the car that Burns had requested... In a dreadful week for Peugeot, Harri Rovanperä retired from fifth when his clutch failed in the final leg, while a broken output shaft eliminated Gilles Panizzi's Bozian-run, works specification car... Jari-Matti Latvala steadily gained confidence to finish tenth in his M-Sport Focus... Mikko Hirvonen was one of the first retirements, rolling his Focus in Brechfa... Didier Auriol lost three minutes down a bank in the second leg, reducing the Skoda driver to 11th place... Toni Gardemeister survived any amount of transmission trouble, only to crash his works Fabia in the last leg... Daniel Carlsson rounded off his Junior Championship career with a rousing victory for Suzuki, fending off a prolonged assault from Kris Meeke... The Ulsterman's rally ended when he rolled the Team Palmer Corsa on the penultimate stage; he had been neck and neck with Carlsson until the throttle body gave trouble on SS15... Brice Tirabassi became Junior Champion despite retiring in the second leg when his Clio blew its engine... Salvador Canellas was beset by gearbox trouble in his Ignis, returning to Cardiff fourth of the five Junior finishers... MG decided against entering a Super 1600 ZR with its fragile gearbox, Gwyndaf Evans mopping up the two-litre class in the Group N version instead, beating Canellas to boot... The original Mini's World Championship career ended gallantly, Neil Burgess/Jim Holder coaxing their injected Cooper home, despite alternator trouble; they were 39th and last...

PREVIOUS WINNERS SINCE 1971

1971 Stig Blomqvist/Arne Hertz	Saab 96 V4	
1972 Roger Clark/Tony Mason	Ford Escort RS1600	
1973 Timo Mäkinen/Henry Liddon	Ford Escort RS1600	
1974 Timo Mäkinen/Henry Liddon	Ford Escort RS1600	
1975 Timo Mäkinen/Henry Liddon	Ford Escort RS1800	
1976 Roger Clark/Stuart Pegg	Ford Escort RS1800	
1977 Björn Waldegård/Hans Thorszelius	Ford Escort RS	
1978 Hannu Mikkola/Arne Hertz	Ford Escort RS	
1979 Hannu Mikkola/Arne Hertz	Ford Escort RS	
1980 Henri Toivonen/Paul White	Talbot Sunbeam Lotus	
1981 Hannu Mikkola/Arne Hertz	Audi Quattro A1	
1982 Hannu Mikkola/Arne Hertz	Audi Quattro A1	
1983 Stig Blomqvist/Björn Cederberg	Audi Quattro A2	
1984 Ari Vatanen/Terry Harryman	Peugeot 205 Turbo 16	
1985 Henri Toivonen/Neil Wilson	Lancia Delta S4	
1986 Timo Salonen/Seppo Harjanne	Peugeot 205 Turbo 16	
1987 Juha Kankkunen/Juha Piironen	Lancia Delta HF 4x4	
1988 Markku Alén/Ilkka Kivimäki	Lancia Delta HF Integrale	
1989 Pentti Airikkala/Ronan McNamee	Mitsubishi Galant VR-4	
1990 Carlos Sainz/Luis Moya	Toyota Celica GT4	
1991 Juha Kankkunen/Juha Piironen	Lancia Delta HF Integrale	
1992 Carlos Sainz/Luis Moya	Toyota Celica Turbo 4WD	
1993 Juha Kankkunen/Juha Piironen	Toyota Celica Turbo 4WD	
1994 Colin McRae/Derek Ringer	Subaru Impreza 555	
1995 Colin McRae/Derek Ringer	Subaru Impreza 555	
1996 Armin Schwarz/Denis Giraudet	Toyota Celica GT-Four	
1997 Colin McRae/Nicky Grist	Subaru Impreza WRC97	
1998 Richard Burns/Robert Reid	Mitsubishi Carisma GT	
1999 Richard Burns/Robert Reid	Subaru Impreza WRC99	
2000 Richard Burns/Robert Reid	Subaru Impreza WRC2000	
2001 Marcus Grönholm/Timo Rautiainen	Peugeot 206 WRC	
2002 Petter Solberg/Phil Mills	Subaru Impreza WRC2002	

STAGE NUMBERS	1	2	3	4	5	6	7	8	9	10	11	12	13	14	15	16	17	18
Solberg	1	2	2	1	1	1	1	1	1	1	1	1	1	1	1	1	1	1
Loeb	6	1	1	2	2	2	2	2	2	2	2	2	2	2	2	2	2	2
Mäkinen	3	6	4	3	3	3	3	3	3	3	3	3	3	3	3	3	3	3
McRae	8	7	5	4	4	4	4	4	4	4	4	4	4	4	4	4	4	4
Duval	12	8	6	7	7	7	7	6	6	6	6	6	6	6	5	5	5	5
Loix	6	12	10	10	9	9	9	8	8	7	7	7	7	7	6	6	6	6
Stohl	15	15	12	9	10	10	10	9	9	8	8	8	9	8	7	7	7	7
Kresta	17	11	9	8	8	8	7	7	8	9	9	9	8	9	8	8	8	8
Pykälisto	14	13	15	12	11	11	11	10	10	10	11	11	10	10	10	9	9	9
Latvala	19	20	16	13	13	13	12	12	12	12	12	11	11	12	11	11	11	10
Auriol	15	17	14	14	14	14	14	15	15	14	14	14	12	12	11	11	11	11
G'meister	18	16	11	16	15	19	18	19	18	18	18	18	16	15	15	R		
Rovanperä	9	10	8	6	6	5	5	5	5	5	5	5	5	5	5	R		
Solá	13	18	13	11	12	12	12	11	11	10	10	11	R					
Panizzi	9	9	7	5	5	5	6	6	R									
Märtin	2	3	3	R														
Grönholm	3	4	R															
Sainz	5	5	R															
Hirvonen	9	14	R															

WORLD RALLY CHAMPIONSHIP FOR DRIVERS

ROUND		1	2	3	4	5	6	7	8	9	10	11	12	13	14	TOTAL
1	PETTER SOLBERG	R	3	R	6	4	6	10	1	8	10	R	10	4	10	72
2	SEBASTIEN LOEB	10	2	R	5	R	R	6	10	4	8	10	0	8	8	71
3	CARLOS SAINZ	6	0	10	0	8	8	4	3	5	4	5	8	2	R	63
4	RICHARD BURNS	4	6	8	8	6	5	R	6	6	6	2	1	R	-	58
5	MARKKO MÄRTIN	5	5	3	R	R	10	R	4	10	EX	6	R	6	R	49
6	MARCUS GRÖNHOLM	0	10	0	10	10	R	R	8	R	R	R	5	3	R	46
7	COLIN MCRAE	8	4	5	R	R	1	5	5	R	5	3	4	0	5	45
8=	FRANÇOIS DUVAL	2	R	6	0	1	R	R	2	R	0	4	6	5	4	30
8=	TOMMI MÄKINEN	R	8	1	2	R	4	R	R	3	3	0	2	1	6	30
10	GILLES PANIZZI	R	-	4	-	-	2	R	0	-	-	8	3	10	R	27
11	HARRI ROVANPERÄ	-	R	R	R	5	3	8	-	R	2	-	-	-	R	18
12	TONI GARDEMEISTER	R	1	2	4	2	R	R	R	R	0	R	0	0	R	9
13=	DIDIER AURIOL	0	0	R	1	3	0	R	R	R	0	0	R	R	0	4
13=	FREDDY LOIX	R	0	0	R	R	R	R	0	0	1	-	-	3		4
15=	MIKKO HIRVONEN	R	0	R	0	0	R	3	0	R	0	R	0	0	R	3
15=	ALISTER MCRAE	-	-	3	-	-	-	-	-	-	-	-	-	-	-	3
15=	CEDRIC ROBERT	3	-	-	-	-	-	0	-	-	-	0	0	-		3
15=	ARMIN SCHWARZ	1	0	R	R	R	R	2	0	0	0	-	-	-	-	3
19=	MANFRED STOHL	-	-	-	R	-	0	-	0	-	-	-	R	-	2	2
19=	JANNE TUOHINO	-	0	-	-	-	-	2	-	-	-	-	-	-	-	2
21=	PHILIPPE BUGALSKI	-	-	-	-	-	-	-	-	-	-	1	0	0		1
21=	ROMAN KRESTA	0	0	-	-	-	R	-	R	-	-	0	-	0	1	1
21=	ALISTAIR GINLEY	-	-	0	-	-	0	1	-	0	-	-	R	0	R	1
21=	SEBASTIAN LINDHOLM	-	-	-	-	-	-	1	-	-	-	-	-	-	-	1

WORLD RALLY CHAMPIONSHIP FOR MANUFACTURERS

ROUND		1	2	3	4	5	6	7	8	9	10	11	12	13	14	TOTAL
1	CITROEN	18	6	15	5	8	10	11	15	9	13	15	12	10	13	160
2	PEUGEOT	6	16	9	18	16	8	8	14	6	9	11	8	13	3	145
3	SUBARU	0	11	2	9	5	10	10	2	11	14	2	12	5	16	109
4	FORD	10	5	10	1	3	10	4	7	10	1	10	7	11	4	93
5	SKODA	2	1	3	6	7	1	0	0	0	0	1	0	0	2	23
6	HYUNDAI	3	0	0	0	0	0	3	1	3	2	-	-	-	-	12

KEY TO ROUNDS 1-MONTE CARLO; 2-SWEDEN; 3-TURKEY; 4-NEW ZEALAND; 5-ARGENTINA; 6-ACROPOLIS; 7-CYPRUS; 8-DEUTSCHLAND; 9-FINLAND; 10-AUSTRALIA; 11-SANREMO; 12-CORSICA; 13-CATALONIA; 14-GREAT BRITAIN

JUNIOR WORLD CHAMPIONSHIP

ROUND		1	2	3	4	5	6	7	TOTAL
1	BRICE TIRABASSI	10	R	10	8	R	10	R	38
2	SALVADOR CANELLAS	R	8	5	4	8	6	5	36
3	DANIEL CARLSSON	R	R	8	10	R	5	10	33
4=	URMO AAVA	5	R	6	5	R	4	R	20
4=	MIRCO BALDACCI	2	R	R	10	R	R	8	20
6	VILLE-PERTTI TEURONEN	R	R	5	R	5	3	R	19
7	GUY WILKS	R	6	3	6	3	0	R	18
8	ALESSANDRO BROCCOLI	6	R	R	3	R	R	4	13
9=	KOSTI KATAJAMÄKI	EX	10	R	R	R	R	R	10
9=	MARCOS LIGATO	8	R	R	2	R	-	-	10

KEY TO ROUNDS 1-MONTE CARLO; 2-TURKEY; 3-ACROPOLIS; 4-FINLAND; 5-SANREMO; 6-CATALONIA; 7-GREAT BRITAIN

PRODUCTION CAR DRIVERS

ROUND		1	2	3	4	5	6	7	TOTAL
1	MARTIN ROWE	6	5	-	8	8	10	6	43
2	TOSHIHIRO ARAI	R	10	10	10	-	R	8	38
3=	KARAMJIT SINGH	8	3	6	R	5	8	-	30
3=	STIG BLOMQVIST	10	1	-	6	4	5	4	30
5	DANIEL SOLA	-	0	8	R	10	4	R	22
6	NIALL MCSHEA	-	2	R	R	R	6	10	18

KEY TO ROUNDS 1-SWEDEN; 2-NEW ZEALAND; 3-ARGENTINA; 4-CYPRUS; 5-DEUTSCHLAND; 6-AUSTRALIA; 7-CORSICA

LOSER TAKES ALL

REVIEW Junior World Championship By David Williams

There is a lobby within Super 1600 circles for the introduction of a manufacturers' award within the Junior World Championship. The theory is that it will give the car makers an added incentive and it will lessen the hypocrisy thrust upon the series at the outset: the pretence that even the leading competitors are 'privateers' can be done away with and Suzuki, for example, could paint out the words 'Customer Support Unit' – a risible sop to the regulations – on the side of one of its bigger lorries.

Hypocrisy is to be deplored and it's questionable whether the privateers' pretence does anything to reduce costs, far less help genuine privateers, but to argue for a manufacturers' championship is to miss the point. Recent history suggests that it's hardly worth having a drivers' championship. There's no harm in awarding points and giving a prize to the driver with the most at the end of the season – no more so than there is in all championships, with their joyless emphasis on consistency, at least – but in the Junior series, the list of winners and losers is utterly at variance with the points table.

The results portray Brice Tirabassi, Salvador Canellas, Daniel Carlsson, Urmo Aava and Mirco Baldacci as the most successful drivers in 2003. By the designated FIA measure, this was certainly the case, but there can be no doubt either that the true winner was Suzuki's Swede, Carlsson.

A year ago, Suzuki's chances of winning a Junior Championship round with the ungainly Ignis, far less the championship itself, looked about the same as a camel's of winning the Grand National. The car was too narrow and too tall, condemned by maladroit homologation in the first place. By the time Carlsson romped to a convincing class victory on the Rally GB, it was tempting to blame his impetuousness for his failure to carry off the trophy. The loquacious Swede is a maddening talent: he put the opposition to the sword on the first leg of the Monte, only to be detained by French police for his driving on a road section – a sobering thought in itself – until he had exceeded his maximum lateness. In Turkey, he looked on course to make amends until he got a puncture, then destroyed the front suspension in a red-mist charge to regain second. At Sanremo, when Tirabassi had run into brake trouble and a wall in quick succession, Carlsson threw away a sure second and

the championship lead with an accident.

There were technical improvements, of course, including new shock absorbers and a healthy dose of negative camber at the rear to enhance stability on fast, loose-surface rallies, but Monster Sport Europe staff were adamant that the transformation was in the driver line-up and above all, in hiring Carlsson; no other Ignis driver seemed a likely winner in 2003. After taking an obedient second place on the Acropolis, he scored a resounding success in Finland, despite stopping to change a puncture on a stage, then rounded off his Junior career triumphantly in Britain. By then, he had long since signed a contract to drive a works-backed 206 in 2004.

In a Puma in 2002, Carlsson could have been forgiven for wondering what had possessed him to walk away from his Corolla WRC. By the time he left Wales, he had no regrets.

'It's really difficult as a driver to learn you don't have to win every stage. It's been unbelievable good experience, these two years in Junior,' he promised, echoing another larger-than-life Scandinavian, Petter Solberg.

The points table demotes Guy Wilks to seventh, with 19 points to Tirabassi's 38. In practice, the Darlington driver illustrated the danger of placing blind faith in statistics, for although he didn't distinguish himself on the autumn asphalt rallies, he was the find of the season. At the start of the year, he had little international experience and no international standing. While Carlsson had been making waves in a Corolla, Wilks had been driving a Ka. In 2002, he was generally flattened by Gwyndaf Evans in Britain – and no one supposed the low-budget ZR was a true match for a Puma.

Chris Birkbeck's men have patiently refined Ford's coupe into a far more manageable beast, but the fact is that it's a comparatively old design, struggling for performance and none too durable either. Nevertheless, Wilks would have been in the points on his first attempt at the Monte if it hadn't been for sheared wheel studs, took a gritty third in Turkey, losing second near the end thanks to gearbox trouble, then finished a brilliant third on his first visit to Finland. In four rallies, he had displayed the speed and resolve to convince an international audience; he's less accident-prone than some of his rivals and has the priceless

ability to make accurate pace notes too. Works support beckons: at 23, there's no danger of his joining the twilight ranks of drivers once thought to have had potential.

Like Wilks, Tirabassi had a car problem, albeit of a very different kind. The Frenchman is four years older than Ford's front runner, but didn't have much international experience at the beginning of the year either. He displayed admirable nerve and stamina in winning the Acropolis with a boiling engine that forced him to drive with the heater on in 30-degree heat, while an excellent second place on his first visit to Finland confirmed his preference for dirt. His problem was that he drove a Clio. Simon Jean-Joseph's array of class wins in 2002 had suggested that the Renault was the ticket to success and while Tirabassi collected maximum points three times on his way to the title, it was impossible to erase the nagging suspicion that the Oreca-prepared car was making him look better than he was. The Renaults were curiously off the pace in Britain, even before Tirabassi's engine blew up, but on most rallies, they were in a different league, stunningly superior, in fact, given the restrictive nature of Super 1600 regulations.

Certainly, Tirabassi wasn't stretched on his way to maximum points on the Monte and in Catalonia – not once the *Gendarmerie* had done for Carlsson on the former, anyway – and his French Championship results, against Jean-Joseph and factory 206s, may be a better gauge of his abilities. He is taking the risky course of returning to the Junior series in 2004. There is no reason to suppose that he isn't good enough to win it again, but the fact that Carlsson has the WR Car drive indicates that in Tirabassi's case, reservations linger.

A 21st-century Polo is as big as the original Golf and the news that Karl-Heinz Goldstein, the engineer behind some of the most successful 1980s Opels and Toyotas, was responsible for the design suggested that it was poised to emulate the feats of a succession of Golf rally cars. Instead Kosti Katajamäki and the Swede, Oscar Svedlund, found themselves in the worst predicament of all. Far from having the promised works support, once the Danish former racing driver, Kris Nissen, took charge of VW Racing, they had no support whatsoever. Katajamäki ought to have been second on the Monte, only for a homologation over-sight to lead to his exclusion for using undersized rear brakes. Having rebounded to take victory in Turkey, he failed to finish another rally all season. Development ceased, reliability dwindled. At least Volkswagen made no attempt to dishonour a contract in his case, as it did at Sanremo to Svedlund; the stewards decided that under the circumstances, no penalty for missing the rally should be imposed. But Katajamäki had done enough to win support from Marcus Grönholm and to attract the interest of Suzuki.

Three Ignis drivers in the top four underlined the worth of factory backing, but it isn't necessarily vital and from a Junior perspective, Kris Meeke's eight points trumped Urmo Aava's 20 and Ville-Pertti Teuronen's 18. Their performances were generally workmanlike, whereas Meeke's were often exasperating, but he was never mediocre. While he scored points only once, taking second in Catalonia, he was on course for second in Italy and gave Carlsson a run for his money for much of the distance in Britain. However, both rallies ended with the Corsa off the road.

A good deal of the credit for Meeke's gathering speed should go to Team Palmer. In the absence of any support from the Opel Performance Centre, the British team did a fine job of refining the Corsa, along much the same principles that Birkbeck brought to the Puma: Swindon developed a more flexible engine, while suspension and differential settings were modified to make the car easier to drive. The Corsa is a newer design than the Puma and some reckon that it's the pick of the Super 1600 bunch; no wonder Meeke wondered if it might not be better to stick to a known quantity for 2004. It would be fair to say in this context that the Ulsterman's confidence burgeoned too, as his results in Britain against Evans and the works MG proved. Nevertheless, he admitted that he was still foxed occasionally abroad, finding it difficult to make accurate pace notes for the wider stages in Catalonia when lorry drivers going about their business obscured the best line; the admission would have brought a wry smile to the faces of Carlos Sainz or his manager, through S-Mac, Colin McRae.

Meeke was some distance behind Baldacci at Sanremo, when the latter scored a crushing victory for Fiat, but the San Marino driver is no mere Tarmac expert, for although he didn't harry Carlsson, he finished a strong second in Wales. He scored more than twice as many points as Meeke, but he had something of an international reputation before. In a season blighted somewhat by mechanical problems, he took one pace forward to Meeke's three.

Spare a thought for the runner-up. Canellas gave Suzuki sterling service. He was in his element on tar, naturally, and had Baldacci retired and Suzuki chosen to shuffle the pack in Wales, he might just have deprived Tirabassi of the crown. Instead, after a rally dogged by gearbox problems, he ended up two points short. He is too old to return in 2004 and risks becoming a footnote in some future history of Suzuki in rallying. The age limit introduced for 2003 has increased the element of unpredictability, because the drivers tend to be even less experienced and consequently more prone to error, but it hasn't altered the brutal application of natural selection that has applied to the series from the start.

Reliability has improved markedly as the formula has found its feet and it's worth noting in this context that punctures played far less of a part in deciding rallies than they did in previous years. Michelin deserves

Daniel Carlsson was an irresistible force. Fortunately for Brice Tirabassi, he had an occasional tendency to meet with immovable objects. Salvador Canellas was Suzuki's linchpin, while Mirco Baldacci was the pick of the Fiat drivers (anti-clockwise from top left).

much of the credit, but Catalan road engineers should be mentioned in dispatches too: many of the most vicious, wheel-wrecking road edges had been bevelled since 2002.

It would be good to think that the Corsa will remain competitive, but the signs are that the Junior series is moving into a new phase and that older machinery will soon be as outgunned as an Impreza WRC99 is against a 2003 version. Renault has flung down the gauntlet with an exemplary machine designed on Mégane principles. It has close to 200mm of suspension travel all round, which is not only well in excess of a Puma's, but more than an Accent World Rally Car's. In response, Suzuki is switching to the five-door Ignis chiefly because homologation restrictions have all but exhausted the potential of the three-door, while Ford has laboured diligently on the Fiesta and Citroën is taking the C2 so seriously that Ford claimed that the French maker sent a spy to an autumn Fiesta test in France.

The idea that a Puma or a Saxo – a curiously, utterly neglected car in 2003, considering that it had been beaten only twice in the previous two years – will stand any chance is difficult to credit. In the meantime, costs are set to rise in tandem and the championship co-ordinator, Nini Russo, is suggesting that the notional 100,000 price cap should be raised to 150,000. It's a realistic assessment of current practice, but there is a danger that it would merely

hike costs further instead of stamping out the nefarious habit of providing 'optional extras' to favoured customers. The FIA is making some effort to extend its cost clampdown into the Super 1600 class, forcing Renault to use up four of its 'jokers' to change the Clio's dampers, while Suzuki is relying on a mixture of Ohlins and KYB units for the same reason.

The 100,000 limit was an admirable goal and even though the Junior series looks in better health than the main attraction at present, the price ceiling in a driver development formula should not be discarded lightly.

Photographs by Ross Hyde

In last year's review of the Asia-Pacific Rally Championship it was suggested that the future of the series lay in attracting those at the top of the sport in their own countries who wanted a new challenge, yet were never likely to join a factory World Championship team. For 2003, Armin Kremer, Geof Argyle and Fumio Nutahara, all past national or international championship winners, answered the call. Between them, this diverse trio managed to keep the defending champion, Karamjit Singh, on his mettle as the series headed for a dramatic four-way crescendo in India. That the 2003 Asia-Pacific Championship was so hotly fought was a remarkable achievement, given what was happening on the world stage before the series commenced.

Months of sabre-rattling were followed by the US-led invasion of Iraq in late March. A few days earlier, international travellers had started donning surgical masks en masse when the World Health Organisation released a global alert on the SARS virus, which originated in southern China.

The timing, just a month before the opening rally in Australia, could hardly have been worse for those keen to build on the positive momentum of 2002 and attract a truly international field to the Asia-Pacific region. When the New Caledonia round, scheduled for June, withdrew from the calendar for financial reasons around the same time, the championship looked set for a serious tumble.

That it held its own was due in part to the new structure, which extended the contest to seven rounds, without a rally in Asia until September. The presence of that extra event (the season finale in India) provided sufficient padding to cope with the exit of New Caledonia and the subsequent cancellation of the China Rally. Further, the late start of the Asian leg meant that teams did not face travel to the more exotic locations until fears about SARS had subsided.

In the circumstances, the presence of 11 Asia-Pacific Championship-registered drivers in Canberra represented a better start than could reasonably have been hoped for, even though it was four down on the 2002 total. Indeed, the longest shadow hanging over Canberra was caused not by world events, nor even the bush fires that reduced to a barren wasteland many of the forests through which the rally ran. Rather, it came with the absence of the multiple Asia-Pacific and Australian Champion, 'Possum' Bourne. The New Zealander had sustained terrible head injuries in a freak accident the week before and died soon after the rally.

Karamjit was also a late withdrawal from Canberra, for more prosaic reasons: the sponsorship he required to run in both the World and the Asia-Pacific Champion-ships simply wasn't available. In his absence the 2002 Asia-Pacific Group N Champion, Nico Caldarola, headed the field in his Top Run Lancer Evo VII.

Particular attention surrounded the Indian MRF Team, which ditched the services of New Zealand's Stu Warren and its local Indian drivers in favour of two paying Europeans, the former European Champion, Kremer, and the Austrian, David Doppelreiter. The team once again ran Group N Lancer Evo VIIs fitted with its own MRF tyres.

Despite the absence of Bourne and Warren, New Zealanders were out in force, the twice national champion, Argyle, committing himself to an Asia-Pacific campaign for the first time. He joined a trio who had contested the series in 2003. Two of them – the young gun, Andrew Hawkeswood, and the old hand, Brian Green – were also running under the Argyle Motorsport banner in Group A Lancers. The third, Reece Jones (another former double national champion), entered his own Group N Lancer.

The presence of another former national champion, Nutahara, gave the Japanese Asia-Pacific contingent the greatest credibility it had enjoyed since Katsuhiko Taguchi took the crown in 1999. Nutahara, driving a Group N Lancer, was joined by another Mitsubishi driver, Atsushi Masumura, and the championship regular, Haruo Takakuwa, at the wheel of an Impreza. The array was completed by the rising Australian star, Chris Atkinson, taking Nobuhiro 'Monster' Tajima's place in the Suzuki Sport Ignis as the sole two-wheel-drive entry for 2003.

Fittingly in the circumstances, and after a good scrap with the Australian series import, Juha Kangas, outright victory in Canberra went to Bourne's protegé and erstwhile Subaru Australia team-mate,

NEW BLOOD KEEPS SERIES ALIVE

REVIEW Asia-Pacific Rallying Championship

By David Thomson

Roads such as these draw adventurous Europeans – Norberto Cangani in this case – to the Far East (left). Karamjit Singh (centre) remains the man to beat in his Group A Proton, but found that Fumio Nutahara took some beating when both drove Group N cars.

Cody Crocker. The local drivers, Scott Pedder, Dean Herridge and Ed Ordynski filled the next three places, leaving Kremer to claim the top Asia-Pacific Championship spot and fifth place after a see-saw battle with Argyle and Nutahara. It was a sign of things to come.

The German was forced to work hard for his first-up Asia-Pacific Championship success, snatching the win from Argyle by just three-tenths of a second on the final stage. Nursing an ailing car, Argyle was also hard pressed to keep Nutahara at bay, but managed to do so by a matter of seconds.

Atkinson was the next of the Asia-Pacific Championship contingent, in an excellent tenth overall in the Super 1600 machine. Green, Doppelreiter, Masumura and Takakuwa also managed to make the finish and claim points. Caldarola headed the list of those out of luck: his rally ended on leg one when his Lancer's motor died on a road section. Engine problems also accounted for Jones and Hawkeswood, both during leg two.

Round two of the series, the Rotorua International Rally, marked Karamjit's return to the fray. He had secured a last-minute injection of funds from the Malaysian Ministry of Sport and arranged the loan of an Evo VI (hurriedly fitted with Proton badges) from Reece Jones.

However, no one had beaten Bruce Herbert on the Rotorua event since 1997, and the multiple Kiwi champion wasn't about to let that change in his swansong year in the sport. Argyle, who like Herbert was also gunning for New

Zealand Championship honours, did his best to stop his Subaru-mounted rival's winning run. He grabbed the lead on leg one and extended it at the start of leg two, only to see his hopes go up in smoke when the turbo blew. From that moment, the rally belonged to Herbert for another year.

The battle for runner-up honours and Asia-Pacific supremacy raged between Singh and Nutahara, with Caldarola and Hawkeswood initially in hot pursuit. Amazingly, the Malaysian and the Japanese finished the event in a dead heat, although the tiebreak awarded second place overall and maximum Asia-Pacific points to the latter by virtue of his fastest time on SS1. Hawkeswood held on to claim fourth overall, but Caldarola slipped to eighth and fifth in the Asia-Pacific Championship pack, behind the first-time visitor Kremer, whose car had struggled for grip on the smooth but slippery New Zealand roads. With Doppelreiter tenth, Green 17th, Masumara 19th and Argyle recovering much lost ground to finish 21st, the completion rate amongst the Asia-Pacific pack was high for the second event in a row.

The two casualties, Jones and Atkinson, both retired with damaged steering after sliding off on the fearsome Motu stage that opened the event. Atkinson would return to fight again, but a frustrated Jones announced his retirement from driving at the end of the day. Nutahara's result, an outstanding achievement on his first visit to the rally, was enough to hand him a five-

point lead from Kremer as he headed for home territory.

Hokkaido attracted unprecedented interest, as its place in the 2004 World Championship was by then all but assured, although the biggest name of all – Sébastien Loeb – came only for the reconnaissance.

The event was held in unseasonably wet and changeable conditions for the second year in a row, and was won handsomely for Subaru by Japan's most accomplished rally driver, Toshihiro Arai. Biding his time while several of the Japanese drivers went hard at the start only to strike trouble, Argyle slid and slithered to runner-up honours, and a

two-point Asia-Pacific lead.

Nutahara slipped to second in the series, having led for the first three stages, only to retire later after a heavy landing. It left him one point clear of Kremer, who was third of the Asia-Pacific contenders in Hokkaido. Singh was forced to rejoin to rack up three precious bonus points, after retiring with gearbox problems before completing the first stage.

Although outdone by his team-mate, Daniel Carlsson, in the overall results, the Swede finishing a sensational fifth, Atkinson brought his Ignis home strongly in tenth. Hawkeswood could count himself unlucky, having set several top three stage times between an early engine cut-out and later turbocharger problems. Caldarola bade farewell to the Group N title and the 2003 Asia-Pacific Championship after crashing in the first leg.

China should have been next, but in late August the organisers announced the rally's cancellation, apparently after the local government withdrew its support for the event in the wake of the SARS epidemic. Attention therefore turned to Thailand. Held once again in the province of Ryong, it was the first event on which an Asia-Pacific-registered driver took outright victory. That driver was Singh, who, with the Production World Championship season over, re-appeared with his Group A Proton and emerged with the win he needed to stay in contention for a third successive Asia-Pacific crown.

While the Malaysian's eventual winning margin was comfortable enough, he faced a tough scrap with Argyle and Hawkeswood over the opening stages. Argyle led at the end of leg one, but his run was hindered by meeting non-competing vehicles on a couple of stages and his challenge faltered further with boost problems. Hawkeswood, who had gained the lead with some impressive stage wins, was sidelined with a blown motor a couple of stages later.

While Singh focused on consolidating his lead and scoring maximum bonus points for the leg, Argyle dropped into the clutches of Kremer, whose team

MRF's Lancer squad demonstrated India's growing industrial power, with European drivers such as Armin Kremer hired to make the most of its latest tyres. Suzuki's hunt for emerging talent is worldwide, the Australian Chris Atkinson showing genuine promise in his Ignis.

was making full use of a new MRF tyre with improved sidewalls. The New Zealander had the edge until he locked up and slid wide on the final stage, handing the German second place by three seconds. Thailand was also notable for the appearance of four of China's top rally drivers, headed by the Hong Kong-based Chan Chi Wah. Hua Qing Xian was the best of them at the end, finishing 13th in a Lancer Evo V. The result set the scene for a dramatic Indian showdown in Pune.

In 2004, New Caledonia is expected to slot in between Australia and New Zealand to complete the Pacific leg of the series, and China will retain its October slot as round five. Hokkaido is likely to gain dispensation to remain in the series despite its World Championship status.

Until late in the year it seemed that Group A would continue to be sanctioned in a limited form, but the decision was taken to restrict the championship to Group N and Super 1600 at the same time as the 2004 calendar was released. The change should level

out the playing field for the 2004 championship. That said, the current Group A cars in the series are older Evo VI or 6.5-based machines, prepared well short of the limit of the Group A regulations, so the performance gap to fully developed Lancer Evo VII or Evo VIII Group N opposition is not that great. This was demonstrated by the results of the first four rounds of the 2003 series, in which Group N cars took Asia-Pacific honours on two rounds and won two outright.

Faced with a regulation change that demands new Group N cars in 2004, drivers such as Argyle will have to deal with escalating costs, at least in the short term. In building a car to Group A specification he might, for example, sidestep the expensive luxury of a dog gearbox. It can also be argued that the greater freedom of Group A rules allow teams to build stronger cars that require less maintenance during the season, although the reliability record of such machinery in 2003 didn't support this.

Ultimately, the decision must be seen as inevitable, made sooner rather than later in accord with changing times: Group A has steadily lost its international relevance since being replaced by the World Rally Car class at the top of the sport and its demise as a regional championship formula from 2004 was signalled by the FIA last year. It has already been dropped, or is being phased out, as a national championship category in almost all of the countries that host Asia-Pacific rounds.

A new format of two-day events preceded by two days of reconnaissance is also set to come into force for most rounds and this, combined with the elimination of pre-event shakedowns, will reduce costs by drastically cutting the time spent in each country.

Perhaps if calmer times prevail on the global stage and dissatisfaction over the radical changes to the World Championship remains high, the Asia-Pacific Championship will yet prosper in 2004. In the meantime though, mere survival through a turbulent 2003 must count as quite an achievement.

Play word association with 'European Rally Championship', and the chances are that 'heroic,' 'engrossing' and 'nailbiting' won't immediately spring to mind. Over the years, the title has been a reward for persistence and tenacity, even long service in the case of certain Lancia drivers, but the championship rarely produces a close finish or even much of a contest; one mediocre year is apt to merge into another. But 2003 joyously defied the trend. It produced drama and controversy, an enthralling finish and a new champion in Bruno Thiry, who beat Miguel Campos on a tiebreak. It was like watching a caterpillar turn into a butterfly.

minute penalty incurred in a dispute with a marshal.

After that, Thiry was on the back foot, under constant pressure not only to finish, but to beat a redoubtable opponent. Peugeot Portugal builds its cars to the highest standards – its Team Manager, Carlos Dos Barros, was Peugeot's chief mechanic in the Group B era – and Campos has an exceptionally safe pair of hands. He finished every event he contested in 2003 and has now completed more than 60 rallies in succession. In contrast, there were occasional weaknesses in the Belgian car, for in addition to the 1000 Miglia setback, Thiry did well to retain second when the clutch began to slip badly just before the end of the Polish Rally.

Campos displayed a fine turn of speed besides, withstanding intense pressure to triumph in Poland and on home ground in Madeira. The winning margin of close to three minutes in Klodzko belied an electrifying duel, in which the Peugeot men were never separated by more than 5.6 seconds in 150 miles of stages until Thiry's clutch wilted; in Madeira, just 4.8 seconds divided the two.

But Campos was under pressure too. Money was tight, and Peugeot Portugal and Total were more interested in results at home. He therefore missed Bulgaria and the Tofas, and while he retained his championship lead, the 400 unchallenged points kept Thiry in the championship race.

Yet while the Portuguese invariably finished, he wasn't infallible under pressure. He clawed his way back to third after skidding off at Ieper and another excursion cost him victory on the Barum, handing the Czech event to Vaclav Pech, whom he beat by ten minutes a month later at Antibes.

By then, experience and determination had begun to tell. While unseasonably early snow led to cancelled stages at Antibes and prevented Campos from launching a last-gasp bid for glory, Thiry made full use of his greater knowledge of the Alpes-Maritimes and an effective testing programme to outpoint his rival. He was under intense pressure himself: retirement from the Barum thanks to an electronic problem in parc ferme had left no further room for error.

But Thiry had a joker up his sleeve. Second place in Antibes gave Campos an eighth finish, the maximum permitted for points-scoring purposes. Absence and unreliability had left his older adversary with an 80-point deficit, but a result in hand. If Thiry could finish in the top two on home ground, on the Condroz Rally, a co-efficient-10 round of the sprawling European series, he would snatch the championship on a tiebreak, with five wins to Campos's four.

Campos considered entering, hoping against hope that while he couldn't score himself, he might prevent Thiry from adding to his total. But while it was a good entry, there was no one capable of troubling Thiry

Rivalry between Miguel Campos (above left) and Bruno Thiry was good natured, but ferocious. Thiry (below) won the tiebreak. Volkan Isik's sparkling performances in Fiat Turkey's Palio gave a hint of the championship's possible future.

THE BRIDESMAID WINS!

REVIEW European Championship By David Williams

It was perhaps the most hotly fought European Championship since 1988, when Thiry's fellow Belgian, Patrick Snijers, narrowly failed to deprive Fabrizio Tabaton of the crown, and it was some recompense for Thiry, whose works Xsara kit car was outgunned by Henrik Lundgaard's four-wheel-drive Corolla in 2000. Yet the genial Belgian made an unlikely champion and not simply because at the ripe old age of 41, he had never previously won a championship in his life.

When the El Corte Inglés organisers declined to shift their rally's date, it became necessary to use two cars to contest all the highest-scoring co-efficient 20 rounds of the series. Thiry's team, Kronos, decided that this was a luxury that it could not afford and rather than rent a 206, Thiry was obliged to skip the principal Spanish round, presenting Campos with an easy victory and a 200-point head start. When the Kronos car snapped its propshaft as it began the seventh stage of the 1000 Miglia, Campos bagged another 200 points, despite a puncture and a three-

Campos might argue that money told, that thanks to Bastos and Peugeot Belgium, he was outspent rather than outsprinted. He was unlucky too in Greece, when a bizarre accident resulted in the death of a local driver, Dimitris Koliopanos, on the third test. When all the Greek drivers withdrew as a mark of respect, the organisers declared the results final rather than stage the rest of the event for three drivers, Thiry, Campos and Thiry's Russian team-mate, Evgeny Vasin, driving the Itera 206. It was tragic, but absurd, as it transpired that in contrast to most FIA championships, European Championship regulations make no provision for awarding half points if less than half the distance is covered. Campos therefore finished a handful of seconds and 40 points behind Thiry.

other than Freddy Loix, who was his team-mate on this occasion and thus bound to help rather than hinder. Even in Campos's absence, Thiry was acutely conscious that he had to finish, however, and heavy rain made the stages uncomfortably slippery in the final leg. He prudently relinquished the lead to Loix and made sure of second.

It wasn't an anti-climax exactly, but it was certainly an uncomfortable reminder of the European Championship's bad old, co-efficient-playing past. Yet it didn't tarnish Thiry's achievement. When both Peugeots were on song, he took three wins to Campos's two. It was a near-run thing; both men would have made worthy champions, but ultimately Campos had as much reason to regret tiny errors in Belgium and the Czech Republic as his absence from two co-efficient-20 events in early summer. Peugeot's Sports Director, Jean-Pierre Nicolas, has raised the possibility of giving him some support for a World Championship programme in 2004. It was a fair

tribute to the impact he had made.

No one else approached the leading duo, as the points table makes clear. Vasin is perhaps getting a little long in the tooth to make the most of a World Rally Car, but much younger, theoretically promising drivers such as the Czech, Roman Kresta, struggled to match the championship contenders on home ground. It was truly a vintage year for the European Championship.

Dwarfed by the World Championship, the European mirrors it in at least one respect, in that the competitors are at odds with the FIA and in this case, deeply resentful of the ban on WR Cars implemented at the end of 2003.

The WR Car advocates have a case. Teams such as Peugeot Portugal and Kronos are nothing if not professional. Kronos has 20 staff, for instance, and not only works for Toyota in racing, but runs a large Porsche dealership. Both front-running teams had worthwhile sponsorship and made sure that the national press in their countries were given

opportunities to report each rally. They had found a sustainable and attractive level of competition. It's difficult to see the new order, which notionally makes Group N the top category, producing anything to match the speed and excitement of the duel between Campos and Thiry, at least in the short term.

In Poland, Jean-Pierre Mondron, Marc Van Dalen's partner at Kronos, made a persuasive, if doomed plea for leaving well alone.

'The World Championship is out of reach for a private team. I think the value of a European Championship is more than to be first privateer in the World Championship. If you look at the battle here, it's good, it's really nice,' he said.

He emphasised too that the visual resemblance between the WR Cars used at World and European level was misleading.

'We know the differences between the cars, but the man in the main street doesn't see it. It's a big difference, bigger than ever,' he said. Whether he would include the Rallies Commission President,

Shekhar Mehta, among his men in the main street is open to question. His point was that Thiry's car has only one active differential, the centre, that it has a manual gearchange and few of the budget-busting electronics increasingly prevalent on works cars.

It amounted to a call for WRC2, the long-discussed WR Car sub-category that may finally come into force in 2004. WRC2 won't apply to the European series, however, because the FIA's stability rules don't permit such sudden changes of tack. Instead, it will nominally become a championship for Regional Rally Cars, the cheaper four-wheel-drive prototypes with naturally aspirated engines.

As no manufacturer has yet built a Regional Rally Car, the category defaults to Group N, which means that it is entirely feasible that the 2004 European Champion will drive either a Subaru or a Mitsubishi. One can imagine Mondron's distaste. Imprezas and Lancers are quick, robust cars now, but they have the aural appeal of a milkfloat and on Tarmac, they're no visual substitute for a WR Car either.

There's another point of view though. Tomas Czopik has been one of Poland's most successful Group N drivers latterly and scraped together the money for a WR Car in 2003. It was an Impreza WRC99 – a fundamentally sound car, but showing its age. He held third for much of the distance on home soil, but once Vasin hit his stride in the second leg, the Subaru was simply no match for the Russian's Peugeot.

Midway through the leg, Czopik recognised an unequal struggle.

'The last stage I drove the fastest I have this rally. I know that stage, I like that stage and he beat me seven seconds. Today's stages are very fast. This car is enough for Poland, but not for the European Championship,' he said.

Mehta would like to give drivers such as Czopik a leg up and that means bringing the rungs of the ladder closer together. It remains to be seen if Regional Rally Cars achieve that goal, unless, as some works teams already suspect, the long-term plan is that they should replace WR Cars altogether, in which case manufacturers have no choice but to build them.

It is worth noting too that while Thiry and Campos invariably made short work of local opposition, that opposition is increasingly confined to Super 1600 cars, as national authorities recognise that WR Cars have become too expensive. To that extent, winning

A Peugeot remained the car to have at European level, Miguel Campos (far left) usually having little difficulty seeing off Vaclav Pech's Focus. Cheaper cars – a Group N Subaru in this case – ensured that even the likes of Piero Longhi (right) didn't trouble the visitors on the 1000 Miglia. To the well-organised Bulgarian spectator, groups and classes are mere alphabet soup, but all equally tasty.

European Championship Results

became easier.

Doing good by stealth, the FIA is bringing a little order to the overgrown thicket the European Championship had become. It still includes an absurd number of rallies, but championship contenders have to concentrate almost exclusively on the highest-scoring co-efficient-20 events, which means that drivers have a coherent programme, while the lesser rallies are granted the prestige to satisfy the mayor and the tourist board. In other respects, their status merely grants them the distant prospect of climbing the co-efficient pyramid sufficiently to gain true international eminence. Further reductions in the number of co-efficient-20 rallies are on the way and no bad thing either, when the 2003 calendar was so clumsily planned that two cars were needed to contest the series in full and the outcome was settled on a rally on which only one of the title contenders could score.

Despite the upheavals and the discontent, the 2004 series could be thoroughly entertaining. A good Super 1600 car is capable of giving a Group N Japanese turbo a run for its money and in favourable circumstances, it could outpace it on asphalt. Thiry reckons that the two-wheel-drive machine could be a better bet. Even though the FIA has shrunk from imposing Super 1600, the European Championship could become a beguiling example of the law of unintended consequences.

Yet there isn't the least sign of it becoming the next step up the ladder from the Junior World Championship, as Mehta has suggested. To do that, it will need to switch its emphasis from asphalt to dirt, which could well involve turning its back on its strongholds in southern and eastern Europe. Things change, but tectonic plates shift faster than that.

MILLE MIGLIA, 3-5 April, Italy

1	M. Campos/	Peugeot 206 WRC
	C. Magalhaes	3h 35m 49.7s
2	L. Pedersoli/	Peugeot 306 Maxi
	D. Vernuccio	3h 36m 12.1s
3	G. Basso/	Fiat Punto S1600
	F. Guglielmi	3h 38m 20.8s
4	P. Longhi/	Subaru Impreza STi
	L. Baggio	3h 38m 34.4s
5	G. Cunico/	Mitsubishi Lancer E7
	L. Pirollo	3h 39m 14.0s
6	R. Travaglia/	Peugeot 206 XS
	F. Zanella	3h 39m 14.8s
7	A. Aghini/	Peugeot 206 XS
	L. Roggia	3h 39m 28.1s
8	P. Andreucci/	Fiat Punto S1600
	A. Andreussi	3h 40m 46.8s

EL CORTE INGLES RALLY, 11-12 April, Spain

1	M. Campos/	Peugeot 206 WRC
	C. Magalhaes	3h 02m 31.0s
2	M. Fuster/	Citroën Saxo 1600
	J. Medina	3h 08m 35.6s
3	A. Ponce/	Skoda Octavia 2.0
	R. Gonzalez	3h 10m 06.2s
4	S. Vallejo/	Fiat Punto
	C. Larrode	3h 12m 04.1s
5	J-M Ponce/	VW Polo 1600
	C. Larrode	3h 12m 54.1s
6	D. Garcia/	Citroën Saxo 1600
	Y. Mujica	3h 12m 55.6s
6	S. Concepcion/	Mitsubishi Lancer E6
	V. Del Rosario	3h 15m 12.9s
6	V. Delgado/	Mitsubishi Carisma E6
	J. Perez	3h 16m 25.2s

TOFAS RALLY, 16-18 May, Turkey

1	B. Thiry/	Peugeot 206 WRC
	J-M Fortin	3h 02m 28.7s
2	S. Yazici/	Ford Focus WRC
	C. Okan	3h 09m 49.5s
3	P. Andreucci/	Fiat Palio S1600
	A. Andreussi	3h 13m 57.3s
4	E. Kazaz/	Citroën Saxo S1600
	M. Gür	3h 14m 57.0s
5	V. Isik/	Fiat Palio S1600
	E. Güleren	3h 16m 38.5s
6	E. Genim/	Renault Mégane
	A. Atilgan	3h 19m 53.8s
6	C. Gülerhan/	Mitsubishi Lancer E7
	A. Dinçer	3h 20m 51.8s
6	M. Akdelik/	Subaru Impreza WRX
	U. Ulocak	3h 21m 04.5s

POLISH RALLY, 29-31 May, Poland

1	Miguel Campos/	Peugeot 206 WRC
	Carlos Magalhaes	2h 24m 18.9s

2	B. Thiry/	Peugeot 206 WRC
	J-M Fortin	2h 26m 59.8s
3	E. Vasin/	Peugeot 206 WRC
	A. Shchukin	2h 31m 12.1s
4	T. Czopik/	Subaru Impreza WRC99
	L. Wronski	2h 32m 03.7s
5	S. Frycz/	Mitsubishi Lancer E5
	J. Gieras	2h 35m 11.7s
6	M. Bebenek/	Mitsubishi Lancer E5
	G. Bebenek	2h 35m 42.2s
7	M. Lubiak/	Mitsubishi Lancer E5
	Wislawski	2h 38m 13.9s
8	D. Jurczak/	Fiat Punto S1600
	R. Ciupka	2h 39m 52.7s

RALLY BULGARIA, 13-15 June, Bulgaria

1	B. Thiry/	Peugeot 206 WRC
	J-M Fortin	2h 46m 21.5s
2	J. Popov/	Skoda Octavia WRC
	D. Popov	2h 52m 23.8s
3	K. Donchev/	Peugeot 306 Maxi
	R. Manolov	2h 57m 15.5s
4	I. Tzarski/	Ford Escort WRC
	L. Tevekelov	2h 58m 02.7s
5	R. Kozlekov/	Mitsubishi Lancer E7
	P. Sivov	2h 58m 23.9s
6	V. Isik/	Fiat Punto S1600
	E. Güleren	2h 58m 56.1s
7	G. Geradziev/	Mitsubishi Lancer E6
	N. Popov	2h 59m 13.3s
5	I. Marinov/	Mitsubishi Lancer E6
	S. Cholakov	2h 59m 22.5s

IEPER-WESTHOEK RALLY, 27-29 June, Belgium

1	B. Thiry/	Peugeot 206 WRC
	J-M Fortin	2h 51m 21.3s
2	P. Tsjoen/	Toyota Corolla WRC
	E. Chevaillier	2h 53m 00.0s
3	M. Campos/	Peugeot 206 WRC
	C. Magalhaes	2h 59m 30.1s
4	B. Munster/	Subaru Impreza 555
	Y. Haghedooren	3h 03m 41.0s
5	L. Cols/	Fiat Punto S1600
	F. Godde	3h 05m 35.1s
6	J. de Winkel/	VW Golf Mk4 2.0
	R. Van Hoek	3h 06m 13.4s
7	B. Colsoul/	Mitsubishi Lancer E7
	T. Colsoul	3h 07m 05.3s
8	X. Bouche/	Mitsubishi Lancer E7
	C. Pirotte	3h 07m 59.9s

MADEIRA RALLY, 1-2 August, Portugal

1	M. Campos/	Peugeot 206 WRC
	C. Magalhaes	3h 00m 42.9s
2	B. Thiry/	Peugeot 206 WRC
	J-M Fortin	3h 00m 47.7s
3	F. Delecour/	Peugeot 206 WRC
	A-C Pauwels	3h 04m 40.9s

4	V. Sá/	Peugeot 306 Maxi
	O. Camacho	3h 07m 57.0s
5	A. Campos/	Peugeot 306 Maxi
	J. Camacho	3h 08m 41.6s
6	J. Camacho/	Peugeot 306 Maxi
	M. Cabral	3h 12m 27.7s
7	P. Gomes/	VW Golf Mk 4 2.0
	N. Rodrigues	3h 13m 07.0s
8	F. Freitas/	Opel Astra 2.0
	D. Figueiros	3h 15m 20.2s

BARUM RALLY, 12-14 September, Czech Republic

1	V. Pech/	Ford Focus WRC
	P. Uhel	2h 34m 57.0s
2	M. Campos/	Peugeot 206 WRC
	C. Magalhaes	2h 36m 08.4s
3	J. Kopecky/	Skoda Octavia WRC
	F. Schovánek	2h 36m 50.1s
4	T. Cserhalmi/	Ford Focus WRC
	J. Palivec	2h 39m 25.7s
5	K. Trojan/	Skoda Octavia WRC
	R. Nesvadba	2h 42m 28.5s
6	T. Enge/	Skoda Octavia WRC
	P. Gross	2h 43m 03.7s
7	M. Jandík/	Mitsubishi Lancer E7
	R. Chastecky	2h 46m 16.8s
8	E. Triner/	Seat WRC E3
	E. Horniacek	2h 46m 57.1s

ELPA RALLY, 26-28 September, Greece

1	B. Thiry/	Peugeot 206 WRC
	J-M Fortin	23m 51.2s
2	M. Campos/	Peugeot 206 WRC
	C. Magalhaes	23m 57.4s
3	E. Vasin/	Peugeot 206 WRC
	J. Baran	25m 16.0s

ANTIBES RALLY, 23-26 October, France

1	B. Thiry/	Peugeot 206 WRC
	J-M Fortin	3h 13m 38.7s
2	M. Campos/	Peugeot 206 WRC
	c. Magalhaes	3h 14m 03.8s
3	V. Pech/	Ford Focus WRC
	P. Uhel	3h 24m 10.6s
4	T. Van Parijs/	Mitsubishi Lancer E6
	Y. Peyskens	3h 34m 05.5s
5	R. Bartolini/	Mitsubishi Lancer E6
	J-C Descamps	3h 36m 38.6s
6	B. Casier/	Citroën Saxo S1600
	F. Miclotte	3h 39m 35.1s
7	F. Fiandino/	Peugeot 206 XS
	D. Badano	3h 40m 38.7s
8	E. Verola/	Renault Clio RS
	L. Bonnamy	3h 44m 20.8s

European Championship Final Standings
1 B. Thiry 1400; 2 M. Campos 1400; 3 V. Pech 565.

A GLASS HALF EMPTY

REVIEW British Rally Championship

By Hannah Curry, Deputy Rallies Editor, Motorsport News

The results of the 2003 British Rally Championship suggest it enjoyed a pretty healthy year. Jonny Milner successfully defended his title in his Corolla WRC, but only after a season-long battle with another former champion, Tapio Laukkanen, driving private Imprezas. The results point to a closely fought contest: Laukkanen won three events, whereas Milner took maximum points four times.

Additional competition came from the likes of the 18-year-old Finnish hotshot, Jari-Matti Latvala, driving a works-tended Focus, the 2002 British Touring Car Champion, James Thompson (Lancer E6.5) and the veteran Dubliner Austin McHale, in another Subaru. Some of British rallying's foremost drivers, such as the Scottish Champion, Barry Johnson, and that regular Kumho Championship event winner, Julian Reynolds, also threw their hats into the ring.

The Super 1600 category was well supported, largely by young drivers viewing it as a step to the World Rally Championship, but also in the shape of former British Champions such as Gwyndaf Evans, driving the works MG, and Mark Higgins in RED's Clio. Through no fault of their own, neither achieved much in the way of results. Both provided a valuable yardstick.

In the end, youth vanquished experience, the 23-year-old Kris Meeke beating his childhood hero Evans fair and square. Granted, Evans's ZR was conspicuously unreliable, but whenever the pair had the chance to go the distance in a fair fight, the stage times got quicker and quicker, with the duel usually resolved in favour of Meeke and the Team Palmer Corsa. If the Super 1600 category was all about bringing new talent to the fore, it did its job in 2003. But while the drivers were getting on with the business of driving, clouds were gathering on the horizon.

It's a cliché to say that 2003 was a crucial year for the British Championship, because that has seemed to be the case almost every year in recent times, but it is no less true for that. It was battling for survival and the noun is used advisedly. With some justice, the championship management proclaimed that there was plenty to be cheerful about, but the 2003 series was played out against a backdrop of uncertainty.

At the end of 2002, it was clear that, once again, the championship structure wasn't working. The demise of the 2001 Formula Rally Championship for Super 1600 machinery had seen off the last of the manufacturers and therefore copying the French Championship model, in which the winner came from the Super 1600 category, wasn't viable.

But as Super 1600 is the Junior World Championship category, it was clearly worth retaining to give young drivers a defined ladder of progression. World Rally Cars had been allowed into the British series for the first time in 2002, with a points-scoring system that allowed drivers in either the Open or Super 1600 categories to win the overall crown. This was confusing for the uninitiated. Try explaining to a novice rally fan that a Super 1600 car is going more slowly than a WR Car, that it will have a lower finishing position, but that it can score more points in the championship and you were likely to get some blank looks.

While the Super 1600 category was well defined, everything else had been lumped into the Open class, ensuring WR Car drivers dominated. However, it was harder for them to score points, because there was more competition.

So for 2003, the championship structure changed yet again. In a nutshell, the fastest man would get the most points. Super 1600 would remain an integral part of the series, but the drivers would be fighting for their own title. If they did well in the overall standings, they would be awarded points towards the overall championship based on their finishing position outright, not on their position in the category.

There were still critics, who thought that WR Cars had no place in a national championship, and the FIA's announcement of its intention to ban such machinery at regional level raised further doubts, but the change was generally accepted. While it was an admirable goal that the British Championship should be a springboard for new talent and as such, it would make sense for

the champion to come from the category aimed at up-and-coming drivers, it was impossible to achieve in the absence of widespread manufacturer and importer assistance. That support was still missing in 2003, Peugeot being the only team to stump up the £10,000 needed to run as a manufacturer entry.

The Super 1600 category was still important, but it had become necessary for the championship to cater for a different breed of driver – the well-off, experienced competitor who could afford reasonably modern machinery and who would provide the backbone of entries that made organising events financially viable.

In addition, the Production Cup was revived, to provide some incentive for Group N drivers outgunned in the race for the overall title. Classes for less powerful machinery were tweaked, simply named Formula 2000, 1600 and 1400, lumping Group N and

Jonny Milner (above) conquered the Finns with a rally to spare, although Tapio Laukkanen was a shade unlucky, a broken exhaust manifold halting his Manx charge (below). Leon Pesticcio coped with his share of misfortune in the Punto before taking the Super 1600 spoils on the Tempest.

Group A machinery together for simplicity.

While the new system seemed well thought out, it was the fourth change in as many years. If the British rallying public was beginning to tire of the goalposts constantly shifting, the cancellation of the championship opener, the Rally of Wales in March, drained patience further still.

The official reason was a lack of entries. It was worrying enough that the opening round of Britain's so-called premier championship couldn't attract enough competitors to make it viable, but of more concern was the mud-slinging that soon commenced between the rally organisers and British Championship Licensing, the new company set up to manage the series.

The championship had previously been run by ABIRO, an association made up of event organisers who had plenty of expertise in running rallies, but little experience in the promotional and logistical aspects of keeping a championship together. By bringing those organisers together with International Motor Sports, the commercial arm of the MSA, it was hoped that the series would have a coherent overall structure and improved promotion.

But when the Rally of Wales organisers blamed the British Championship management for not providing enough support and the championship manager, Mark Taylor, pointed the finger at the event's organising team for failing to communicate with the series management, it was clear that something wasn't working as it should.

Such public squabbling was hardly a glowing advertisement for the stability of the British Championship, but the whole affair raised an even more worrying question: if the first round couldn't get enough entries,

did this herald the championship's demise?

The age-old excuses were trotted out: the rallies were too long and too expensive, and people needed to take too much time off work to contest them. Organisers were soon encouraged to stage more compact events or to run at National A status in what seemed like desperate attempts to get some competitors – any competitors – on board.

For once, the sport's governing body, the MSA, had anticipated a crisis. At the end of 2002, the rally study group was commissioned to undertake a comprehensive review of the structure of British rallying and make recommendations to secure its future, the majority of the work being undertaken by the respected former co-driver, Mike Broad.

When the results and recommendations were announced in July, the championship had managed to get off the starting blocks and was ticking along satisfactorily, with unimpressive but adequate entry levels on events. Nevertheless, that report's conclusion added to the sense of uncertainty.

The four-tier system proposed in the review seemed to suggest that there wouldn't be room in future for both the British and the ANCRO Championships, the popular series that provided one-day National A events. The recommendation was that the foremost championship should consist of a mixture of British and ANCRO Championship events, raising questions as to who would run it. There was to be no change until 2005 and none likely until 2006 for the British series, because BRCL had a contract with the MSA to run the series for the next two years. But with the MSA's Chief Executive, Colin Hilton, admitting that that contract might be terminated early and the ANCRO Chairman, John Trevethick, openly stating that his association would bid to run the top-level championship, it was time to shape up and prove that there really was a market for the British series in its existing form.

In fact, when the competition finally commenced with the Gateshead-based Pirelli International Rally in April, there had been a real sense of hope in the air. The main field consisted of only 43 crews, but that number included former British champions, up-and-coming international drivers and an impressive 13 Super 1600 cars, including several entries from Junior World Championship contenders.

Laukkanen had raised eyebrows when he put in a late entry, jumped in the 1998-spec Impreza WRC for the first time on the start ramp, and proceeded to lock Milner into an event-long battle before emerging as victor. Here was a real upset, and the potential for a tight season-long battle between a current and former champion. But as Milner was crowned champion on the Trackrod Rally Yorkshire in September, with one round still to go, it was difficult not to feel short-changed by the 2003 championship.

Yes, the organisers of June's Scottish Rally lived up to their promise to provide better stage conditions and a service area that wasn't in a boggy field. The Jim Clark Memorial Rally was marred by a large number of accidents and competitors complained about the amount of road mileage, but for the international field, it was largely a smooth run. While the Manx and Ulster Rallies involved expensive ferry travel for many championship contenders, the big names all made it to both.

But with the exception of the Production Cup, which went down to the wire between the popular Lancer drivers, Neil Buckley and Roy White, all the titles were decided before the final round, the Tempest Stages in October.

Although Milner appeared to have come up against tougher opposition than he had in 2002, when his main rivals were the Super 1600 drivers, he wasn't often pushed to come up with his best in 2003. He benefitted when Laukkanen was slowed by a puncture on the Scottish Rally and extended his points lead still further when the Finn crashed out of the Jim Clark, then retired from the Manx with a cracked exhaust manifold.

Laukkanen was the only serious threat. Latvala and Thompson pushed Milner at times, but both were sufficiently inexperienced to fall off the road at regular intervals. Their personalities might have won over the fans, but on the stages their challenge amounted to little. McHale never displayed the pace that won him five Irish Tarmac titles, while Reynolds and Johnson pulled out too early in the season to pose any kind of challenge.

In reality, Milner's true rivals were pretty thin on the ground. With the exception of the Pirelli, when he fought back from a puncture to finish second, the Driffield man was pushed to be consistent but he was never pushed to be quick. Victories on the Scottish and the Manx came rather more easily.

After another season of driving to finish rather than driving to win, Milner could be forgiven if he chooses to seek pastures new in 2004. Aged 34, he openly admits he has missed the boat as far as making it into the World Championship goes, but the Yorkshireman has contested several rounds of the increasingly popular US SCCA Pro Rally Championship. Soon after winning his title in September, he disclosed that he was considering a season in the United States.

It is also unlikely that Laukkanen will choose to return in 2004. He's already taken one British title and volunteered that winning it again wasn't a priority. Likewise, Latvala has learned a great deal of his craft in Britain, but as an ambitious young driver who had already contested several world-level events, it wouldn't be surprising if his priorities lie further up the ladder in 2004. Thompson ran out of money towards the end of the season and while he said he was desperate to return to the scene, he conceded it was unlikely that he would be back the following year.

So as British Championship Licensing announced that the 2004 scoring system would run along the same lines as in 2003, it was difficult to see who the leading competitors might be. Indeed, it raised doubts as to whether there is a pool of talented drivers in World Championship machinery, who want to contest a domestic championship made up of two-day events and recces.

Despite Meeke's success, Super 1600 had its fair share of problems, many of these stemming from the 'promotional package' through which some teams paid to have preferential seeding and television coverage. Evidently, some thought this was worth paying for, even though the footage from events was usually shown early on a Saturday morning while most of the nation was tucked up in bed.

On the Pirelli, the Super 1600 drivers who'd bought the package ran at the front, ahead of the WR Cars, with the other competitors in the category scattered throughout the field. It was confusing for spectators and frustrating for drivers, because they had no way of comparing times when their main rivals were running a long way ahead of or behind them. Organisers tried to counter the problem by grouping all the drivers together at the front of the field on subsequent events, but this merely annoyed drivers of quicker machinery.

The glory days may have gone, but the British Championship still throws the spotlight on rising stars. Beyond question, the most exciting newcomers were Jari-Matti Latvala, seen on his way to third on the Ulster in the M-Sport Focus, and the Super 1600 Champion Kris Meeke (right) in his Corsa.

The numbers were healthy at the start of the year, but by the Ulster in September there were just six regular Super 1600 drivers left. There might have been a good battle at the front and the less experienced drivers had noticeably raised their game by the end of the season, but the numbers were still a concern.

The bald truth was that interest steadily declined: fewer than 30 registered British Championship contenders entered each of the last six rounds and just 11 drivers contested all of the first six.

Several Irish competitors had shown enthusiasm and attempted to register for the British series when the Toshiba Irish Tarmac Championship visited the Jim Clark. But those in the latest machinery were turned away, because the British regulations didn't allow WR Cars under two years old and the rest were told that they needed to have registered by the third round. If you counted the events that ran, then the Jim Clark was indeed round three. But the championship management insisted that the cancelled Rally of Wales remained the first round, thereby turning away a group of competitors who might have enlivened the title race, as well as bringing valuable revenue.

However, the foreign competitors who came over for full or partial championship assaults couldn't speak highly enough of the British Championship. Fiat's best bet in the Junior World Championship, Mirco Baldacci, openly said his three outings in Britain had helped his international campaign. The Norwegian Junior Champion, Markus Foss, won the Formula 2000 category, while the Peugeot 206 Super Cup and VW

Castrol Polo Challenge one-make championships, which ran at the back of several events, attracted entries from Greece, Spain, Sweden and Finland.

It seemed the murmurs of discontent that were flying around in Britain hadn't yet reached foreign shores. From an international point of view, it was encouraging that the British series still appealed to competitors unscarred by memories of Formula Rally and foot and mouth.

However, as a British competition, it badly needed home-grown drivers and to remain an integral part of the rallying ladder. If the championship wanted to do this, then the announcement of the 2004 calendar brought one or two surprises. The Rally of Wales was to be reinstated, despite British Championship management's criticism of its organising team early in the year. The Tempest Stages, a 50-mile blast around some uninteresting forests in Hampshire, was also retained as the final round, despite again receiving very tepid support from the championship contenders.

Broad's report served to undermine Taylor's insistence that the British Championship was to be a bona fide international series, and that it should live or die by that standard.

'Maybe we've just got to start admitting that there are only about 30 drivers in Britain who want to do an international championship. It might not be a huge demand, but it's demand all the same. We should start thinking about quality and not just quantity,' he said.

Some of the rule changes appeared to be along the right lines. WR Cars would be allowed, regardless of age. It might upset some, but if it meant more competitors, it had to be the right move. The junior championship would be extended to include all 1600cc machinery, not just the Super 1600 cars. The class structure would follow FIA prescriptions for maximum clarity.

The management finally seemed to accept that dwindling manufacturer interest wasn't likely to pick up and scrapped the manufacturers' title in favour of a new teams cup for privateers.

Yet reform created a task of gargantuan proportions. To be a successful international series, the British Championship needed more competitors, more television coverage and greater commercial investment. At the same time, events needed to be more compact, while retaining their individual characteristics. Against the backdrop of general uncertainty in the British rallying community, partly generated by the possibility of change in 2005 as a result of Broad's review, it was difficult to see how all this could happen if no one could guarantee a stable future beyond 2004.

Then, having provided a backbone of entries, the one-make championships dealt a final blow. The 206 Cup, the Polo Challenge and the Ka Championship, all of which had run at some or all British Championship rounds, announced that they would give their allegiance to different competitions in 2004. The British Championship gave them a certain prestige, but that was outweighed by the benefits of running in cheaper and shorter events.

The detractors asserted that ANCRO already provided a playground for established drivers in WR Cars, while if Super 1600 drivers wanted to prove their pedigree, they could always go to France. While the championship management harped on about attracting foreigners, they couldn't dispel a very real sense of foreboding, exacerbated by uncertainty over the consequences of the review. The authorities had evidently decided that there was no future for the championship in its present form. The domestic market for the championship was unquestionably diminishing. The management team appeared to be making the right decisions and clearly had the best interests of the championship at heart, but they couldn't extinguish the fear that the contest was on a downward spiral that no amount of tweaking could halt.

MONEY TOO TIGHT TO MENTION

All eyes might have been on the battle in the Open and Super 1600 categories, but in 2003 the British Championship also ran new 'formula' classes, in the hope of attracting stronger support.

As their names implied, F2000, F1600 and F1400 catered for machinery up to two litres, 1600cc and 1400cc respectively, with entry fees staggered, depending on engine size. The thinking behind this was that drivers who ran near the back of the field had rougher stage conditions and therefore shouldn't pay as much as those at the front. The production classes were also amalgamated with Group A, doing away with a plethora of titles.

The success of the formulae can best be described as limited. While the Formula 2000 class provided a season-long battle between Foss, driving an Almera, and the up-and-coming Brit, Steve Loveridge, in a ZR, only five drivers registered for the category and only three contested all the rounds.

Elsewhere, support bordered on the dismal. Formula 1600 received just two registrations, neither driver completing the full season. Formula 1400 had four registered drivers, with only two crews contesting anything that resembled the full championship. These weren't going to be difficult titles to win.

There was no F1600 champion, because the leading driver, James Gloster (106) didn't start the required five rounds. Shelley Taunt did enough to claim both the F1400 and Ladies' titles in her Micra, but beating only one person to each didn't add a great deal of lustre to her accolades.

The phrase 'everyone's a winner' springs to mind. If you wanted a British title to put on your rallying CV, there wasn't much more you needed to do than turn up in a smaller car and get to the end of the rallies.

The entry fees might have been reduced, but competing on British rounds still involves more time off work and more stage miles than lesser championships. Group N drivers such as Loveridge were a little aggrieved that amalgamation pitted them against much more highly modified and therefore expensive opposition, but in general, it was further gloomy evidence that if the budget won't stretch to a big car, it probably won't stretch to an international championship either.

Pirelli British Championship Results

PIRELLI INTERNATIONAL RALLY, Gateshead, 25-26 April

1	Tapio Laukkanen/ Miika Anttila	Subaru Impreza WRC98 1h 38m 24.3s.
2	Jonny Milner/ Nicky Beech	Toyota Corolla WRC 1h 38m 33.6s.
3	Mark Higgins/ Bryan Thomas	Renault Clio 1600 1h 39m 31.4s.
4	Gwyndaf Evans/ Claire Mole	MG ZR 1600 1h 41m 34.0s.
5	Kris Meeke/ Chris Patterson	Vauxhall Corsa 1600 1h 44m 38.7s.
6	James Thompson/ Plug Pulleyn	Mitsubishi Lancer E6.5 1h 45m 23.8s.
7	Simon Hughes/ Calvin Cooledge	Renault Clio 1600 1h 45m 26.7s.
8	Mirco Baldacci/ Giovanni Bernacchini	Fiat Punto 1600 1h 45m 34.8s.
9	Dougi Hall/ Steve Egglestone	Mitsubishi Lancer E6 1h 45m 48.9s.
10	Jari-Matti Latvala/ Carl Williamson	Ford Focus WRC01 1h 45m 56.4s.

Championship points. Drivers: 1 Laukkanen 15; 2 Milner 12; 3 M. Higgins10.

SCOTTISH RALLY, Dumfries, 7-8 June.

1	Jonny Milner/ Nicky Beech	Toyota Corolla WRC 1h 30m 11.1s.
2	Tapio Laukkanen/ Miika Anttila	Subaru Impreza WRC 1h 30m 39.1s.
3	Jari-Matti Latvala/ Carl Williamson	Ford Focus WRC01 1h 33m 58.3s.
4	Austin McHale/ Brian Murphy	Subaru Impreza WRC 1h 35m 28.3s.
5	Gwyndaf Evans/ Claire Mole	MG ZR 1600 1h 35m 57.1s.
6	Julian Reynolds/ Ieuan Thomas	Subaru Impreza 555 1h 36m 25.8s.
7	Barry Johnson/ Stewart Merry	Subaru Impreza 1h 36m 39.3s.
8	Kris Meeke/ Chris Patterson	Vauxhall Corsa 1600 1h 37m 52.4s.
9	Mirco Baldacci/ Simone Scattolin	Fiat Punto 1600 1h 38m 35.6s.
10	Neil Buckley/ Doug Redpath	Mitsubishi Lancer E5 1h 39m 13.0s.

Championship points. Drivers: 1 Milner, Laukkanen 27; 3 Evans 17.

JIM CLARK MEMORIAL RALLY, Edinburgh, 12-13 July

1	Andrew Nesbitt/ James O'Brien	Subaru Impreza WRC 1h 58m 05.1s.
2	Jonny Milner/ Nicky Beech	Toyota Corolla WRC 1h 58m 52.2s.
3	Derek McGarrity/ Dermot O'Gorman	Subaru Impreza WRC 1h 59m 10.1s.
4	Peadar Hurson/ Ian Porter	Subaru Impreza WRC 1h 59m 36.4s.
5	Eugene Donnelly/ Paul Kiely	Subaru Impreza WRC 1h 59m 49.3s
6	Austin McHale/ Brian Murphy	Subaru Impreza WRC 2h 01m 45.1s
7	Tim McNulty/ Anthony Nestor	Subaru Impreza WRC 2h 03m 22.8s
8	James Thompson/ Plug Pulleyn	Mitsubishi Lancer E6.5 2h 04m 19.0s
9	Kris Meeke/ Chris Patterson	Opel Corsa 1600 2h 06m 27.6s
10	Seamus Leonard/ Paul McLaughlin	Subaru Impreza WRX 2h 06m 56.4s

Championship points. Drivers: 1 Milner 42; 2 Laukkanen 27; 3 McHale, Meeke 23.

MANX INTERNATIONAL RALLY, Douglas, July 31-2 August

1	Jonny Milner/ Nicky Beech	Toyota Corolla WRC 2h 38m 28.3s.
2	Ken McKinstry/ Noel Orr	Subaru Impreza WRC 2h 43m 27.7s.
3	Derek McGarrity/ Dermot O'Gorman	Subaru Impreza WRC 2h 44m 40.5s.
4	Austin McHale/ Brian Murphy	Subaru Impreza WRC 2h 45m 59.5s.
5	Eamonn Boland/ Francis Regan	Subaru Impreza WRC 2h 46m 04.4s.
6	Seamus Leonard/ Paul McLaughlin	Subaru Impreza WRX 2h 52m 03.8s.
7	Garry Jennings/ Gordon Noble	Peugeot 206XS 2h 54m 30.0s.
8	Patrick White/ James McKee	Subaru Impreza WRC 2h 55m 54.2s.
9	John Cope/ Donna Harper	Ford Escort Cosworth 2h 56m 13.5s.
10	Aaron McHale/ Damien Connolly	Mitsubishi Lancer E8 3h 02m 02.2s

Championship points. Drivers: 1 Milner 57; 2 McHale 35; 3 Laukkanen 27.

ULSTER RALLY, Armagh, 5-6 September

1	Tapio Laukkanen/ Ilkka Riipinen	Subaru Impreza WRC 1h 59m 25.6s.
2	Derek McGarrity/ Dermot O'Gorman	Subaru Impreza WRC 2h 01m 13.1s.
3	Jari-Matti Latvala/ Miika Anttila	Ford Focus WRC01 2h 01m 18.3s.
4	Jonny Milner/ Nicky Beech	Toyota Corolla WRC 2h 01m 47.4s.
5	Austin McHale/ Brian Murphy	Subaru Impreza WRC 2h 02m 11.8s.
6	Kris Meeke/ David Senior	Vauxhall Corsa 1600 2h 04m 13.0s.
7	Gwyndaf Evans/ Claire Mole	MG ZR 1600 2h 04m 17.2s.
8	Dougi Hall/ Steve Egglestone	Mitsubishi Lancer E6 2h 07m 40.7s.
9	Maurice Gass/ Andrew Cullen	Subaru Impreza WRC 2h 07m 56.4s.
10	Ryan Champion/ Cliff Simmons	Ford Puma 2h 07m 58.5s.

Championship points. Drivers: 1 Milner 69; 2 McHale 44; 3 Laukkanen 42.

TRACKROD RALLY, Malton, 27-28 September

1	Tapio Laukkanen/ Ilkka Riipinen	Subaru Impreza WRC 1h 38m 11.6s.
2	Jonny Milner/ Nicky Beech	Toyota Corolla WRC 1h 39m 00.2s.
3	Jari-Matti Latvala/ Miika Anttila	Ford Focus WRC01 1h 39m 38.6s.
4	Austin McHale/ Brian Murphy	Subaru Impreza WRC 1h 41m 30.9s.
5	Steve Petch/ John Richardson	Hyundai Accent WRC 1h 42m 51.5s.
6	Barry Johnson/ Stewart Merry	Subaru Impreza WRC 1h 43m 21.8s.
7	Chris Mellors/ Craig Thorley	Ford Escort WRC 1h 44m 13.6s.
8	Kris Meeke/ Chris Patterson	Opel Corsa 1600 1h 47m 31.1s.
9	Aki Teiskonen/ Miika Teiskonen	Citroen Saxo 1600 1h 48m 32.3s.
10	Neil Buckley/ Doug Redpath	Mitsubishi Lancer E6 1h 48m 33.5s

Championship points. Drivers: 1 Milner 81; 2 Laukkanen 57; 3 McHale 53.

TEMPEST RALLY, Aldershot, 26 October

1	Jari-Matti Latvala/ Miika Anttila	Ford Focus WRC01 49m 40.7s.
2	Ryan Champion/ Cliff Simmons	Subaru Impreza 555 50m 51.0s.
3	Julian Reynolds/ Ieuan Thomas	Toyota Corolla WRC 50m 56.4s.
4	Austin McHale/ Brian Murphy	Subaru Impreza WRC 51m 26.7s.
5	Phil Morgan/ Martin Douglas	Subaru Impreza WRC 53m 20.9s.
6	Will Nicholls/ Nick Broom	Subaru Impreza WRC 53m 57.6s.
7	Roy White/ Greg Shinnors	Mitsubishi Lancer E7 54m 16.5s.
8	John Lloyd/ Pauline Gullick	Subaru Impreza 54m 56.6s.
9	Neil Buckley/ Doug Redpath	Mitsubishi Lancer E6 55m 30.4s.
10	Mark I'Anson/ Toby I'Anson	Mitsubishi Lancer E6 55m 43.4s

Championship points. Drivers: 1 Milner 81; 2 McHale 60; 3 Laukkanen 57.

Never let it be said that championships are the first resort of the mediocre. Over the past few years we have seen numerous examples of British national championships being clinched at the last gasp after the eventual winner had spent the whole season building up to a title-clinching drive on the final round. The other way of clinching it is to attack it like a bull at a gate.

Step forward, Raymond Munro. His declared intention was to win the New Pig Scottish Championship. The records will show that he succeeded, but it was the manner of his success that was worthy of note. Co-driven by Neil Ewing, the Impreza driver from Culloden won the opening encounter, the Snowman, outright. He took the next round, the Border Counties, in similar fashion, then the third, fourth, fifth and sixth so that, after the Jim Clark at the beginning of July, Munro's score card was showing six maximums. A competitor's seven best scores, from nine rounds, count towards their final tally north of the border and, while Munro could manage only second on the McRae Stages, the full house was completed on the Speyside in August.

Andy Burton collected the Dunlop Gold Star Championship in a similar, but less cavalier vein in his home-built, four-wheel-drive Peugeot-Cosworth. In doing so, he and his co-driver, Rob Morgan, became the first crew to win both BTRDA Gold and Silver Stars since Will Sparrow and Nigel Raeburn in 1971. Burton's prowess at BTRDA level is beyond doubt; at the start of the year, he planned to combine it with a season of Kumho National Championship events, one rung up the ladder.

The team's first appearance was in early February on the Wyedean Forest Rally, which proved to be the best possible start to his Dunlop/BTRDA Championship campaign, as it yielded a win and maximum points. Having been down in the far south of England at the end of the month for the Rallye Sunseeker, the first Kumho round, he elected to miss the Lakeland-based Malcolm Wilson, the second BTRDA qualifier. By returning victoriously for the North Humberside and Somerset Stages, Burton was already in the pound seat, if not actually leading the BTRDA series. Although the full calendar includes ten events, each driver's best six scores from their first nine starts form the basis for the all-important maths. Thus by Easter, Burton had already dropped one score, leaving him in need of three more good ones from the remaining six events.

The 306 had taken a hammering on its first visit to the Tarmac of the Isle of Man in early May and consequently it was missing from the Red Dragon a fortnight later. Normal service was resumed on the Dukeries when another victory put Burton up alongside Roger Clark and more recently, Brian Bell, as a three-time winner of the Nottinghamshire event. Missing the Quinton Stages left him requiring two scores from the last three rounds, but he needn't have worried: straight victories on both the Woodpecker and Plains sealed the title, with the Cambrian still to run.

In a year in which some event organisers have been left wondering where all their competitors have gone, the Dunlop Gold Star Championship attracted entries that almost without exception would make others weep. It does not take much in-depth analysis to establish that the British economy, especially in terms of 'luxury' industries such as motorsport, is not in a particularly healthy state. It remains to be seen whether much of 2003's action has been funded by credit cards and 2004 is when it will end in tears, but as far as BTRDA organisers are concerned, it has been a case of making hay while the sun shines.

The Kumho National Championship has also experienced a resurgence in popularity in terms of numbers. This, it must be said, is partly due to the upsurge in support for the Mitsubishi Evolution Challenge which has formed part of each round. For the first time for a number of years, an almost-full entry lined up in Bournemouth for the Rallye Sunseeker and, while Marcus Dodd went on to win his 'home' event for the fourth time, it would be the one occasion on which he scored championship points during the season. His Impreza WRC failed to finish the next three rounds and was subsequently sold, Dodd deciding to have a go at some Historic events in a Mark 2 Escort instead.

During 2002, the seven rounds of the National Championship each produced a different winner and

FULL HOUSE

REVIEW British National Rallying

By Andrew Haill

2003 repeated the pattern, in that no driver grabbed the series by the scruff of the neck. This time it was more a story of dogged determination paying off, with that veteran campaigner, David Mann, at last putting his name on the trophy after more than 20 years of trying. The highlight of the season was the Suffolk mushroom farmer's victory on the Isle of Man in the face of some very stiff opposition, much to the delight of the championship sponsors, Kumho, whose tyres evidently justified their presence on his Impreza.

As the season drew to a close, the points table closely mirrored that of the Formula 1 circus as it headed for the last race in Japan. After a start to the year that was instantly forgettable, the former National Champion, Roger Duckworth, had had a run in which he had taken three maximum scores on the trot, moving him within striking distance of Mann. As he arrived in Shrewsbury for the Bulldog Rally,

Duckworth was cast in the role of Kimi Raikkonen, in that nothing less than a win on the final Kumho counter would do, whereas Mann was Michael Schumacher, needing just to finish in the top nine to make sure the prize spent the next 12 months in Suffolk. In the event, and after much nail biting by all the interested parties, Duckworth could manage only second.

The Mitsubishi Evolution Challenge was in its third season, but this time, the first prize of a funded drive in a Lancer Evo VIII for the 2004 National Championship caught drivers' imagination. At its height, there were 23 of the Group N cars contesting the Mutiny Rally in June. The Ulsterman, Brendan Crealey, who had originally made his name in the Peugeot 205 Challenge, came out of retirement to contest the series and following a string of finishes in the top ten overall on several ANCRO-organised events, he took the title after the Park Systems Stages in Scotland in

September.

At the end of 2002 the National Tarmacadam Championship points-scoring system, which differentiated between homologated and non-homologated cars, had created the unprecedented spectacle of joint champions, John Price, driving a Metro 6R4, and Steve Hendy, at the wheel of an Escort Cosworth. The series reverted to a more conventional method for the new season without deterring either of its champions. Hendy's win had been his first, while Price had already amassed nine on his own and one shared. The 6R4 driver had set his heart on a never-to-be equalled, and certainly not beaten, tenth solo championship. In fact, a higher than usual number of rivals lined up for the first major event of the year on the Epynt Ranges. One of Price's strengths, apart from his obvious skill behind the wheel, has been the reliability of his car, but by the end of the day, things had taken an altogether different turn.

On the very first stage of the rally the Metro's engine had let go in a big way. This was only the beginning of Price's problems. Such are the intricacies of a modern-day 6R4 engine that there are very few people in business building the pukka units. Consequently, it is possible to languish in a queue for a rebuild for several months. As a stop-gap measure, Price borrowed his old car back for the Tour of Cornwall and registered another non-finish, while a hired engine went into his own 6R4 for the Roush Manx National. Realising that his chances for 2003 were already at an end, the most successful driver in the championship's history made a strategic withdrawal from the rest of the series.

In the meantime, David Kynaston's development work on his Audi A3 Quattro had paid off, as outright wins on the Tours of Epynt and Cornwall showed. Hendy was never far away, but even after Kynaston's mediocre run on the Manx, he couldn't get ahead of the Devonian. The Audi topped the points all through the summer, before events took a dramatic turn on the championship's second visit to Epynt for the Mewla National Rally in August. Kynaston was leading when the Audi left the road at high speed, finishing up badly damaged and out of sight of following competitors. Both he and his co-driver, Andy Russell,

Andy Burton (below, inspecting the gearbox) and his self-built 306 are the biggest draws in British national rallying. Most drivers, Bob Ceen (far left) and Roger Duckworth included, are content to buy four-wheel drive off the shelf.

British National Rally Champions

ANCRO	David Mann
BTRDA Gold Star	Andy Burton
BTRDA Silver Star	Jon Ballinger
BTRDA 1400	Shaun Woffindent
Safety Devices	Steve Hendy
Scottish	Raymond Munro

David Mann (below and below right) finally took a thoroughly deserved national title. in his Impreza. While Martin Harrison was one of a number of drivers to keep faith with the 6R4 on asphalt, the stunning effectiveness of the latest Group N Lancer attracted considerable support, spearheaded by Brendan Crealey (top).

were injured and taken to hospital, where it was discovered that Kynaston had broken his neck. Fortunately, no lasting damage had been done, but understandably, his championship was run. Hendy was declared the winner after Wexford, but it was not as he had wanted it, as the season had been shaping up for a tremendous finale.

Steve Fleck took the alternative Tarmac contest, the 'Get Connected' Championship, having fended off the advances of his fellow Impreza drivers, Ken McKinstry and Melvyn Evans, although by the final round, the Fastnet, the only person who could stop Fleck was the Corolla driver, Cahal Arthurs. Always newsworthy for his phenomenal turn of speed in his Mark 2 Escort, Phil Collins has contested the championship for the past couple of seasons, but the Pontrilas man's progress was interrupted by several big accidents in 2003. However, eighth overall on the Isle of Man in his two-wheel-drive car was testament to his commitment.

The Dunlop Silver Star and Silkolene 1400 Championship titles remained undecided until the Cambrian Rally at the start of November. Both had provided the theatre for some superb competition during the season and both went down to the wire. The Silver Star Championship caters purely for two-wheel-drive machinery, and while front-wheel-drive cars are starting to make their presence felt, the old guard still rules the roost. The defending champion, Jon Ballinger, and his Manta was pitted against a trio of

Escorts in the hands of the season-long championship leader, Phil Squires, Robin Bradbury and Jason Lepley. However, a top ten result for Ballinger in North Wales gave him his second consecutive Silver Star by the smallest possible margin. Tying on points with Lepley, he got the nod only after the tie-break was applied.

Since the BTRDA took the bold step of introducing a 1400 Championship, which runs at the front of the field on its qualifying rounds, its popularity has been a revelation. Sponsored in 2003 by Silkolene, 60 drivers in a wide variety of machinery have scored points and the lead of the Championship has changed hands frequently. As ever, most had fallen by the wayside by the final round, making it a straight fight between Shaun Woffinden's Puma and the Nova of the erstwhile leader, Gary Standen. The Vauxhall never emerged from the forests, leaving the former Ka champion Woffinden to claim the title in the best possible way, with a category win.

The health of 'club' rallying, while so often brought into question in the past, would seem to be in pretty good shape at the moment. There are quite obviously competitors able to find events and the championships that suit both their requirements and, chiefly, their budgets. The much-vaunted proposals for the future of British rallying, due to be instigated at the beginning of 2005, seek to bring a 'structure' into the sport, but judging by the aforementioned championships, there doesn't seem to be much amiss with what is on offer at this level.